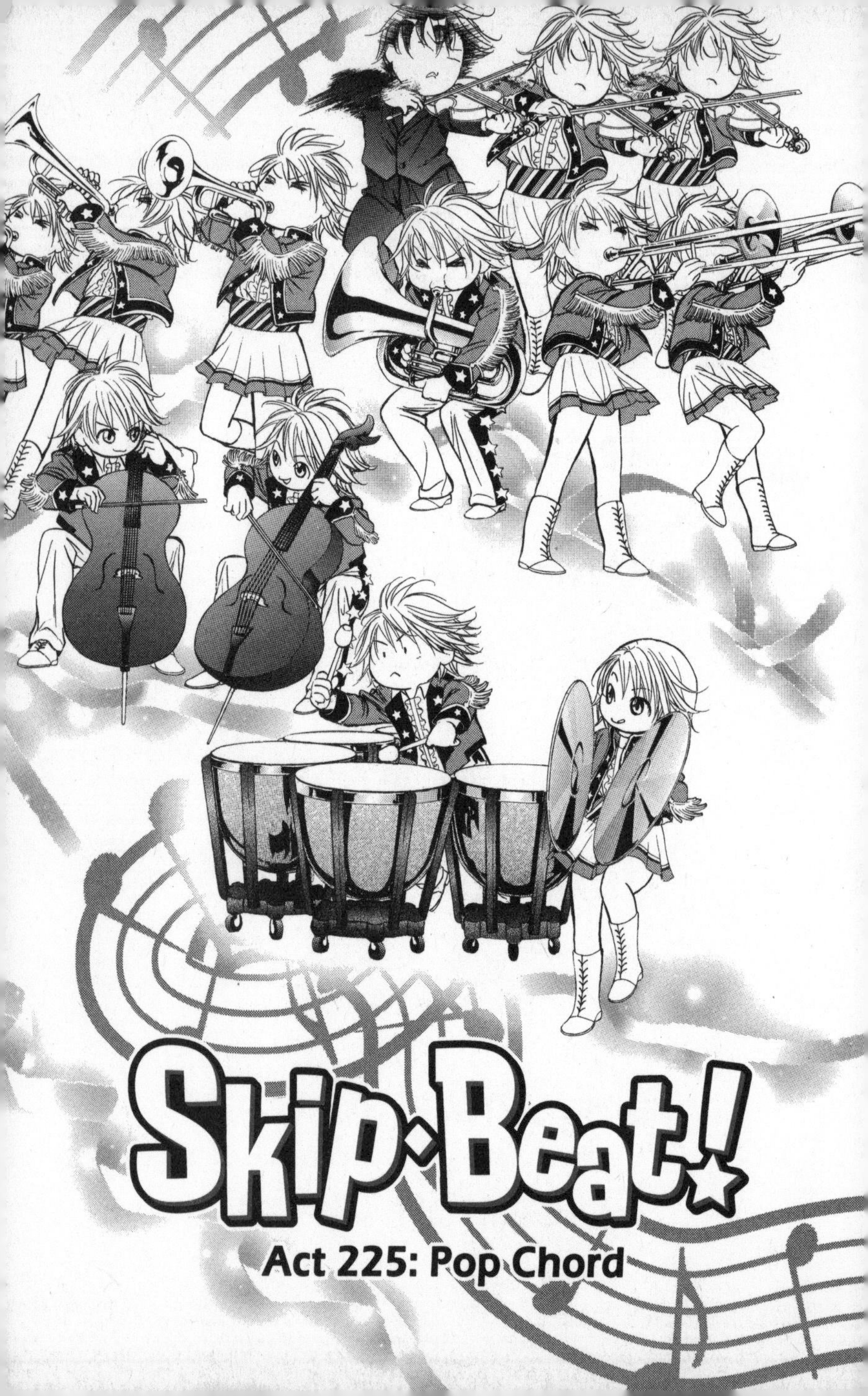
Skip·Beat!
Act 225: Pop Chord

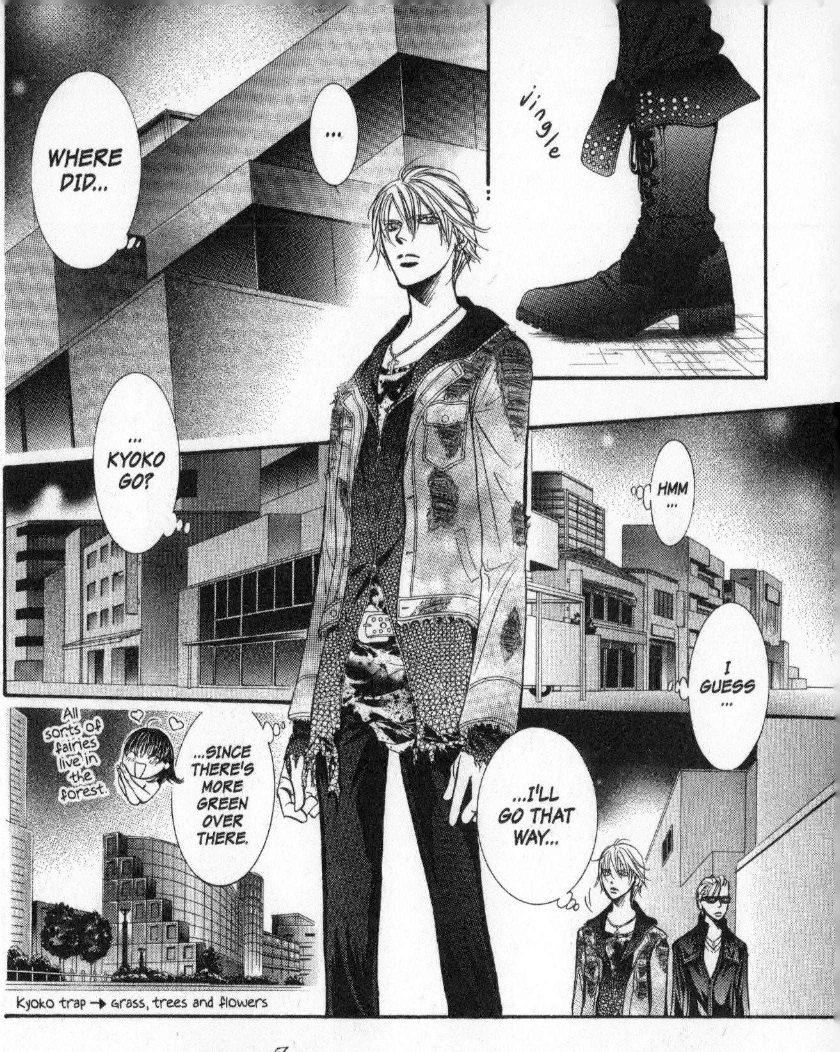
jingle
...
WHERE DID...
... KYOKO GO?
HMM ...
I GUESS ...
...I'LL GO THAT WAY...
...SINCE THERE'S MORE GREEN OVER THERE.
All sorts of fairies live in the forest.
Kyoko trap → Grass, trees and flowers

Act 225 chapter title page Secret character

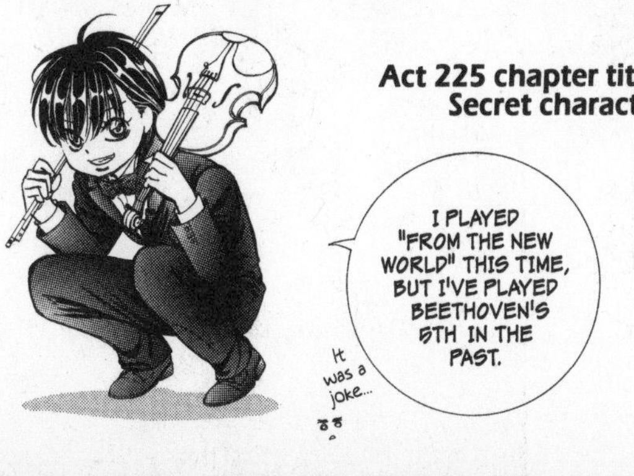
I PLAYED "FROM THE NEW WORLD" THIS TIME, BUT I'VE PLAYED BEETHOVEN'S 5TH IN THE PAST.
It was a joke...

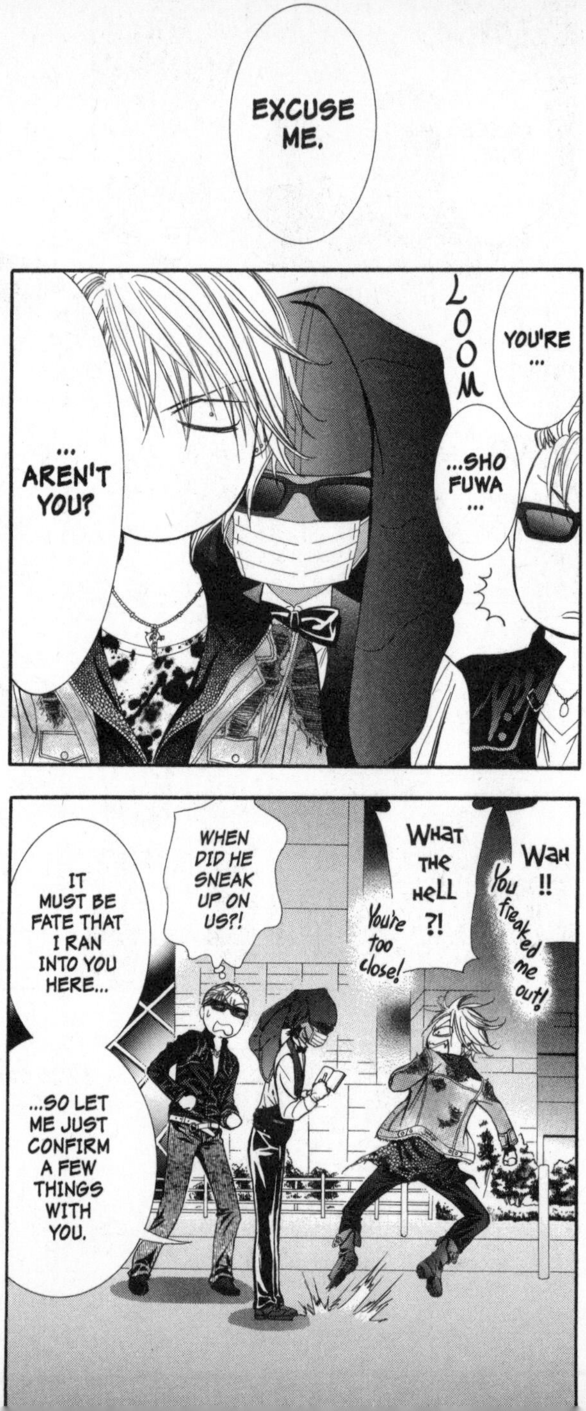
EXCUSE ME.
LOOM
YOU'RE ...
...SHO FUWA ...
... AREN'T YOU?
Wah !! You freaked me out!
What the hell ?!
You're too close!
WHEN DID HE SNEAK UP ON US?!
IT MUST BE FATE THAT I RAN INTO YOU HERE...
...SO LET ME JUST CONFIRM A FEW THINGS WITH YOU.

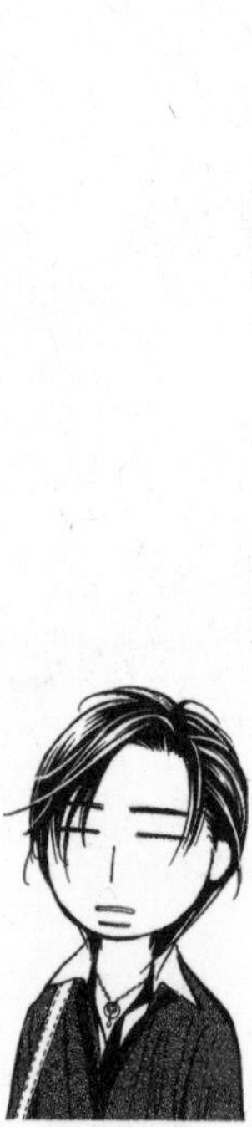

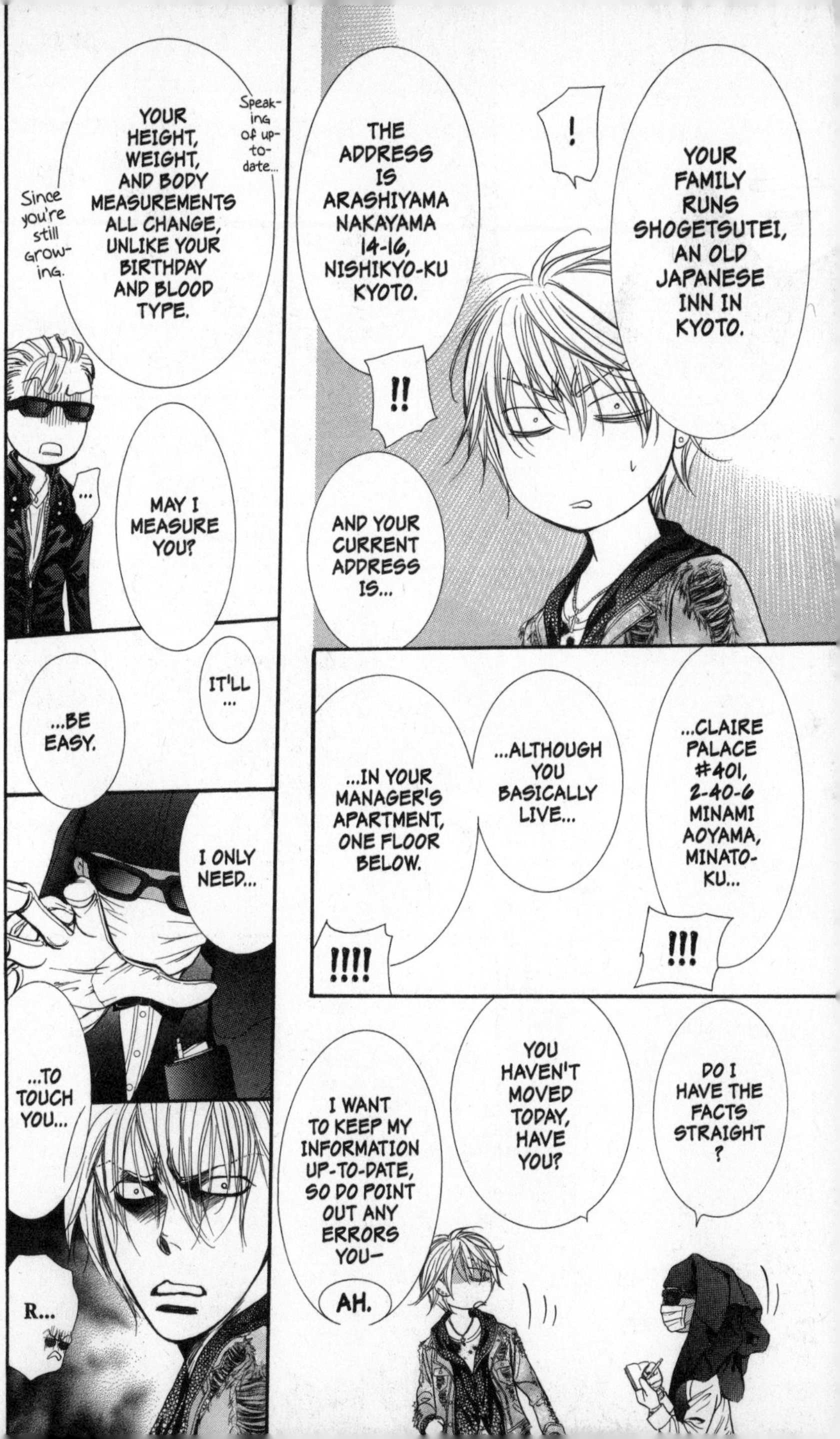
YOUR FAMILY RUNS SHOGETSUTEI, AN OLD JAPANESE INN IN KYOTO.
!
THE ADDRESS IS ARASHIYAMA NAKAYAMA 14-16, NISHIKYO-KU KYOTO.
!!
AND YOUR CURRENT ADDRESS IS...
...CLAIRE PALACE #401, 2-40-6 MINAMI AOYAMA, MINATO-KU...
!!!
...ALTHOUGH YOU BASICALLY LIVE...
...IN YOUR MANAGER'S APARTMENT, ONE FLOOR BELOW.
!!!!
DO I HAVE THE FACTS STRAIGHT?
YOU HAVEN'T MOVED TODAY, HAVE YOU?
I WANT TO KEEP MY INFORMATION UP-TO-DATE, SO DO POINT OUT ANY ERRORS YOU—
AH.
Speaking of up-to-date...
YOUR HEIGHT, WEIGHT, AND BODY MEASUREMENTS ALL CHANGE, UNLIKE YOUR BIRTHDAY AND BLOOD TYPE.
Since you're still growing.
...
MAY I MEASURE YOU?
IT'LL...
...BE EASY.
I ONLY NEED...
...TO TOUCH YOU...
R...

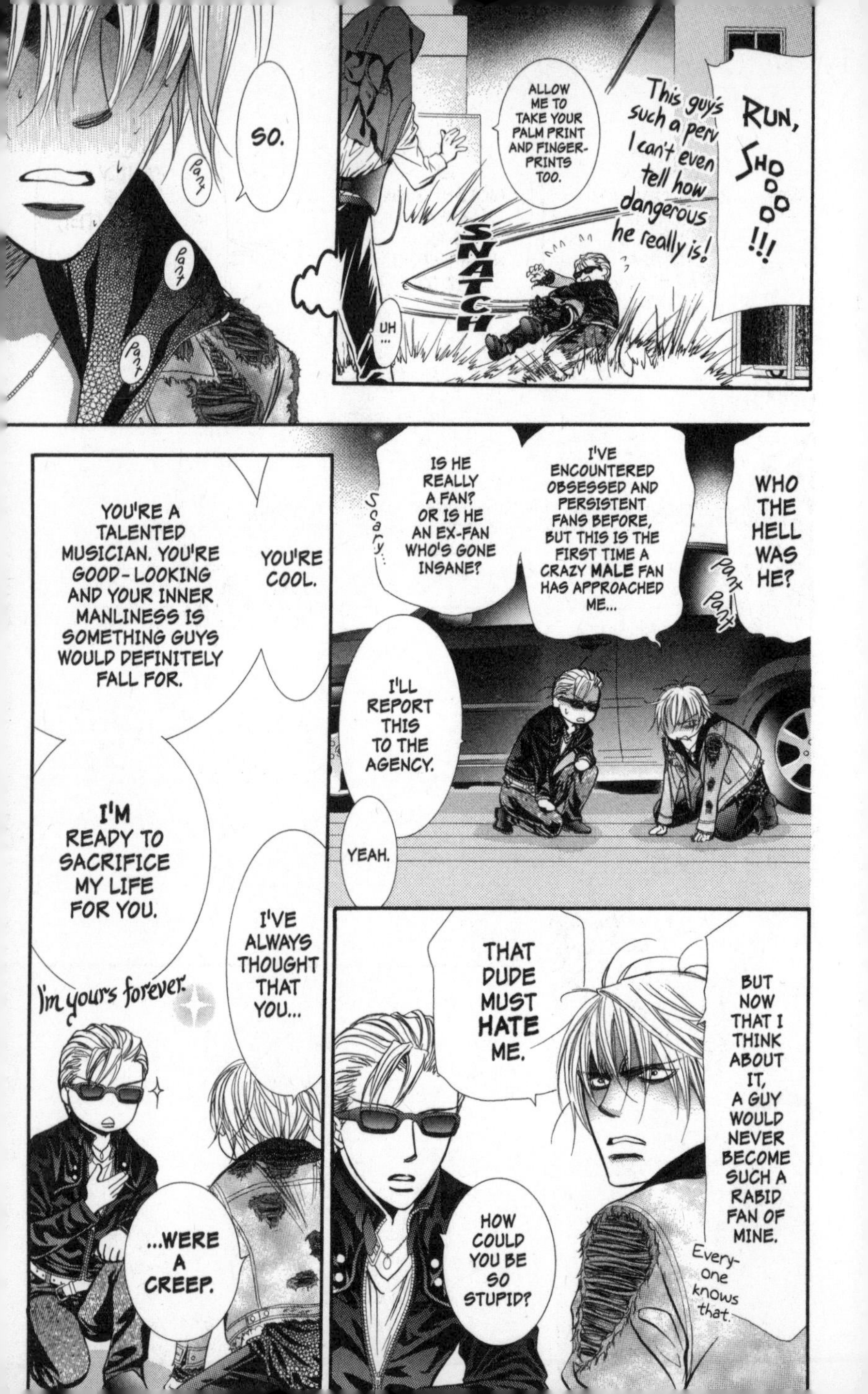
RUN, SHOOOO!!!
This guy's such a perv I can't even tell how dangerous he really is!
ALLOW ME TO TAKE YOUR PALM PRINT AND FINGER-PRINTS TOO.
SNATCH
UH ...
SO.
Pant
Pant
Pant
WHO THE HELL WAS HE?
Pant Pant
I'VE ENCOUNTERED OBSESSED AND PERSISTENT FANS BEFORE, BUT THIS IS THE FIRST TIME A CRAZY MALE FAN HAS APPROACHED ME...
IS HE REALLY A FAN? OR IS HE AN EX-FAN WHO'S GONE INSANE?
Scary...
I'LL REPORT THIS TO THE AGENCY.
YEAH.
BUT NOW THAT I THINK ABOUT IT, A GUY WOULD NEVER BECOME SUCH A RABID FAN OF MINE.
THAT DUDE MUST HATE ME.
HOW COULD YOU BE SO STUPID?
Every-one knows that.
YOU'RE COOL.
YOU'RE A TALENTED MUSICIAN. YOU'RE GOOD-LOOKING AND YOUR INNER MANLINESS IS SOMETHING GUYS WOULD DEFINITELY FALL FOR.
I'M READY TO SACRIFICE MY LIFE FOR YOU.
I'm yours forever.
I'VE ALWAYS THOUGHT THAT YOU...
...WERE A CREEP.

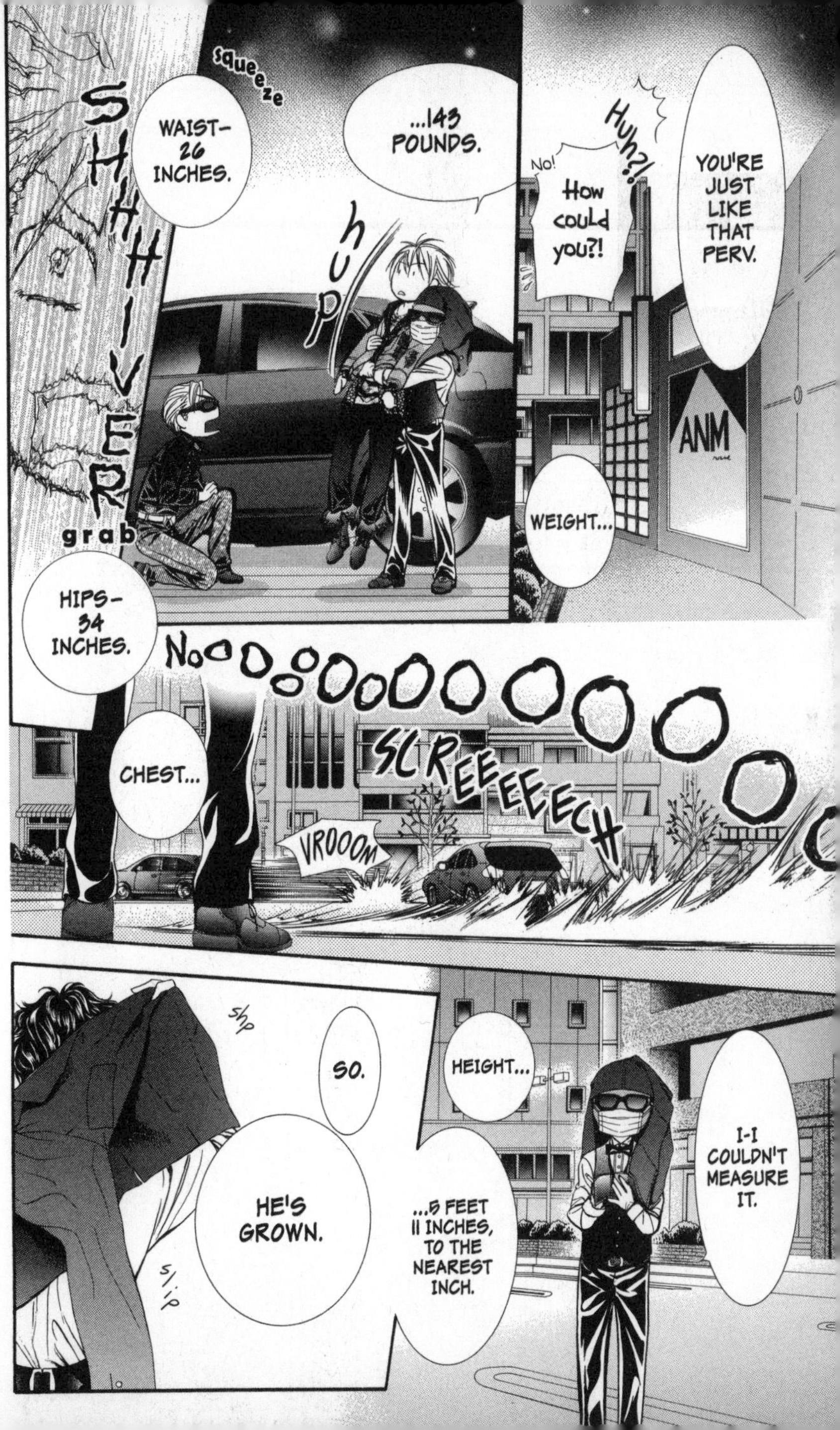
YOU'RE JUST LIKE THAT PERV.
Huh?!
No!
How could you?!
WEIGHT...
...143 POUNDS.
hup
squeeze
WAIST-26 INCHES.
SHHHIVER
grab
HIPS-34 INCHES.
NoOOOOOOOOOOOOO
SCREEEEECH
VROOOM
CHEST...
I-I COULDN'T MEASURE IT.
HEIGHT...
...5 FEET 11 INCHES, TO THE NEAREST INCH.
SO.
HE'S GROWN.
shp
slip

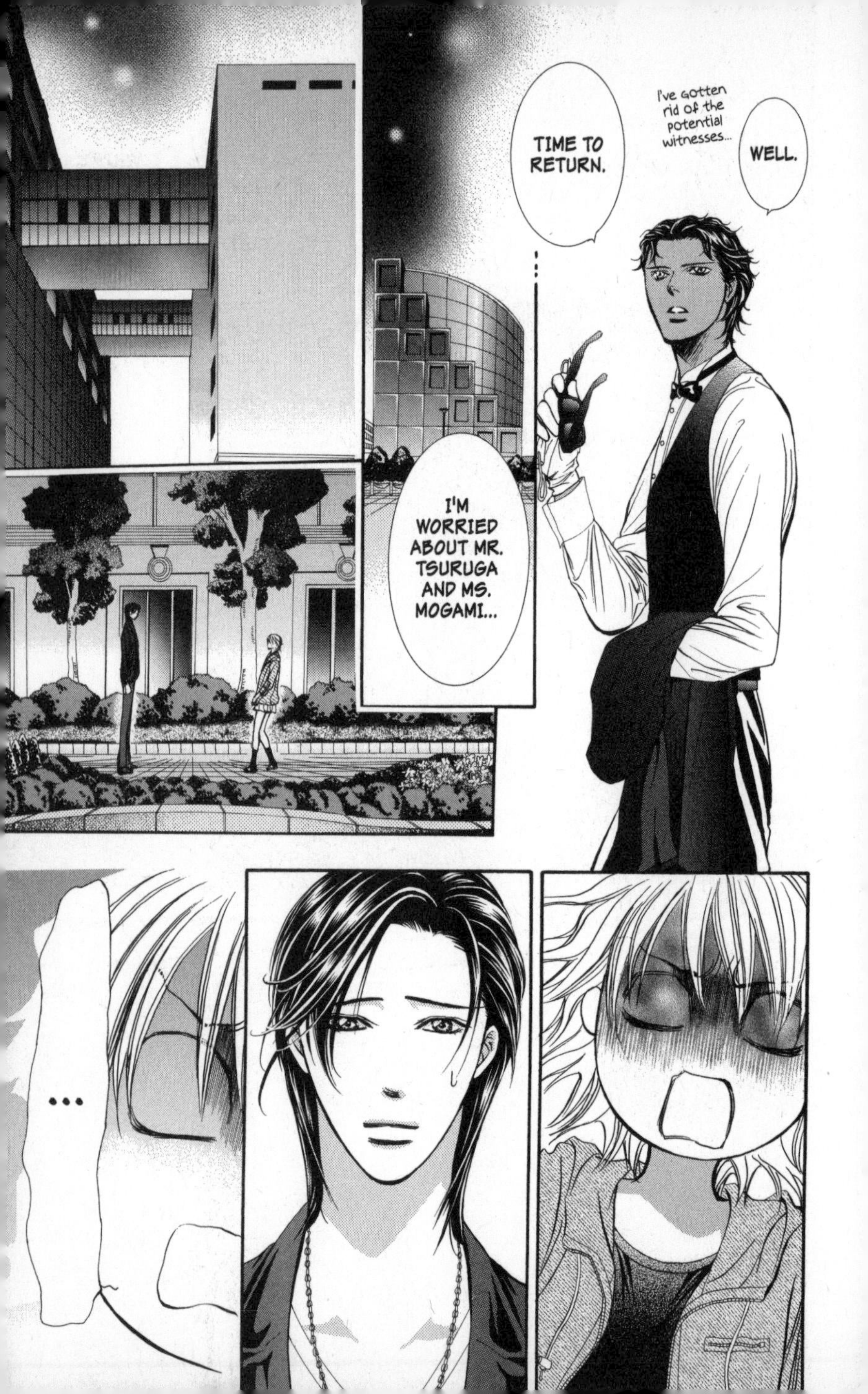
WELL.
I've gotten rid of the potential witnesses...
TIME TO RETURN.
I'M WORRIED ABOUT MR. TSURUGA AND MS. MOGAMI...
...

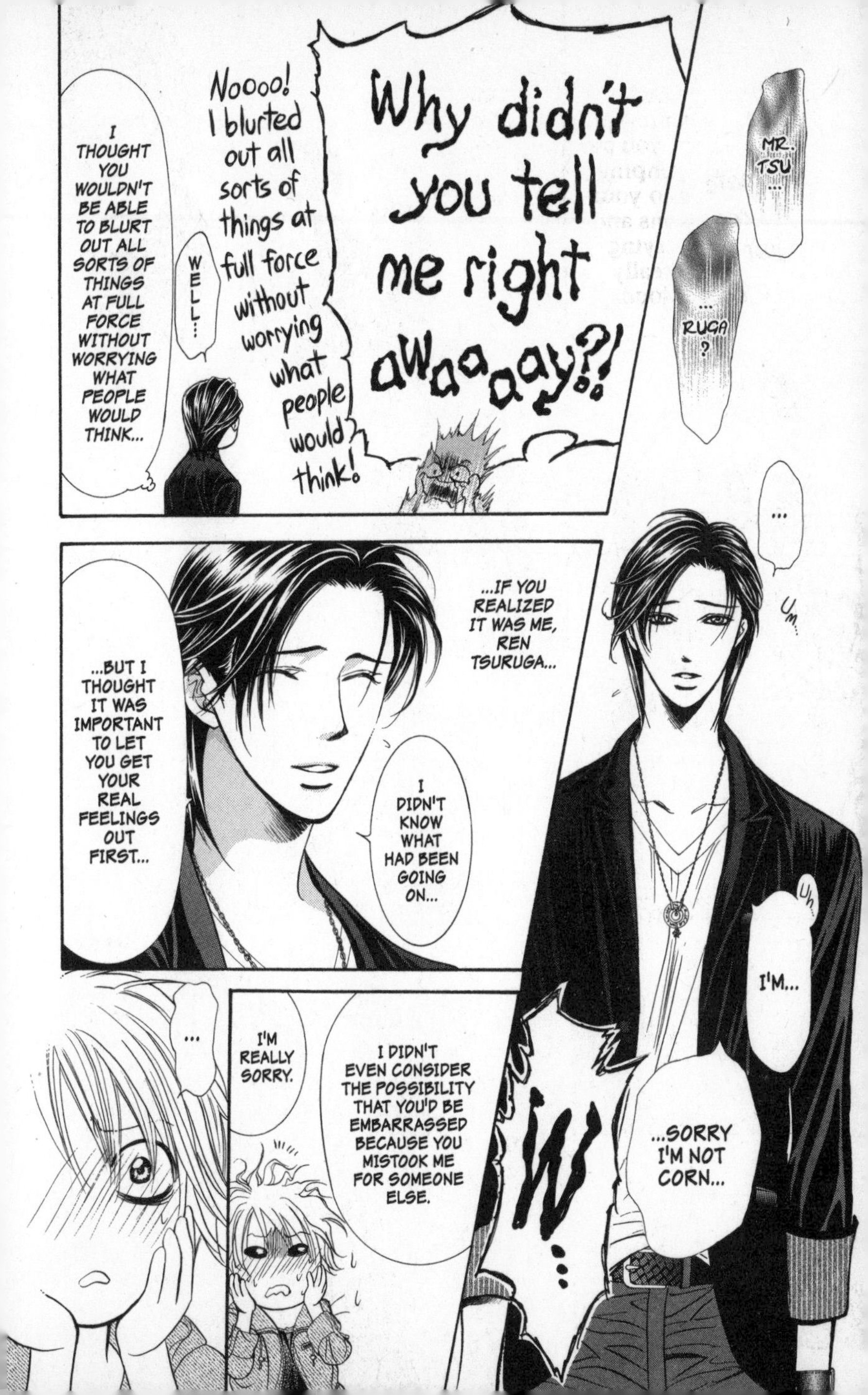
MR. TSU...
...RUGA?
Why didn't you tell me right awaaaay?!
Noooo! I blurted out all sorts of things at full force without worrying what people would think!
WELL...
I THOUGHT YOU WOULDN'T BE ABLE TO BLURT OUT ALL SORTS OF THINGS AT FULL FORCE WITHOUT WORRYING WHAT PEOPLE WOULD THINK...
...
Um...
...IF YOU REALIZED IT WAS ME, REN TSURUGA...
I DIDN'T KNOW WHAT HAD BEEN GOING ON...
...BUT I THOUGHT IT WAS IMPORTANT TO LET YOU GET YOUR REAL FEELINGS OUT FIRST...
Uh...
I'M...
...SORRY I'M NOT CORN...
W...
I DIDN'T EVEN CONSIDER THE POSSIBILITY THAT YOU'D BE EMBARRASSED BECAUSE YOU MISTOOK ME FOR SOMEONE ELSE.
I'M REALLY SORRY.
...

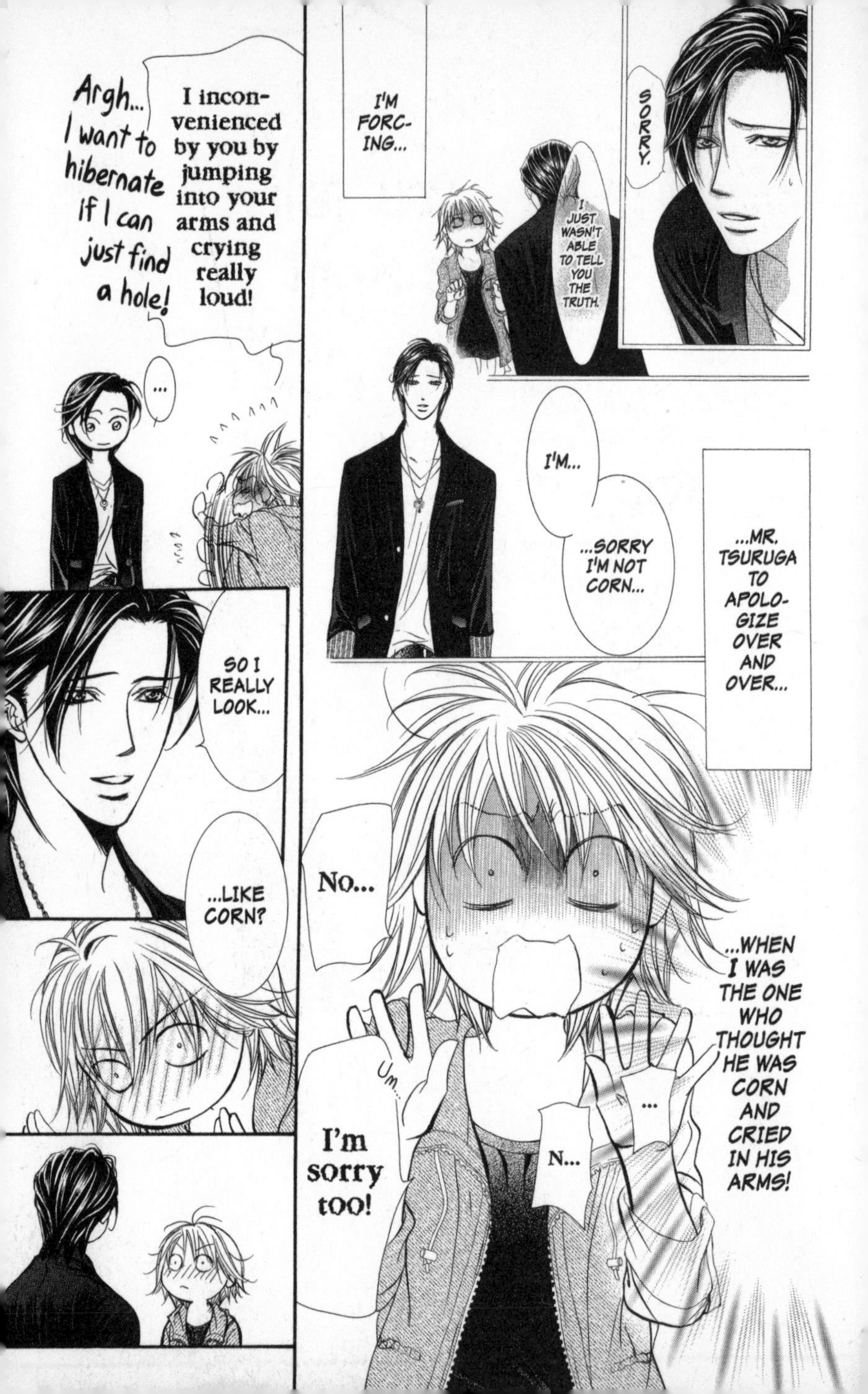
SORRY.
I'M FORCING...
I JUST WASN'T ABLE TO TELL YOU THE TRUTH.
...MR. TSURUGA TO APOLOGIZE OVER AND OVER...
I'M...
...SORRY I'M NOT CORN...
...WHEN I WAS THE ONE WHO THOUGHT HE WAS CORN AND CRIED IN HIS ARMS!
No...
...
N...
Um...
I'm sorry too!
I inconvenienced by you by jumping into your arms and crying really loud!
Argh... I want to hibernate if I can just find a hole!
...
SO I REALLY LOOK...
...LIKE CORN?

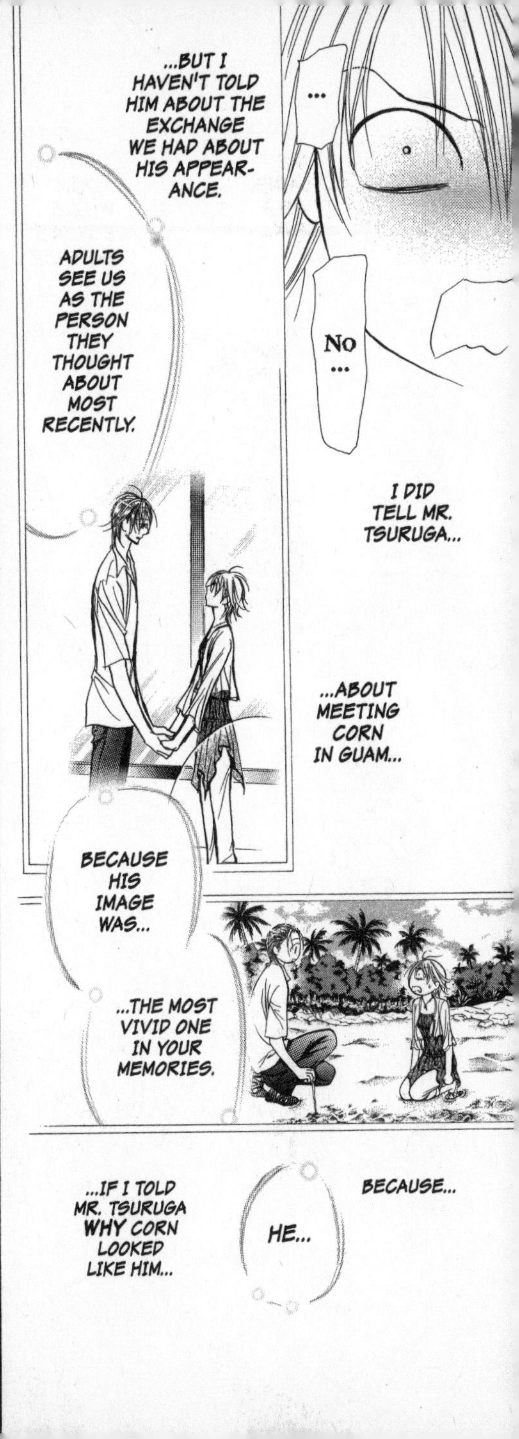
...
No...
I DID TELL MR. TSURUGA...
...ABOUT MEETING CORN IN GUAM...
...BUT I HAVEN'T TOLD HIM ABOUT THE EXCHANGE WE HAD ABOUT HIS APPEAR-ANCE.
ADULTS SEE US AS THE PERSON THEY THOUGHT ABOUT MOST RECENTLY.
BECAUSE HIS IMAGE WAS...
...THE MOST VIVID ONE IN YOUR MEMORIES.
BECAUSE...
HE...
...IF I TOLD MR. TSURUGA WHY CORN LOOKED LIKE HIM...
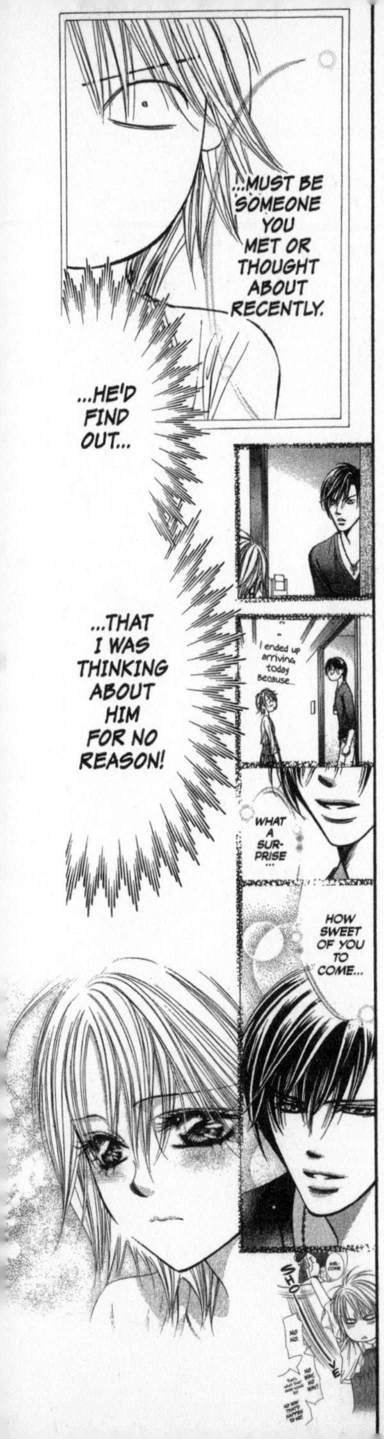
...MUST BE SOMEONE YOU MET OR THOUGHT ABOUT RECENTLY.
...HE'D FIND OUT...
...THAT I WAS THINKING ABOUT HIM FOR NO REASON!
I ended up arriving today because...
WHAT A SUR-PRISE...
HOW SWEET OF YOU TO COME...
WEL-COME.
SHOVE
NO NO.
NO WAY, NO WAY!
NO WAY THAT'D HAPPEN TO ME!

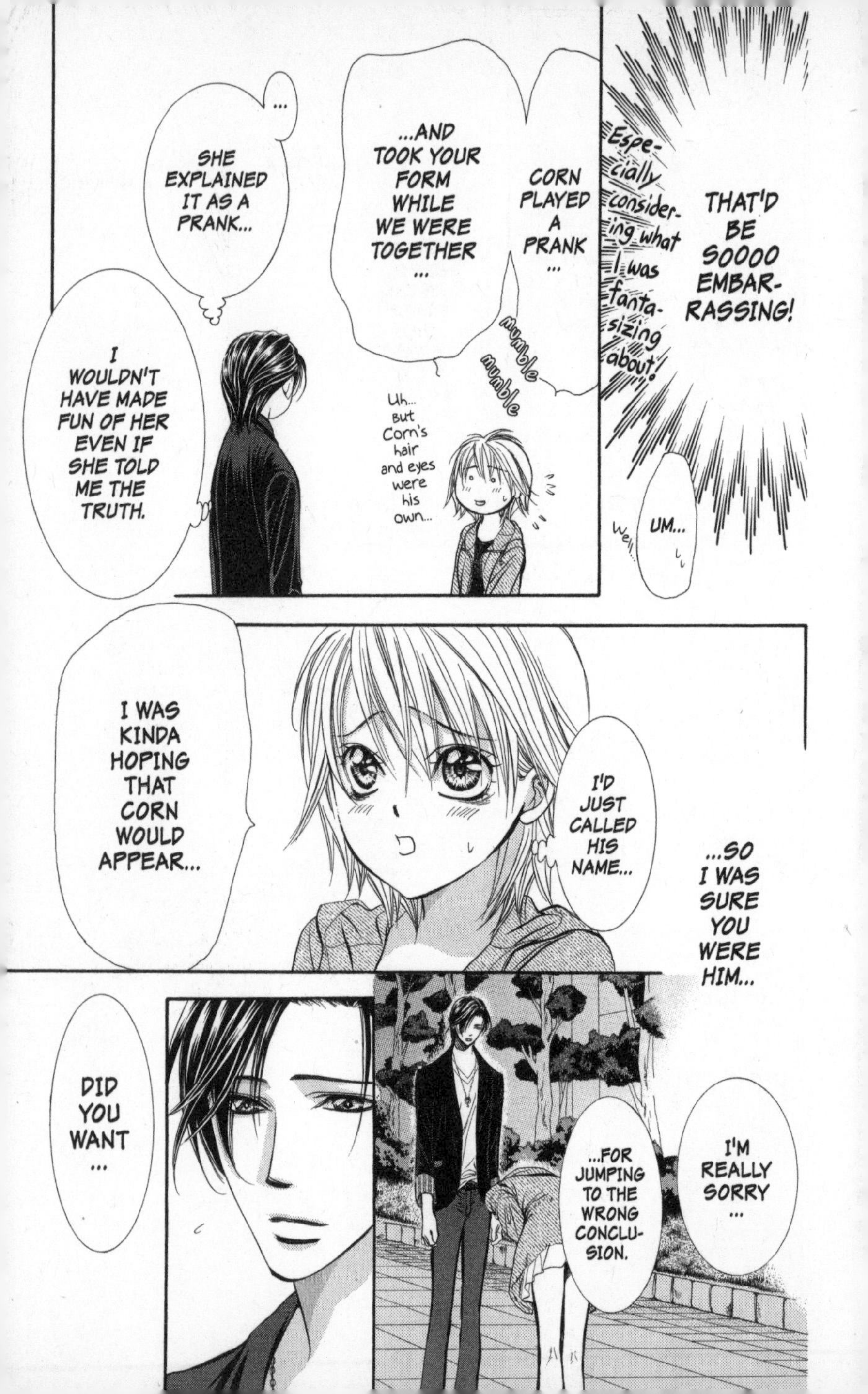
THAT'D BE SOOOO EMBARRASSING!
Especially considering what I was fantasizing about!
CORN PLAYED A PRANK...
...AND TOOK YOUR FORM WHILE WE WERE TOGETHER...
mumble mumble
Uh... but Corn's hair and eyes were his own...
UM...
Well...
...
SHE EXPLAINED IT AS A PRANK...
I WOULDN'T HAVE MADE FUN OF HER EVEN IF SHE TOLD ME THE TRUTH.
...SO I WAS SURE YOU WERE HIM...
I'D JUST CALLED HIS NAME...
I WAS KINDA HOPING THAT CORN WOULD APPEAR...
I'M REALLY SORRY...
...FOR JUMPING TO THE WRONG CONCLUSION.
DID YOU WANT...

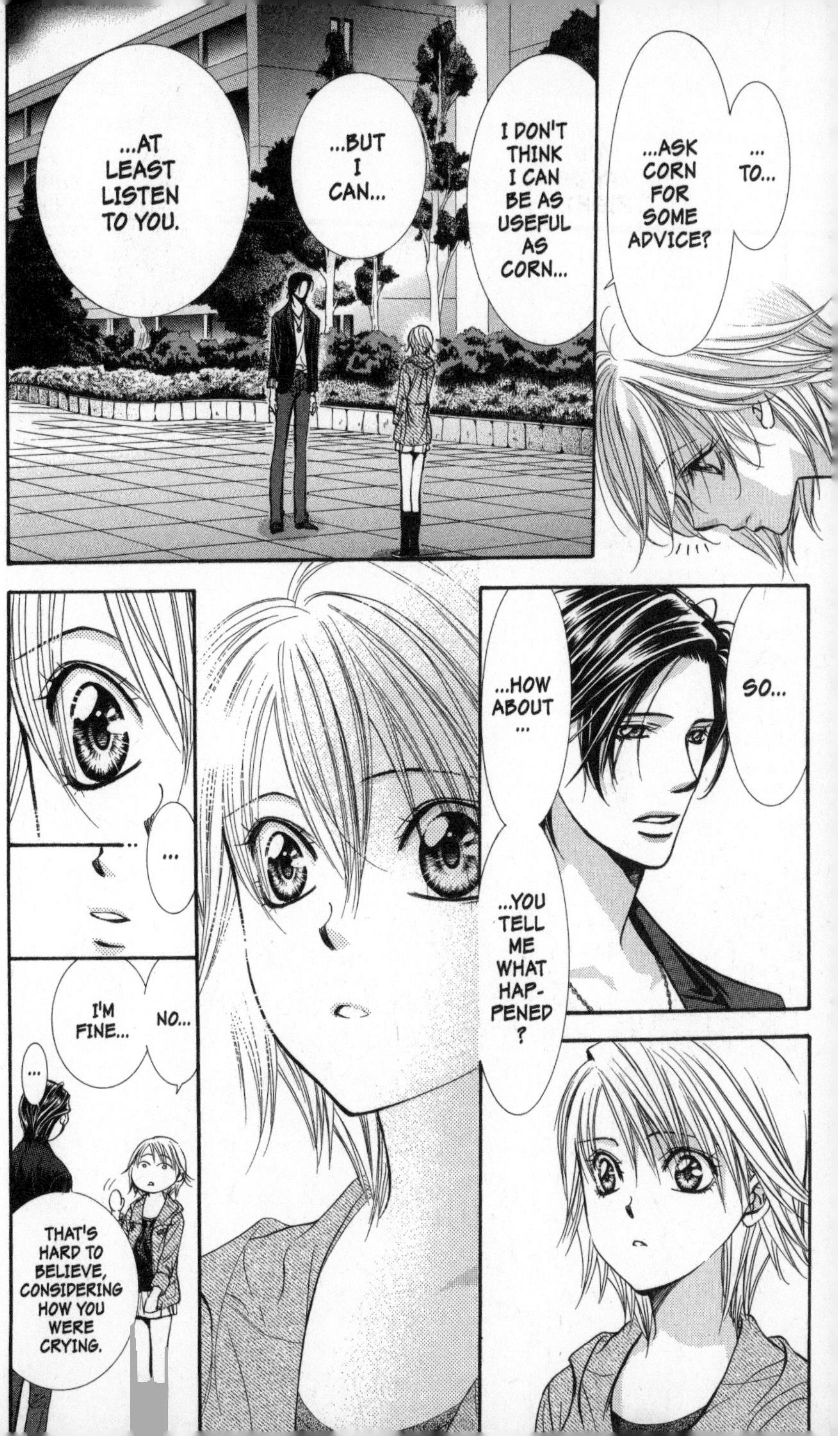
... TO...
...ASK CORN FOR SOME ADVICE?
I DON'T THINK I CAN BE AS USEFUL AS CORN...
...BUT I CAN...
...AT LEAST LISTEN TO YOU.
SO...
...HOW ABOUT ...
...YOU TELL ME WHAT HAP-PENED?
...
NO...
I'M FINE...
...
THAT'S HARD TO BELIEVE, CONSIDERING HOW YOU WERE CRYING.

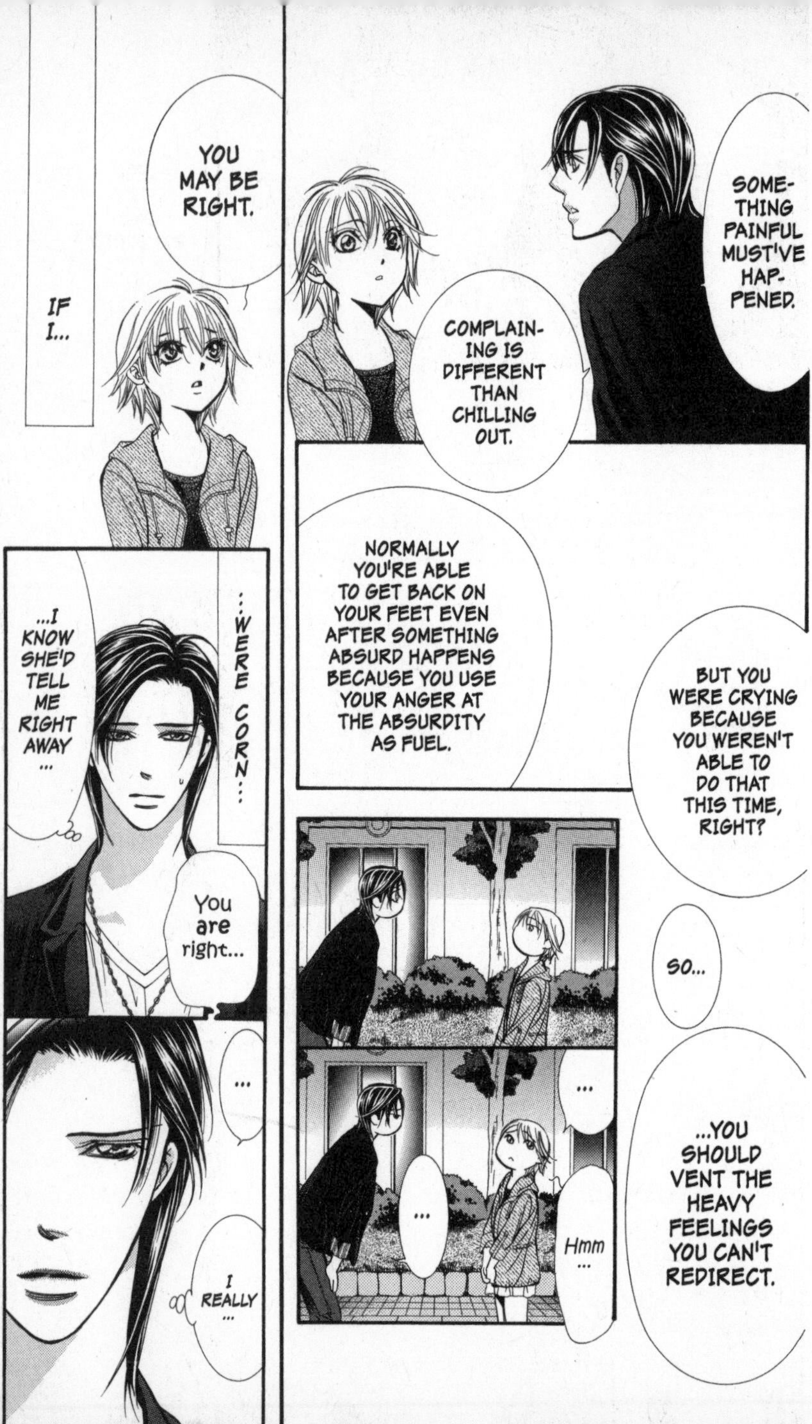
SOME-THING PAINFUL MUST'VE HAP-PENED.
COMPLAIN-ING IS DIFFERENT THAN CHILLING OUT.
NORMALLY YOU'RE ABLE TO GET BACK ON YOUR FEET EVEN AFTER SOMETHING ABSURD HAPPENS BECAUSE YOU USE YOUR ANGER AT THE ABSURDITY AS FUEL.
BUT YOU WERE CRYING BECAUSE YOU WEREN'T ABLE TO DO THAT THIS TIME, RIGHT?
SO...
...YOU SHOULD VENT THE HEAVY FEELINGS YOU CAN'T REDIRECT.
...
Hmm ...
...
YOU MAY BE RIGHT.
IF I...
...WERE CORN...
...I KNOW SHE'D TELL ME RIGHT AWAY ...
You are right...
...
I REALLY ...

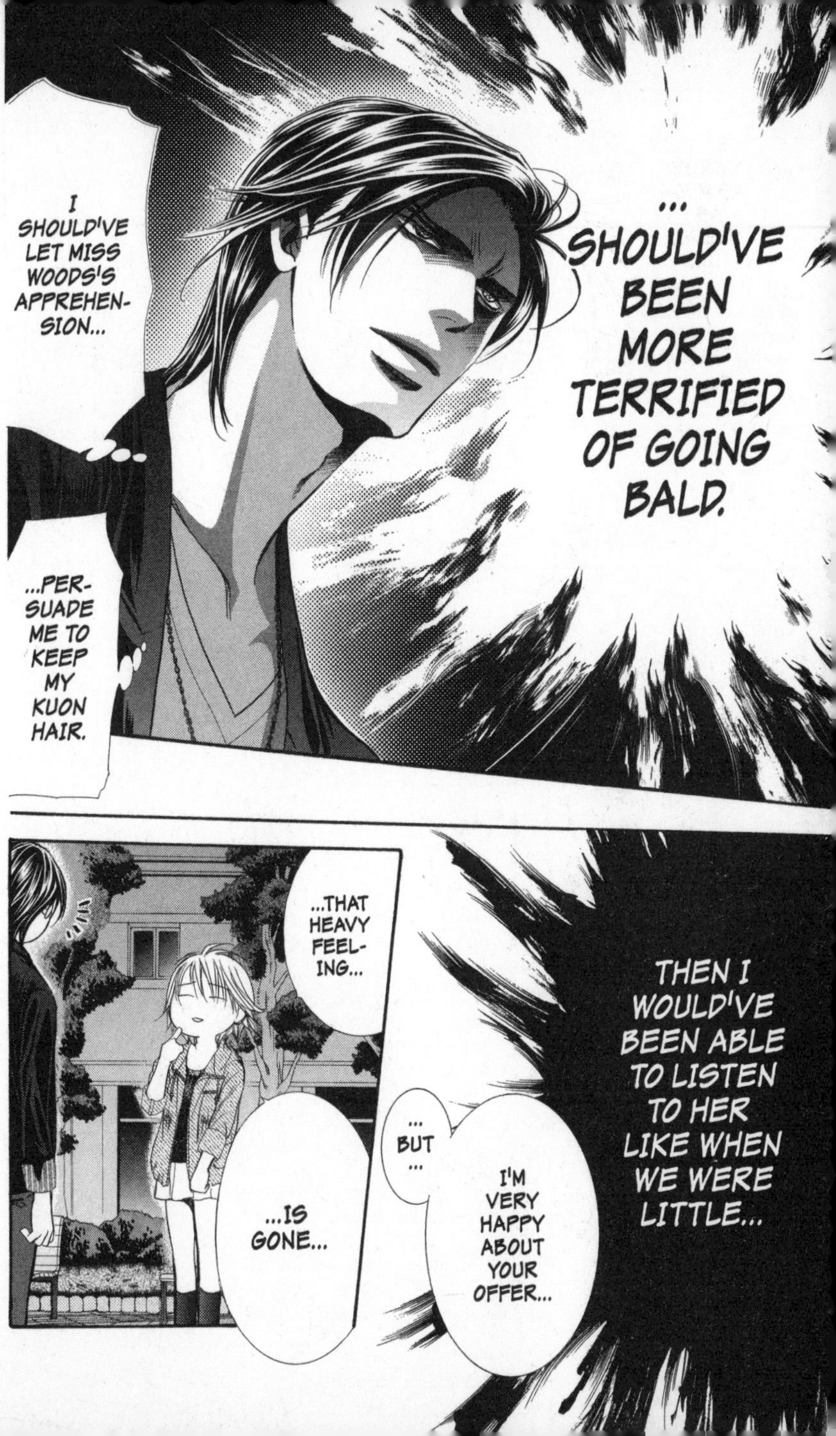
I SHOULD'VE LET MISS WOODS'S APPREHENSION...
...PERSUADE ME TO KEEP MY KUON HAIR.
...SHOULD'VE BEEN MORE TERRIFIED OF GOING BALD.
THEN I WOULD'VE BEEN ABLE TO LISTEN TO HER LIKE WHEN WE WERE LITTLE...
I'M VERY HAPPY ABOUT YOUR OFFER...
...BUT...
...THAT HEAVY FEELING...
...IS GONE...

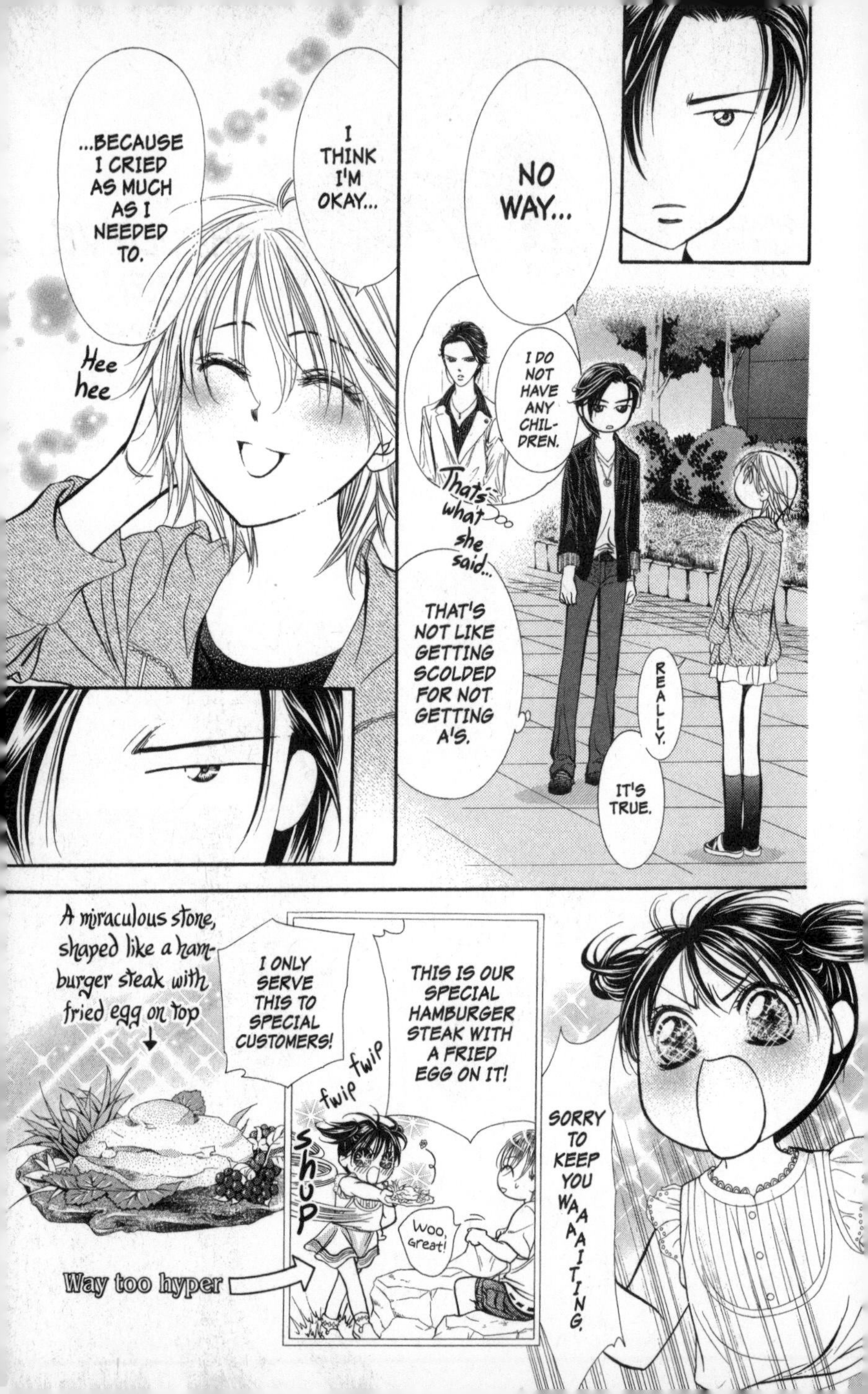
NO WAY...
I DO NOT HAVE ANY CHILDREN.
That's what she said...
THAT'S NOT LIKE GETTING SCOLDED FOR NOT GETTING A'S.
REALLY.
IT'S TRUE.
I THINK I'M OKAY...
...BECAUSE I CRIED AS MUCH AS I NEEDED TO.
Hee hee
SORRY TO KEEP YOU WAAAAAITING.
THIS IS OUR SPECIAL HAMBURGER STEAK WITH A FRIED EGG ON IT!
I ONLY SERVE THIS TO SPECIAL CUSTOMERS!
fwip fwip
SHUP
Woo, Great!
A miraculous stone, shaped like a hamburger steak with fried egg on top
Way too hyper

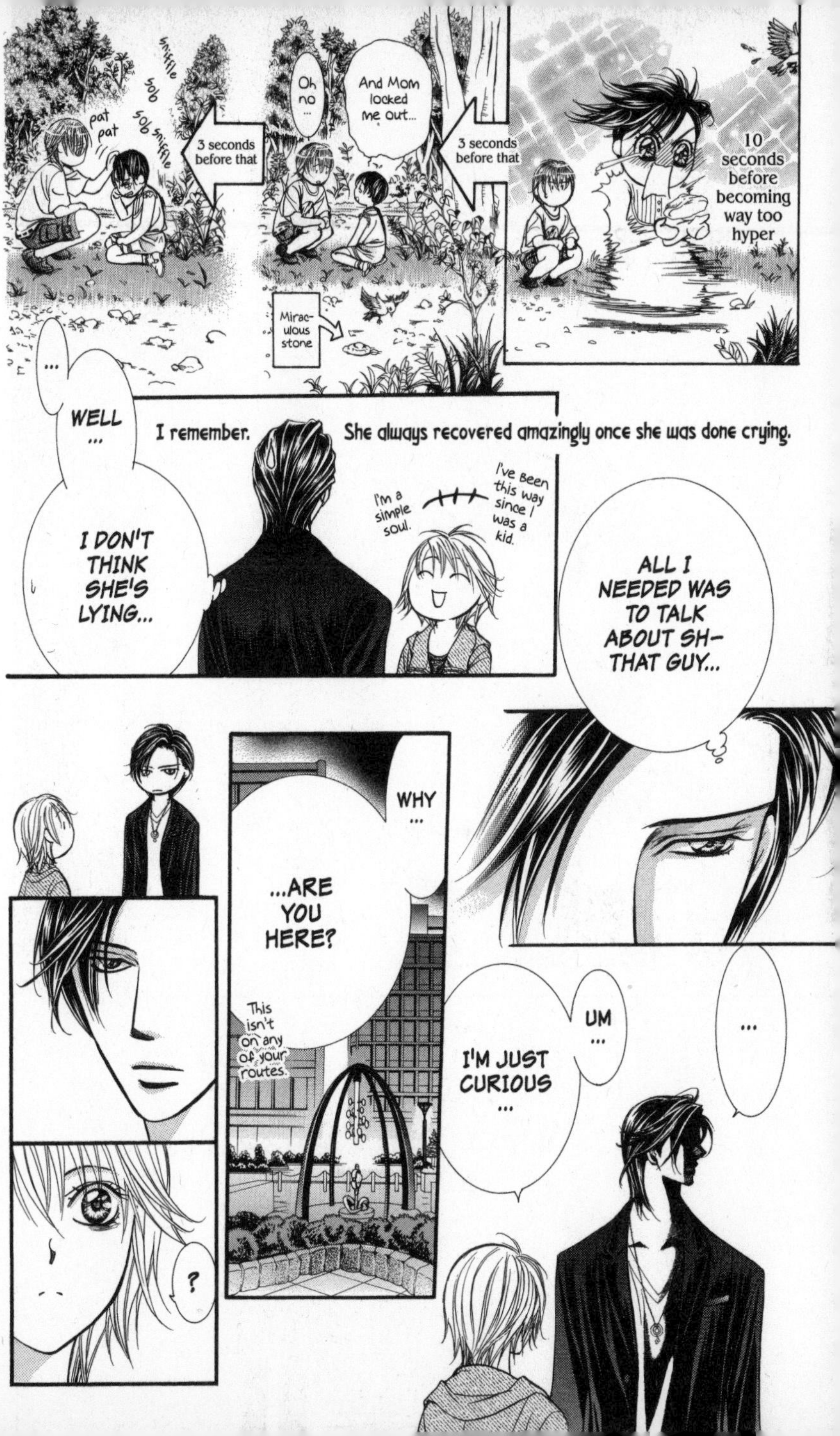
10 seconds before becoming way too hyper
3 seconds before that
And Mom locked me out...
Oh no...
Miraculous stone
3 seconds before that
pat pat
sniffle
sob
sob sniffle
She always recovered amazingly once she was done crying.
I remember.
I've been this way since I was a kid.
I'm a simple soul.
...
WELL...
I DON'T THINK SHE'S LYING...
ALL I NEEDED WAS TO TALK ABOUT SH- THAT GUY...
...
UM...
I'M JUST CURIOUS...
WHY...
...ARE YOU HERE?
This isn't on any of your routes.
?

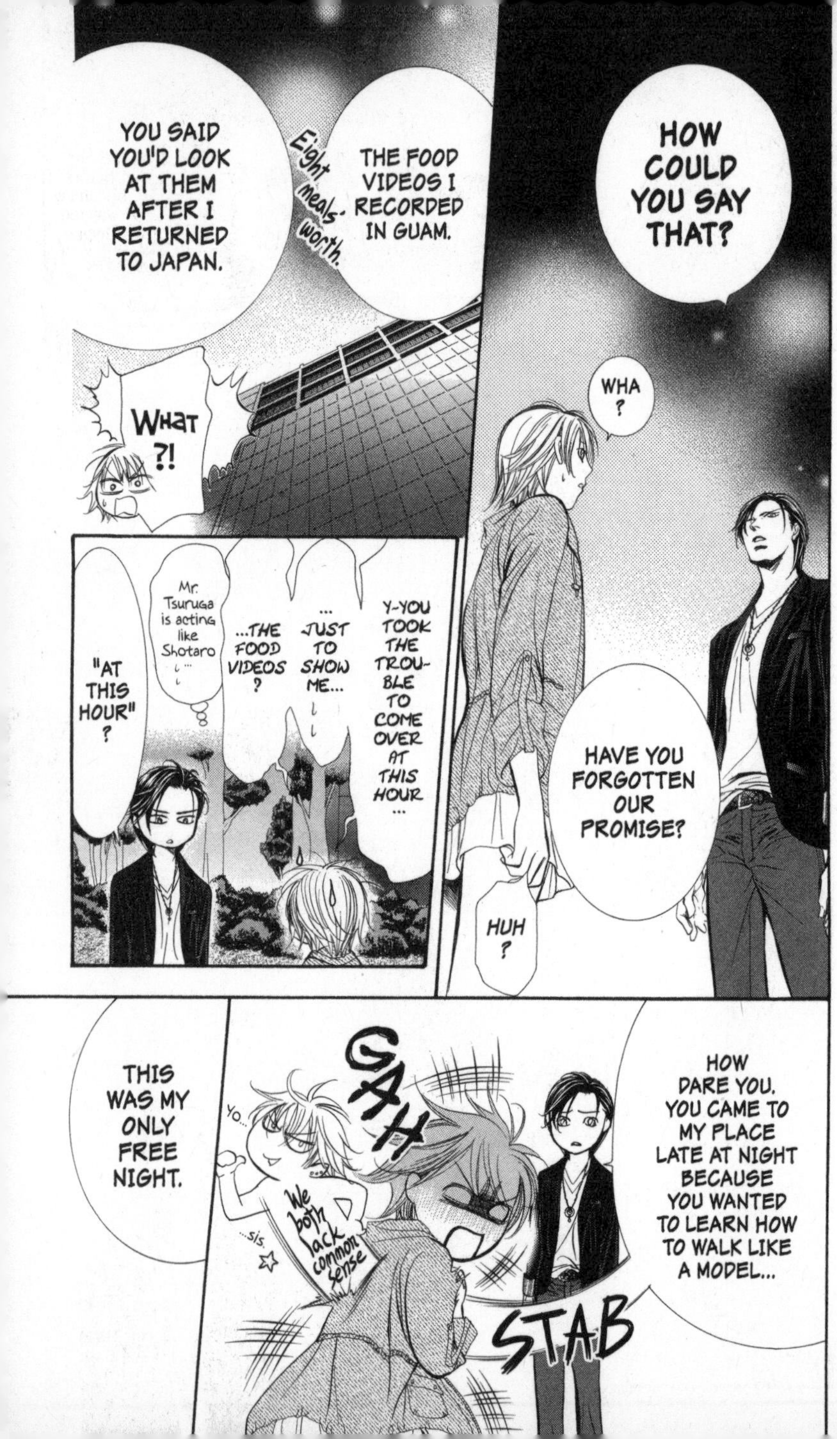
HOW COULD YOU SAY THAT?
WHA?
HAVE YOU FORGOTTEN OUR PROMISE?
HUH?
THE FOOD VIDEOS I RECORDED IN GUAM.
Eight meals' worth.
YOU SAID YOU'D LOOK AT THEM AFTER I RETURNED TO JAPAN.
WHAT?!
Y-YOU TOOK THE TROUBLE TO COME OVER AT THIS HOUR...
...JUST TO SHOW ME...
...THE FOOD VIDEOS?
Mr. Tsuruga is acting like Shotaro...
"AT THIS HOUR"?
HOW DARE YOU. YOU CAME TO MY PLACE LATE AT NIGHT BECAUSE YOU WANTED TO LEARN HOW TO WALK LIKE A MODEL...
STAB
GAH
We both lack common sense
Yo...
...sis.
THIS WAS MY ONLY FREE NIGHT.

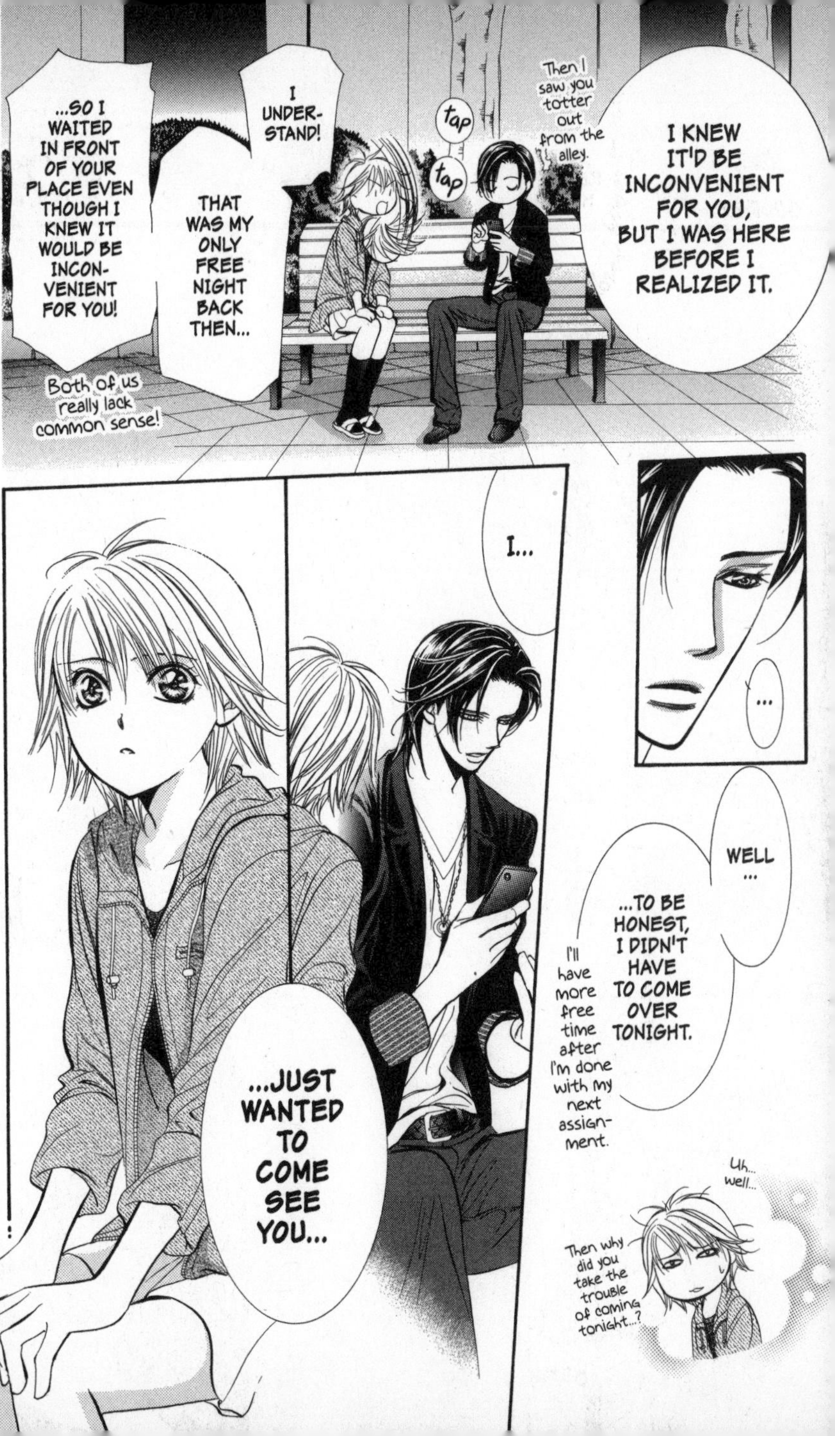
I KNEW IT'D BE INCONVENIENT FOR YOU, BUT I WAS HERE BEFORE I REALIZED IT.
Then I saw you totter out from the alley.
tap
tap
I UNDERSTAND!
THAT WAS MY ONLY FREE NIGHT BACK THEN...
...SO I WAITED IN FRONT OF YOUR PLACE EVEN THOUGH I KNEW IT WOULD BE INCONVENIENT FOR YOU!
Both of us really lack common sense!
...
WELL ...
...TO BE HONEST, I DIDN'T HAVE TO COME OVER TONIGHT.
I'll have more free time after I'm done with my next assignment.
Uh... well...
Then why did you take the trouble of coming tonight...?
I...
...JUST WANTED TO COME SEE YOU...

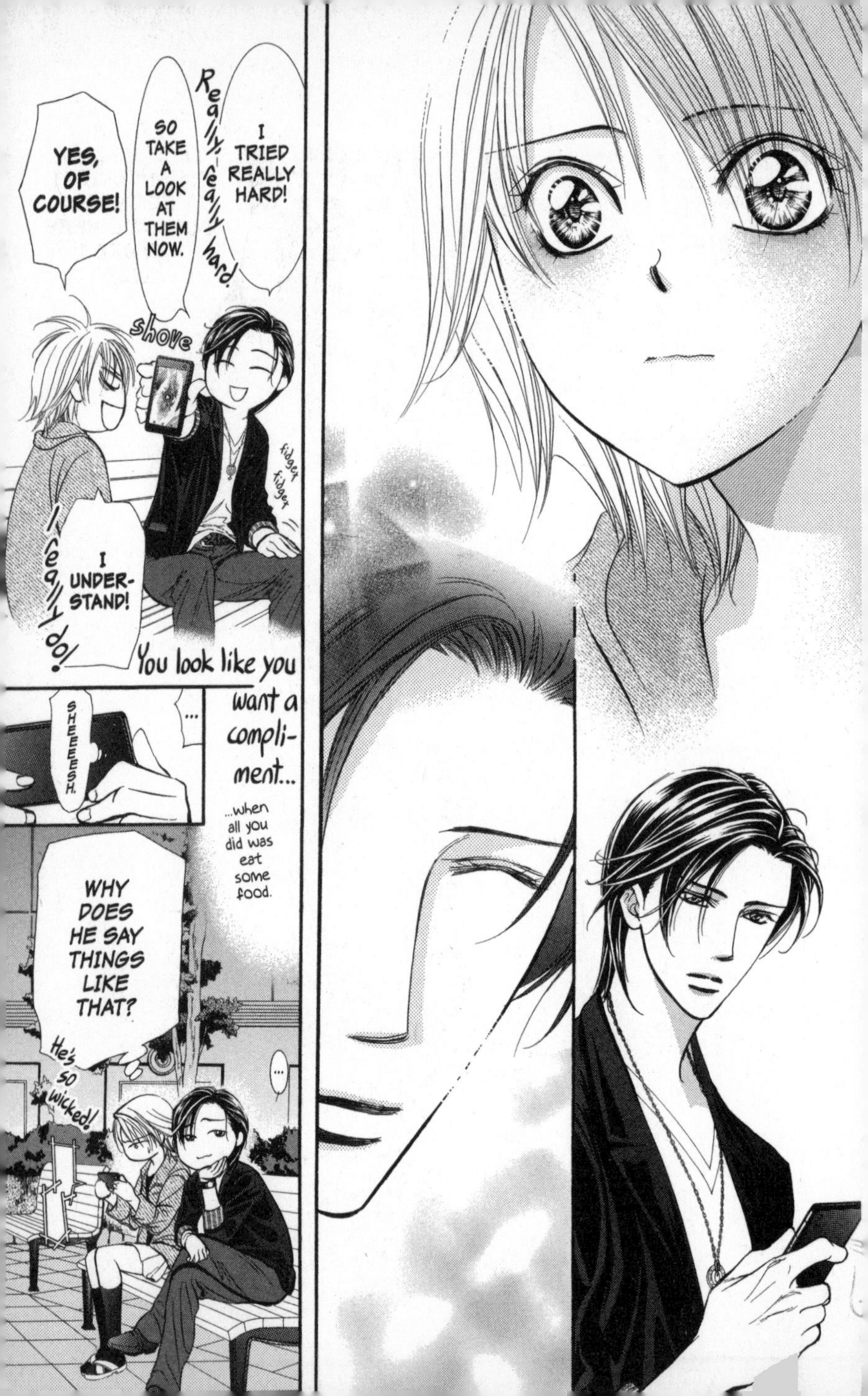
I TRIED REALLY HARD!
Really, really hard.
SO TAKE A LOOK AT THEM NOW.
YES, OF COURSE!
shove
fidget fidget
I UNDERSTAND!
I really do!
You look like you want a compliment...
...
SHEEEEESH.
...when all you did was eat some food.
...
WHY DOES HE SAY THINGS LIKE THAT?
He's so wicked!

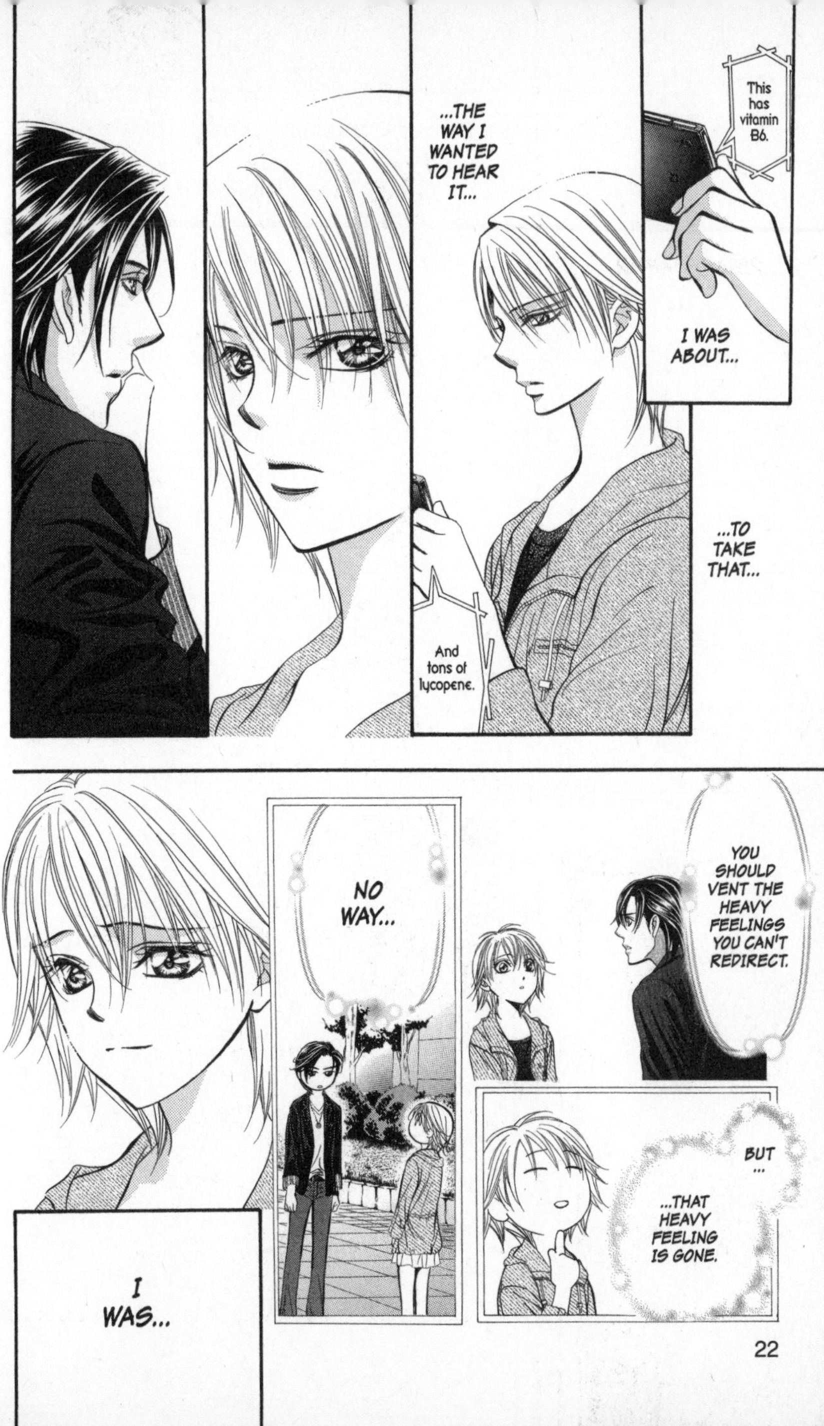
This has vitamin B6.
I WAS ABOUT...
...TO TAKE THAT...
...THE WAY I WANTED TO HEAR IT...
And tons of lycopene.
YOU SHOULD VENT THE HEAVY FEELINGS YOU CAN'T REDIRECT.
BUT ...
...THAT HEAVY FEELING IS GONE.
NO WAY...
I WAS...

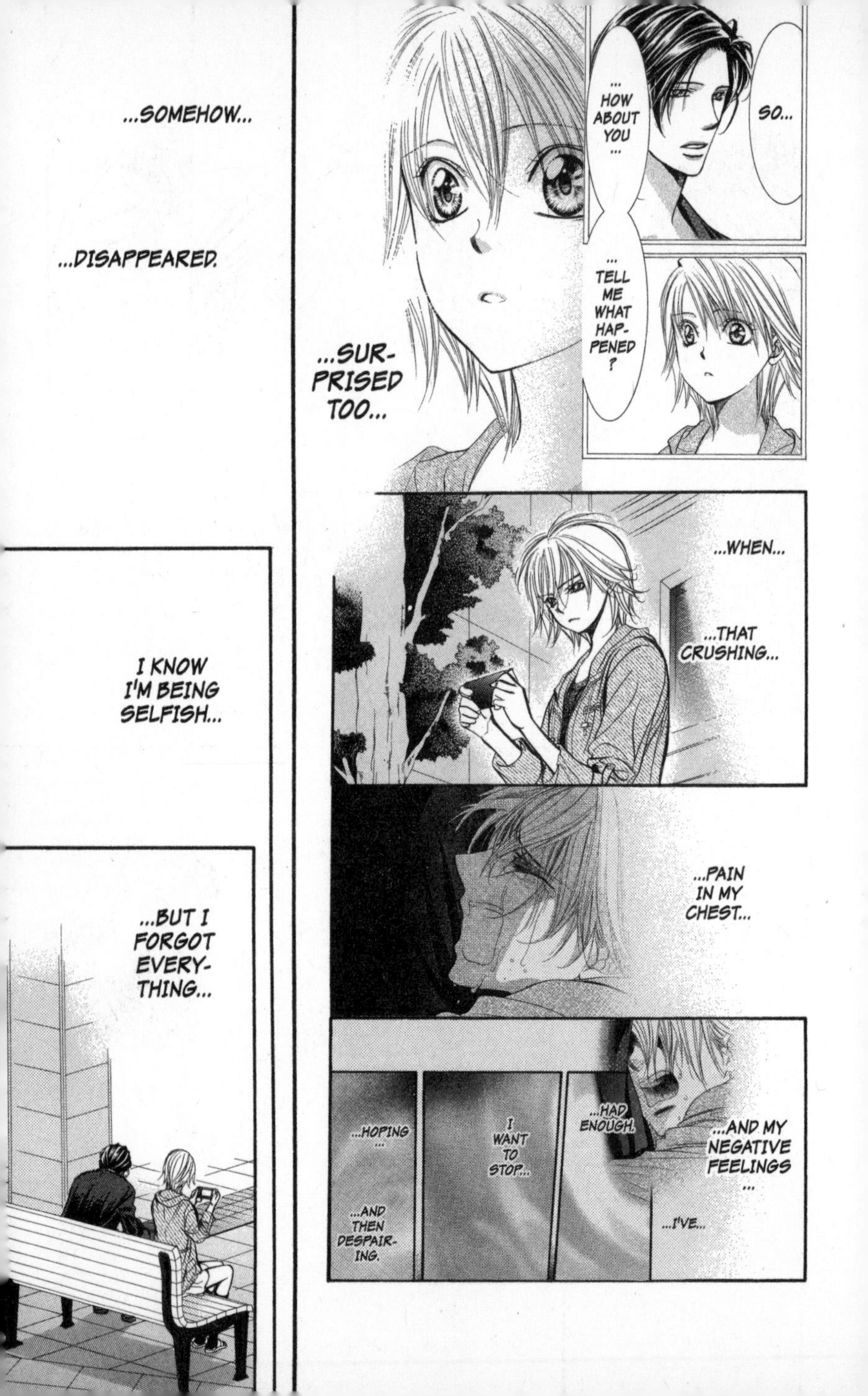
SO...
...HOW ABOUT YOU...
...TELL ME WHAT HAPPENED?
...SURPRISED TOO...
...WHEN...
...THAT CRUSHING...
...PAIN IN MY CHEST...
...AND MY NEGATIVE FEELINGS...
...I'VE...
...HAD ENOUGH.
I WANT TO STOP...
...HOPING...
...AND THEN DESPAIRING.
...SOMEHOW...
...DISAPPEARED.
I KNOW I'M BEING SELFISH...
...BUT I FORGOT EVERYTHING...

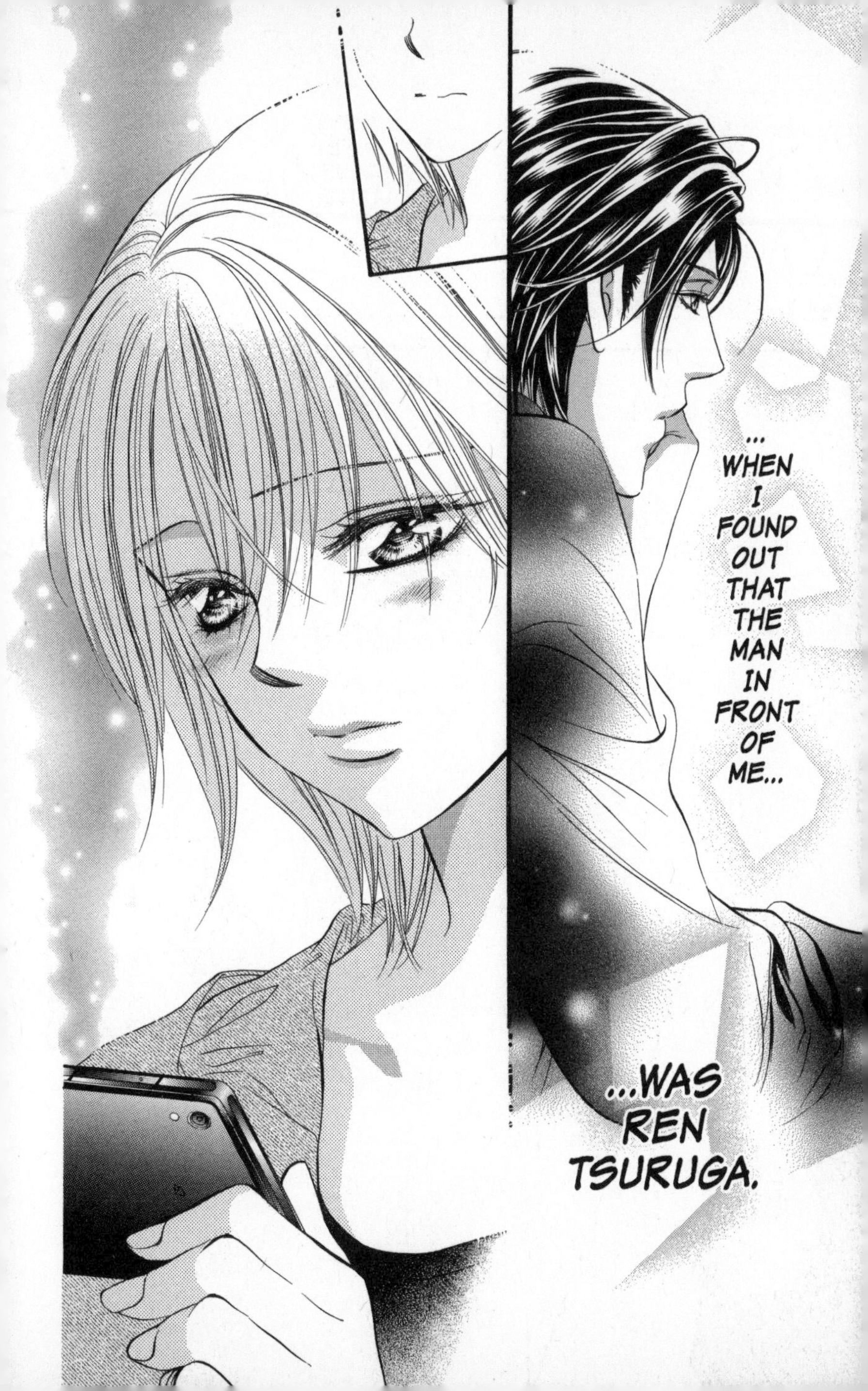
...WHEN I FOUND OUT THAT THE MAN IN FRONT OF ME...
...WAS REN TSURUGA.

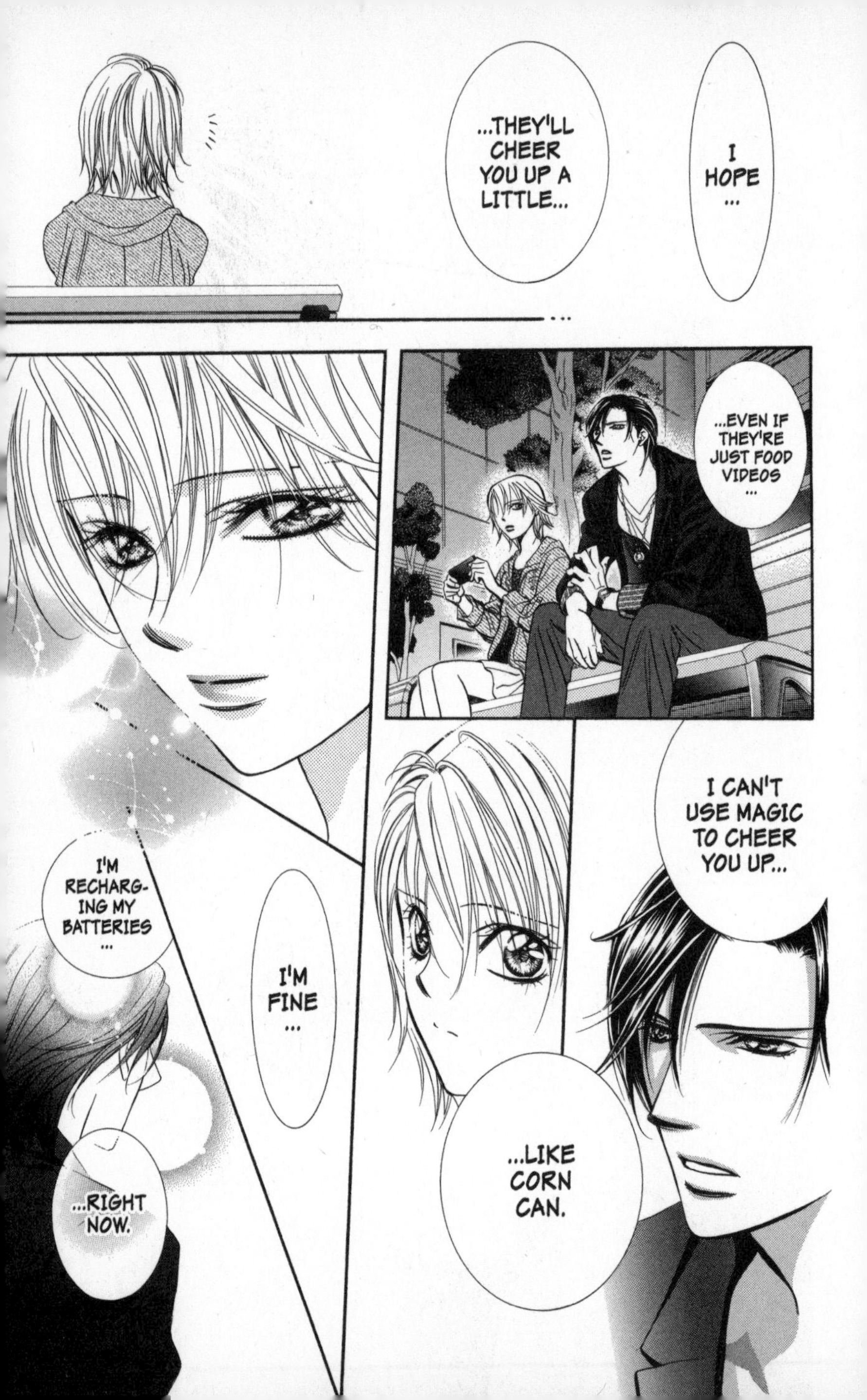

I HOPE ...
...THEY'LL CHEER YOU UP A LITTLE...
...
...EVEN IF THEY'RE JUST FOOD VIDEOS ...
I CAN'T USE MAGIC TO CHEER YOU UP...
...LIKE CORN CAN.
I'M FINE ...
I'M RECHARG-ING MY BATTERIES ...
...RIGHT NOW.

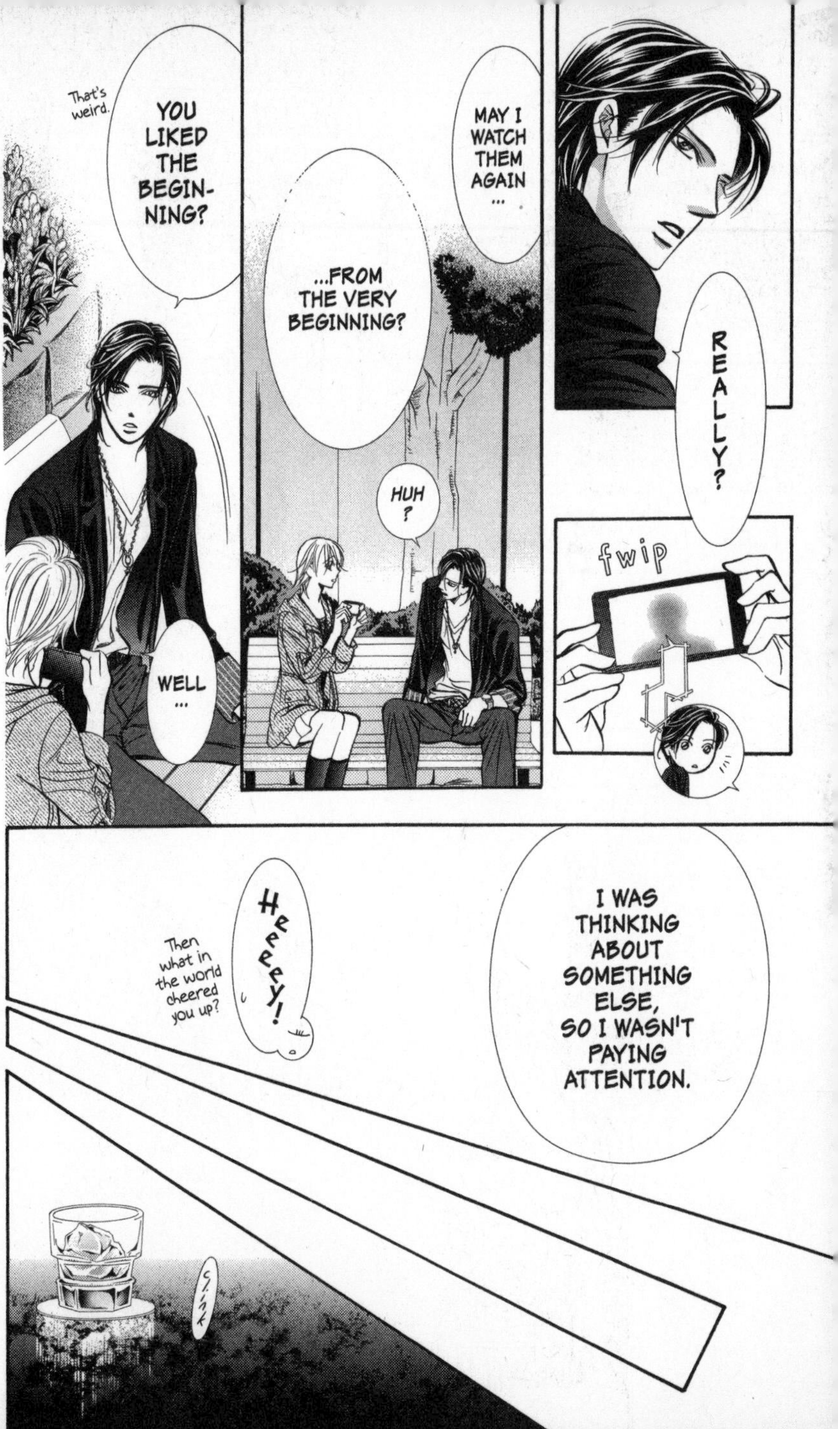
REALLY?
fwip
MAY I WATCH THEM AGAIN...
...FROM THE VERY BEGINNING?
HUH?
YOU LIKED THE BEGIN-NING?
That's weird.
WELL...
I WAS THINKING ABOUT SOMETHING ELSE, SO I WASN'T PAYING ATTENTION.
Heeeey!
Then what in the world cheered you up?
clink

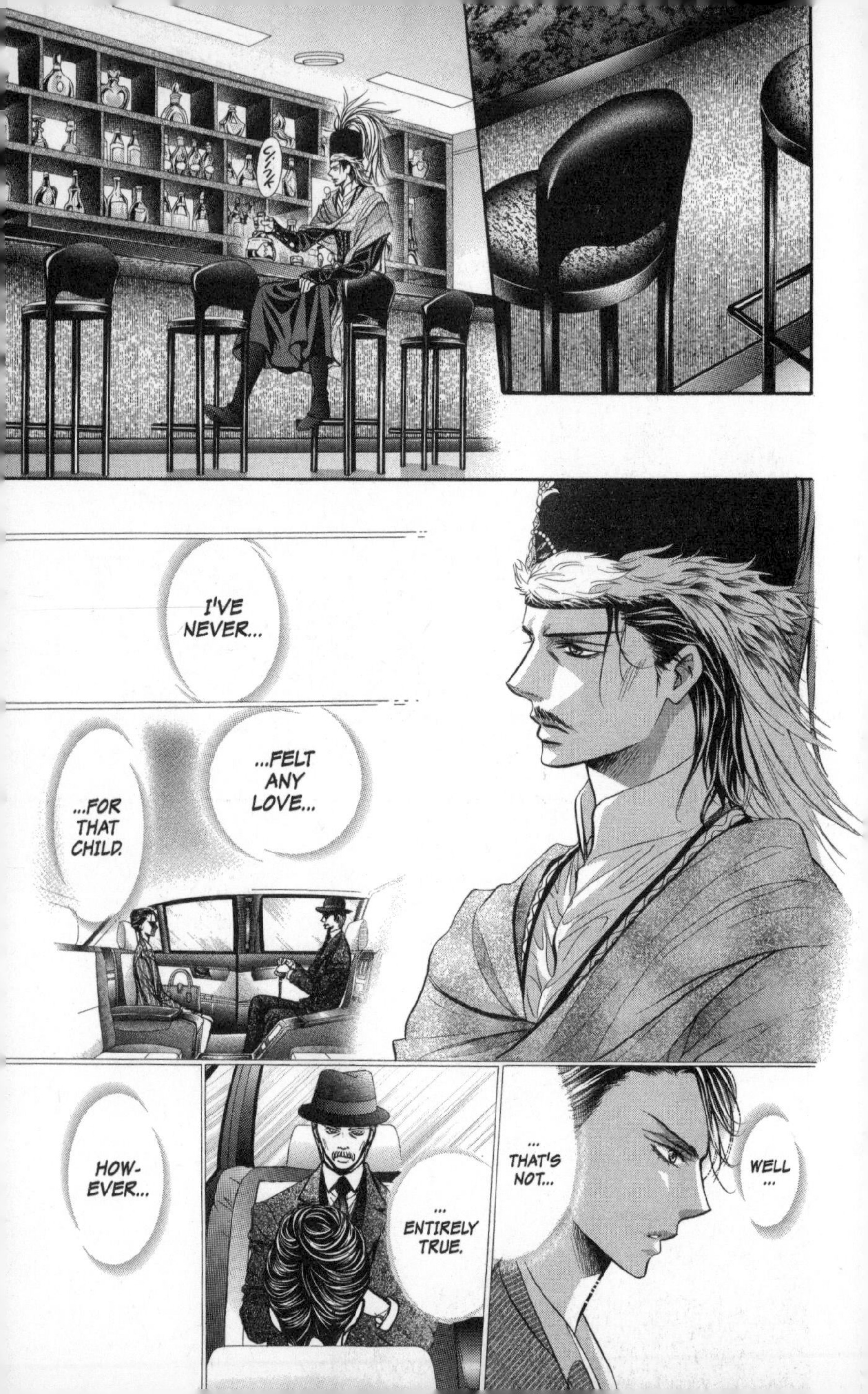
clink
I'VE NEVER...
...FELT ANY LOVE...
...FOR THAT CHILD.
WELL ...
... THAT'S NOT...
... ENTIRELY TRUE.
HOW-EVER...

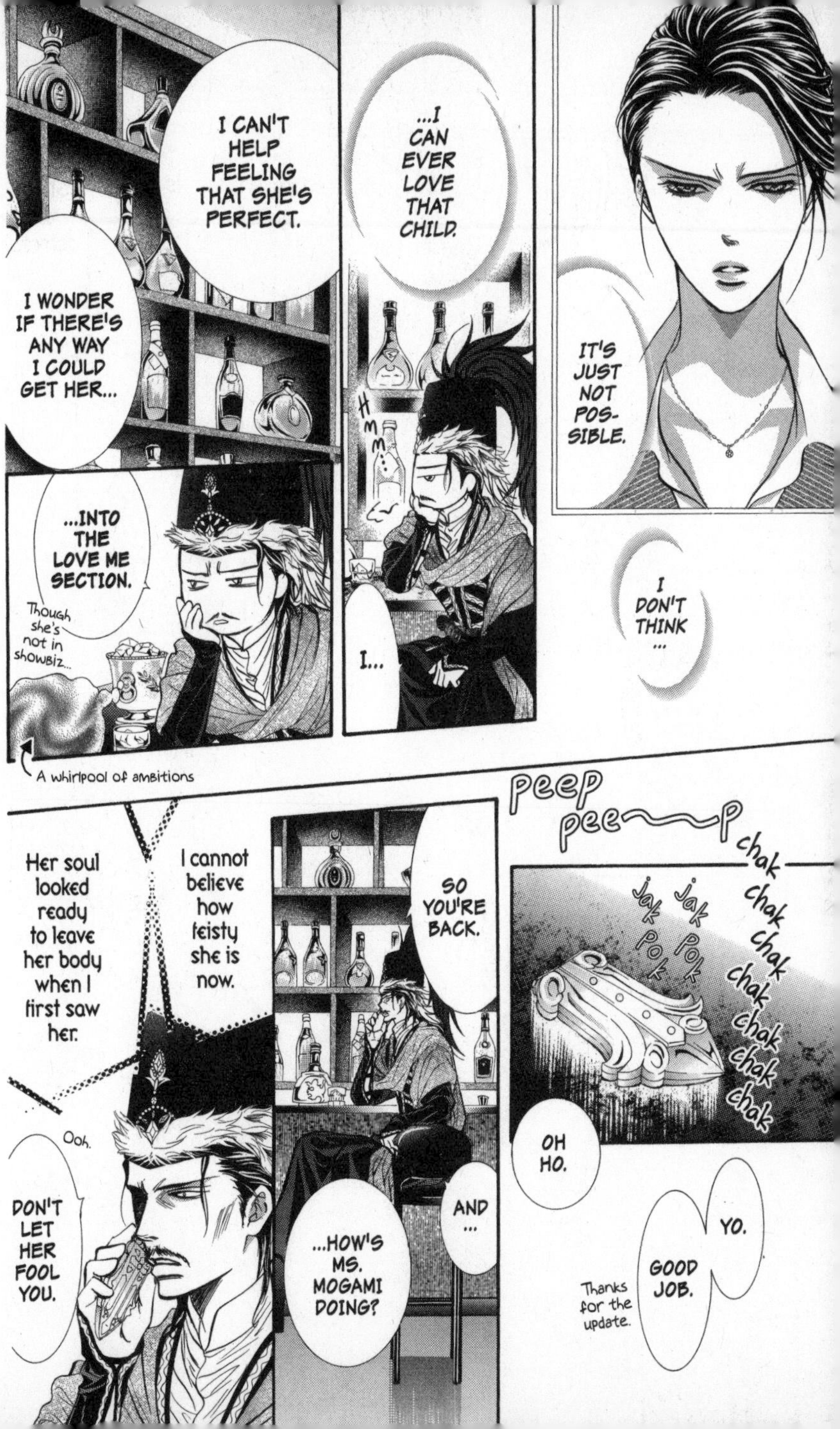
IT'S JUST NOT POSSIBLE.
I DON'T THINK...
I...
...I CAN EVER LOVE THAT CHILD.
HMM...
I CAN'T HELP FEELING THAT SHE'S PERFECT.
I WONDER IF THERE'S ANY WAY I COULD GET HER...
...INTO THE LOVE ME SECTION.
Though she's not in showbiz...
A whirlpool of ambitions
peep pee~~p
chak chak chak chak chak chak chak chak
jak pok jak pok
OH HO.
YO.
GOOD JOB.
Thanks for the update.
SO YOU'RE BACK.
AND...
...HOW'S MS. MOGAMI DOING?
I cannot believe how feisty she is now.
Her soul looked ready to leave her body when I first saw her.
Ooh.
DON'T LET HER FOOL YOU.

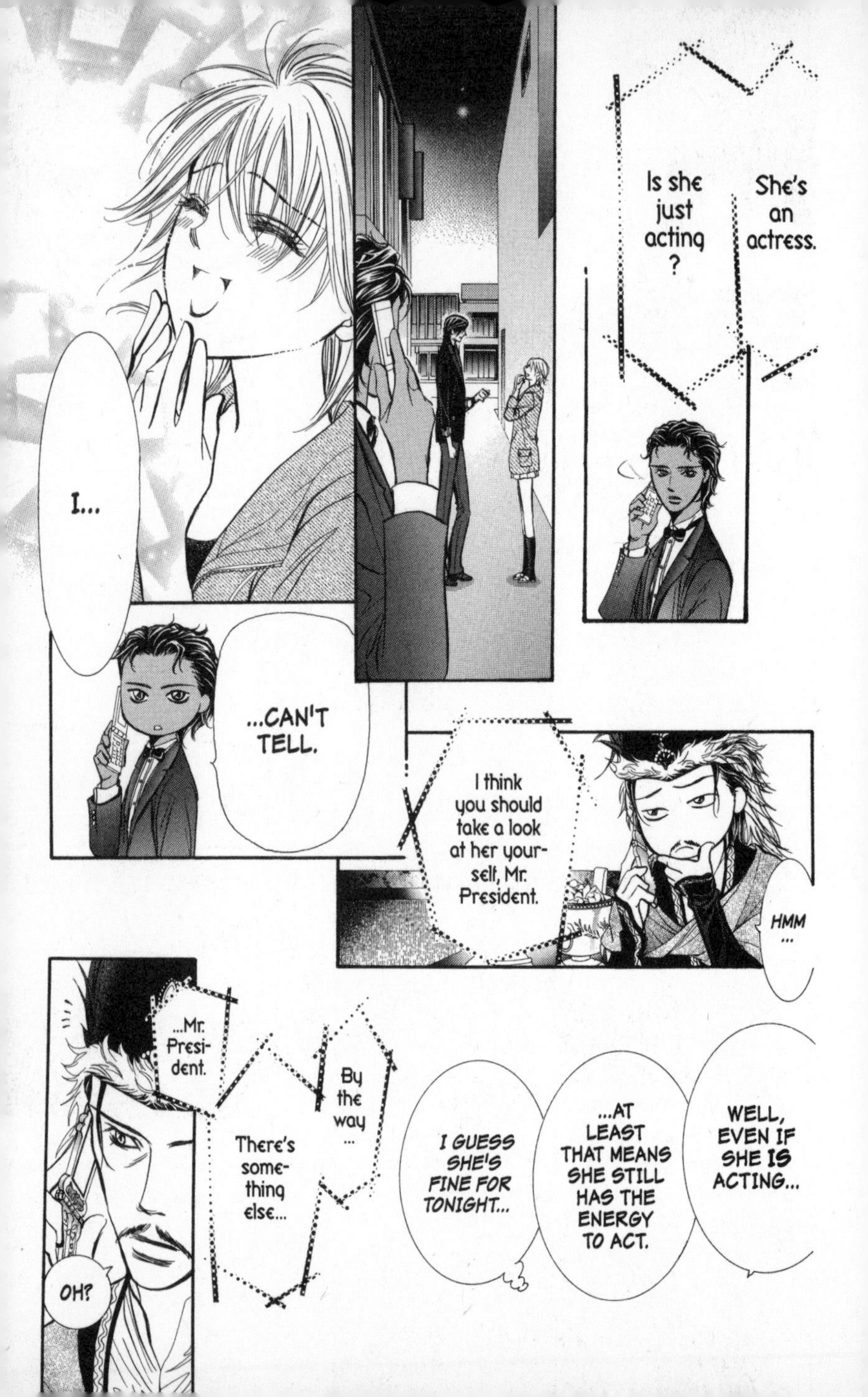
She's an actress.
Is she just acting?
I...
...CAN'T TELL.
I think you should take a look at her your-self, Mr. President.
HMM...
WELL, EVEN IF SHE **IS** ACTING...
...AT LEAST THAT MEANS SHE STILL HAS THE ENERGY TO ACT.
I GUESS SHE'S FINE FOR TONIGHT...
...Mr. Presi-dent.
By the way...
There's some-thing else...
OH?

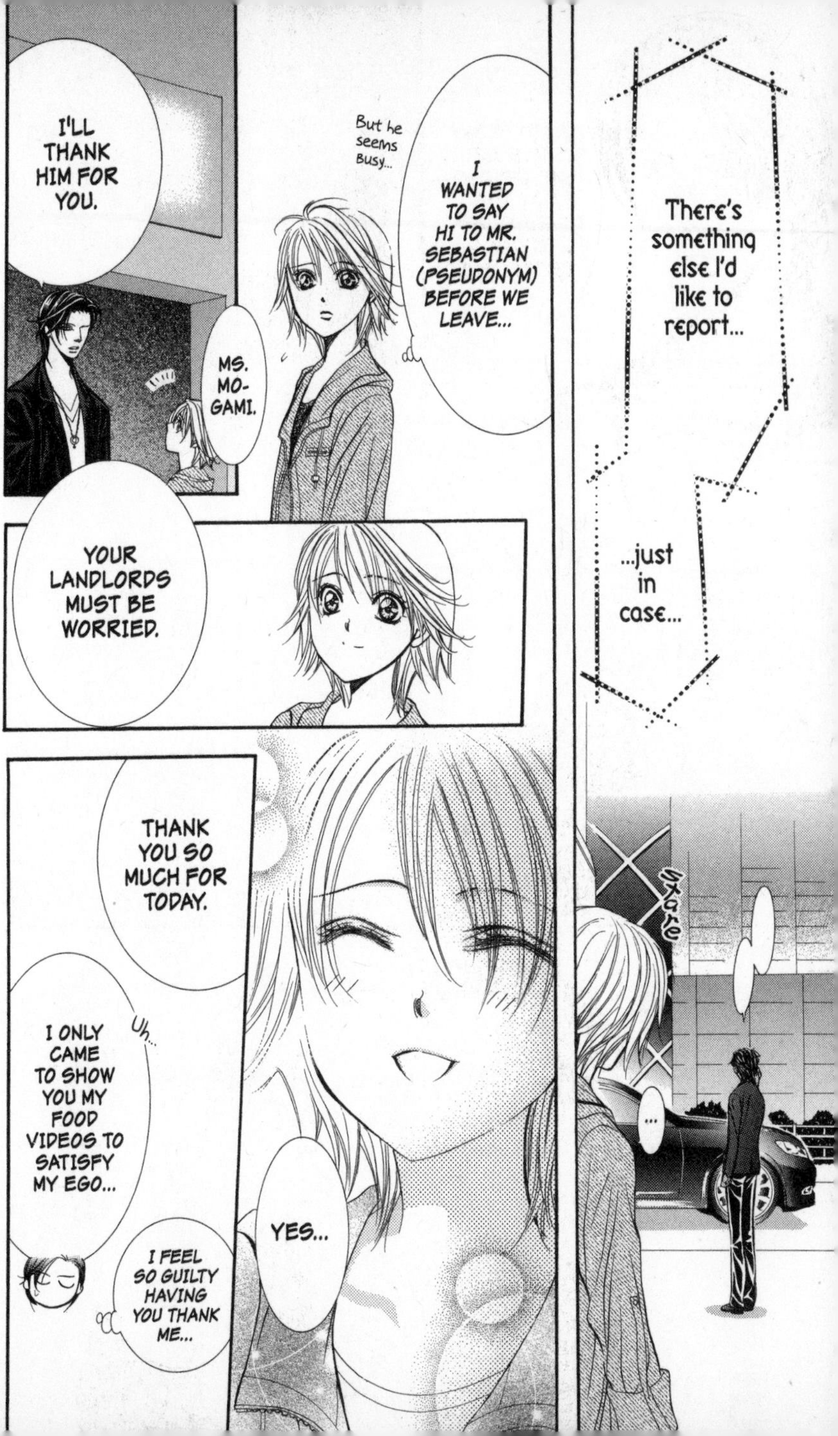
There's something else I'd like to report...
...just in case...
Stare
...
I WANTED TO SAY HI TO MR. SEBASTIAN (PSEUDONYM) BEFORE WE LEAVE...
But he seems busy...
MS. MO-GAMI.
I'LL THANK HIM FOR YOU.
YOUR LANDLORDS MUST BE WORRIED.
THANK YOU SO MUCH FOR TODAY.
YES...
I ONLY CAME TO SHOW YOU MY FOOD VIDEOS TO SATISFY MY EGO...
Uh...
I FEEL SO GUILTY HAVING YOU THANK ME...

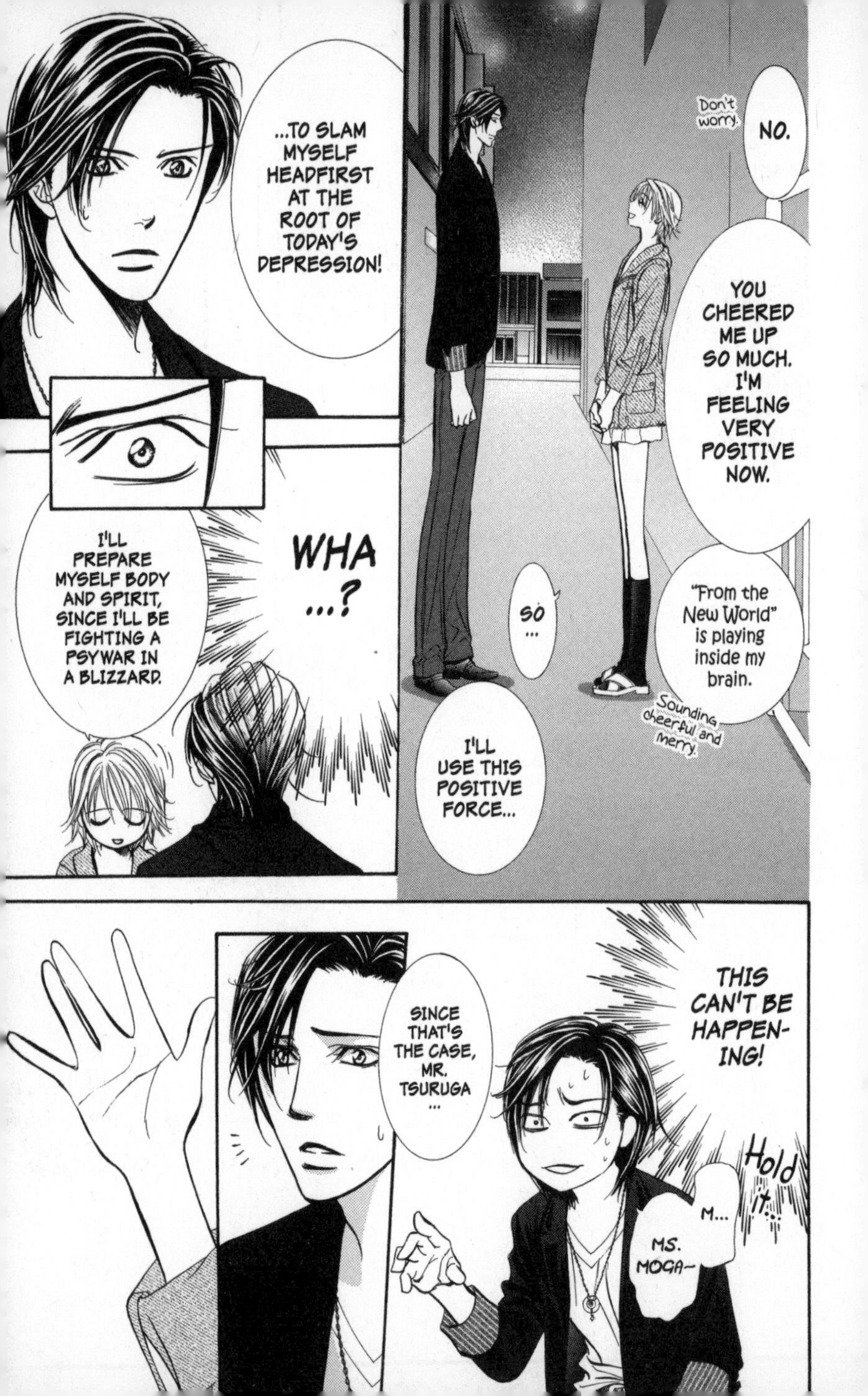
Don't worry.
NO.
YOU CHEERED ME UP SO MUCH. I'M FEELING VERY POSITIVE NOW.
"From the New World" is playing inside my brain.
Sounding cheerful and merry.
SO ...
I'LL USE THIS POSITIVE FORCE...
...TO SLAM MYSELF HEADFIRST AT THE ROOT OF TODAY'S DEPRESSION!
WHA ...?
I'LL PREPARE MYSELF BODY AND SPIRIT, SINCE I'LL BE FIGHTING A PSYWAR IN A BLIZZARD.
THIS CAN'T BE HAPPEN-ING!
Hold it...
M... MS. MOGA~
SINCE THAT'S THE CASE, MR. TSURUGA ...

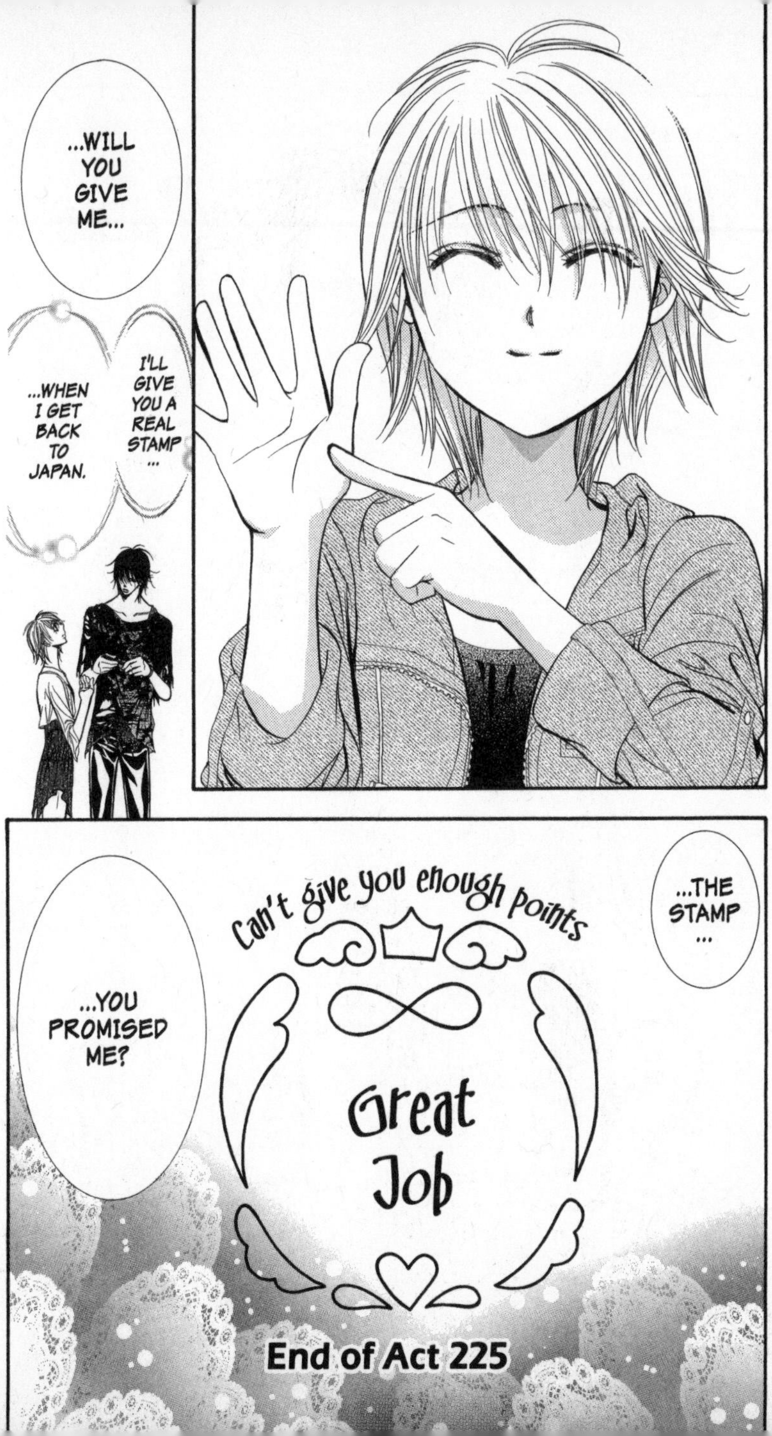
...WILL YOU GIVE ME...
I'LL GIVE YOU A REAL STAMP...
...WHEN I GET BACK TO JAPAN.
...THE STAMP...
...YOU PROMISED ME?
Can't give you enough points
Great Job
End of Act 225

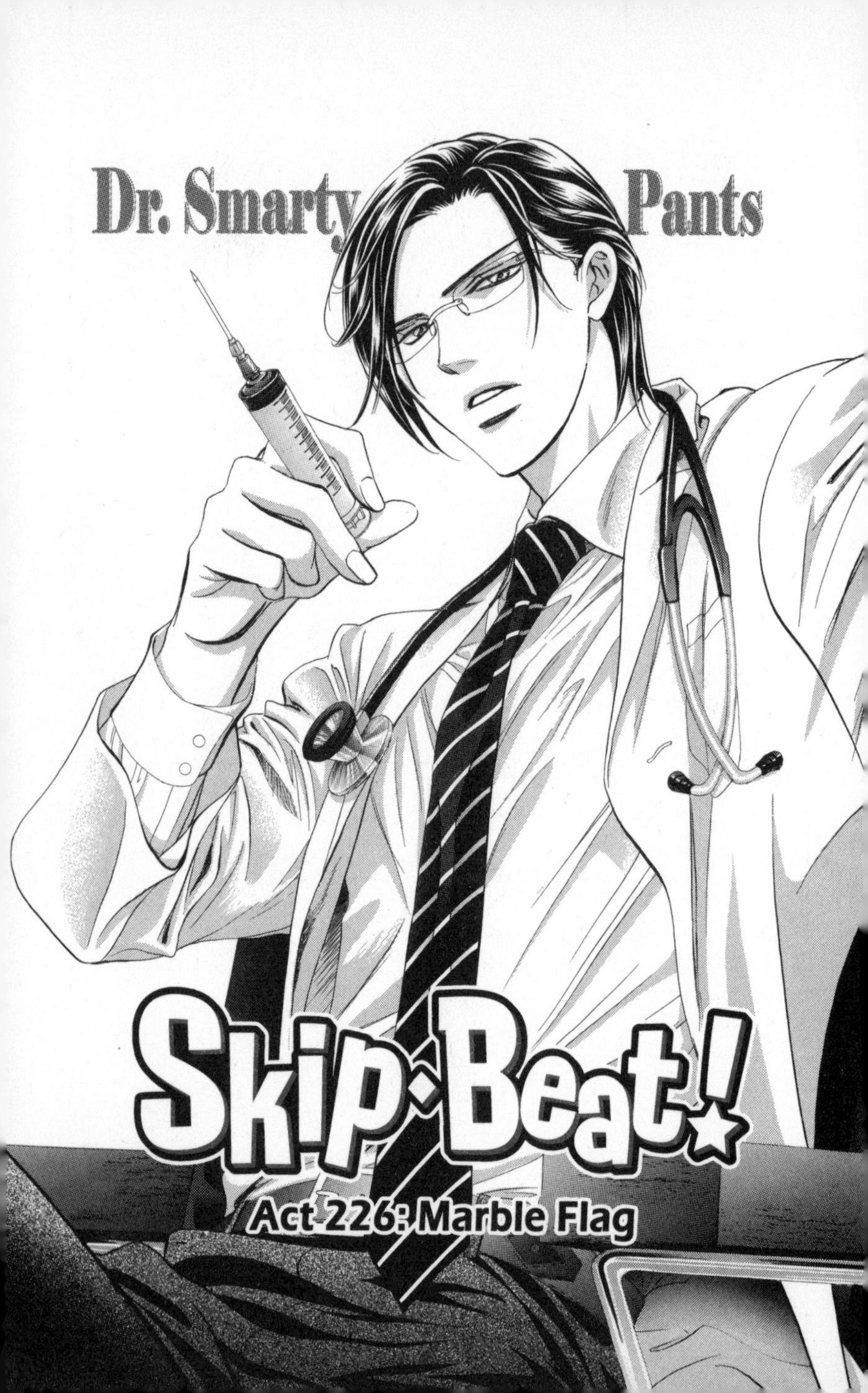
Dr. Smarty Pants
Skip·Beat!
Act 226: Marble Flag

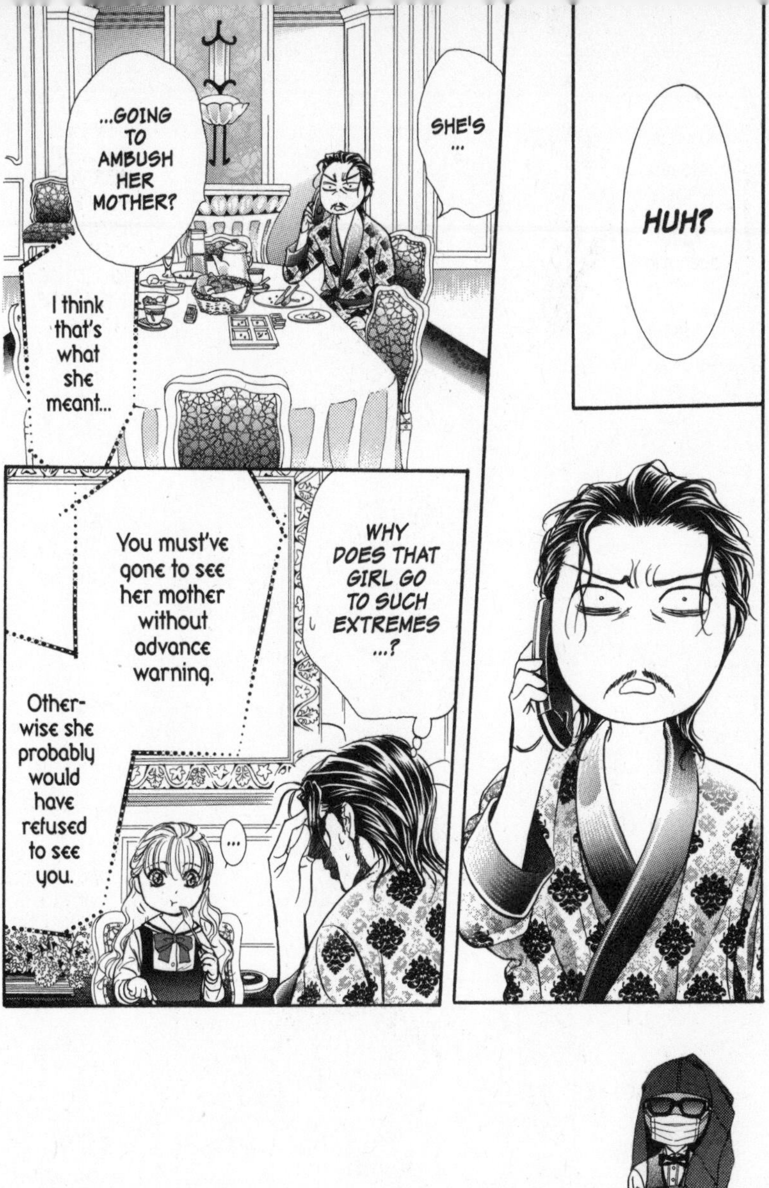
HUH?
SHE'S ...
...GOING TO AMBUSH HER MOTHER?
I think that's what she meant...
WHY DOES THAT GIRL GO TO SUCH EXTREMES ...?
You must've gone to see her mother without advance warning.
Otherwise she probably would have refused to see you.
...
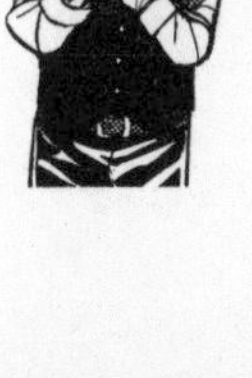

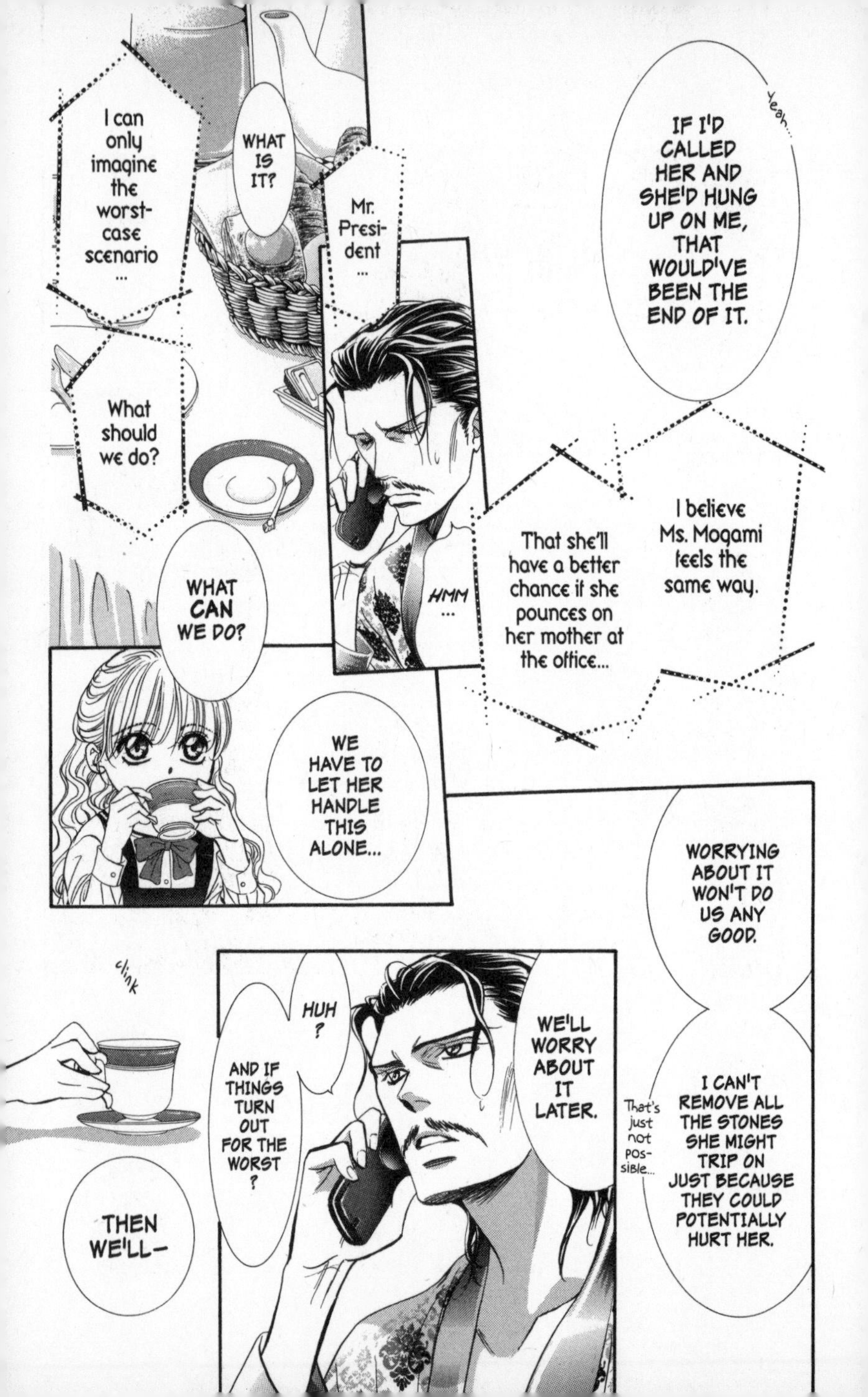

Mr. President...
WHAT IS IT?
I can only imagine the worst-case scenario...
What should we do?
WHAT CAN WE DO?
WE HAVE TO LET HER HANDLE THIS ALONE...
Yeah...
IF I'D CALLED HER AND SHE'D HUNG UP ON ME, THAT WOULD'VE BEEN THE END OF IT.
I believe Ms. Mogami feels the same way.
That she'll have a better chance if she pounces on her mother at the office...
HMM...
WORRYING ABOUT IT WON'T DO US ANY GOOD.
I CAN'T REMOVE ALL THE STONES SHE MIGHT TRIP ON JUST BECAUSE THEY COULD POTENTIALLY HURT HER.
That's just not possible...
WE'LL WORRY ABOUT IT LATER.
HUH?
AND IF THINGS TURN OUT FOR THE WORST?
THEN WE'LL—
clink

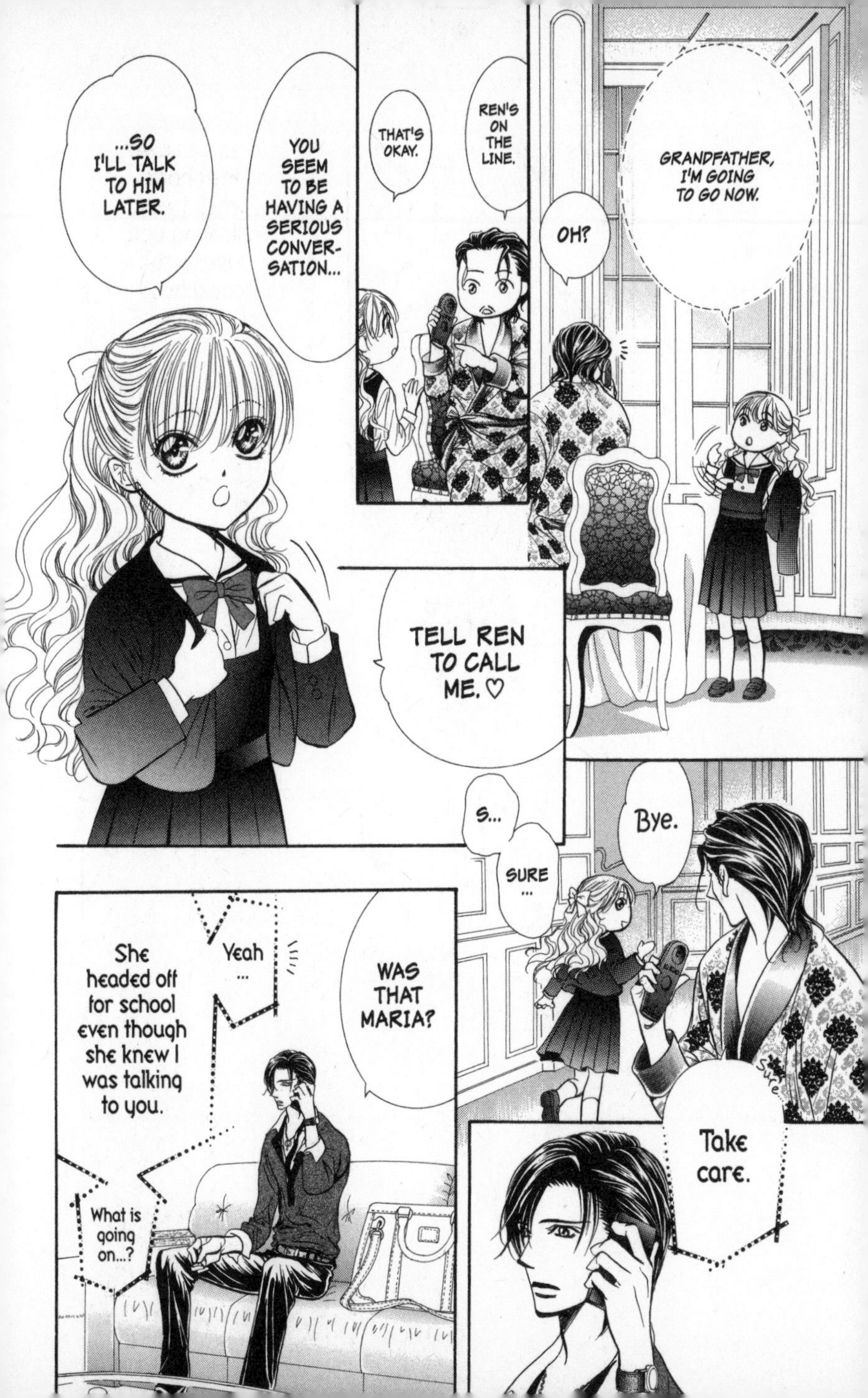
GRANDFATHER, I'M GOING TO GO NOW.
OH?
REN'S ON THE LINE.
THAT'S OKAY.
YOU SEEM TO BE HAVING A SERIOUS CONVERSATION...
...SO I'LL TALK TO HIM LATER.
TELL REN TO CALL ME. ♡
Bye.
S...
SURE...
Sure
Take care.
WAS THAT MARIA?
Yeah...
She headed off for school even though she knew I was talking to you.
What is going on...?

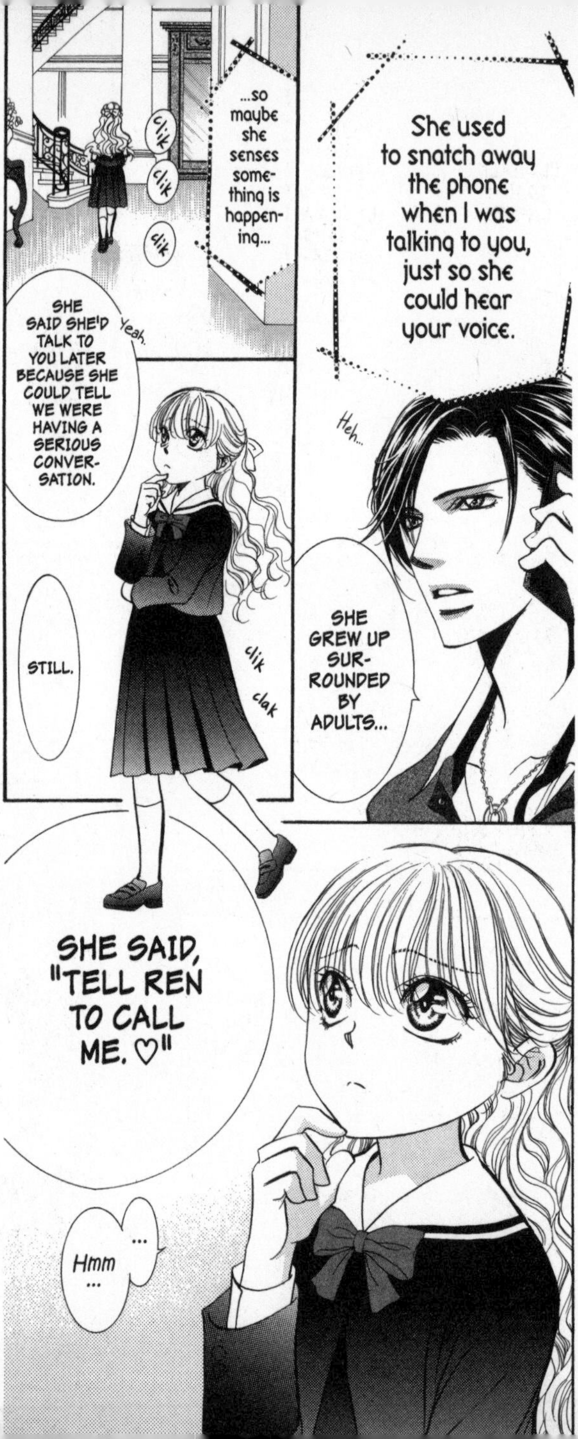
She used to snatch away the phone when I was talking to you, just so she could hear your voice.
Heh...
SHE GREW UP SUR-ROUNDED BY ADULTS...
...so maybe she senses some-thing is happen-ing...
clik
clik
clik
SHE SAID SHE'D TALK TO YOU LATER BECAUSE SHE COULD TELL WE WERE HAVING A SERIOUS CONVER-SATION.
Yeah.
STILL.
clik
clak
SHE SAID, "TELL REN TO CALL ME. ♡"
... Hmm ...

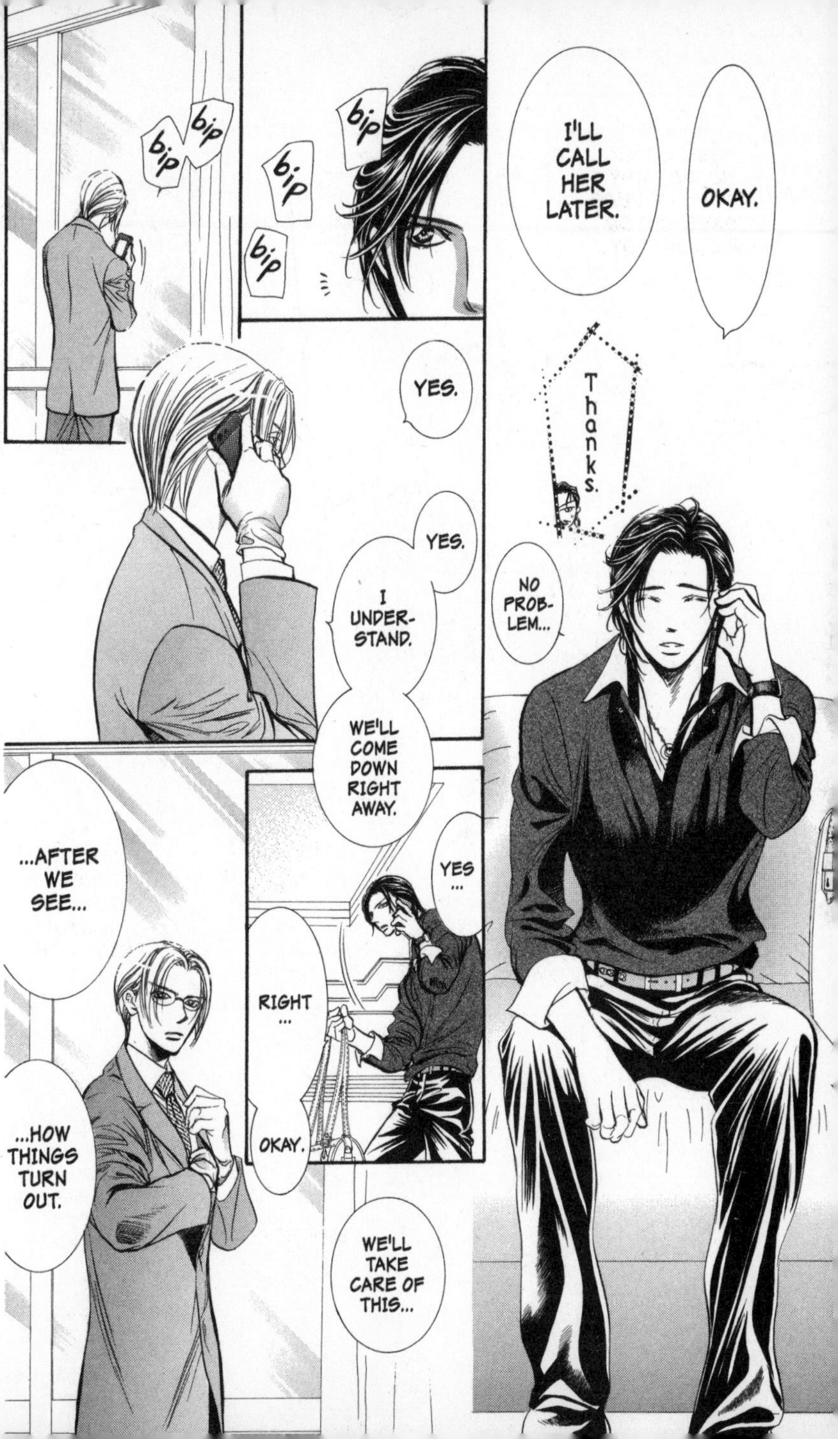
OKAY.
I'LL CALL HER LATER.
Thanks.
NO PROBLEM...
bip
bip
bip
bip
bip
YES.
YES.
I UNDERSTAND.
WE'LL COME DOWN RIGHT AWAY.
YES...
RIGHT...
OKAY.
WE'LL TAKE CARE OF THIS...
...AFTER WE SEE...
...HOW THINGS TURN OUT.

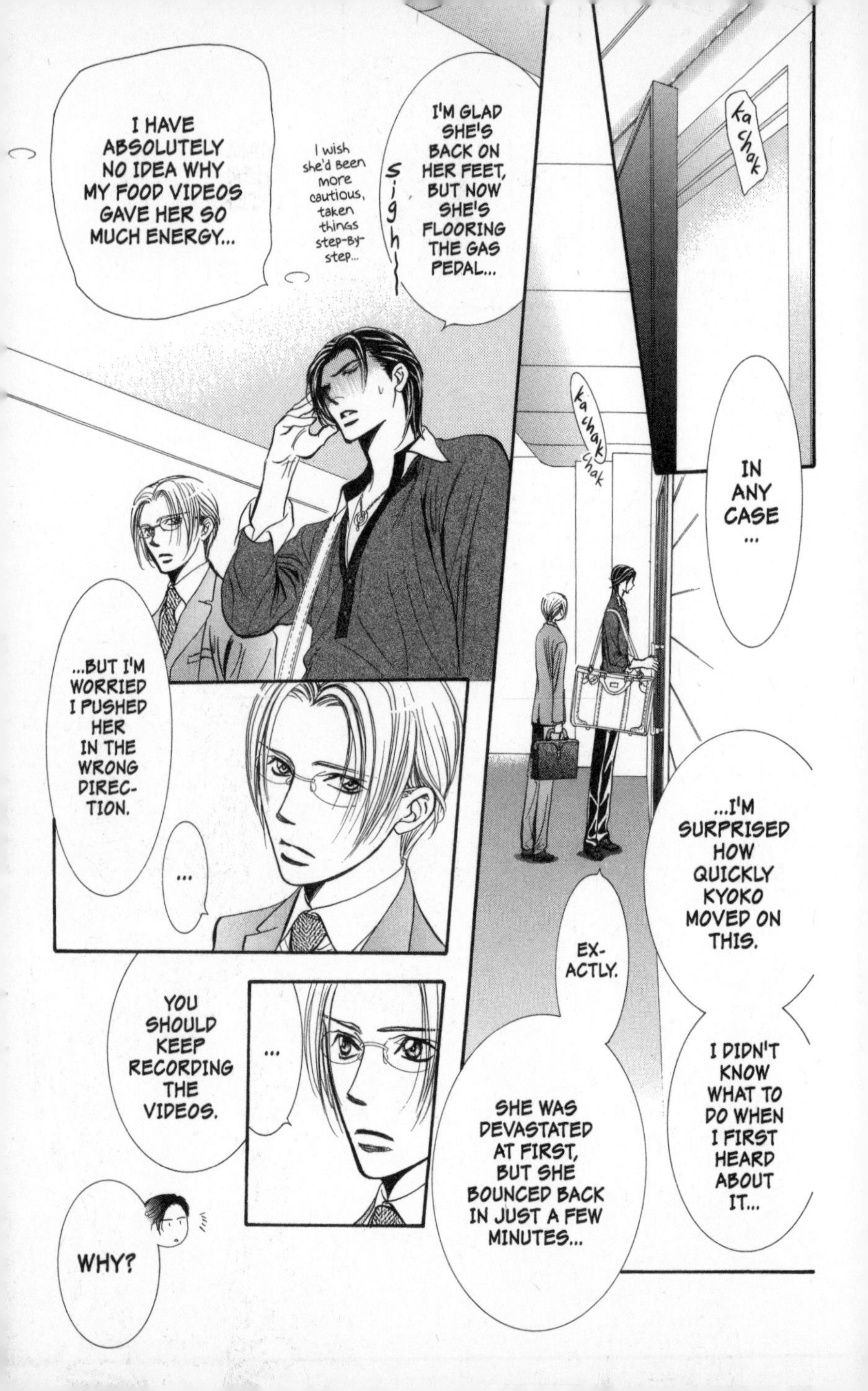
ka chak
ka chak chak
IN ANY CASE...
...I'M SURPRISED HOW QUICKLY KYOKO MOVED ON THIS.
EX-ACTLY.
I DIDN'T KNOW WHAT TO DO WHEN I FIRST HEARD ABOUT IT...
SHE WAS DEVASTATED AT FIRST, BUT SHE BOUNCED BACK IN JUST A FEW MINUTES...
I'M GLAD SHE'S BACK ON HER FEET, BUT NOW SHE'S FLOORING THE GAS PEDAL...
sigh
I wish she'd been more cautious, taken things step-by-step...
I HAVE ABSOLUTELY NO IDEA WHY MY FOOD VIDEOS GAVE HER SO MUCH ENERGY...
...BUT I'M WORRIED I PUSHED HER IN THE WRONG DIRECTION.
...
YOU SHOULD KEEP RECORDING THE VIDEOS.
...
WHY?

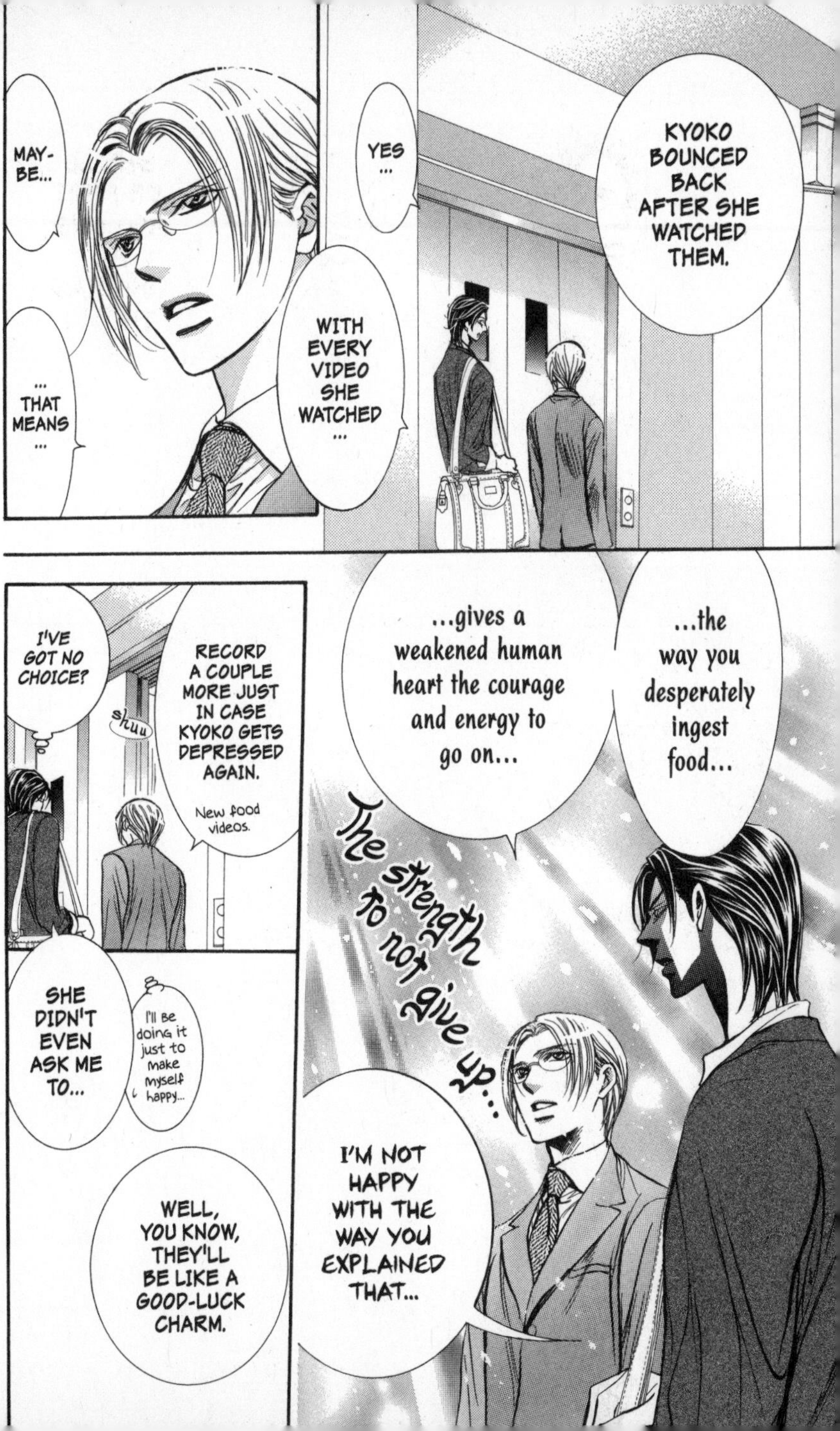
KYOKO BOUNCED BACK AFTER SHE WATCHED THEM.
YES...
WITH EVERY VIDEO SHE WATCHED...
MAY-BE...
...THAT MEANS...
...the way you desperately ingest food...
...gives a weakened human heart the courage and energy to go on...
The strength to not give up...
I'M NOT HAPPY WITH THE WAY YOU EXPLAINED THAT...
RECORD A COUPLE MORE JUST IN CASE KYOKO GETS DEPRESSED AGAIN.
New food videos.
shuu
I'VE GOT NO CHOICE?
I'll be doing it just to make myself happy...
SHE DIDN'T EVEN ASK ME TO...
WELL, YOU KNOW, THEY'LL BE LIKE A GOOD-LUCK CHARM.

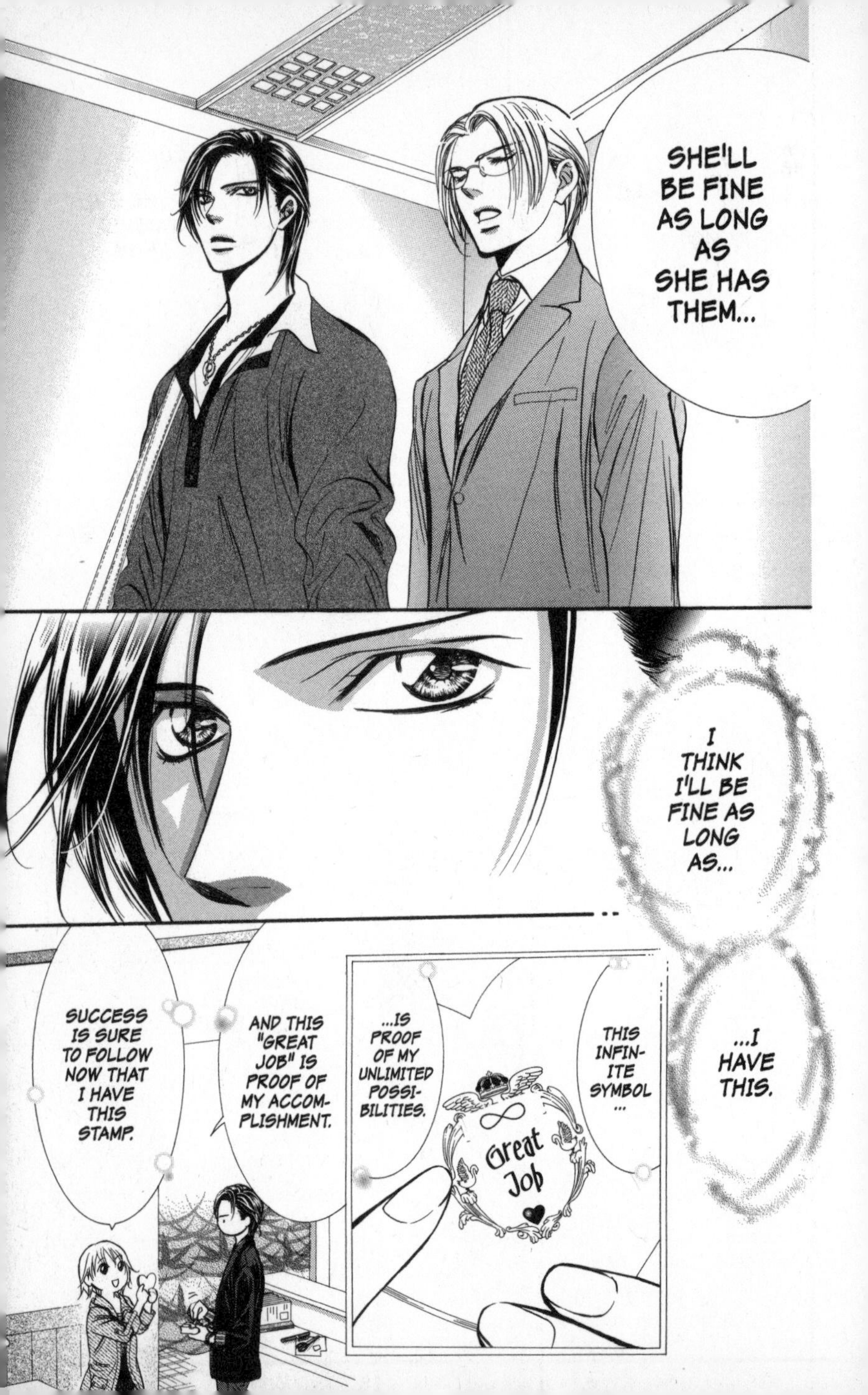
SHE'LL BE FINE AS LONG AS SHE HAS THEM...
I THINK I'LL BE FINE AS LONG AS...
...I HAVE THIS.
THIS INFINITE SYMBOL...
...IS PROOF OF MY UNLIMITED POSSIBILITIES.
Great Job
AND THIS "GREAT JOB" IS PROOF OF MY ACCOMPLISHMENT.
SUCCESS IS SURE TO FOLLOW NOW THAT I HAVE THIS STAMP.

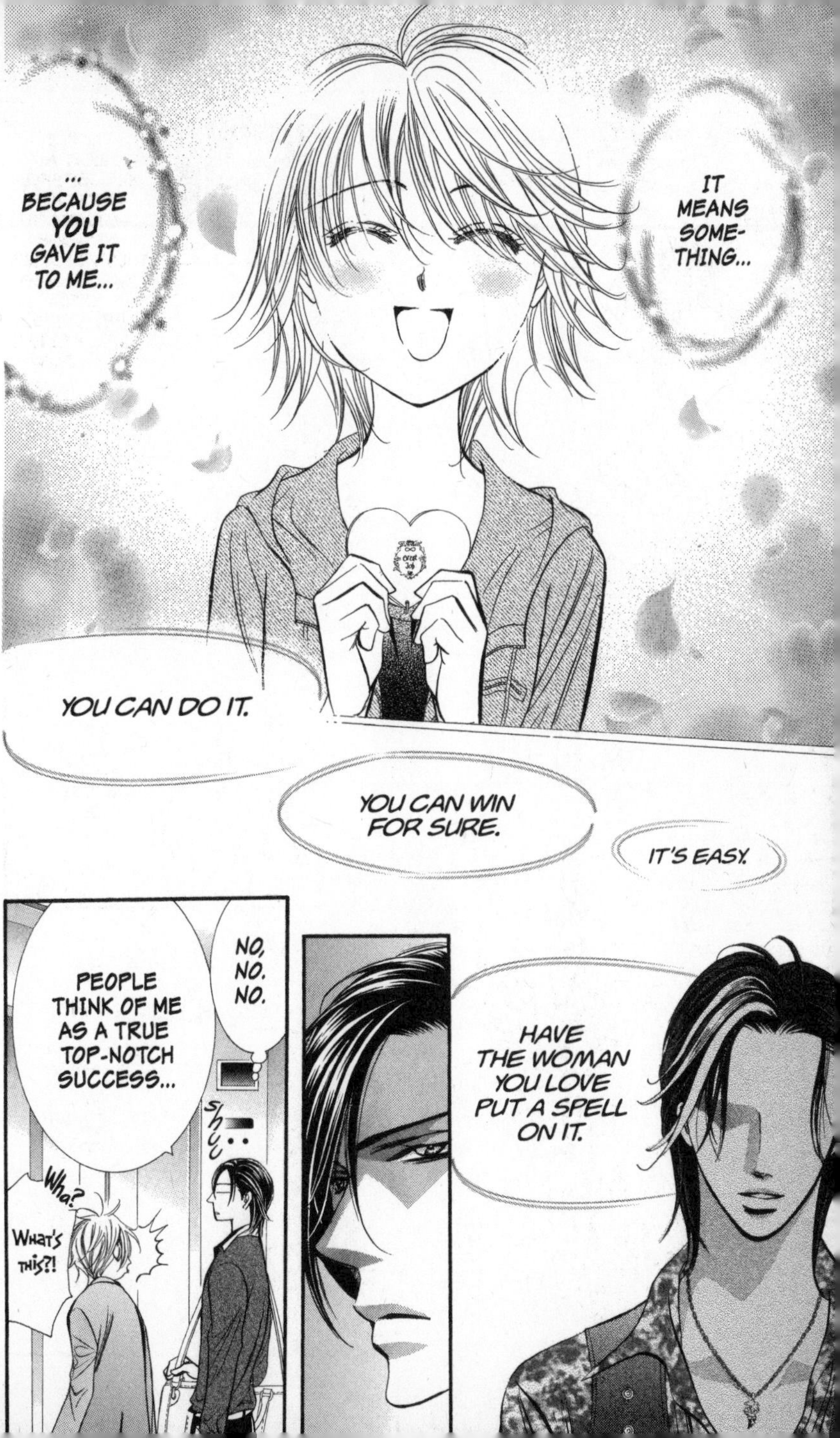
IT MEANS SOMETHING...
...BECAUSE YOU GAVE IT TO ME...
YOU CAN DO IT.
YOU CAN WIN FOR SURE.
IT'S EASY.
HAVE THE WOMAN YOU LOVE PUT A SPELL ON IT.
NO, NO. NO.
PEOPLE THINK OF ME AS A TRUE TOP-NOTCH SUCCESS...
SHUU..
Wha?
What's this?!

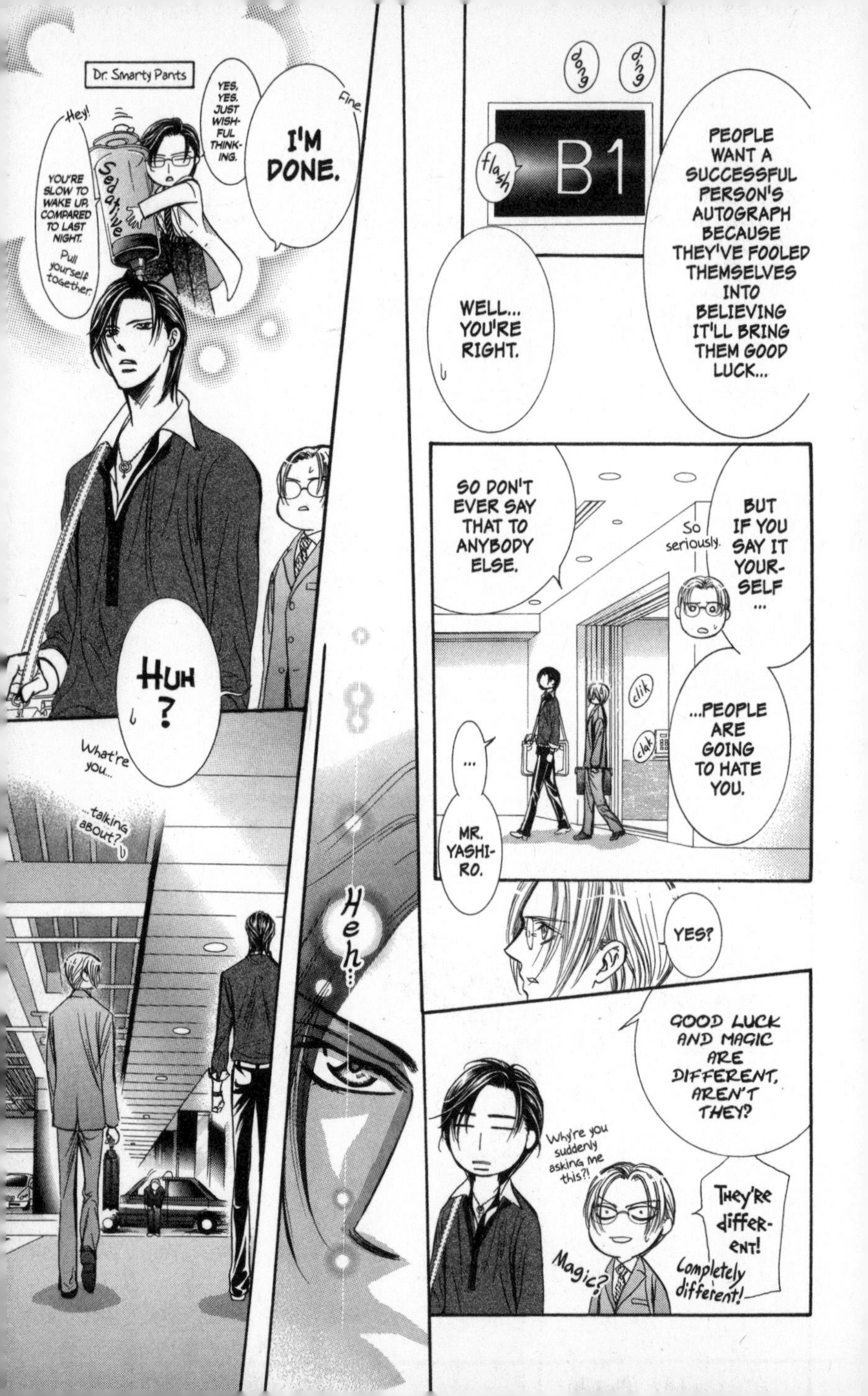
ding
dong
PEOPLE WANT A SUCCESSFUL PERSON'S AUTOGRAPH BECAUSE THEY'VE FOOLED THEMSELVES INTO BELIEVING IT'LL BRING THEM GOOD LUCK...
flash
B1
WELL... YOU'RE RIGHT.
BUT IF YOU SAY IT YOURSELF...
So seriously.
...PEOPLE ARE GOING TO HATE YOU.
SO DON'T EVER SAY THAT TO ANYBODY ELSE.
clik
clak
...
MR. YASHIRO.
YES?
GOOD LUCK AND MAGIC ARE DIFFERENT, AREN'T THEY?
They're different!
Completely different!
Why're you suddenly asking me this?!
Magic?
Fine.
I'M DONE.
YES, YES. JUST WISHFUL THINKING.
Dr. Smarty Pants
Hey!
Sedative
YOU'RE SLOW TO WAKE UP, COMPARED TO LAST NIGHT.
Pull yourself together.
HUH?
What're you...
...talking about?
Heh...

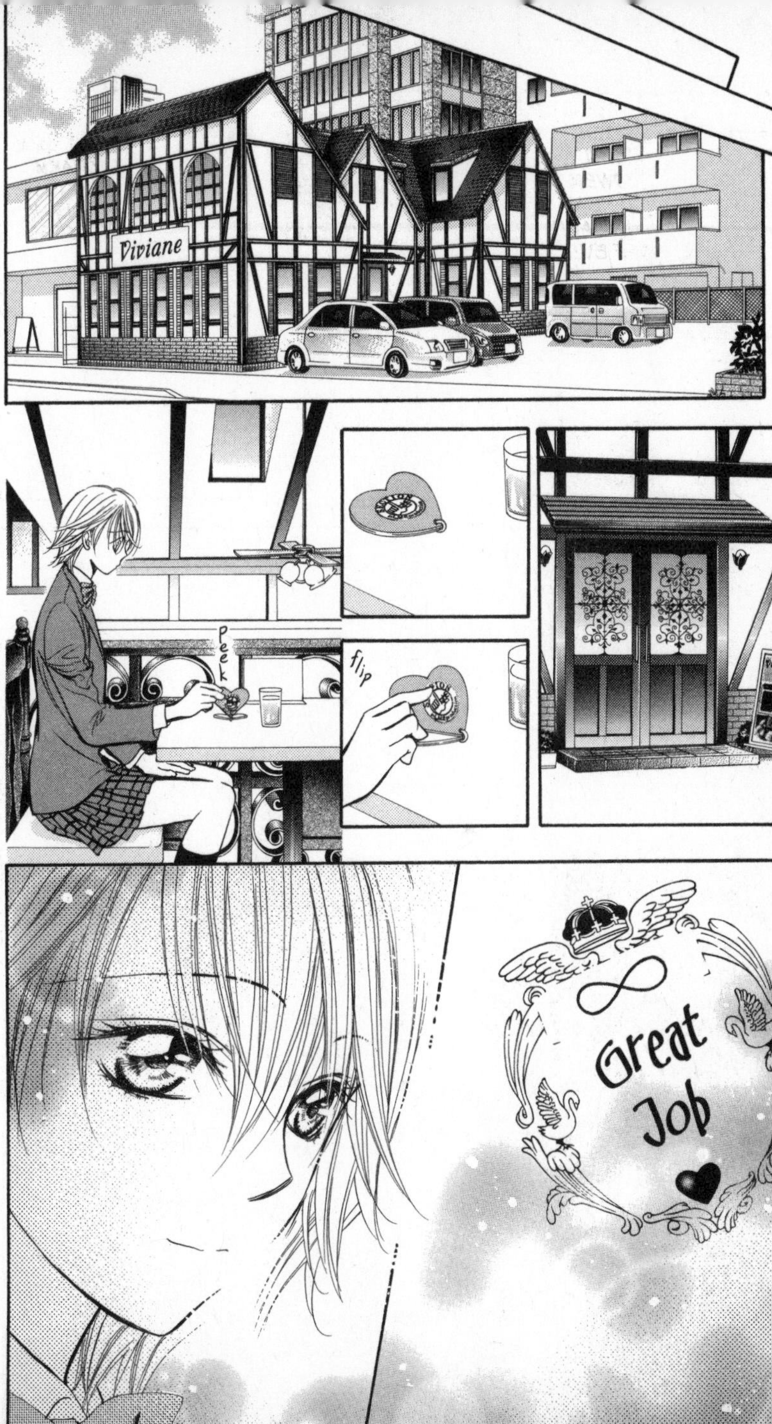
Viviane
flip
Peek
Great Job

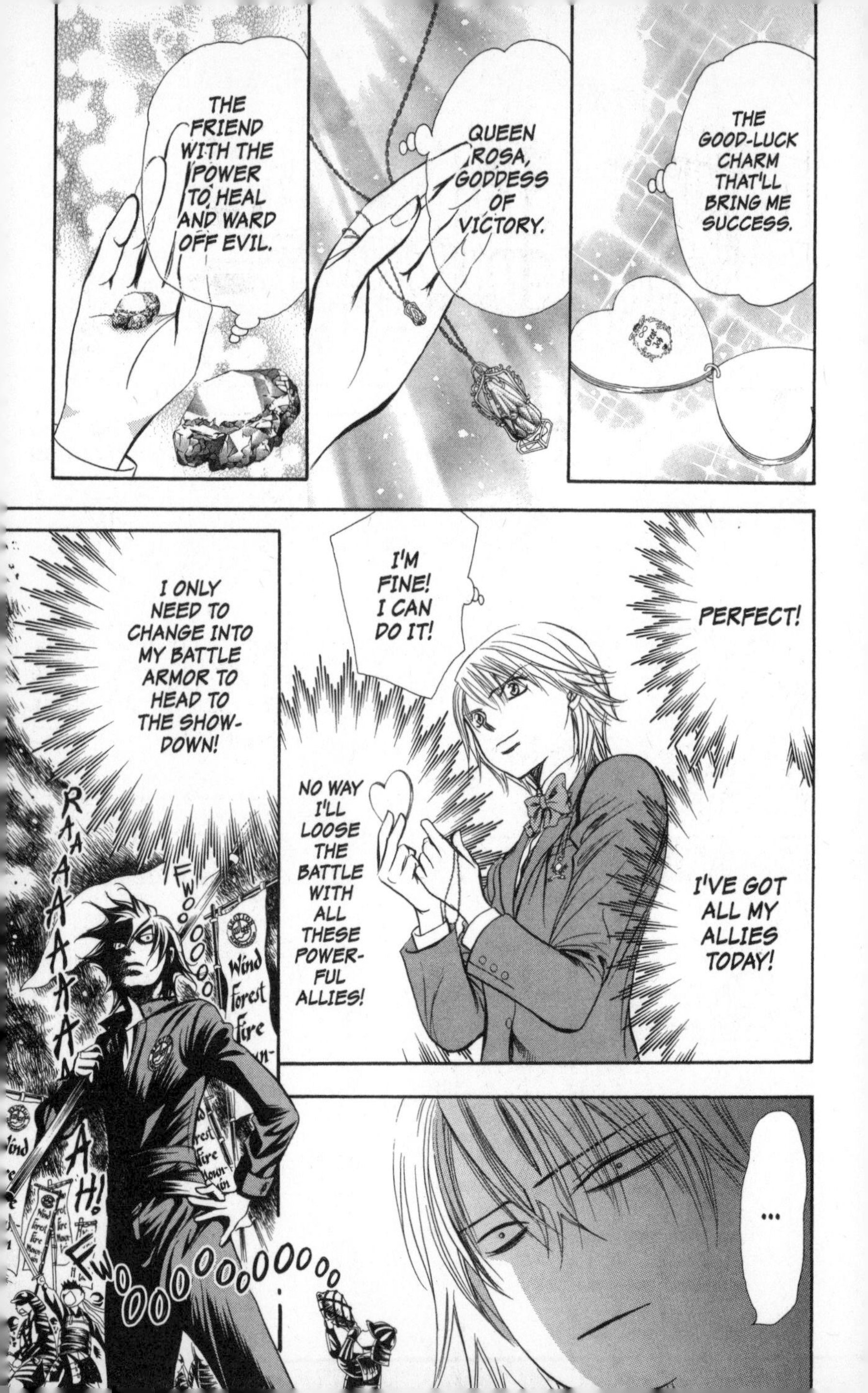
THE GOOD-LUCK CHARM THAT'LL BRING ME SUCCESS.
QUEEN ROSA, GODDESS OF VICTORY.
THE FRIEND WITH THE POWER TO HEAL AND WARD OFF EVIL.
PERFECT!
I'M FINE! I CAN DO IT!
I'VE GOT ALL MY ALLIES TODAY!
NO WAY I'LL LOOSE THE BATTLE WITH ALL THESE POWERFUL ALLIES!
I ONLY NEED TO CHANGE INTO MY BATTLE ARMOR TO HEAD TO THE SHOWDOWN!
RAAAAAAAAAH!
FWOOOOO
Wind Forest Fire
FWOOOOOOOOOOOOOOO
...

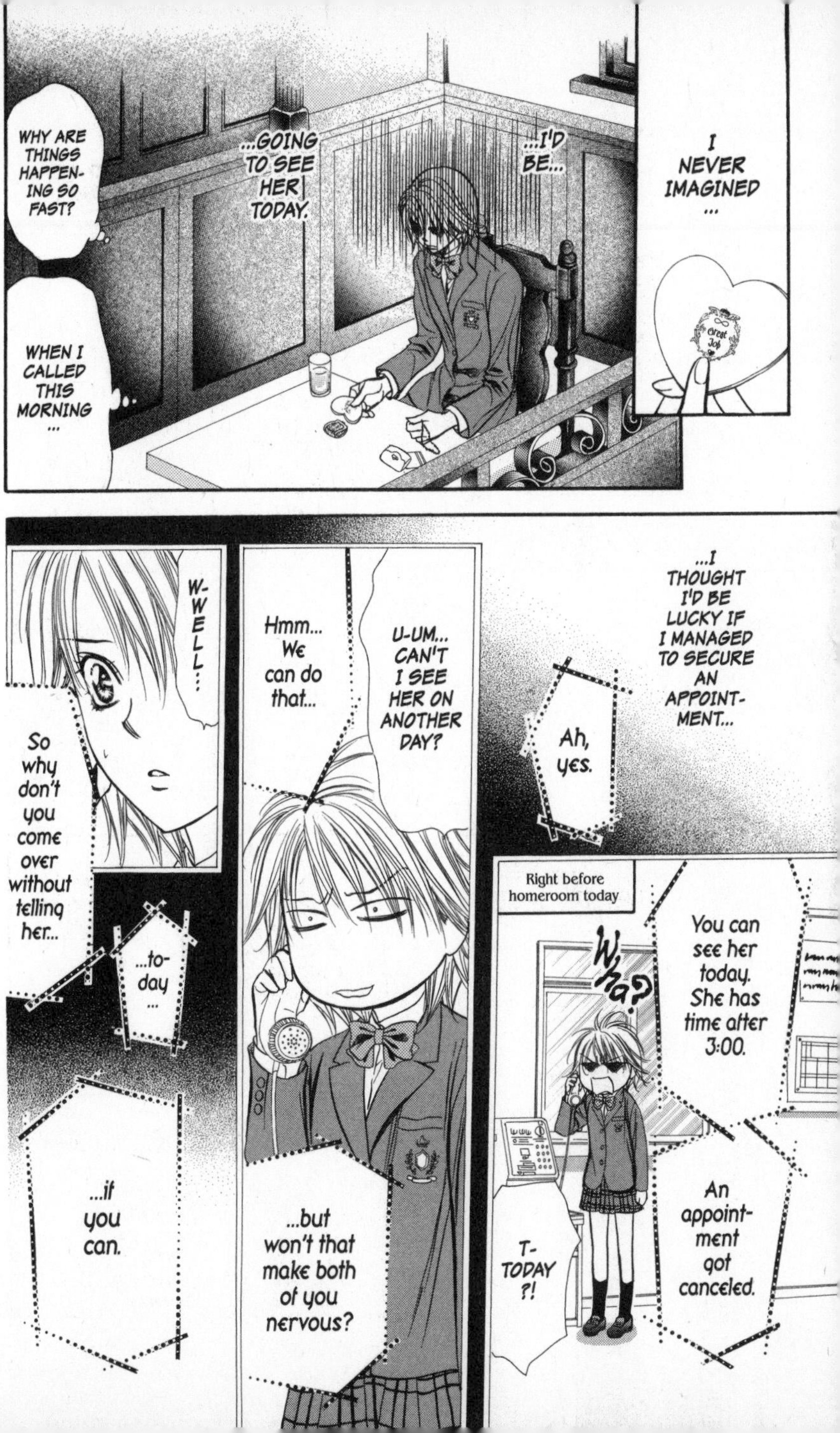
I NEVER IMAGINED ...
...I'D BE...
...GOING TO SEE HER TODAY.
WHY ARE THINGS HAPPENING SO FAST?
WHEN I CALLED THIS MORNING ...
...I THOUGHT I'D BE LUCKY IF I MANAGED TO SECURE AN APPOINTMENT...
Ah, yes.
Right before homeroom today
You can see her today. She has time after 3:00.
Wha?
An appointment got canceled.
T-TODAY?!
U-UM... CAN'T I SEE HER ON ANOTHER DAY?
Hmm... We can do that...
...but won't that make both of you nervous?
W-WELL...
So why don't you come over without telling her...
...to-day...
...if you can.

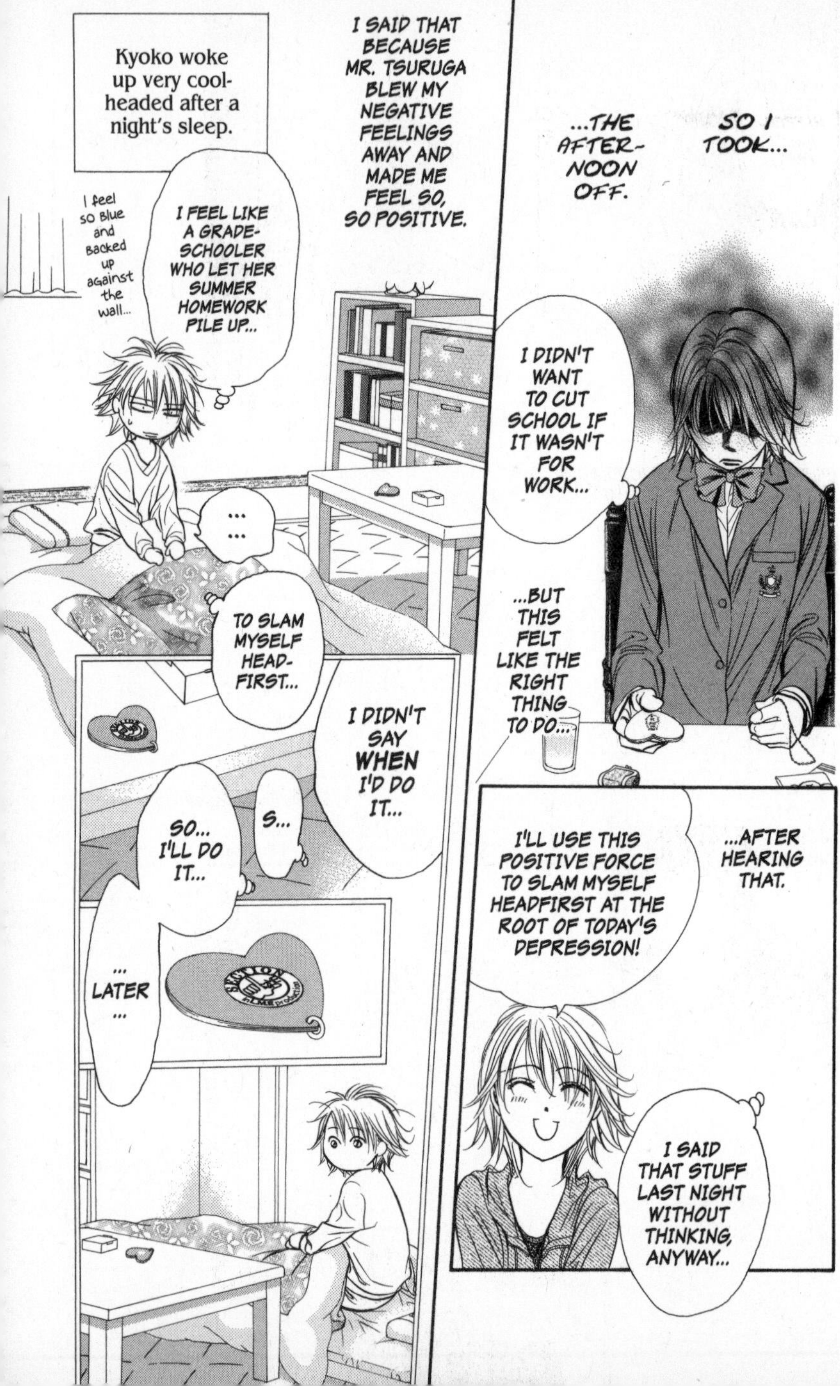
SO I TOOK...
...THE AFTERNOON OFF.
I DIDN'T WANT TO CUT SCHOOL IF IT WASN'T FOR WORK...
...BUT THIS FELT LIKE THE RIGHT THING TO DO...
...AFTER HEARING THAT.
I'LL USE THIS POSITIVE FORCE TO SLAM MYSELF HEADFIRST AT THE ROOT OF TODAY'S DEPRESSION!
I SAID THAT STUFF LAST NIGHT WITHOUT THINKING, ANYWAY...
I SAID THAT BECAUSE MR. TSURUGA BLEW MY NEGATIVE FEELINGS AWAY AND MADE ME FEEL SO, SO POSITIVE.
Kyoko woke up very cool-headed after a night's sleep.
I FEEL LIKE A GRADE-SCHOOLER WHO LET HER SUMMER HOMEWORK PILE UP...
I feel so Blue and Backed up against the wall...
......
TO SLAM MYSELF HEAD-FIRST...
I DIDN'T SAY WHEN I'D DO IT...
S...
SO... I'LL DO IT...
... LATER ...

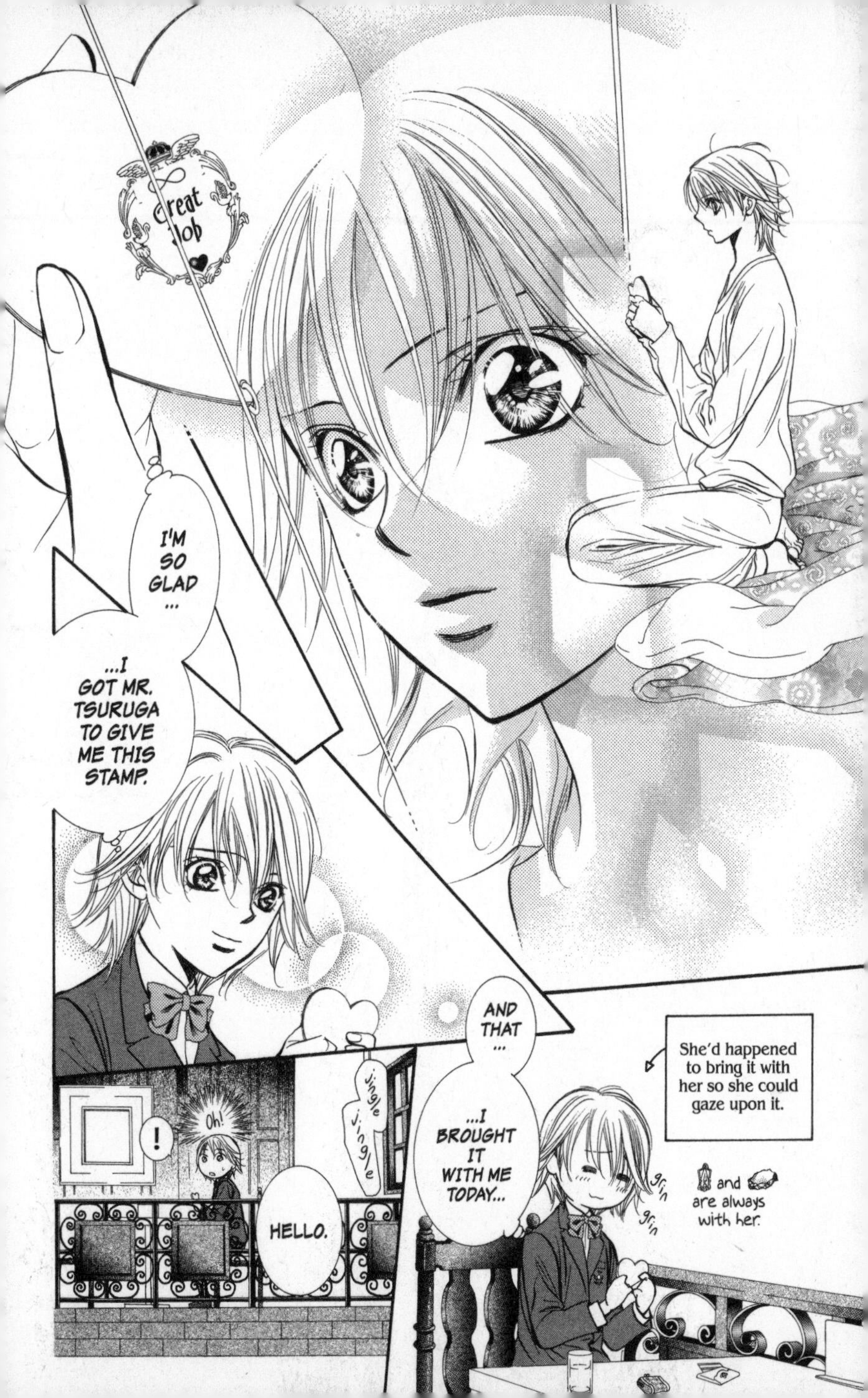
Great Job
I'M SO GLAD ...
...I GOT MR. TSURUGA TO GIVE ME THIS STAMP.
She'd happened to bring it with her so she could gaze upon it.
AND THAT ...
...I BROUGHT IT WITH ME TODAY...
grin grin
and are always with her.
jingle jingle
HELLO.
!
Oh!

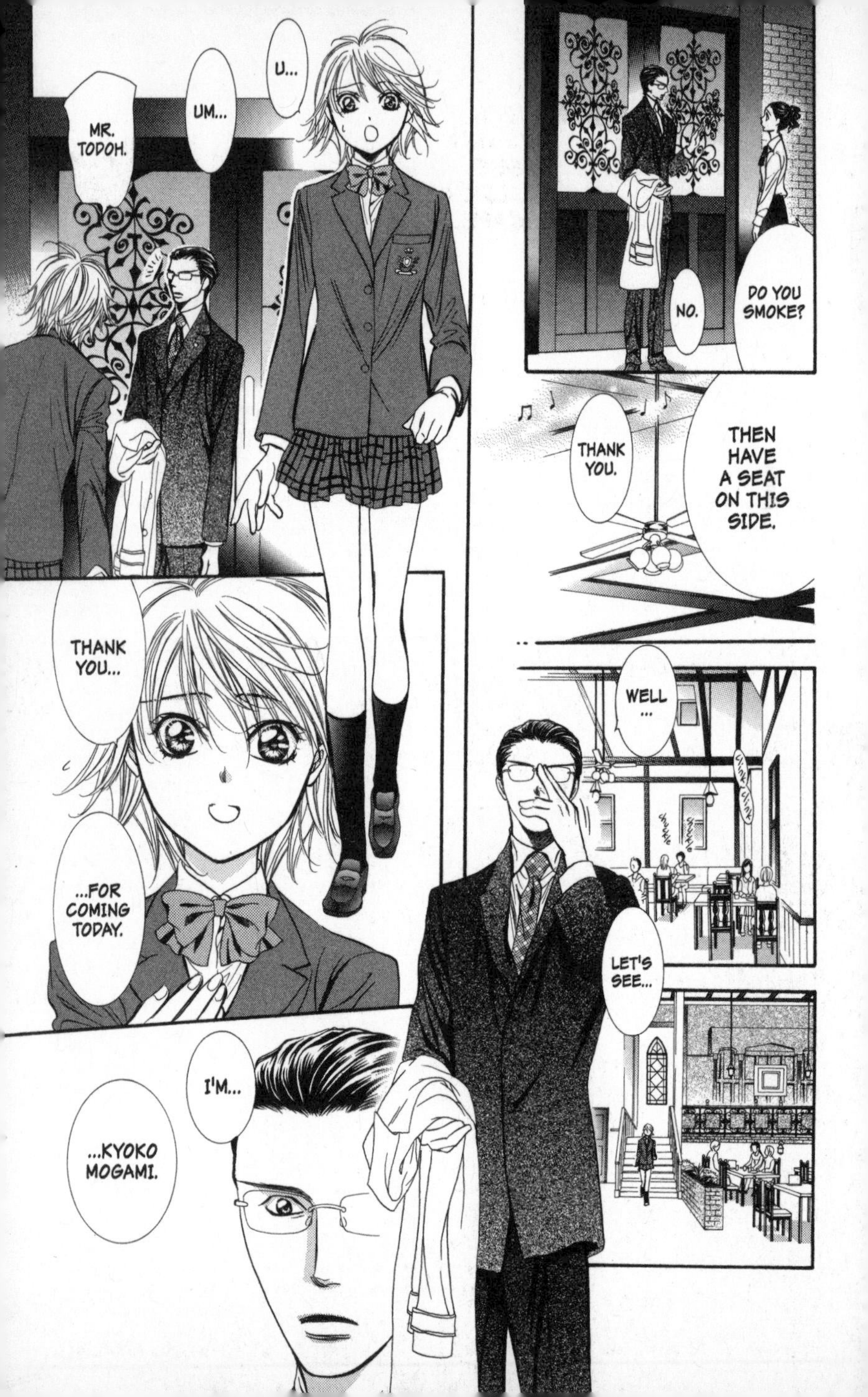
DO YOU SMOKE?
NO.
THEN HAVE A SEAT ON THIS SIDE.
THANK YOU.
WELL ...
clink clink
chuckle
LET'S SEE...
U...
UM...
MR. TODOH.
THANK YOU...
...FOR COMING TODAY.
I'M...
...KYOKO MOGAMI.

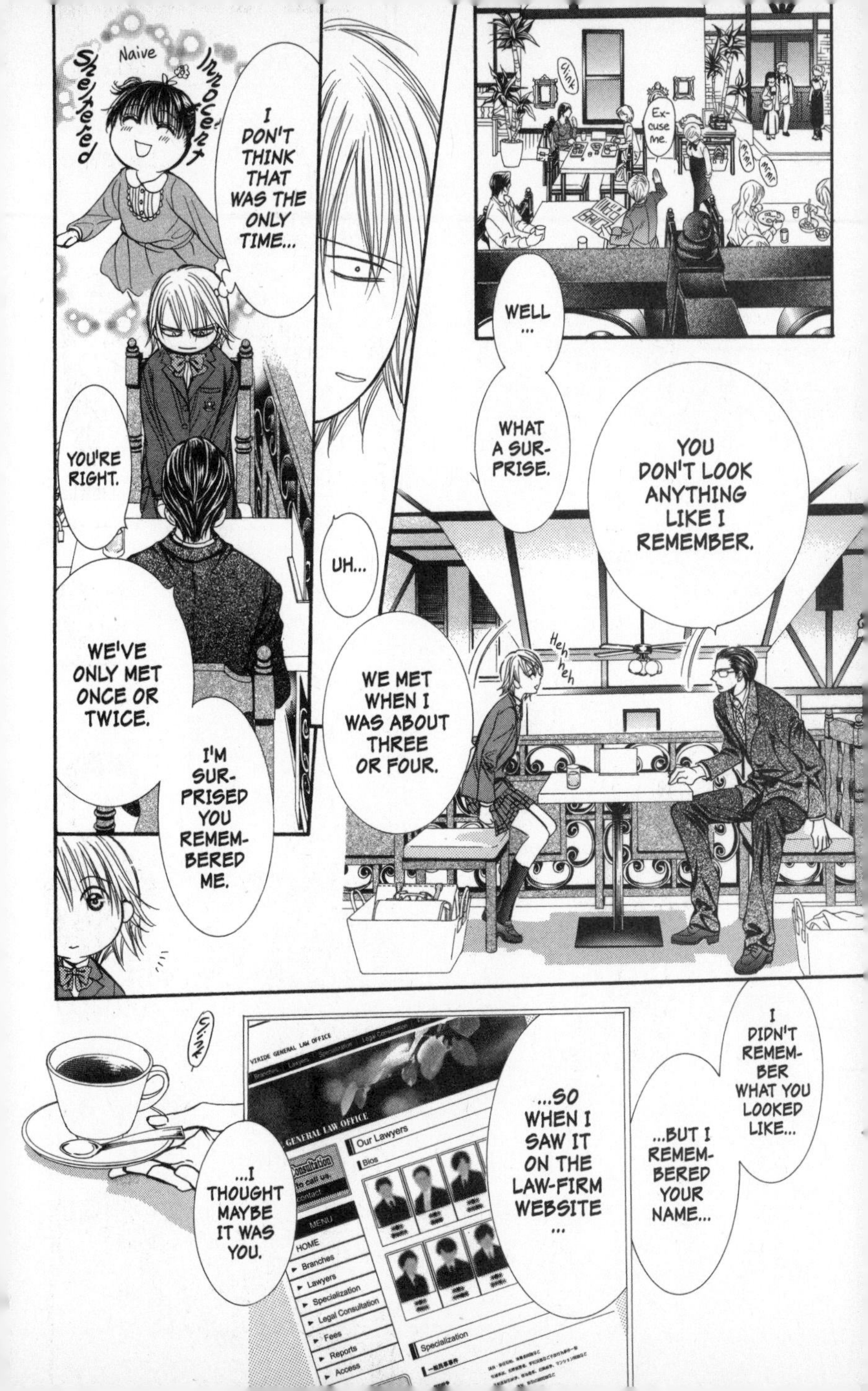
Clink
Ex-cuse me.
murmur
murmur
WELL ...
WHAT A SUR-PRISE.
YOU DON'T LOOK ANYTHING LIKE I REMEMBER.
I DON'T THINK THAT WAS THE ONLY TIME...
UH...
Heh heh
WE MET WHEN I WAS ABOUT THREE OR FOUR.
Naive
Innocent
Sheltered
YOU'RE RIGHT.
WE'VE ONLY MET ONCE OR TWICE.
I'M SUR-PRISED YOU REMEM-BERED ME.
I DIDN'T REMEM-BER WHAT YOU LOOKED LIKE...
...BUT I REMEM-BERED YOUR NAME...
...SO WHEN I SAW IT ON THE LAW-FIRM WEBSITE ...
...I THOUGHT MAYBE IT WAS YOU.
Clink
VIRIDE GENERAL LAW OFFICE
Branches
Lawyers
Specialization
Legal Consultation
GENERAL LAW OFFICE
Our Lawyers
Bios
Consultation
MENU
HOME
Branches
Lawyers
Specialization
Legal Consultation
Fees
Reports
Access
Specialization

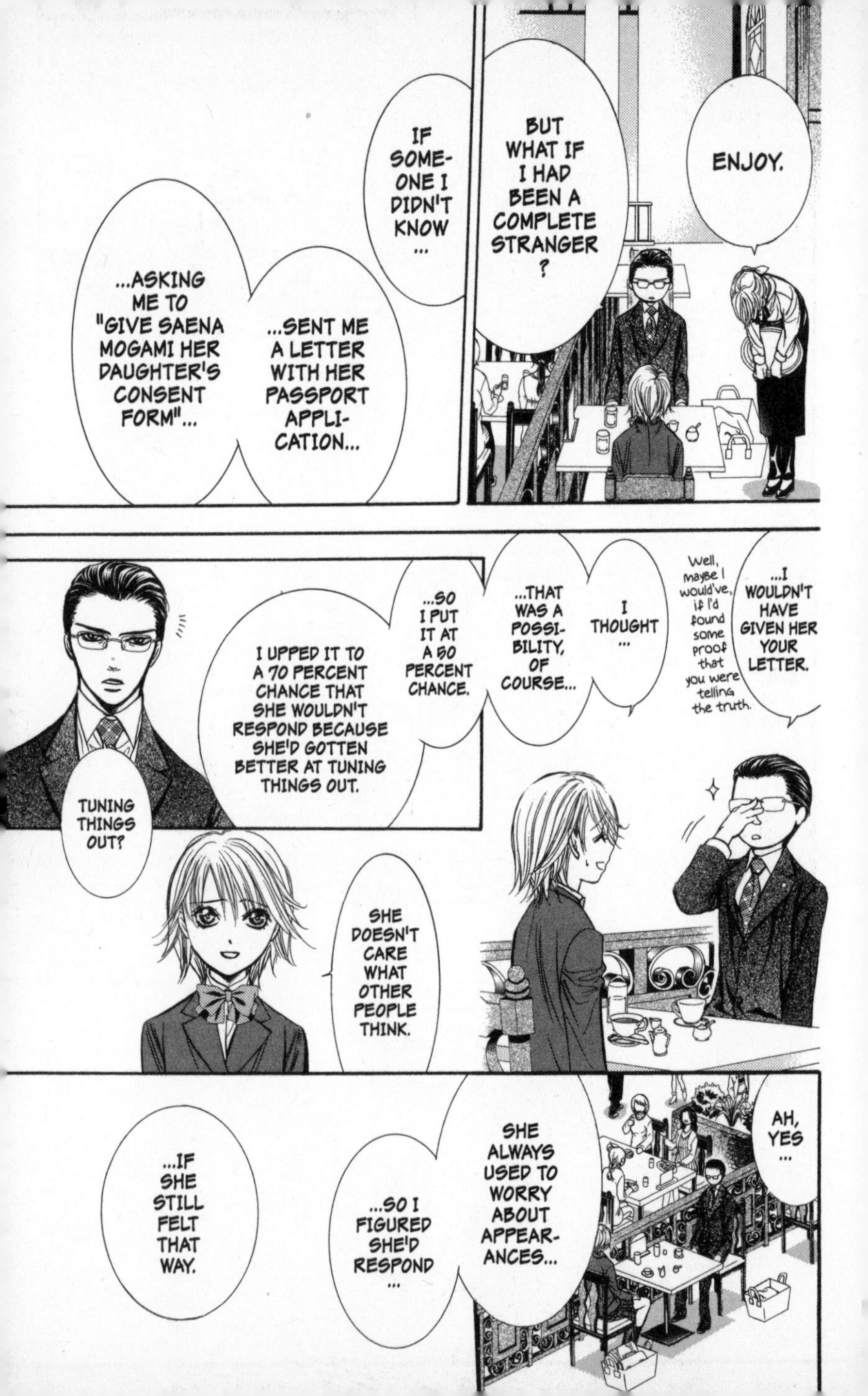
ENJOY.
BUT WHAT IF I HAD BEEN A COMPLETE STRANGER?
IF SOMEONE I DIDN'T KNOW...
...SENT ME A LETTER WITH HER PASSPORT APPLICATION...
...ASKING ME TO "GIVE SAENA MOGAMI HER DAUGHTER'S CONSENT FORM"...
...I WOULDN'T HAVE GIVEN HER YOUR LETTER.
Well, maybe I would've, if I'd found some proof that you were telling the truth.
I THOUGHT...
...THAT WAS A POSSIBILITY, OF COURSE...
...SO I PUT IT AT A 50 PERCENT CHANCE.
I UPPED IT TO A 70 PERCENT CHANCE THAT SHE WOULDN'T RESPOND BECAUSE SHE'D GOTTEN BETTER AT TUNING THINGS OUT.
TUNING THINGS OUT?
SHE DOESN'T CARE WHAT OTHER PEOPLE THINK.
AH, YES...
SHE ALWAYS USED TO WORRY ABOUT APPEARANCES...
...SO I FIGURED SHE'D RESPOND...
...IF SHE STILL FELT THAT WAY.

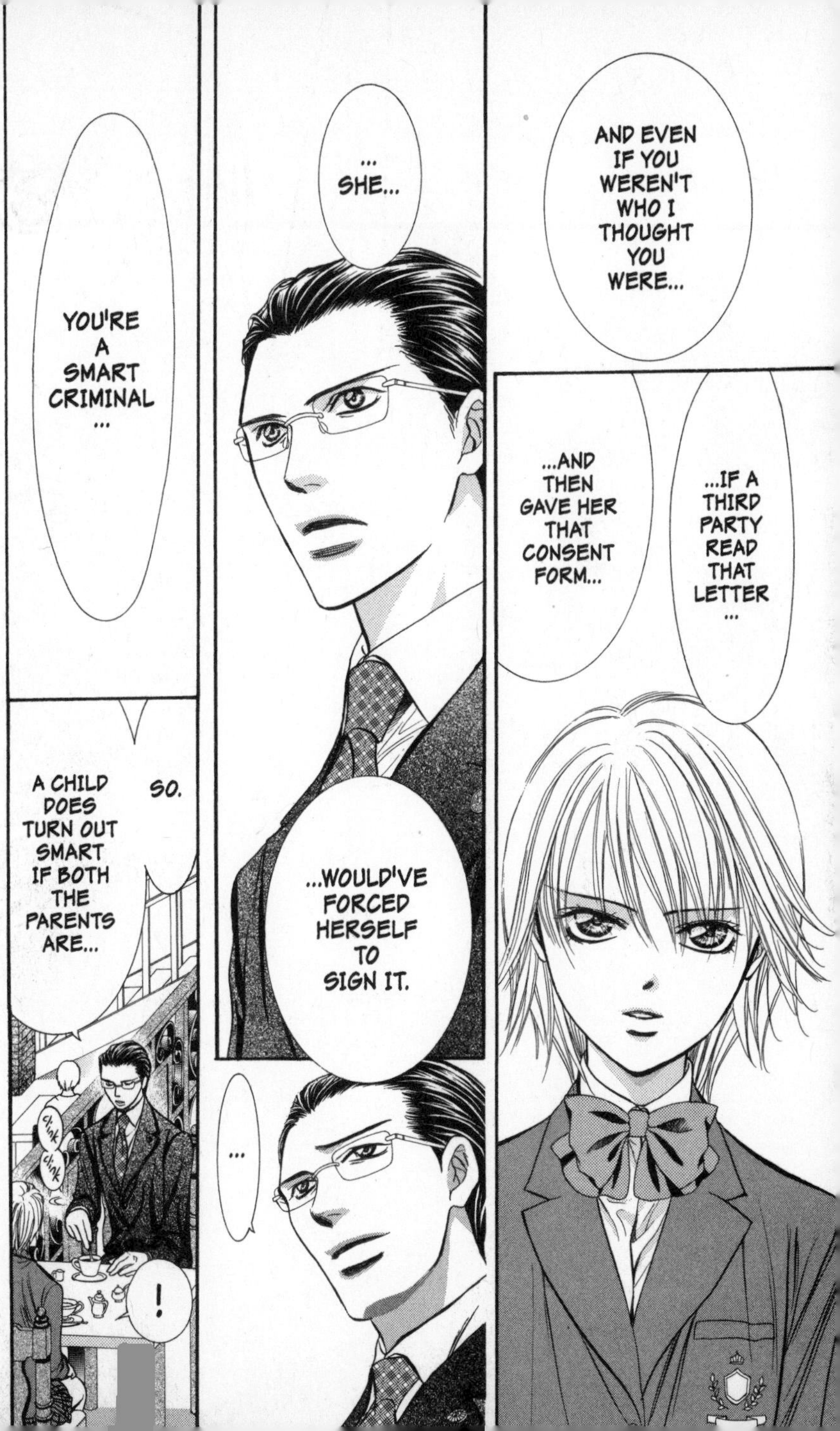
AND EVEN IF YOU WEREN'T WHO I THOUGHT YOU WERE...
...IF A THIRD PARTY READ THAT LETTER...
...AND THEN GAVE HER THAT CONSENT FORM...
...SHE...
...WOULD'VE FORCED HERSELF TO SIGN IT.
...
YOU'RE A SMART CRIMINAL...
SO.
A CHILD DOES TURN OUT SMART IF BOTH THE PARENTS ARE...
clink
clink
!

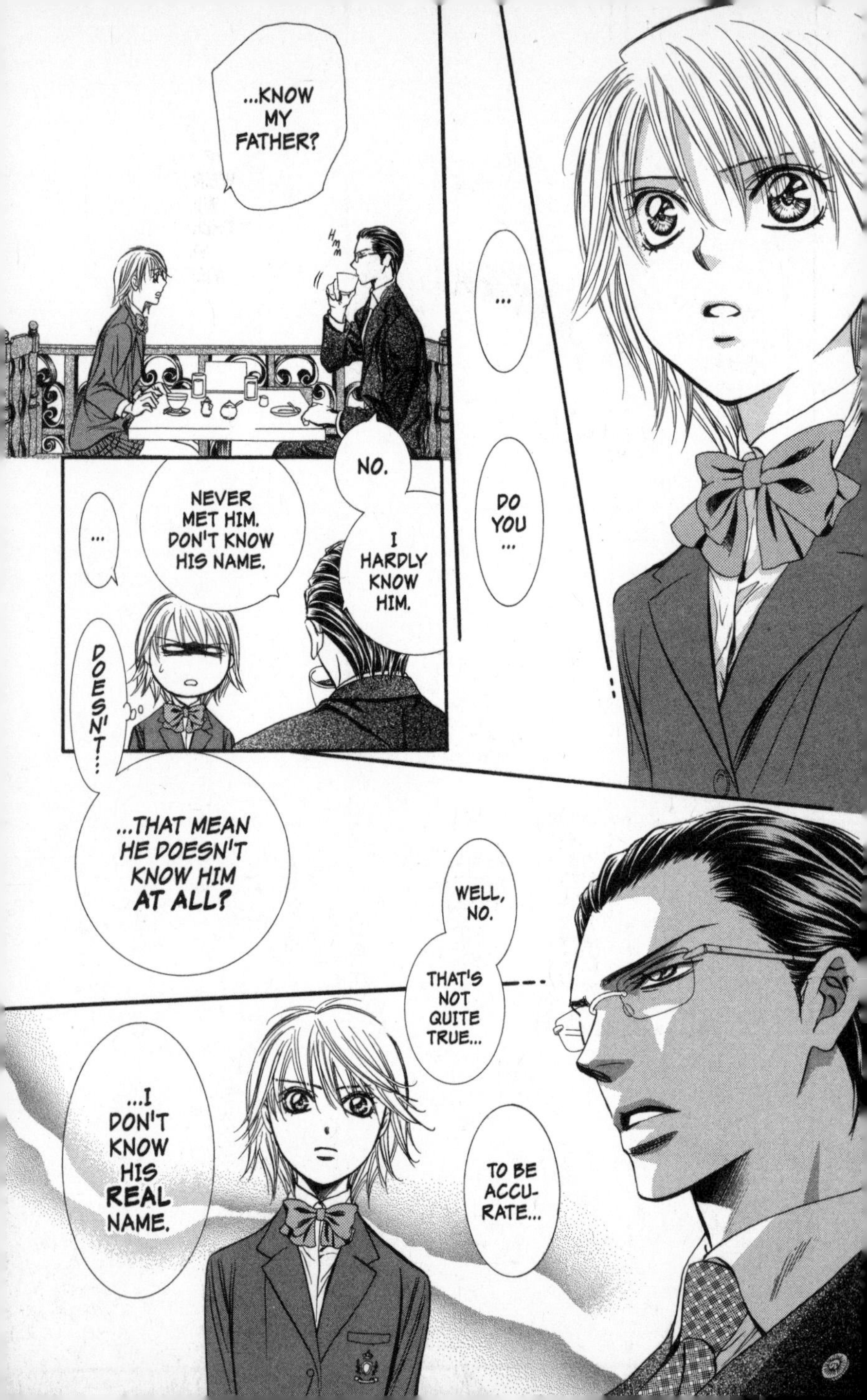
...
DO YOU ...
...KNOW MY FATHER?
Hmm
NO.
I HARDLY KNOW HIM.
NEVER MET HIM. DON'T KNOW HIS NAME.
...
DOESN'T...
...THAT MEAN HE DOESN'T KNOW HIM AT ALL?
WELL, NO.
THAT'S NOT QUITE TRUE...
TO BE ACCU-RATE...
...I DON'T KNOW HIS REAL NAME.

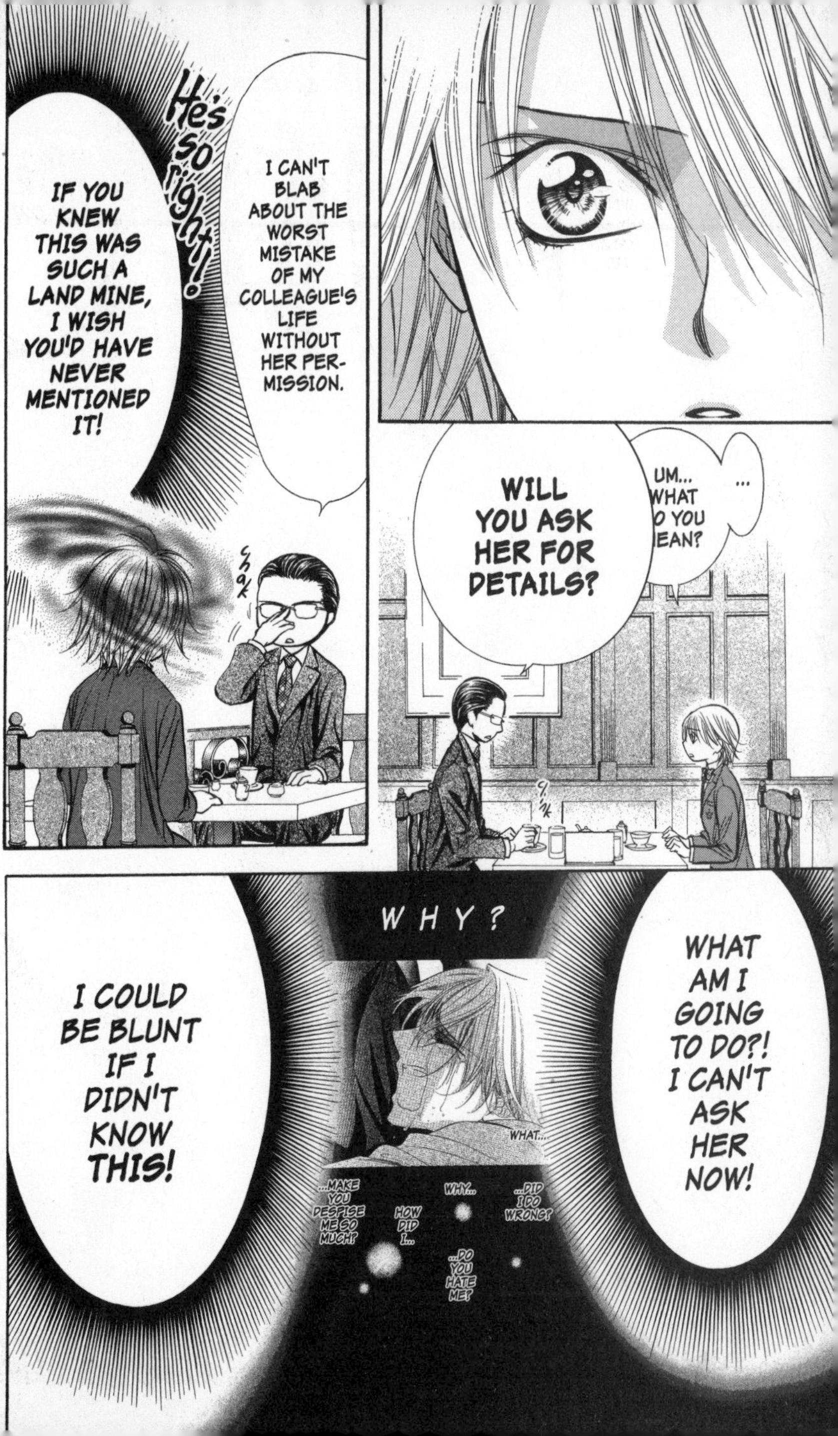
...
UM... WHAT O YOU EAN?
WILL YOU ASK HER FOR DETAILS?
I CAN'T BLAB ABOUT THE WORST MISTAKE OF MY COLLEAGUE'S LIFE WITHOUT HER PER-MISSION.
He's so right!!
IF YOU KNEW THIS WAS SUCH A LAND MINE, I WISH YOU'D HAVE NEVER MENTIONED IT!
WHAT AM I GOING TO DO?! I CAN'T ASK HER NOW!
WHY?
WHAT...
...DID I DO WRONG?
WHY...
...DO YOU HATE ME?
HOW DID I...
...MAKE YOU DESPISE ME SO MUCH?
I COULD BE BLUNT IF I DIDN'T KNOW THIS!

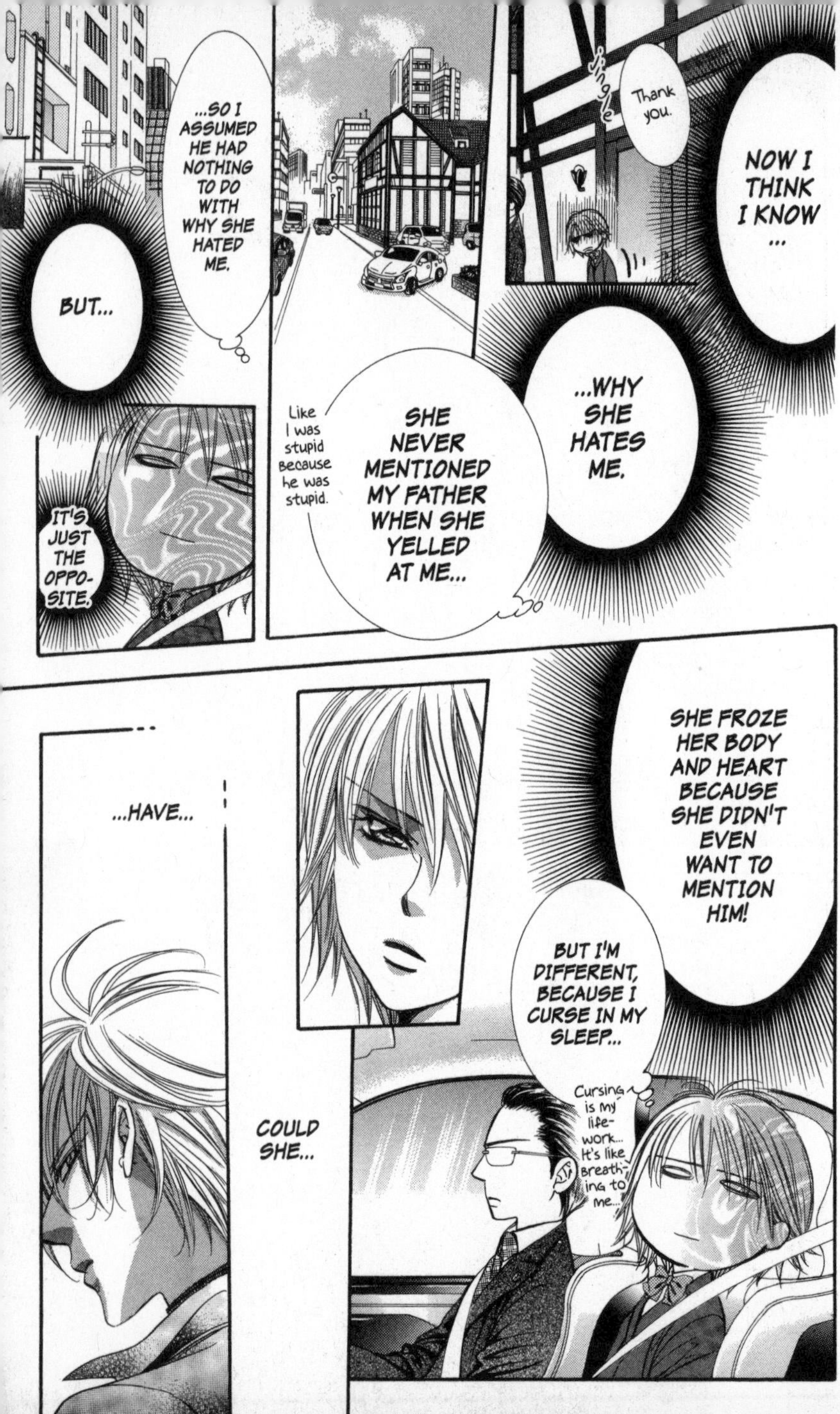

jingle
Thank you.
NOW I THINK I KNOW...
...WHY SHE HATES ME.
SHE NEVER MENTIONED MY FATHER WHEN SHE YELLED AT ME...
Like I was stupid because he was stupid.
...SO I ASSUMED HE HAD NOTHING TO DO WITH WHY SHE HATED ME.
BUT...
IT'S JUST THE OPPOSITE.
SHE FROZE HER BODY AND HEART BECAUSE SHE DIDN'T EVEN WANT TO MENTION HIM!
BUT I'M DIFFERENT, BECAUSE I CURSE IN MY SLEEP...
Cursing is my life-work... It's like breathing to me...
COULD SHE...
...HAVE...

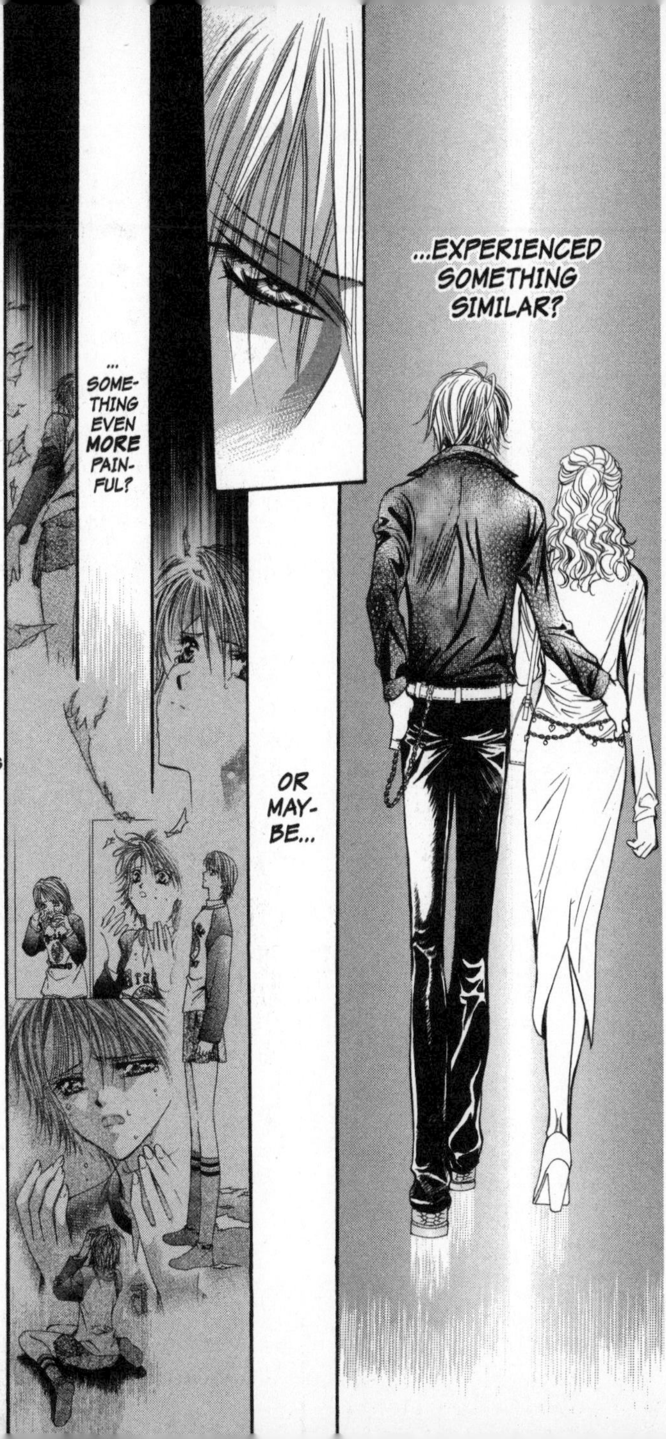
...EXPERIENCED SOMETHING SIMILAR?
OR MAY-BE...
... SOME-THING EVEN MORE PAIN-FUL?
THEN ...
... THERE'S NO WAY...

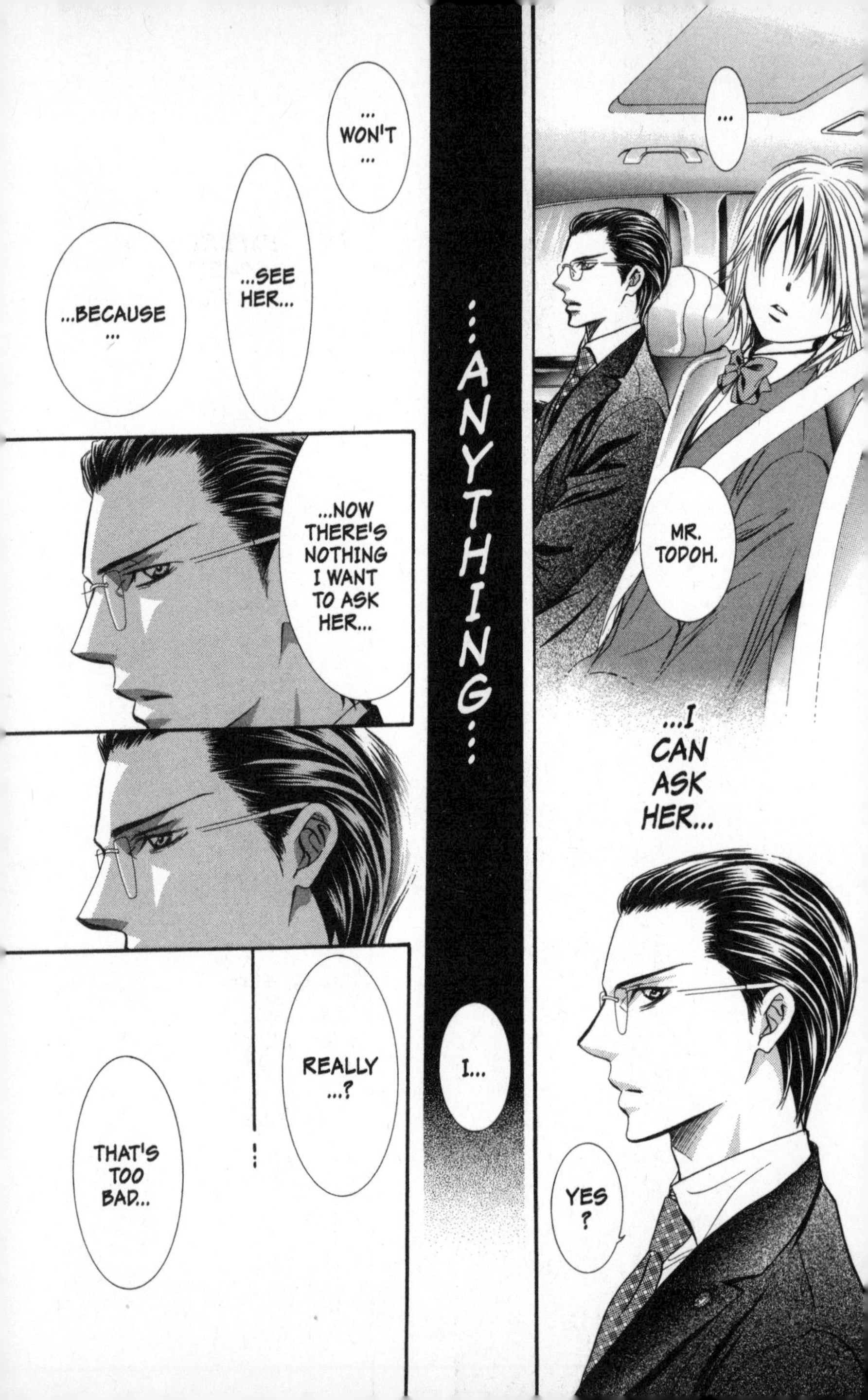
...
MR. TODOH.
YES?
I...
...I CAN ASK HER...
...ANYTHING...
...WON'T...
...SEE HER...
...BECAUSE...
...NOW THERE'S NOTHING I WANT TO ASK HER...
REALLY...?
!
THAT'S TOO BAD...

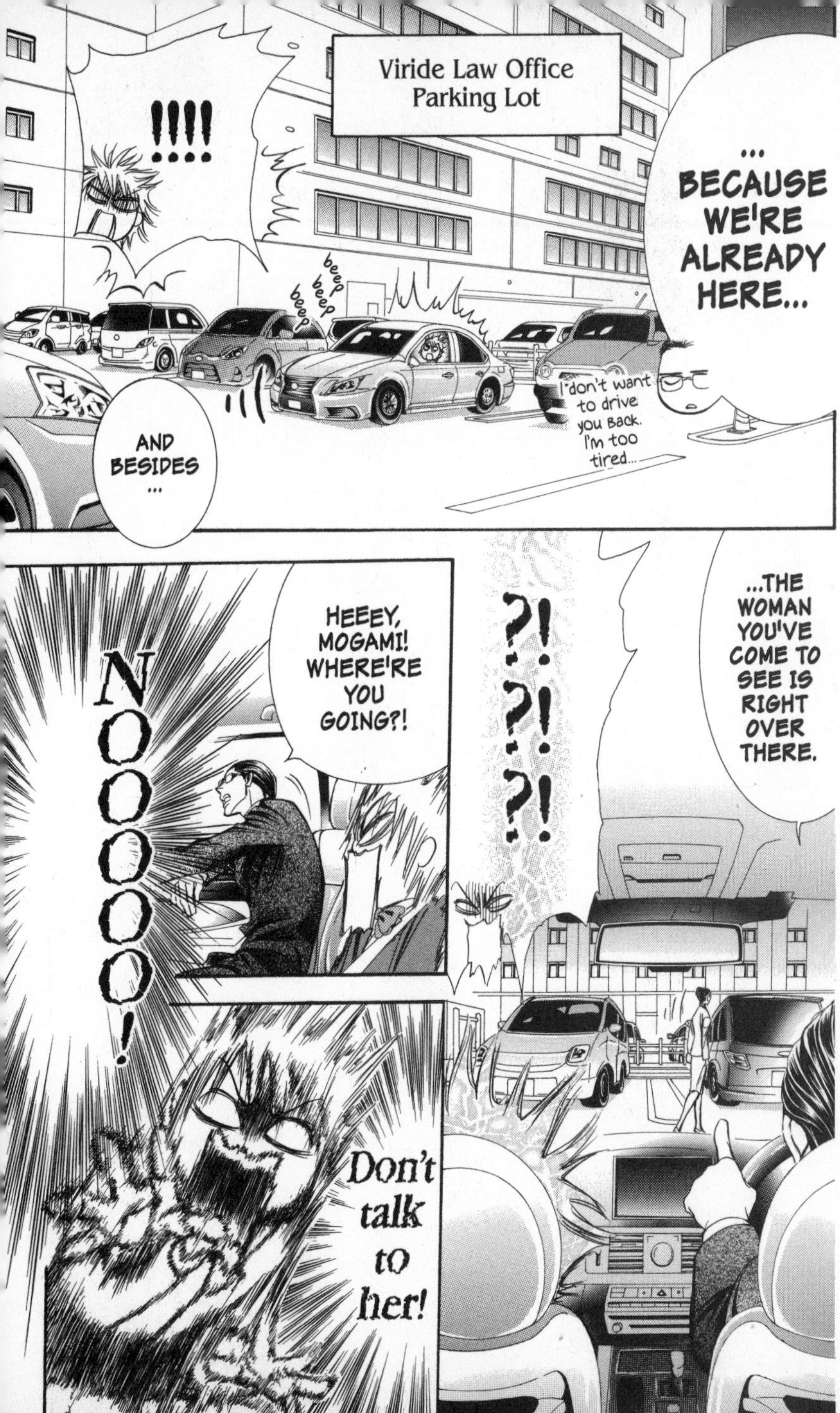

Viride Law Office
Parking Lot
... BECAUSE WE'RE ALREADY HERE...
I don't want to drive you back. I'm too tired...
!!!!
beep beep beep
AND BESIDES ...
...THE WOMAN YOU'VE COME TO SEE IS RIGHT OVER THERE.
?!?!?!
HEEEY, MOGAMI! WHERE'RE YOU GOING?!
NOOOOOO!
Don't talk to her!

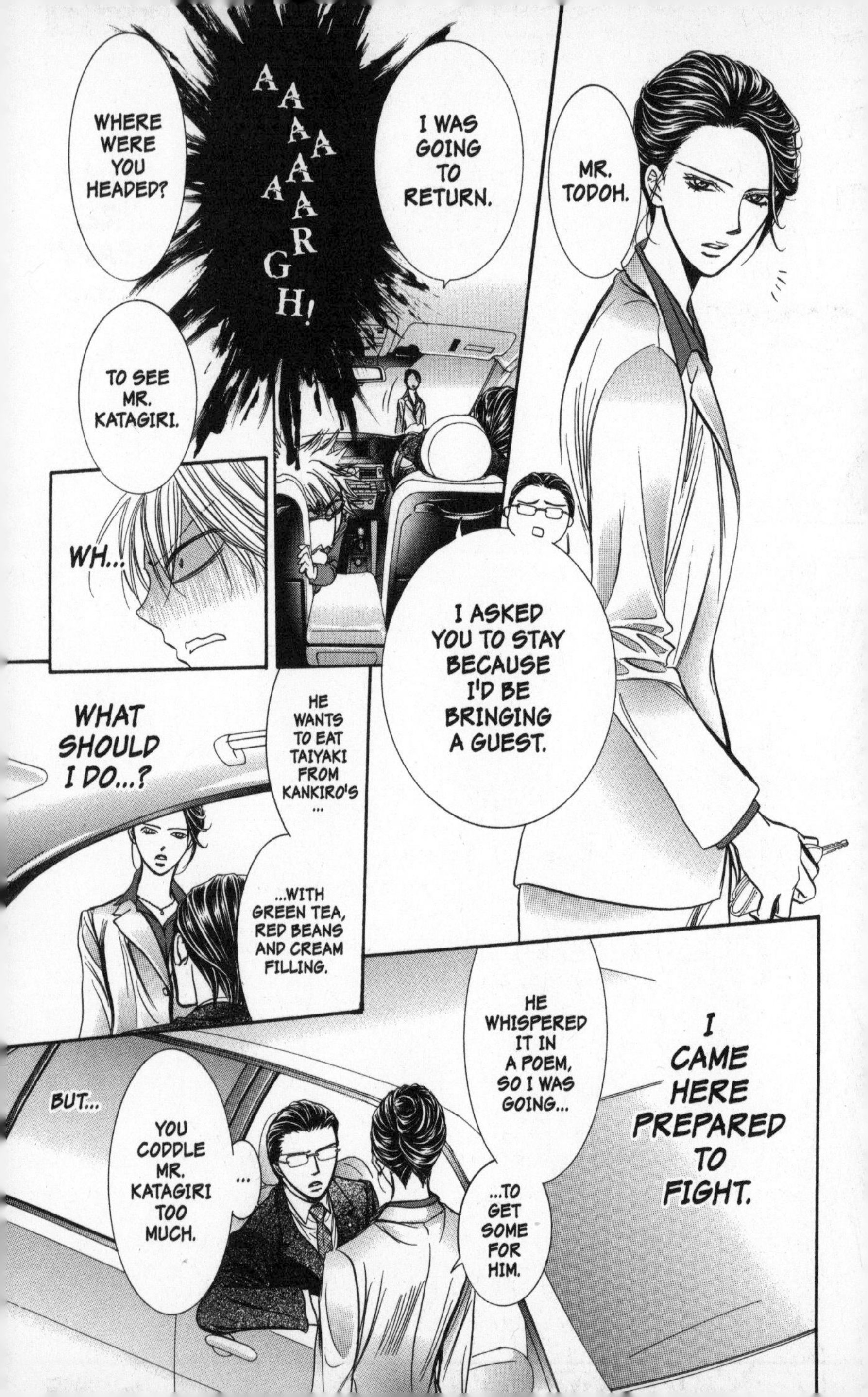
MR. TODOH.
I WAS GOING TO RETURN.
AAAAAAARGH!
WHERE WERE YOU HEADED?
TO SEE MR. KATAGIRI.
WH...
I ASKED YOU TO STAY BECAUSE I'D BE BRINGING A GUEST.
HE WANTS TO EAT TAIYAKI FROM KANKIRO'S ...
...WITH GREEN TEA, RED BEANS AND CREAM FILLING.
WHAT SHOULD I DO...?
I CAME HERE PREPARED TO FIGHT.
HE WHISPERED IT IN A POEM, SO I WAS GOING...
...TO GET SOME FOR HIM.
YOU CODDLE MR. KATAGIRI TOO MUCH.
...
BUT...

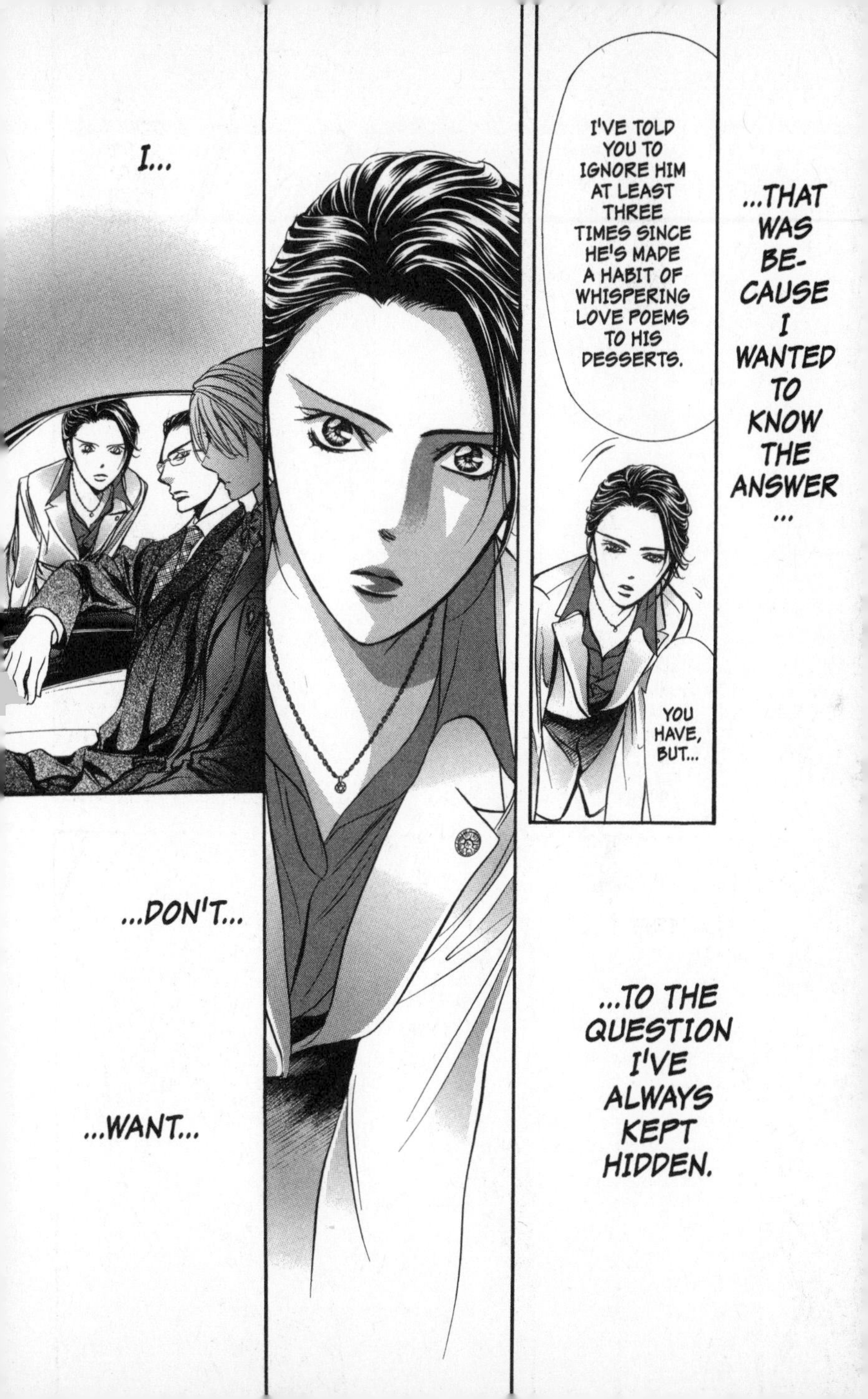
...THAT WAS BE-CAUSE I WANTED TO KNOW THE ANSWER...
I'VE TOLD YOU TO IGNORE HIM AT LEAST THREE TIMES SINCE HE'S MADE A HABIT OF WHISPERING LOVE POEMS TO HIS DESSERTS.
YOU HAVE, BUT...
...TO THE QUESTION I'VE ALWAYS KEPT HIDDEN.
I...
...DON'T...
...WANT...

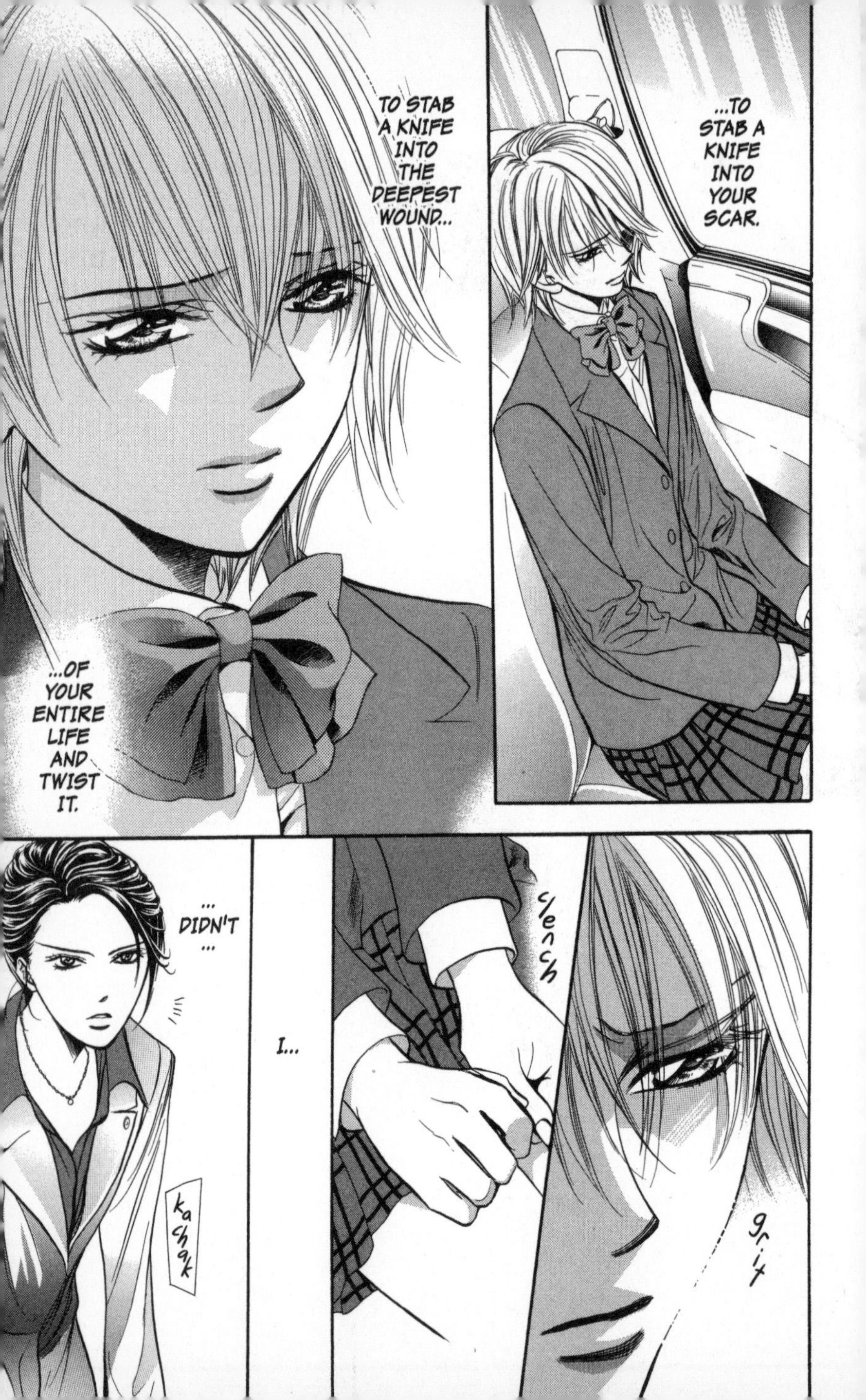
...TO STAB A KNIFE INTO YOUR SCAR.
TO STAB A KNIFE INTO THE DEEPEST WOUND...
...OF YOUR ENTIRE LIFE AND TWIST IT.
grit
clench
I...
...DIDN'T...
kachak

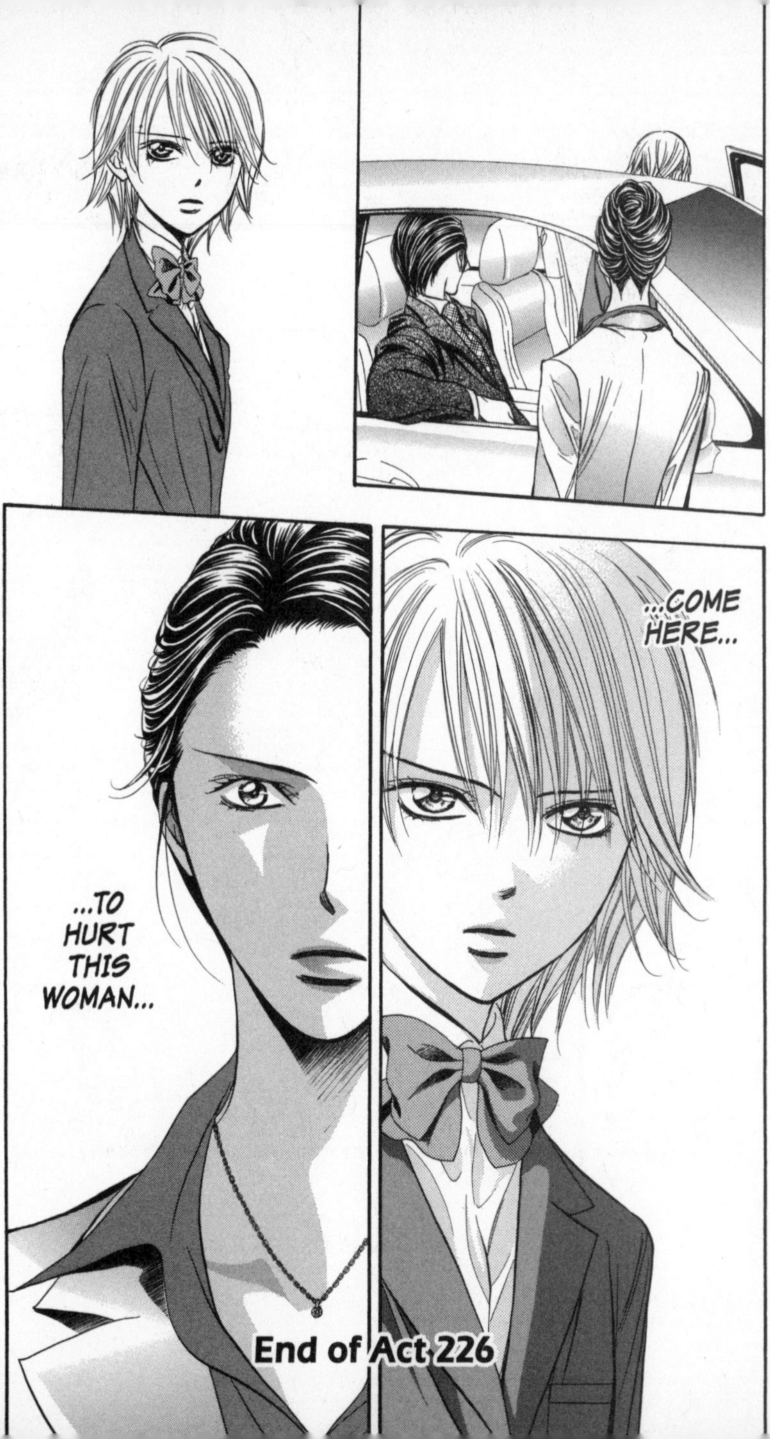
...COME HERE...
...TO HURT THIS WOMAN...
End of Act 226

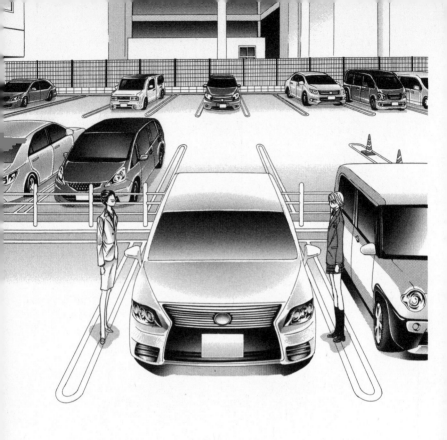

Skip·Beat!

Act 227: Spiral Echo

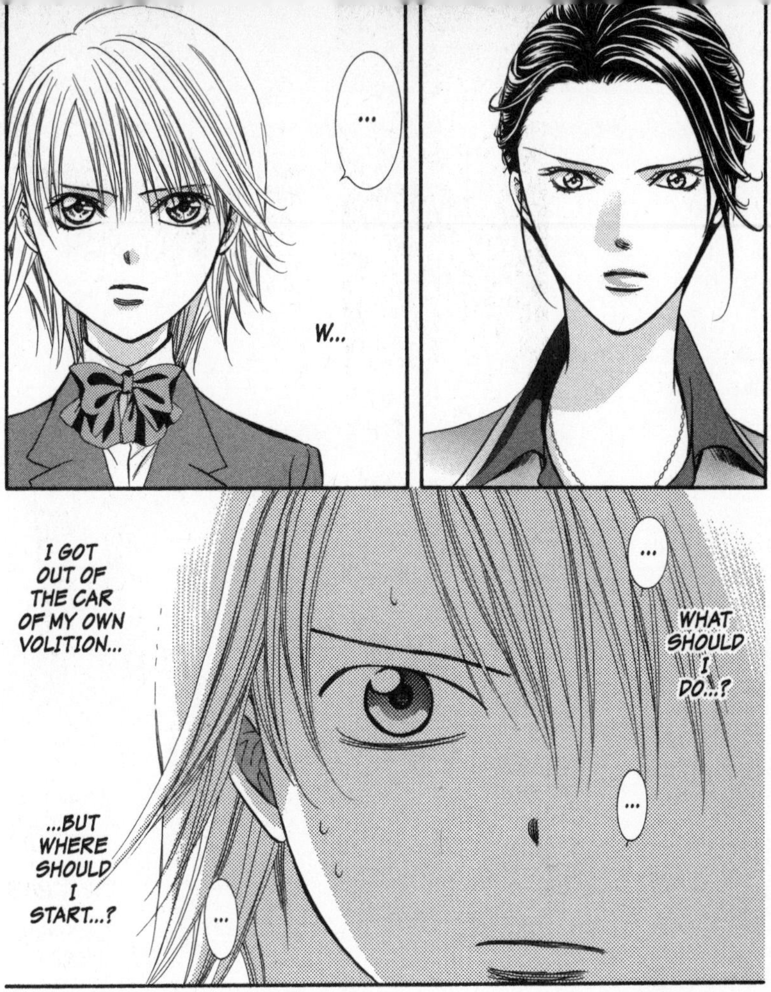
...
W...
...
WHAT SHOULD I DO...?
...
I GOT OUT OF THE CAR OF MY OWN VOLITION...
...BUT WHERE SHOULD I START...?
...

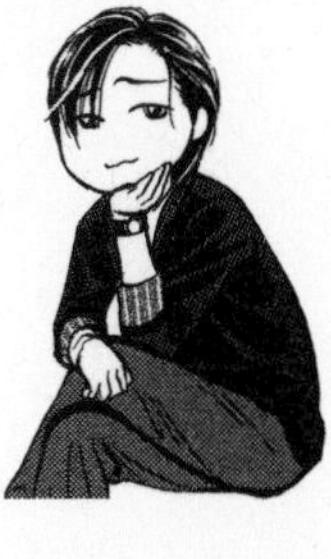

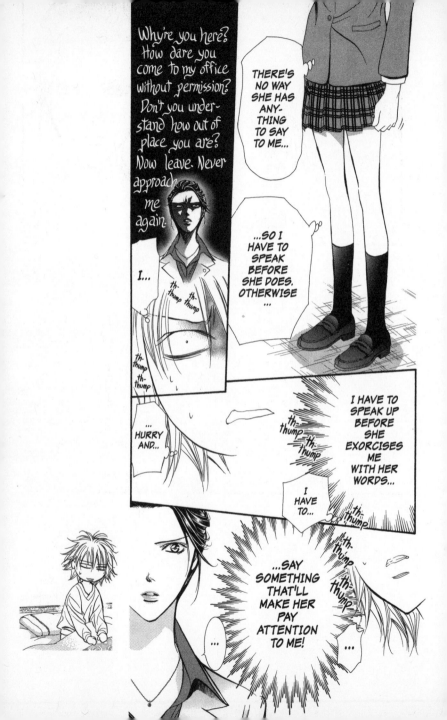

THERE'S NO WAY SHE HAS ANYTHING TO SAY TO ME...
...SO I HAVE TO SPEAK BEFORE SHE DOES. OTHERWISE...
Why're you here? How dare you come to my office without permission? Don't you understand how out of place you are? Now leave. Never approach me again.
I...
th-thump th-thump
th-thump th-thump
I HAVE TO SPEAK UP BEFORE SHE EXORCISES ME WITH HER WORDS...
th-thump th-thump
I HAVE TO...
th-thump
...HURRY AND...
th-thump th-thump
...SAY SOMETHING THAT'LL MAKE HER PAY ATTENTION TO ME!
...
...

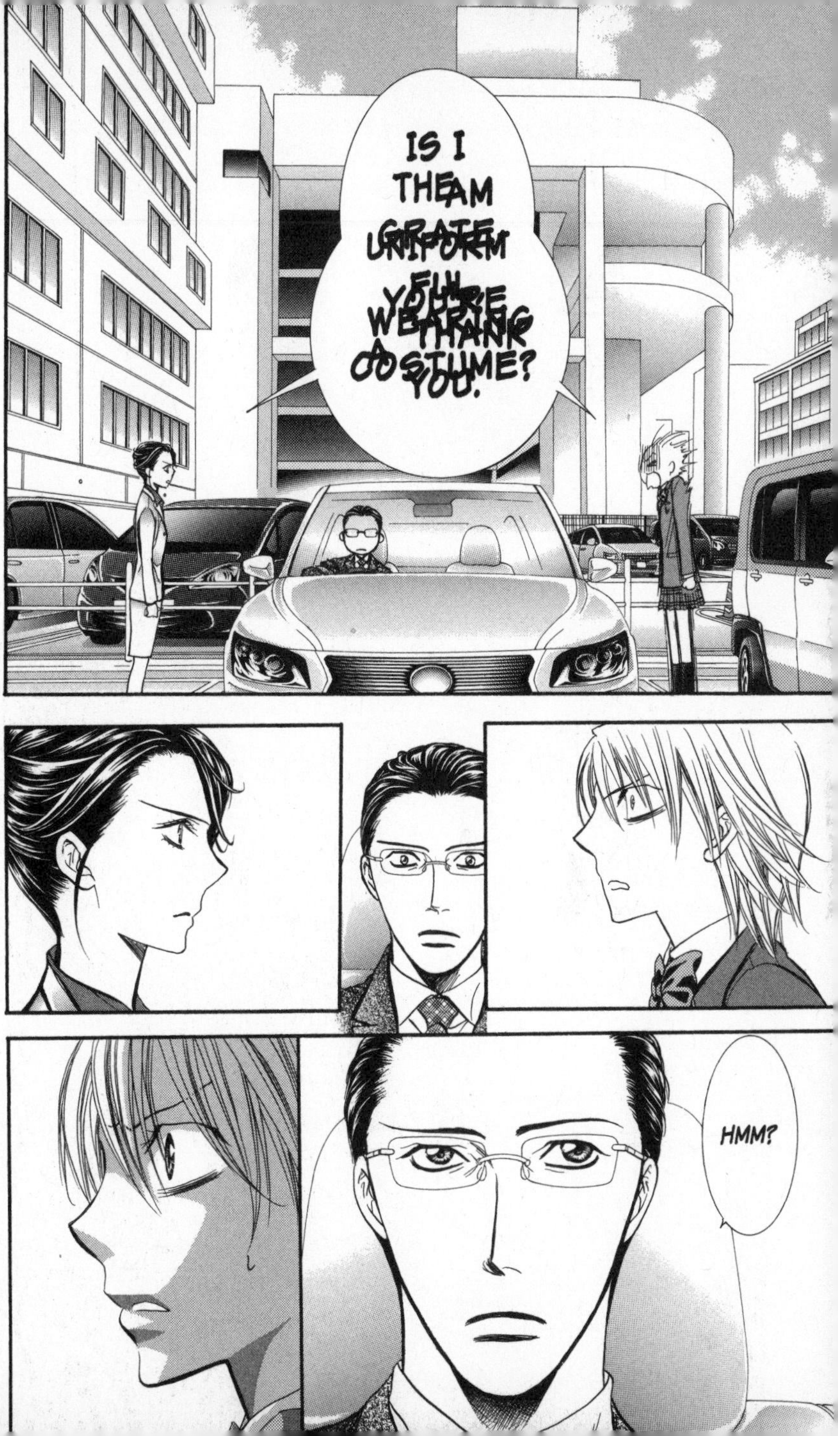
IS THE UNIFORM YOU'RE WEARING A COSTUME?
I AM GRATEFUL THANK YOU.
HMM?

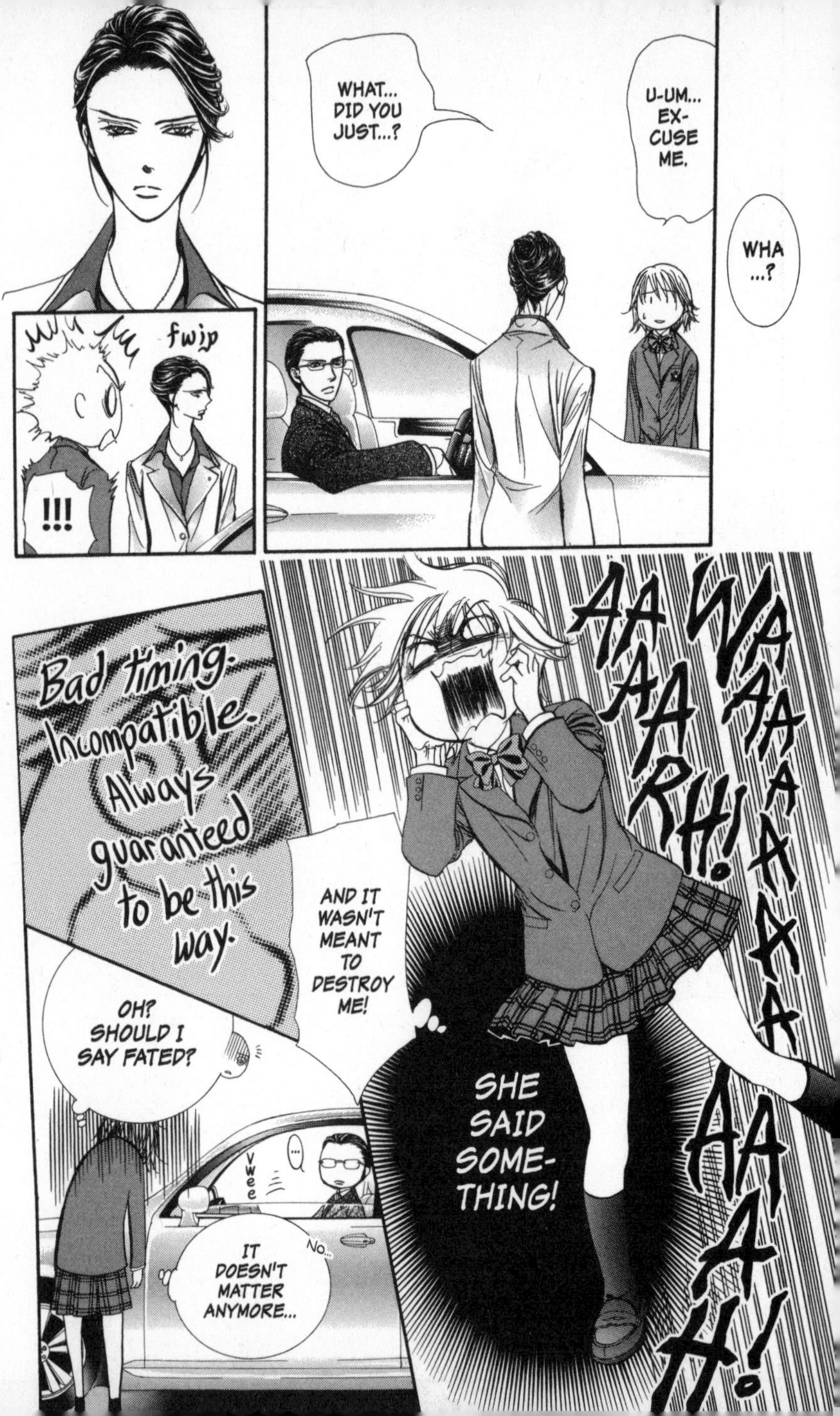
U-UM... EX-CUSE ME.
WHAT... DID YOU JUST...?
WHA...?
fwip
!!!
WAAAAAAAAAAAH!
AAAARH!
SHE SAID SOME-THING!
AND IT WASN'T MEANT TO DESTROY ME!
Bad timing. Incompatible. Always guaranteed to be this way.
OH? SHOULD I SAY FATED?
vwee
...
NO...
IT DOESN'T MATTER ANYMORE...

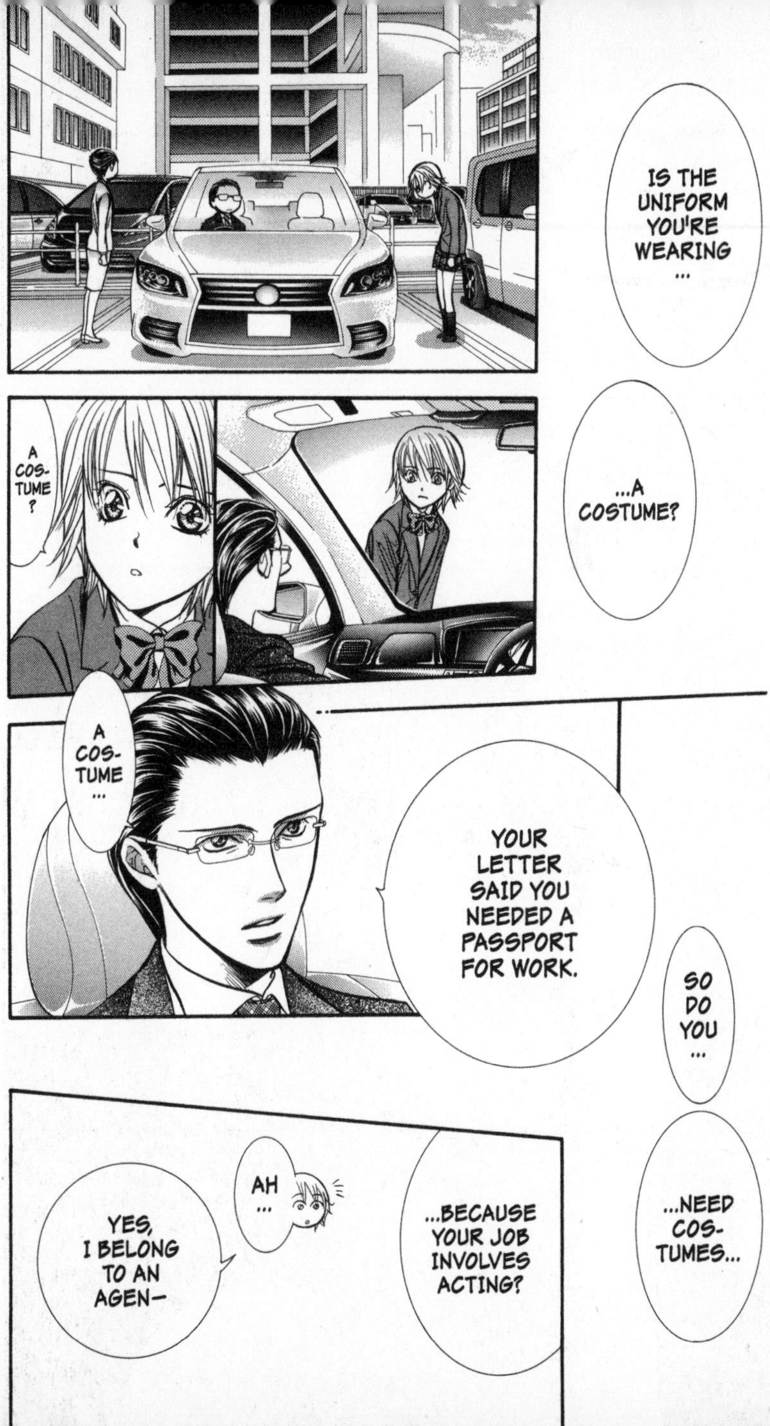

IS THE UNIFORM YOU'RE WEARING ...
...A COSTUME?
A COS- TUME ?
A COS- TUME ...
YOUR LETTER SAID YOU NEEDED A PASSPORT FOR WORK.
SO DO YOU ...
...NEED COS- TUMES...
...BECAUSE YOUR JOB INVOLVES ACTING?
AH ...
YES, I BELONG TO AN AGEN—

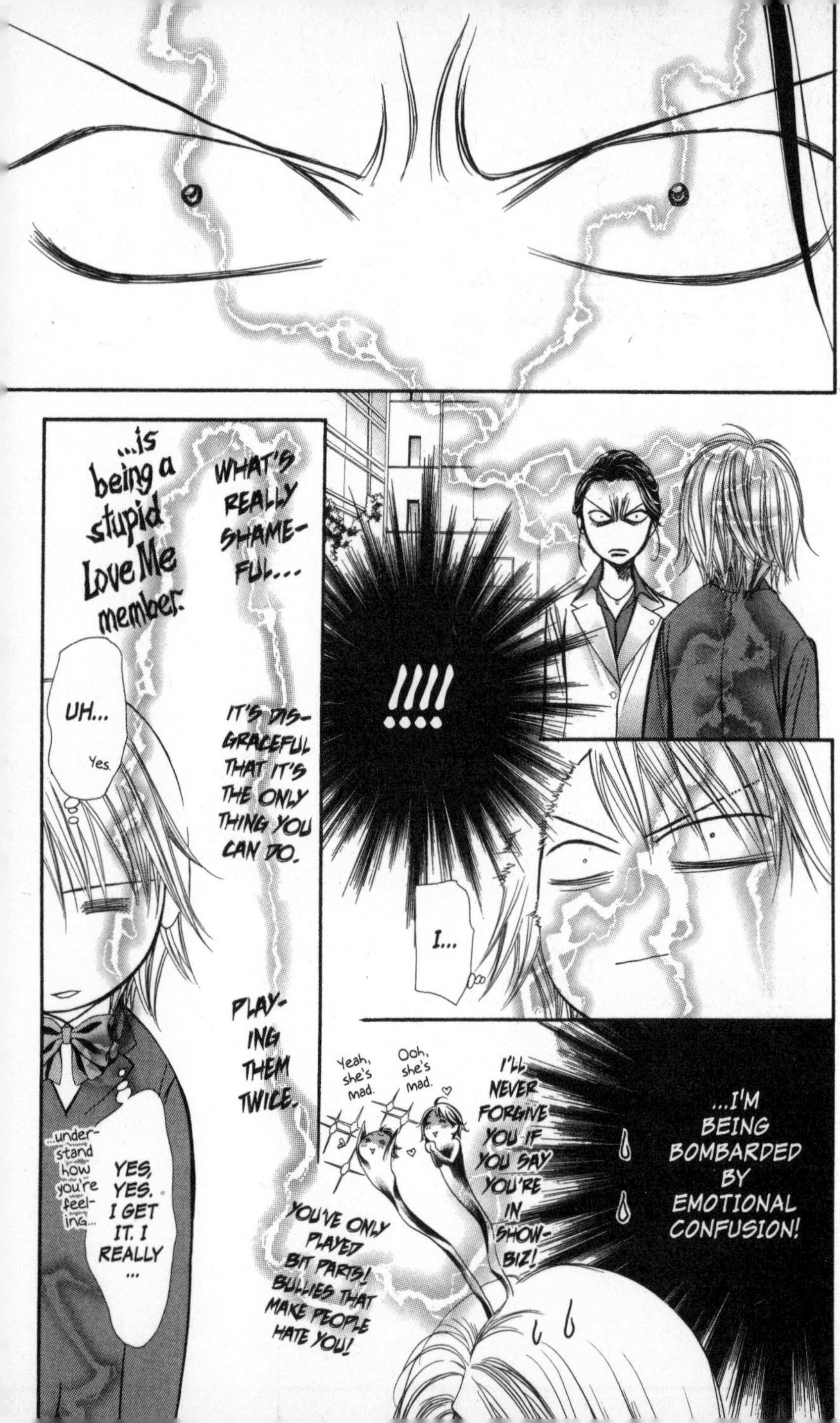
WHAT'S REALLY SHAME-FUL...
...is being a stupid Love Me member.
!!!!
I...
UH...
Yes.
IT'S DIS-GRACEFUL THAT IT'S THE ONLY THING YOU CAN DO.
PLAY-ING THEM TWICE.
...I'M BEING BOMBARDED BY EMOTIONAL CONFUSION!
I'LL NEVER FORGIVE YOU IF YOU SAY YOU'RE IN SHOW-BIZ!
YOU'VE ONLY PLAYED BIT PARTS! BULLIES THAT MAKE PEOPLE HATE YOU!
Ooh, she's mad.
Yeah, she's mad.
YES, YES. I GET IT. I REALLY ...
...under-stand how you're feel-ing...

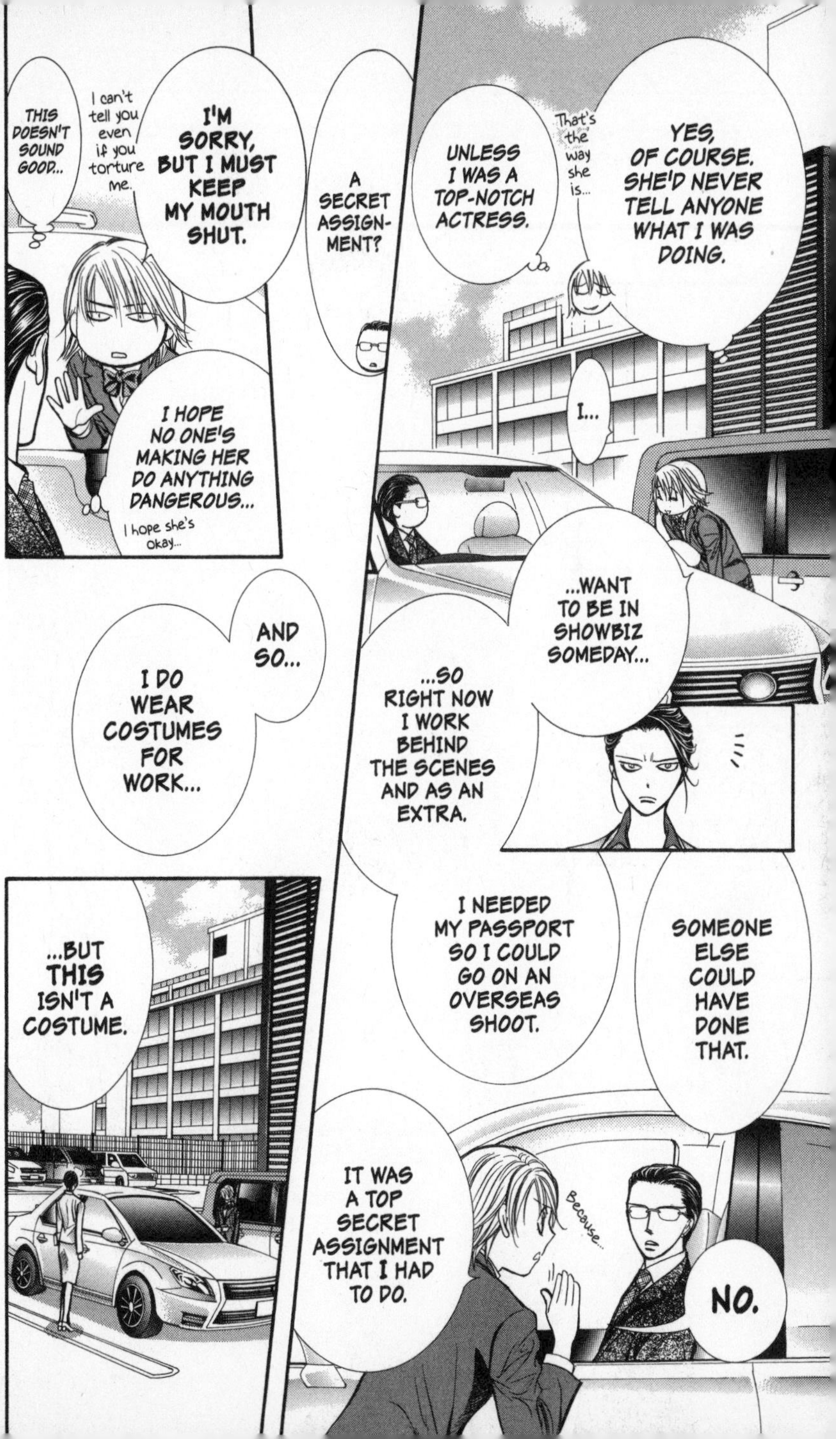
YES, OF COURSE. SHE'D NEVER TELL ANYONE WHAT I WAS DOING.
That's the way she is...
UNLESS I WAS A TOP-NOTCH ACTRESS.
I...
...WANT TO BE IN SHOWBIZ SOMEDAY...
...SO RIGHT NOW I WORK BEHIND THE SCENES AND AS AN EXTRA.
AND SO...
I DO WEAR COSTUMES FOR WORK...
...BUT THIS ISN'T A COSTUME.
I NEEDED MY PASSPORT SO I COULD GO ON AN OVERSEAS SHOOT.
SOMEONE ELSE COULD HAVE DONE THAT.
NO.
Because...
IT WAS A TOP SECRET ASSIGNMENT THAT I HAD TO DO.
A SECRET ASSIGNMENT?
I'M SORRY, BUT I MUST KEEP MY MOUTH SHUT.
I can't tell you even if you torture me.
THIS DOESN'T SOUND GOOD...
I HOPE NO ONE'S MAKING HER DO ANYTHING DANGEROUS...
I hope she's okay...

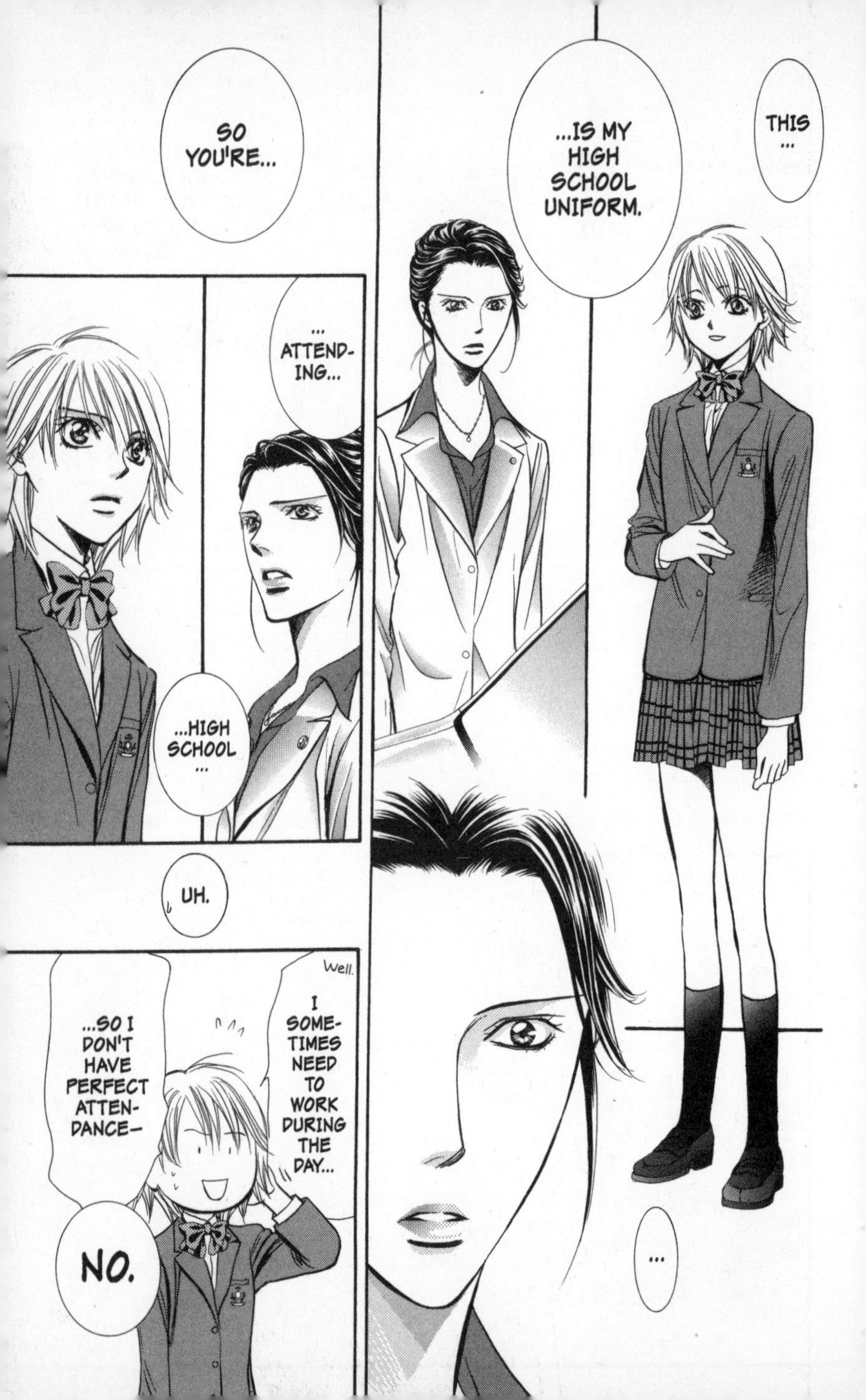
THIS...
...IS MY HIGH SCHOOL UNIFORM.
...
SO YOU'RE...
...ATTENDING...
...HIGH SCHOOL...
UH.
Well.
I SOMETIMES NEED TO WORK DURING THE DAY...
...SO I DON'T HAVE PERFECT ATTENDANCE—
NO.

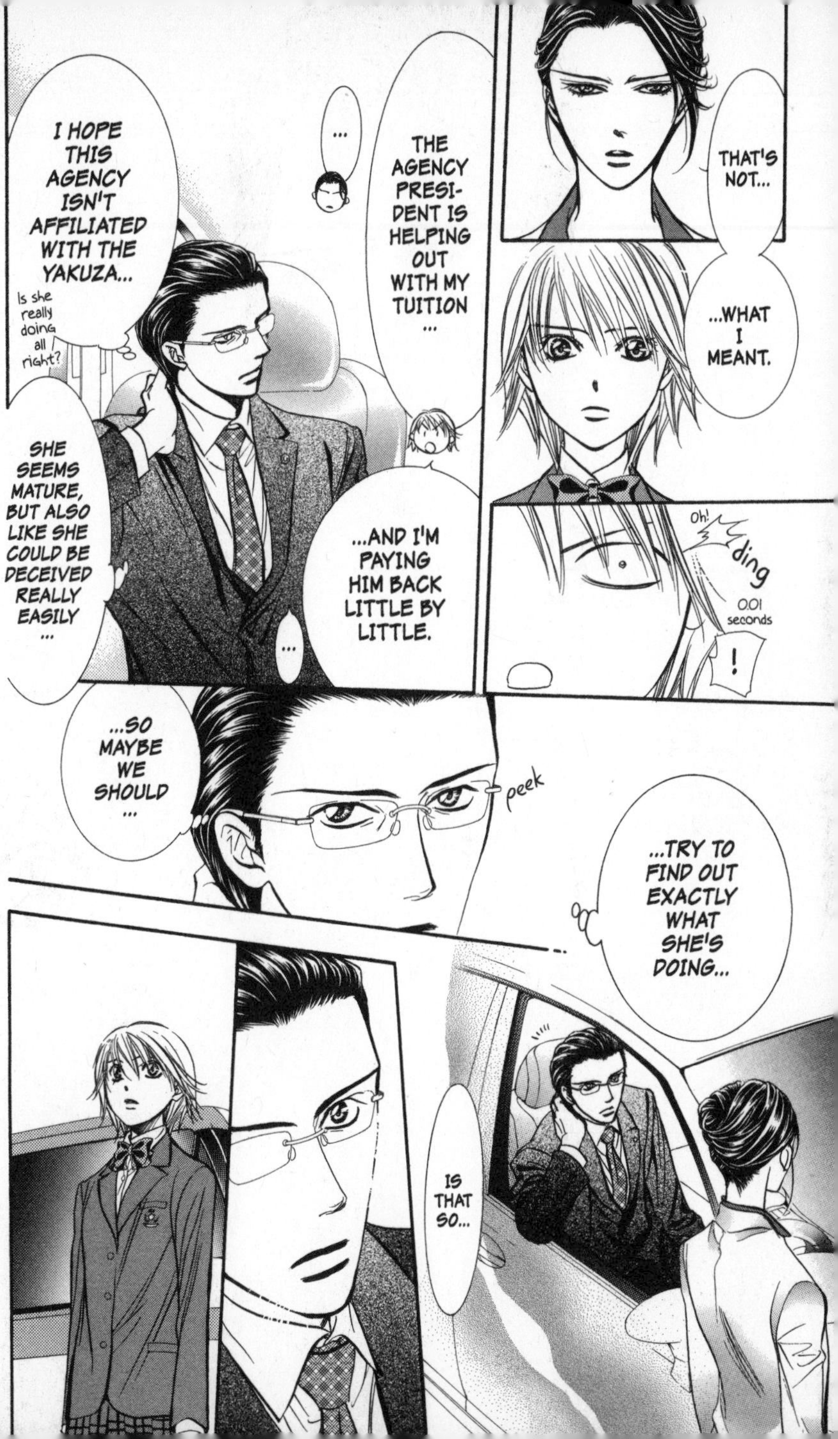
THAT'S NOT...
...WHAT I MEANT.
Oh!
ding
0.01 seconds
!
...
THE AGENCY PRESI-DENT IS HELPING OUT WITH MY TUITION...
I HOPE THIS AGENCY ISN'T AFFILIATED WITH THE YAKUZA...
Is she really doing all right?
...AND I'M PAYING HIM BACK LITTLE BY LITTLE.
...
SHE SEEMS MATURE, BUT ALSO LIKE SHE COULD BE DECEIVED REALLY EASILY...
peek
...SO MAYBE WE SHOULD...
...TRY TO FIND OUT EXACTLY WHAT SHE'S DOING...
IS THAT SO...

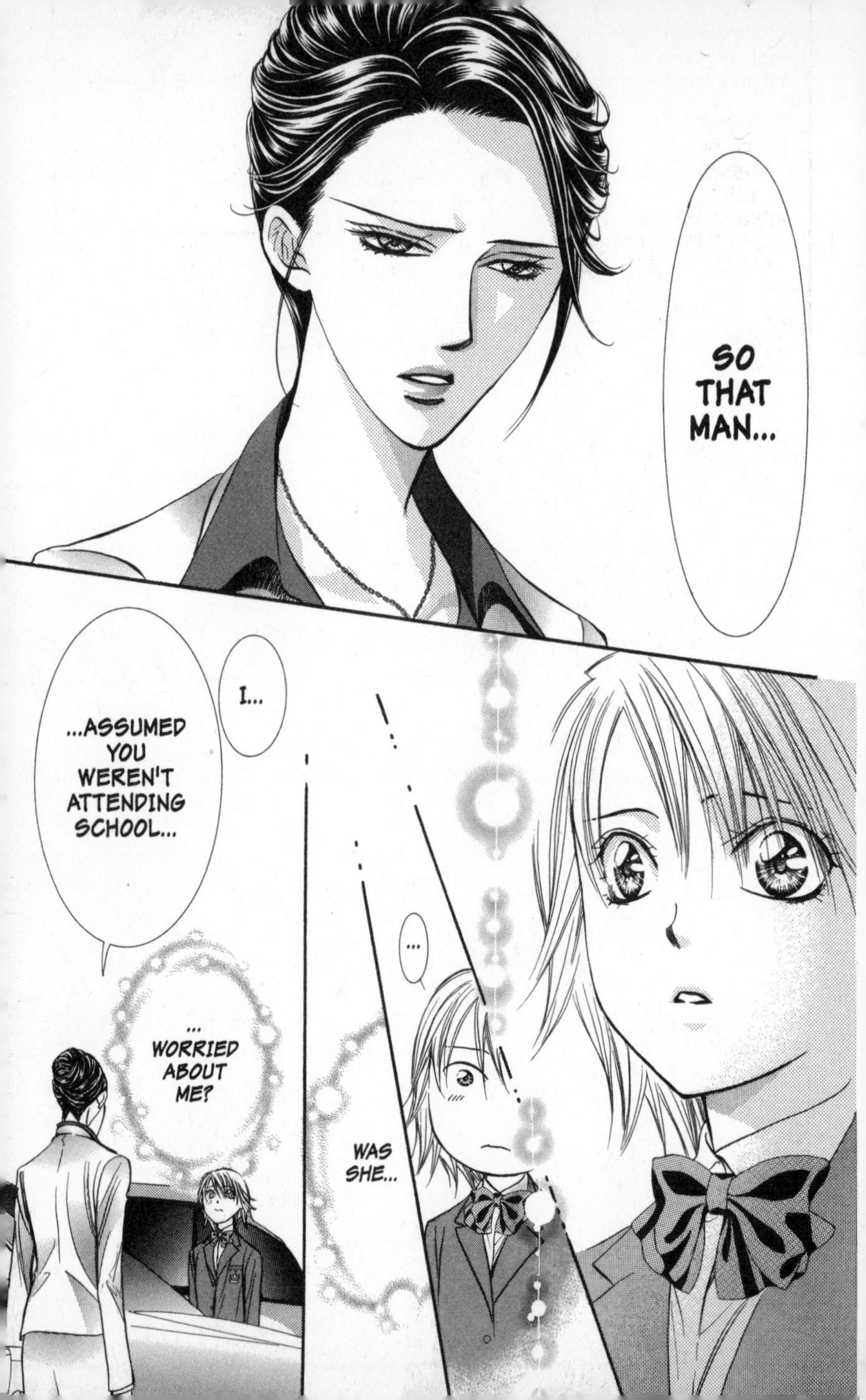
SO THAT MAN...
I...
...ASSUMED YOU WEREN'T ATTENDING SCHOOL...
...
WAS SHE...
...WORRIED ABOUT ME?

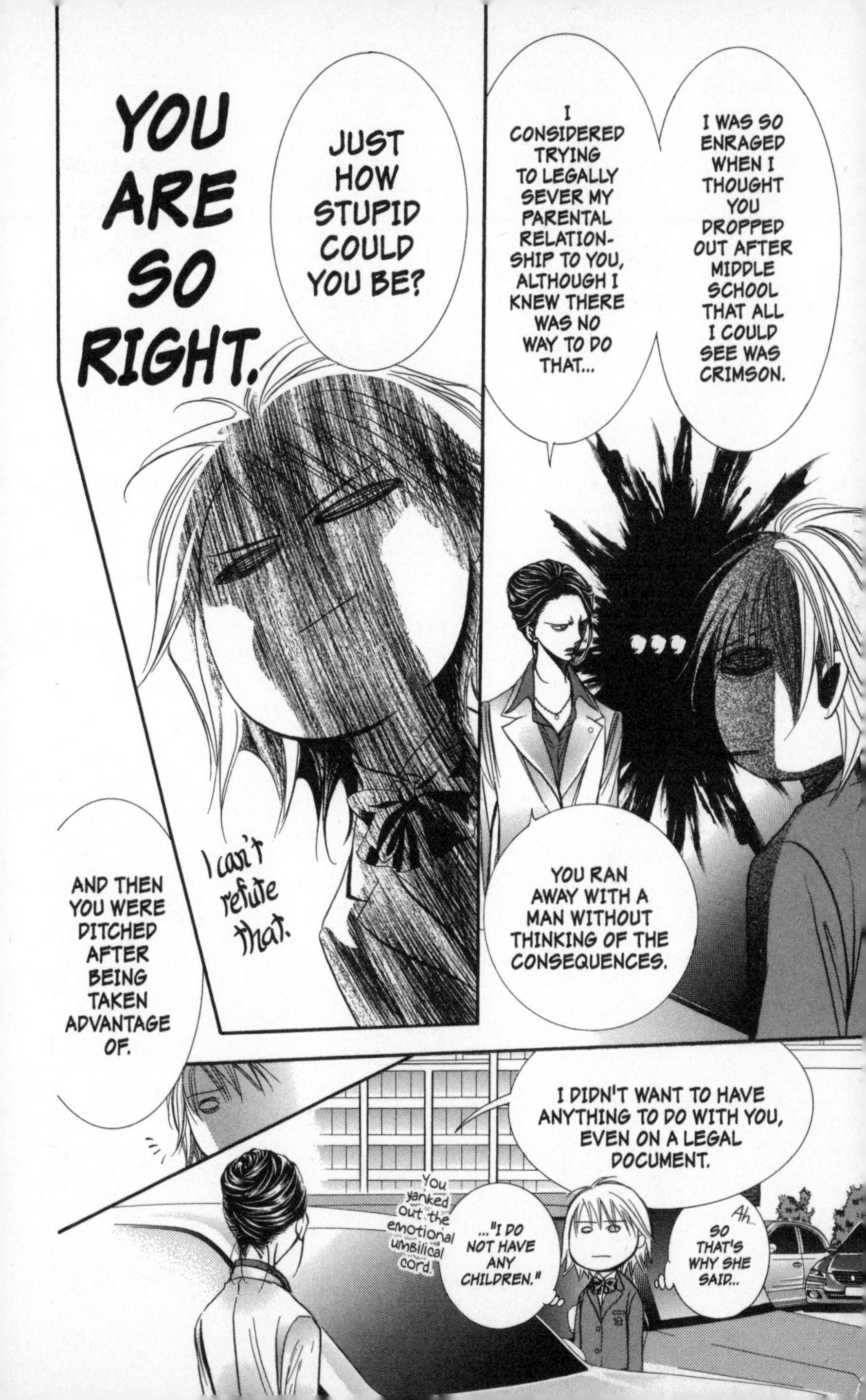
I WAS SO ENRAGED WHEN I THOUGHT YOU DROPPED OUT AFTER MIDDLE SCHOOL THAT ALL I COULD SEE WAS CRIMSON.
I CONSIDERED TRYING TO LEGALLY SEVER MY PARENTAL RELATION-SHIP TO YOU, ALTHOUGH I KNEW THERE WAS NO WAY TO DO THAT...
YOU RAN AWAY WITH A MAN WITHOUT THINKING OF THE CONSEQUENCES.
JUST HOW STUPID COULD YOU BE?
YOU ARE SO RIGHT.
I can't refute that.
AND THEN YOU WERE DITCHED AFTER BEING TAKEN ADVANTAGE OF.
I DIDN'T WANT TO HAVE ANYTHING TO DO WITH YOU, EVEN ON A LEGAL DOCUMENT.
Ah... SO THAT'S WHY SHE SAID...
..."I DO NOT HAVE ANY CHILDREN."
You yanked out the emotional umbilical cord.

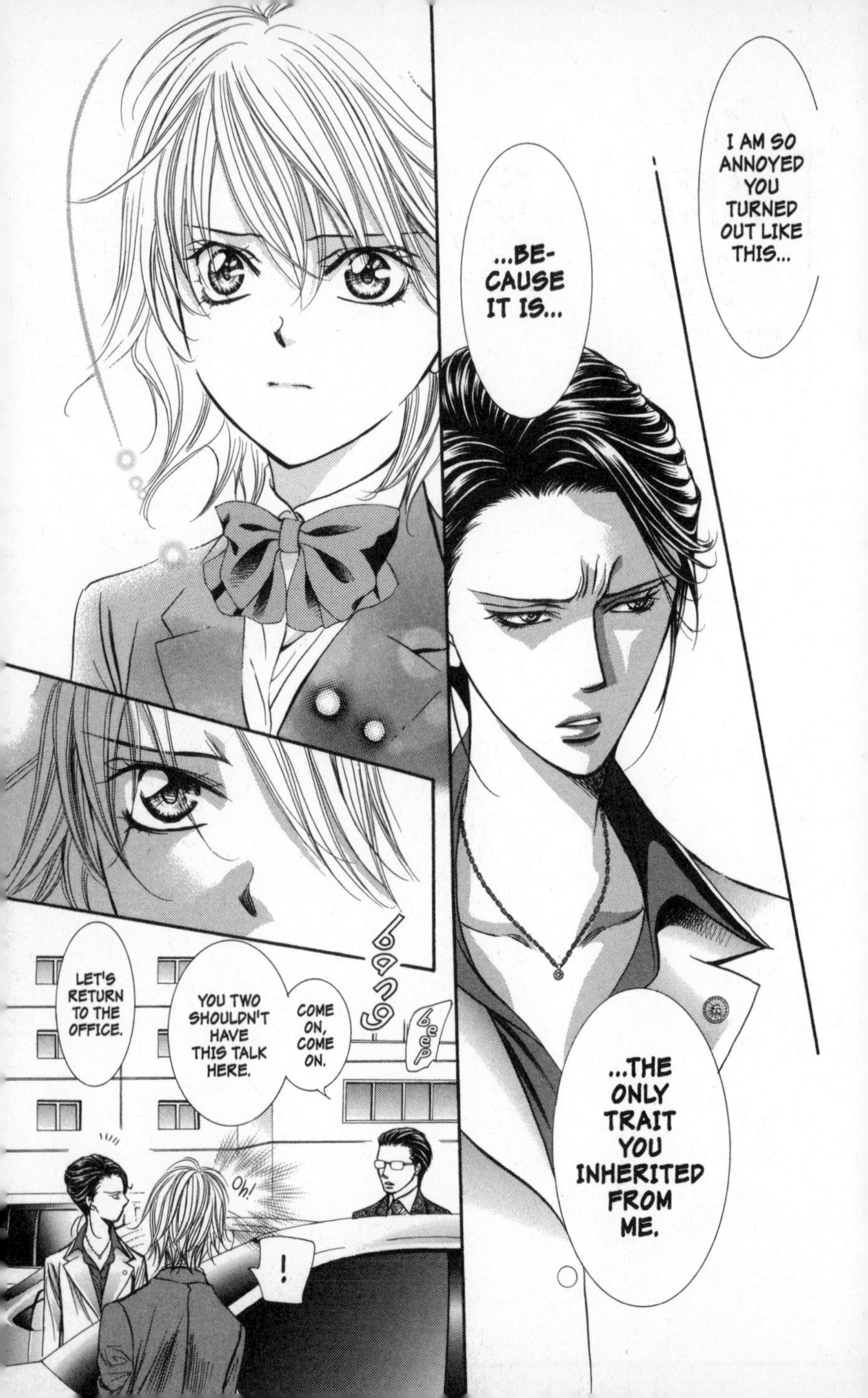
I AM SO ANNOYED YOU TURNED OUT LIKE THIS...
...BE-CAUSE IT IS...
...THE ONLY TRAIT YOU INHERITED FROM ME.
bang
beep
COME ON, COME ON.
YOU TWO SHOULDN'T HAVE THIS TALK HERE.
LET'S RETURN TO THE OFFICE.
Oh!
!

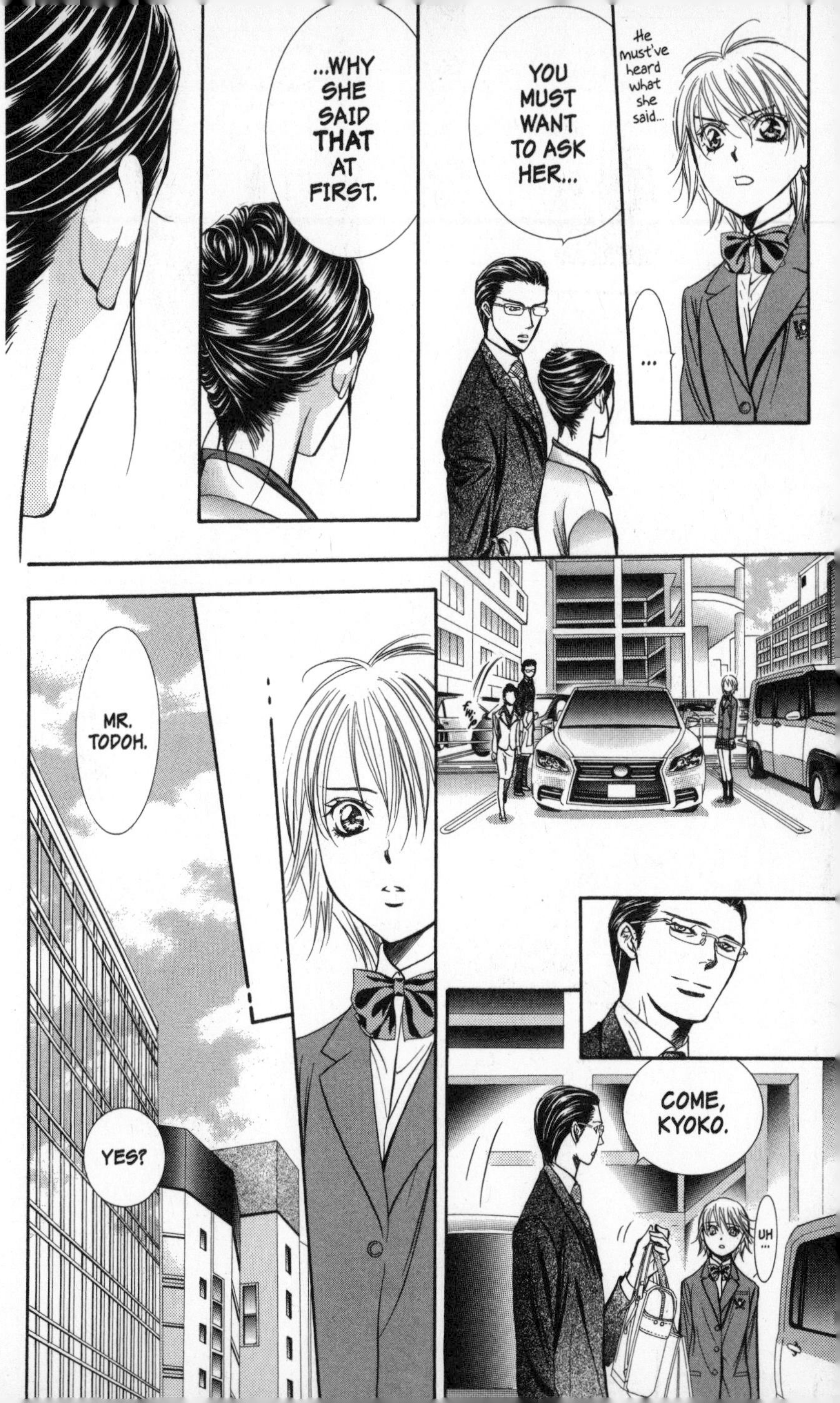
He must've heard what she said...
...
YOU MUST WANT TO ASK HER...
...WHY SHE SAID THAT AT FIRST.
COME, KYOKO.
UH...
MR. TODOH.
YES?

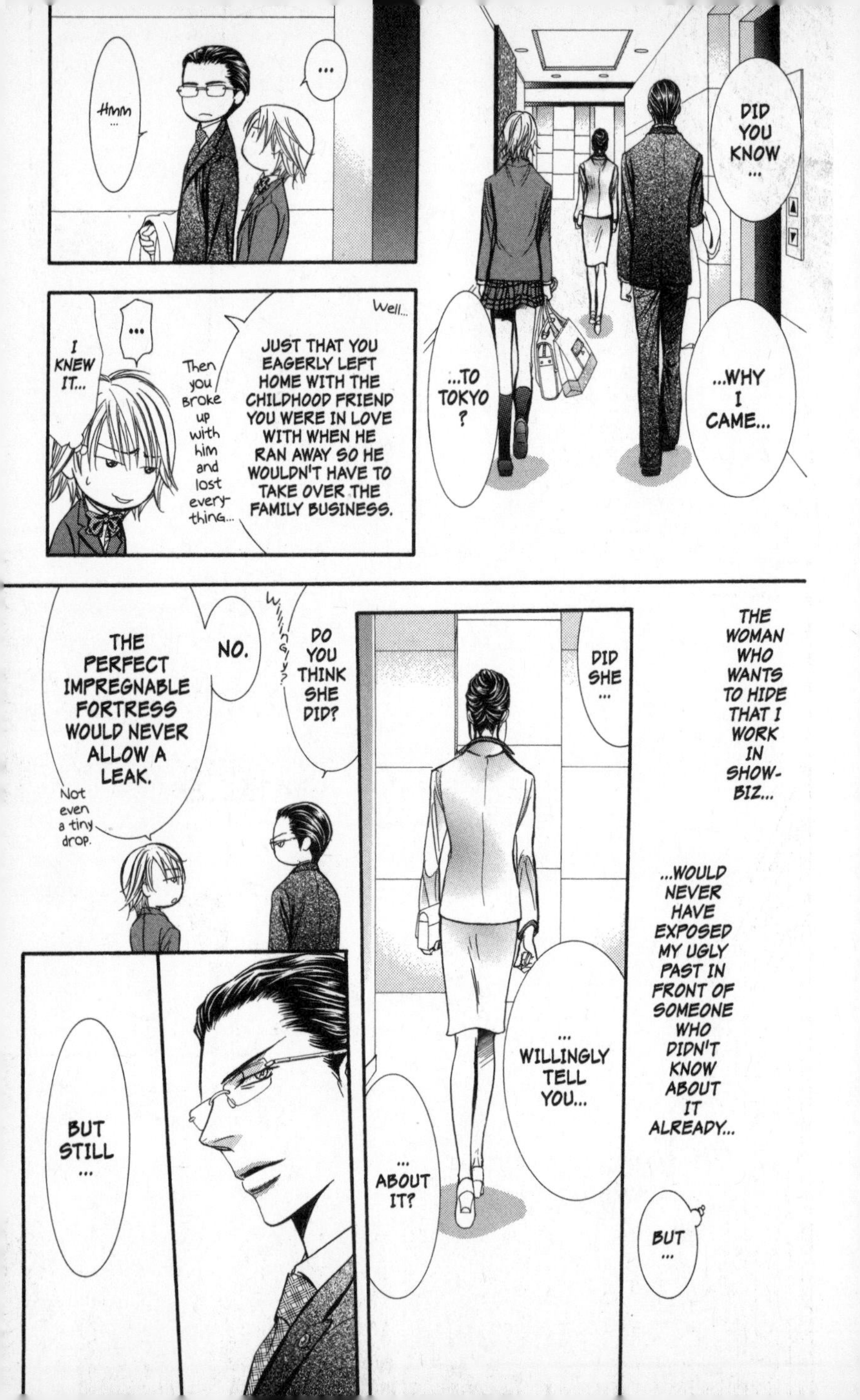
DID YOU KNOW ...
...WHY I CAME...
...TO TOKYO?
...
Hmm ...
Well...
JUST THAT YOU EAGERLY LEFT HOME WITH THE CHILDHOOD FRIEND YOU WERE IN LOVE WITH WHEN HE RAN AWAY SO HE WOULDN'T HAVE TO TAKE OVER THE FAMILY BUSINESS.
Then you broke up with him and lost every-thing...
...
I KNEW IT...
THE WOMAN WHO WANTS TO HIDE THAT I WORK IN SHOW-BIZ...
...WOULD NEVER HAVE EXPOSED MY UGLY PAST IN FRONT OF SOMEONE WHO DIDN'T KNOW ABOUT IT ALREADY...
BUT ...
DID SHE ...
... WILLINGLY TELL YOU...
... ABOUT IT?
DO YOU THINK SHE DID?
Willingly?
NO.
THE PERFECT IMPREGNABLE FORTRESS WOULD NEVER ALLOW A LEAK.
Not even a tiny drop.
BUT STILL ...

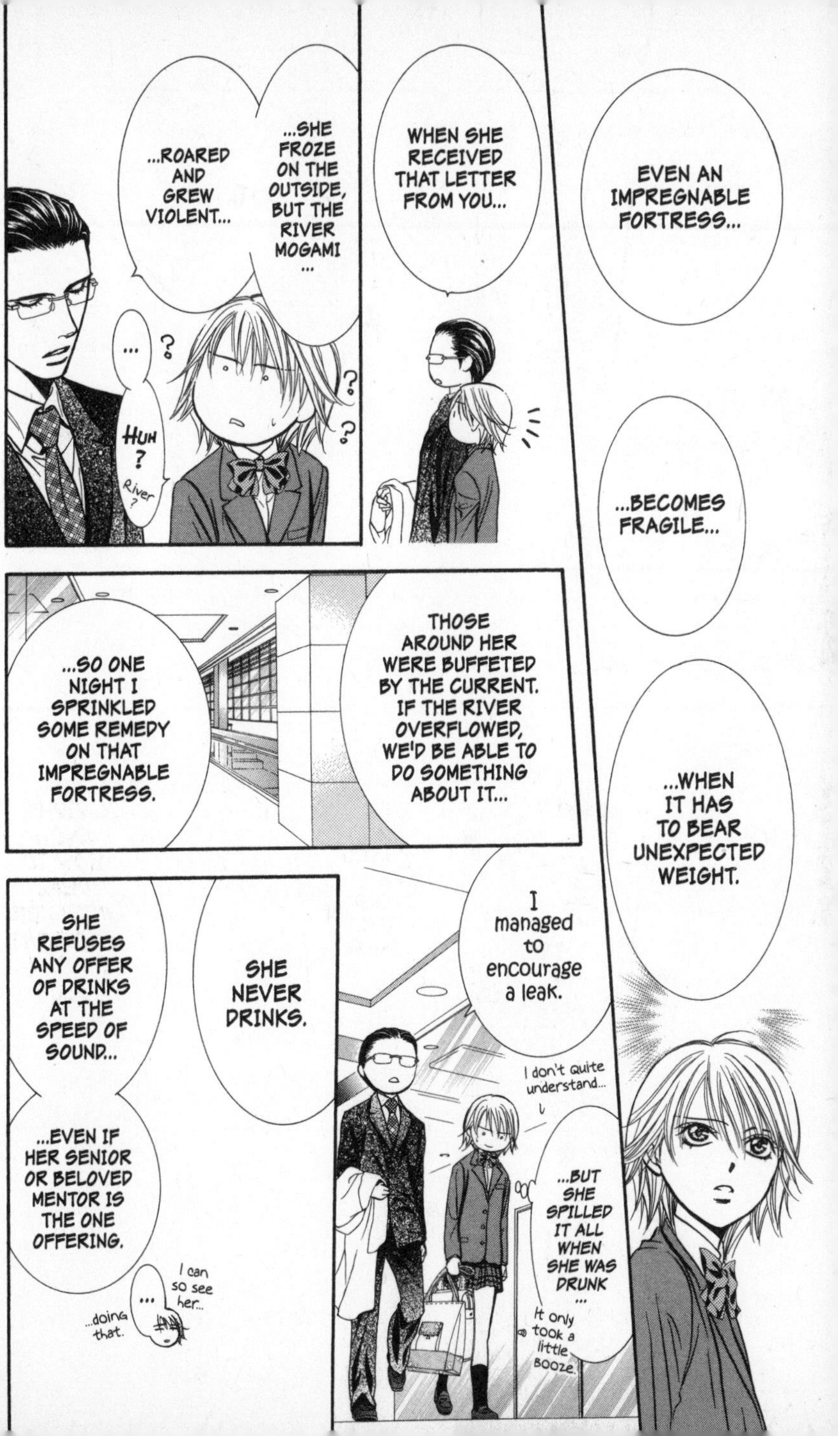
EVEN AN IMPREGNABLE FORTRESS...
...BECOMES FRAGILE...
...WHEN IT HAS TO BEAR UNEXPECTED WEIGHT.
WHEN SHE RECEIVED THAT LETTER FROM YOU...
...SHE FROZE ON THE OUTSIDE, BUT THE RIVER MOGAMI...
...ROARED AND GREW VIOLENT...
...
HUH?
River?
THOSE AROUND HER WERE BUFFETED BY THE CURRENT. IF THE RIVER OVERFLOWED, WE'D BE ABLE TO DO SOMETHING ABOUT IT...
...SO ONE NIGHT I SPRINKLED SOME REMEDY ON THAT IMPREGNABLE FORTRESS.
I managed to encourage a leak.
I don't quite understand...
...BUT SHE SPILLED IT ALL WHEN SHE WAS DRUNK...
It only took a little booze.
SHE NEVER DRINKS.
SHE REFUSES ANY OFFER OF DRINKS AT THE SPEED OF SOUND...
...EVEN IF HER SENIOR OR BELOVED MENTOR IS THE ONE OFFERING.
...
I can so see her...
...doing that.

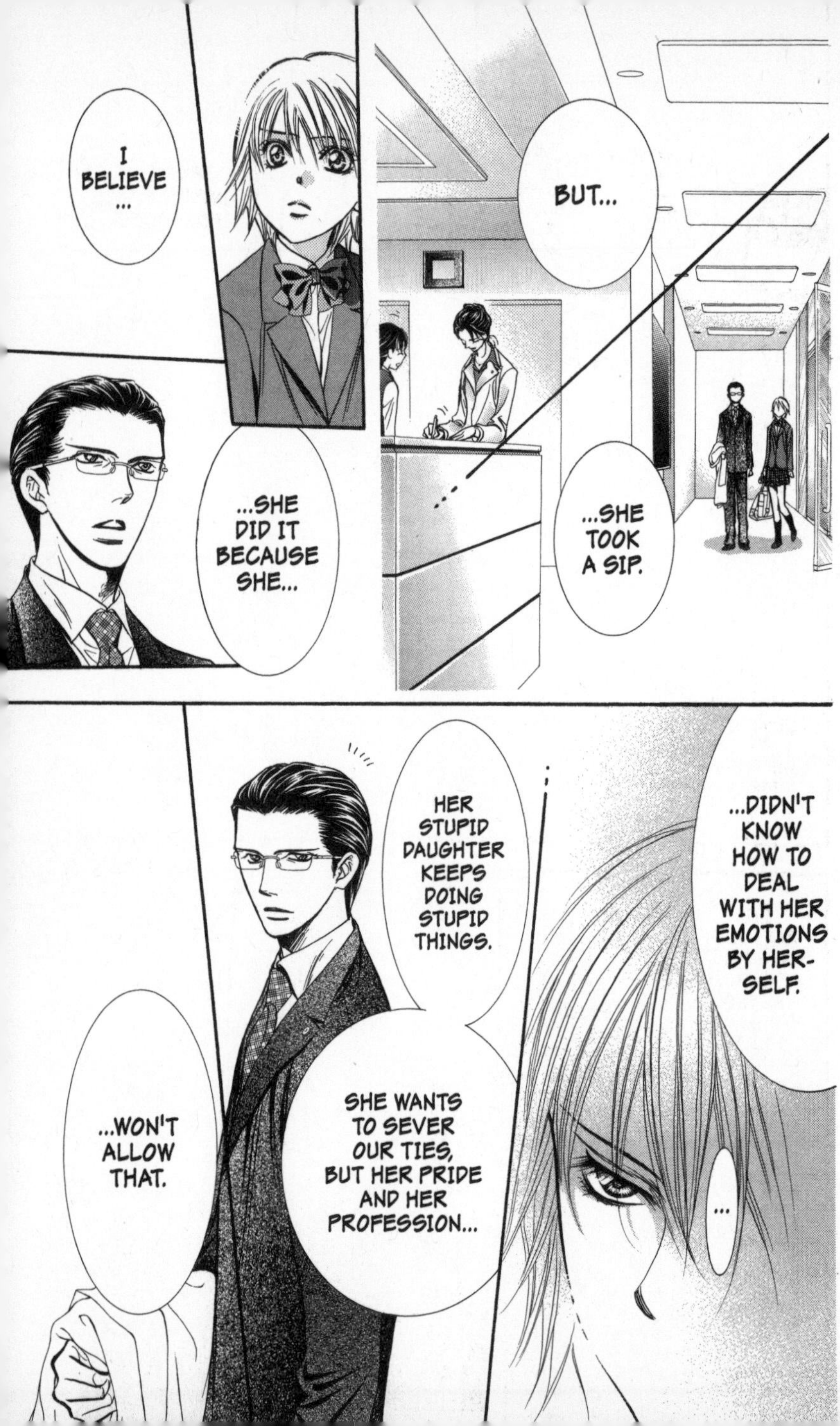
BUT...
...SHE TOOK A SIP.
I BELIEVE ...
...SHE DID IT BECAUSE SHE...
...DIDN'T KNOW HOW TO DEAL WITH HER EMOTIONS BY HER-SELF.
...
HER STUPID DAUGHTER KEEPS DOING STUPID THINGS.
SHE WANTS TO SEVER OUR TIES, BUT HER PRIDE AND HER PROFESSION...
...WON'T ALLOW THAT.

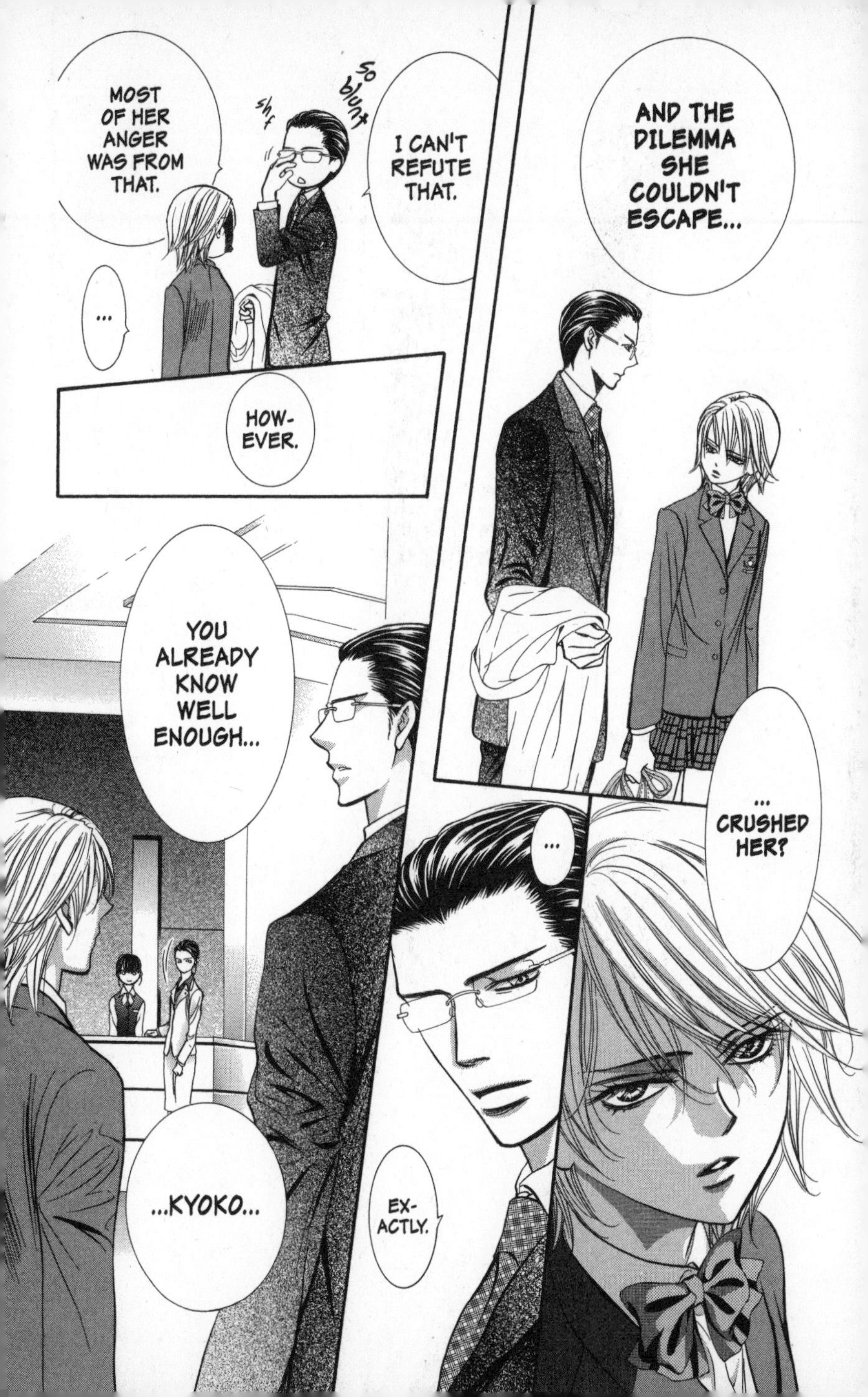
I CAN'T REFUTE THAT.
so blunt
shf
MOST OF HER ANGER WAS FROM THAT.
...
HOW-EVER.
AND THE DILEMMA SHE COULDN'T ESCAPE...
... CRUSHED HER?
...
EX-ACTLY.
YOU ALREADY KNOW WELL ENOUGH...
...KYOKO...

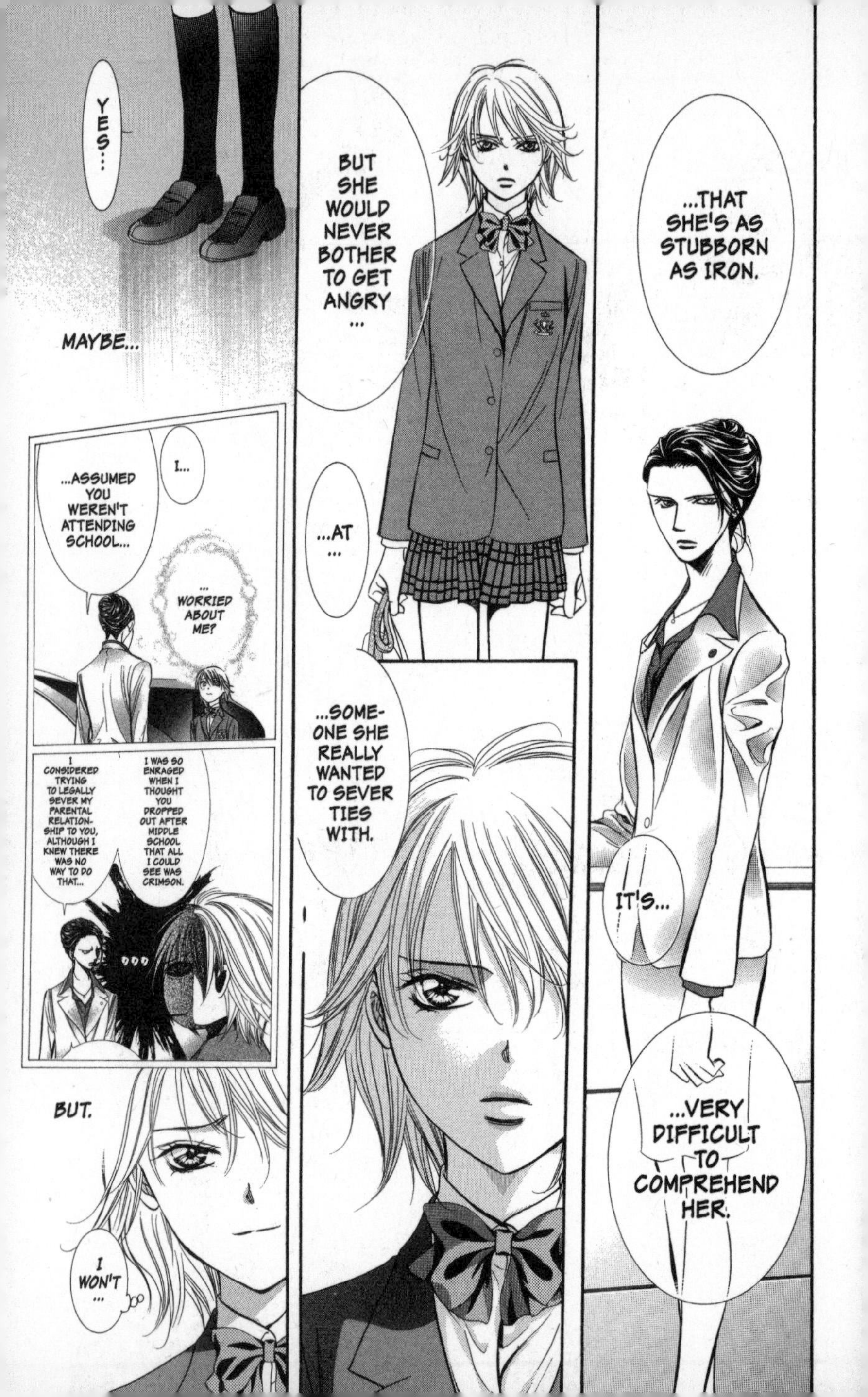
...THAT SHE'S AS STUBBORN AS IRON.
IT'S...
...VERY DIFFICULT TO COMPREHEND HER.
BUT SHE WOULD NEVER BOTHER TO GET ANGRY...
...AT...
...SOME-ONE SHE REALLY WANTED TO SEVER TIES WITH.
YES...
MAYBE...
I...
...ASSUMED YOU WEREN'T ATTENDING SCHOOL...
...WORRIED ABOUT ME?
I WAS SO ENRAGED WHEN I THOUGHT YOU DROPPED OUT AFTER MIDDLE SCHOOL THAT ALL I COULD SEE WAS CRIMSON.
I CONSIDERED TRYING TO LEGALLY SEVER MY PARENTAL RELATION-SHIP TO YOU, ALTHOUGH I KNEW THERE WAS NO WAY TO DO THAT...
BUT.
I WON'T...

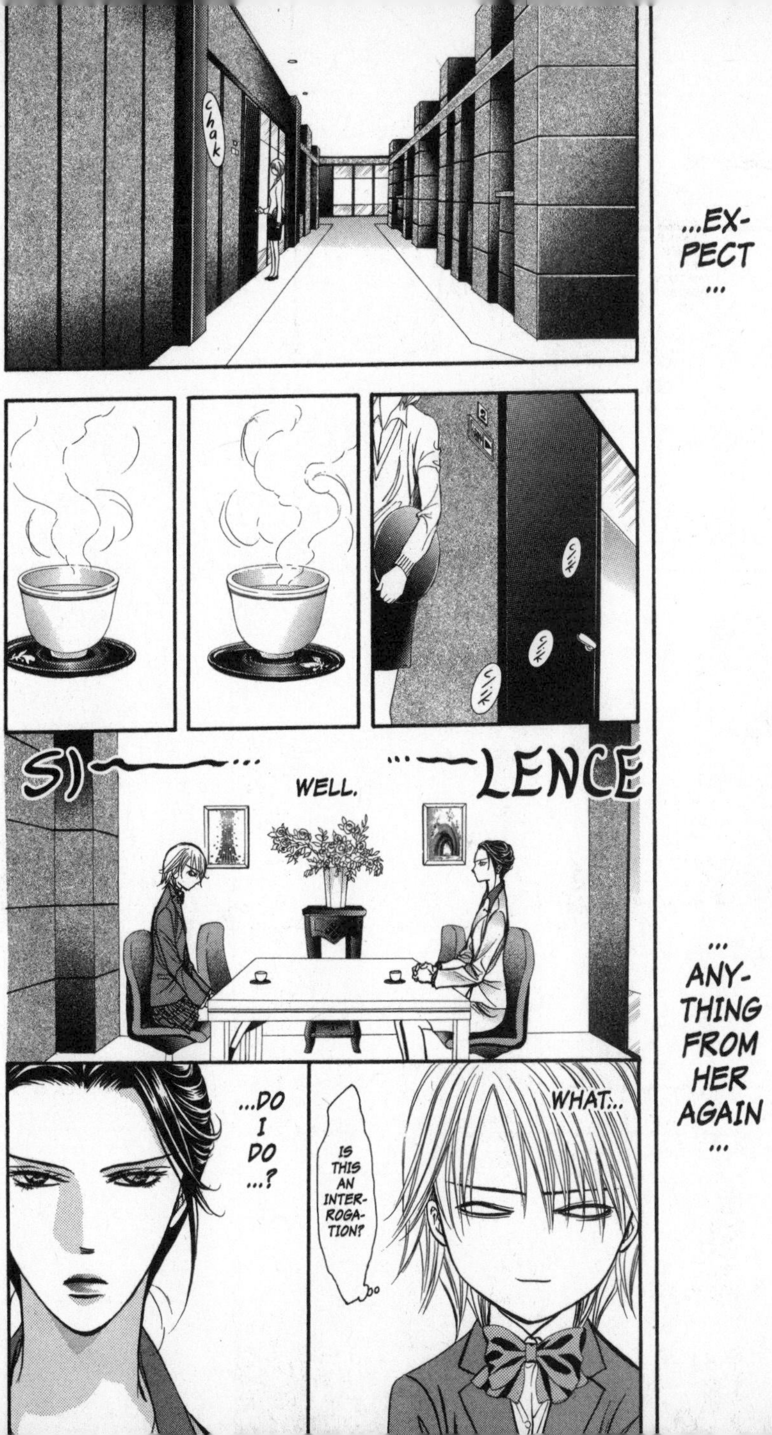
...EXPECT...
chak
clik
clik
clik
SI———... ...———LENCE
WELL.
WHAT...
IS THIS AN INTERROGATION?
...DO I DO...?
...ANYTHING FROM HER AGAIN...

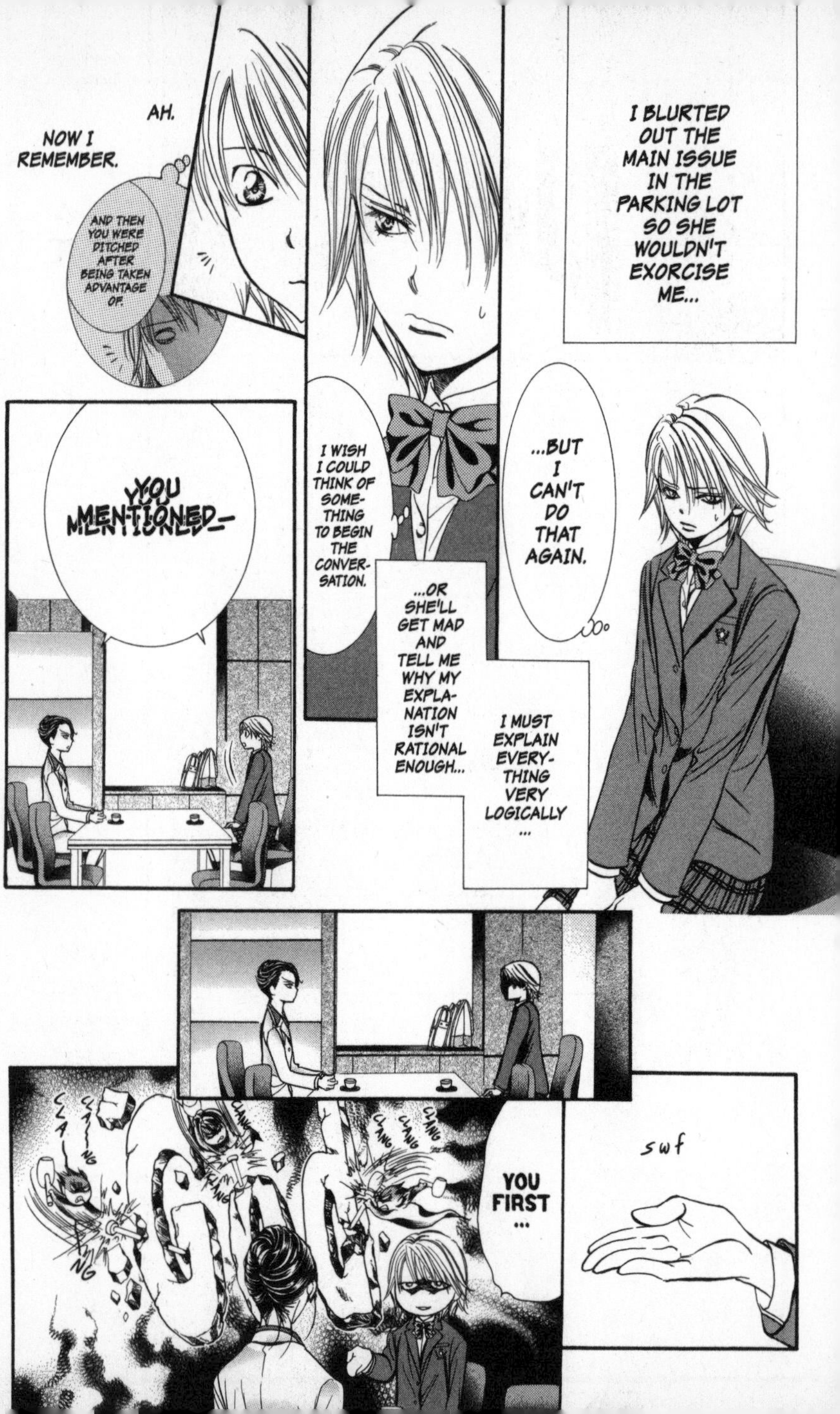
I BLURTED OUT THE MAIN ISSUE IN THE PARKING LOT SO SHE WOULDN'T EXORCISE ME...
AH.
NOW I REMEMBER.
AND THEN YOU WERE PITCHED AFTER BEING TAKEN ADVANTAGE OF.
...BUT I CAN'T DO THAT AGAIN.
I MUST EXPLAIN EVERYTHING VERY LOGICALLY...
...OR SHE'LL GET MAD AND TELL ME WHY MY EXPLANATION ISN'T RATIONAL ENOUGH...
I WISH I COULD THINK OF SOMETHING TO BEGIN THE CONVERSATION.
YOU MENTIONED—
swf
YOU FIRST...
CLANG
CLANG
CLANG
CLANG
CLA-A-NG
CLA-NG

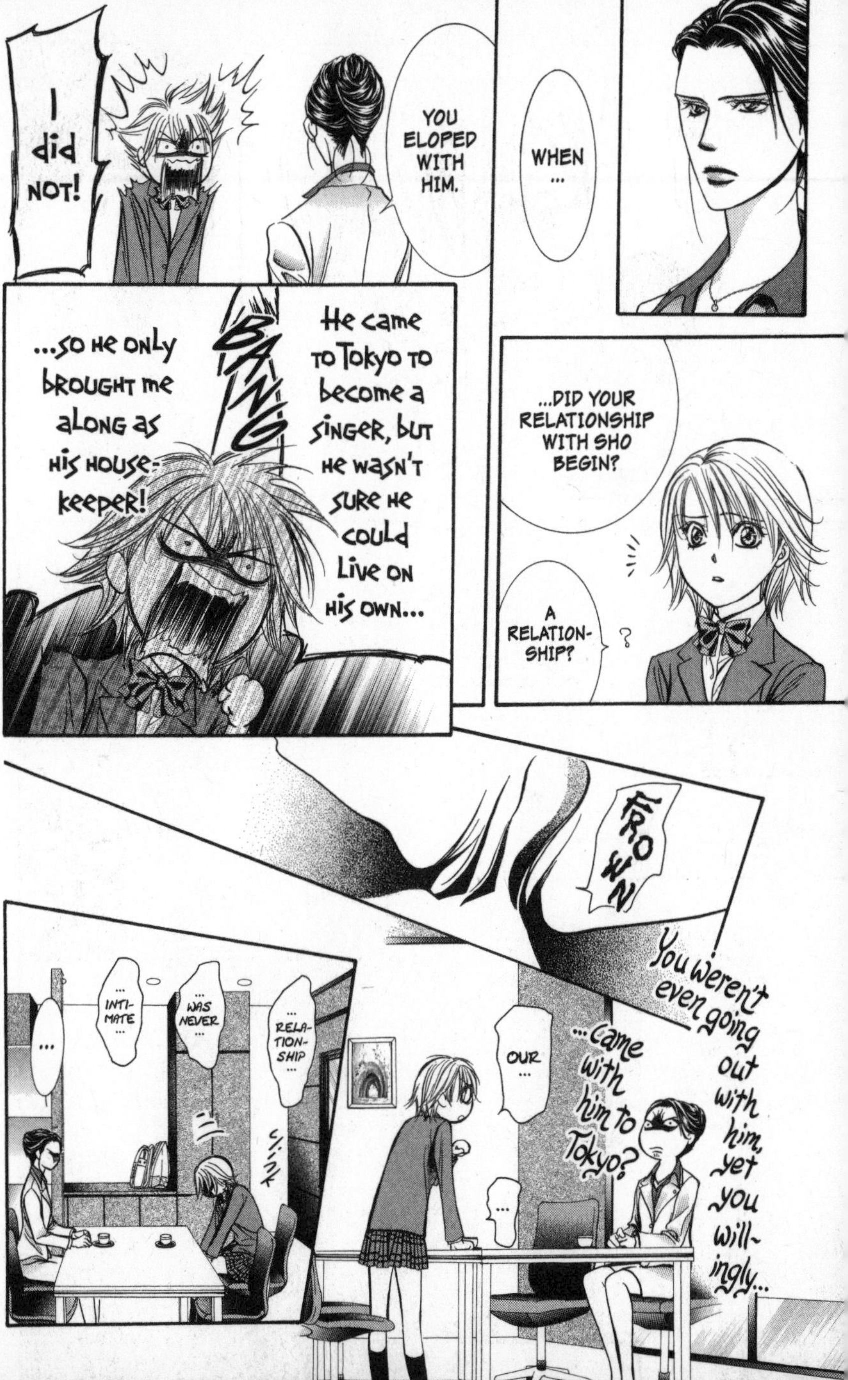
WHEN ...
...DID YOUR RELATIONSHIP WITH SHO BEGIN?
A RELATIONSHIP?
YOU ELOPED WITH HIM.
I did NOT!
BANG
He came to Tokyo to become a singer, but he wasn't sure he could live on his own...
...so he only brought me along as his house-keeper!
FROWN
You weren't even going out with him, yet you willingly...
...came with him to Tokyo?
OUR ...
...
... RELATIONSHIP ...
... WAS NEVER ...
... INTIMATE ...
...

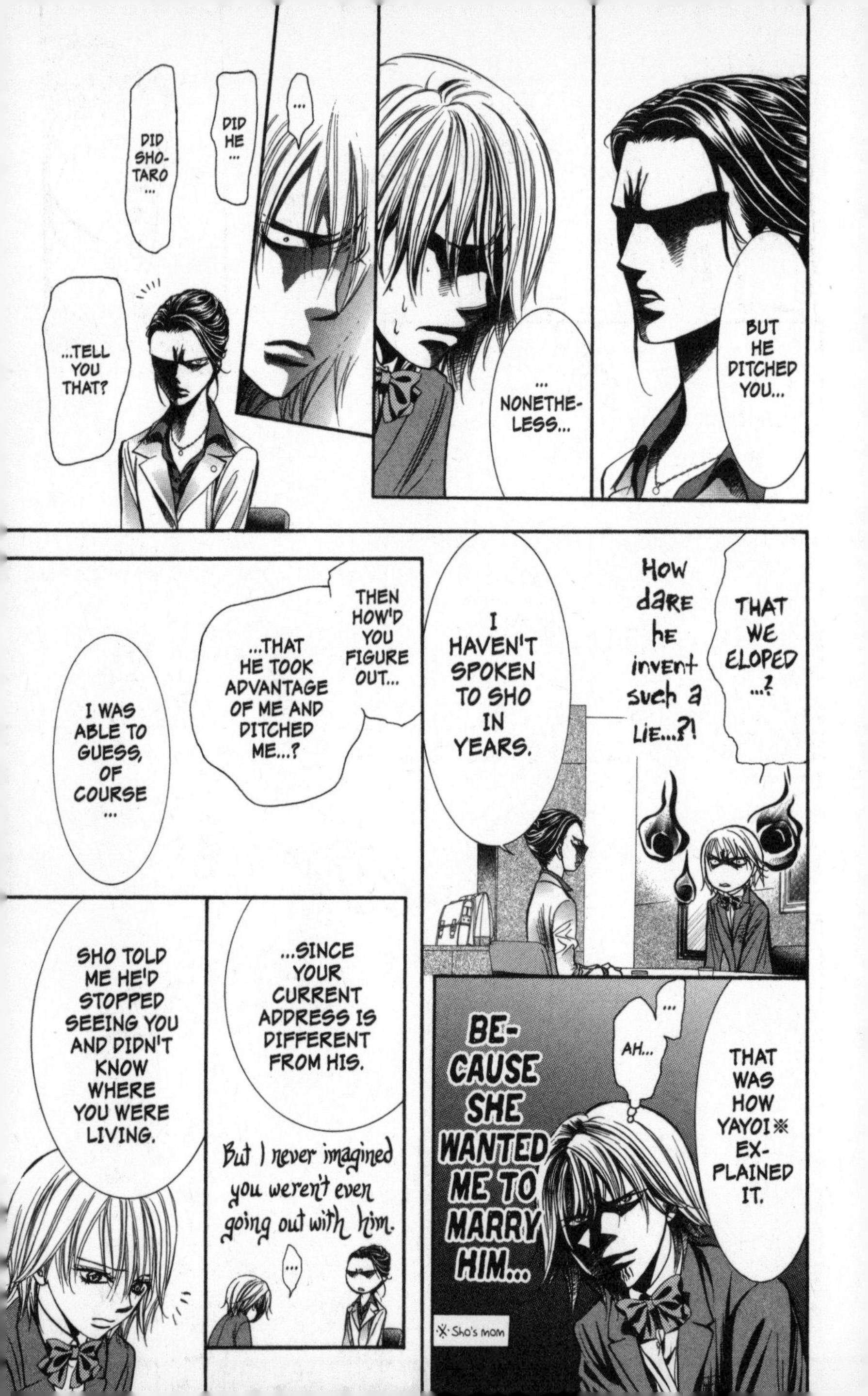

BUT HE DITCHED YOU...
... NONETHE-LESS...
...
DID HE ...
DID SHO-TARO ...
...TELL YOU THAT?
THAT WE ELOPED ...?
How dare he invent such a lie...?!
I HAVEN'T SPOKEN TO SHO IN YEARS.
THEN HOW'D YOU FIGURE OUT...
...THAT HE TOOK ADVANTAGE OF ME AND DITCHED ME...?
I WAS ABLE TO GUESS, OF COURSE ...
THAT WAS HOW YAYOI※ EX-PLAINED IT.
...
AH...
BE-CAUSE SHE WANTED ME TO MARRY HIM...
※ Sho's mom
...SINCE YOUR CURRENT ADDRESS IS DIFFERENT FROM HIS.
But I never imagined you weren't even going out with him.
...
SHO TOLD ME HE'D STOPPED SEEING YOU AND DIDN'T KNOW WHERE YOU WERE LIVING.

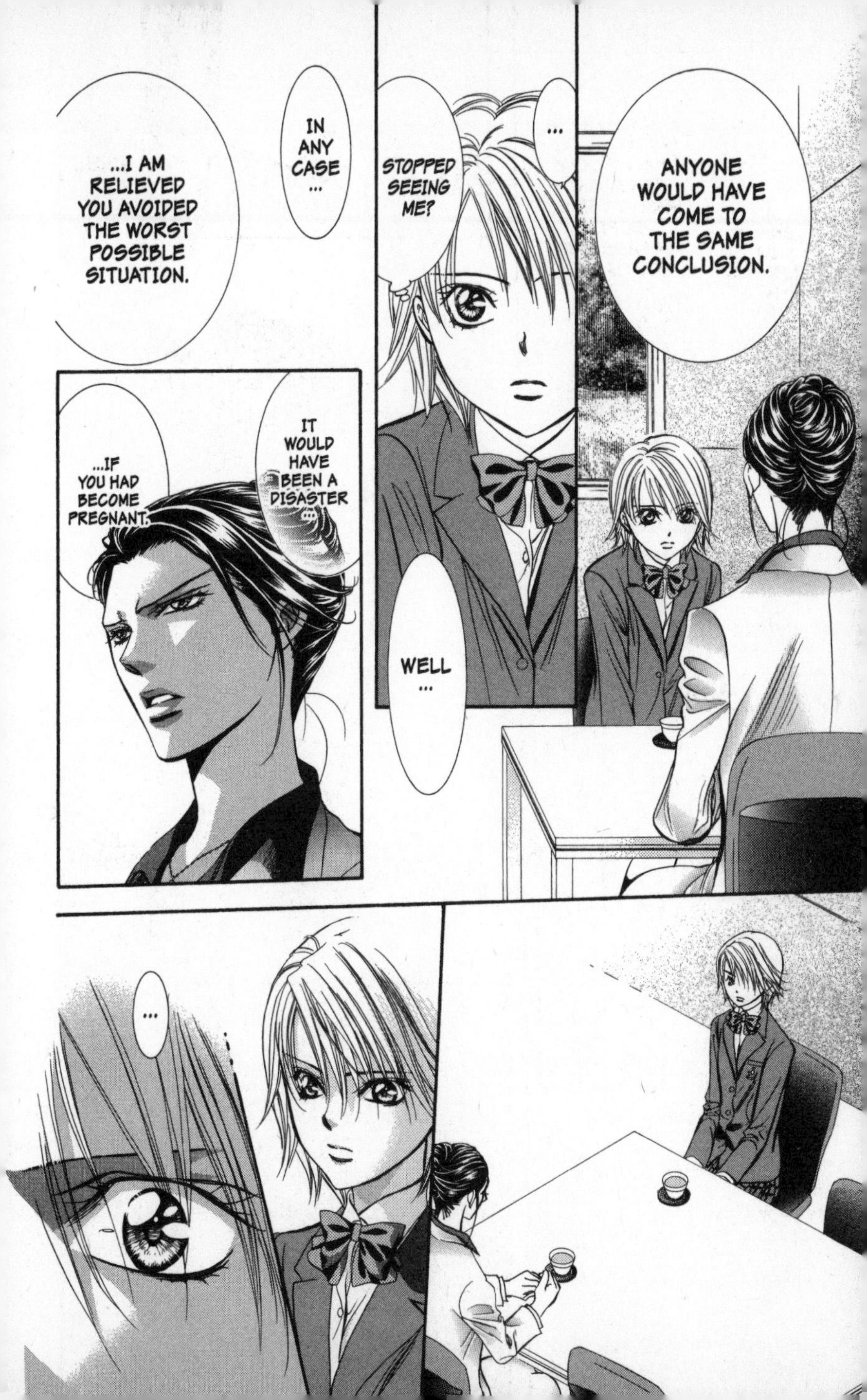
ANYONE WOULD HAVE COME TO THE SAME CONCLUSION.
...
STOPPED SEEING ME?
WELL ...
IN ANY CASE ...
...I AM RELIEVED YOU AVOIDED THE WORST POSSIBLE SITUATION.
IT WOULD HAVE BEEN A DISASTER ...
...IF YOU HAD BECOME PREGNANT.
...

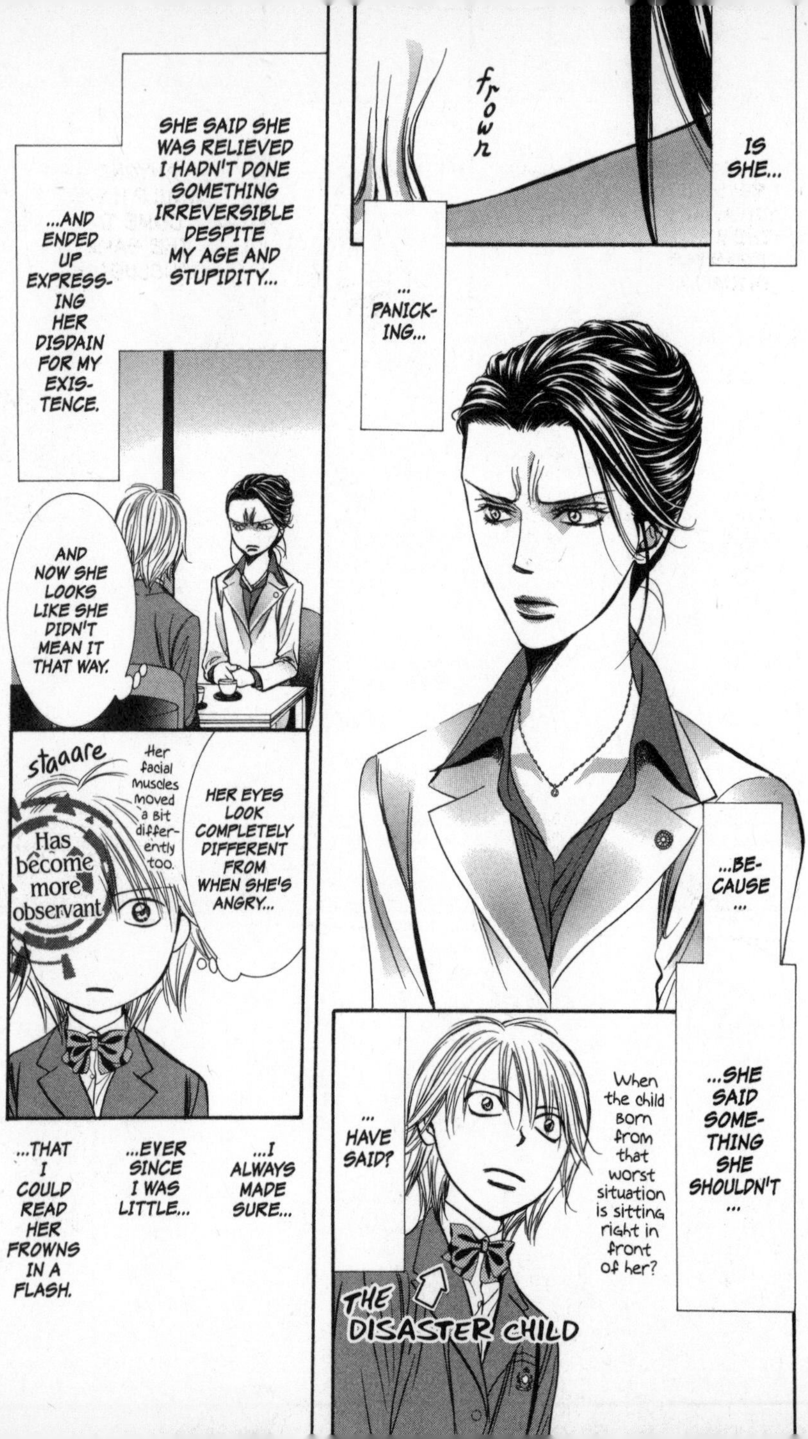
frown
IS SHE...
...PANICKING...
...BECAUSE...
...SHE SAID SOMETHING SHE SHOULDN'T...
When the child born from that worst situation is sitting right in front of her?
...HAVE SAID?
THE DISASTER CHILD
SHE SAID SHE WAS RELIEVED I HADN'T DONE SOMETHING IRREVERSIBLE DESPITE MY AGE AND STUPIDITY...
...AND ENDED UP EXPRESSING HER DISDAIN FOR MY EXISTENCE.
AND NOW SHE LOOKS LIKE SHE DIDN'T MEAN IT THAT WAY.
HER EYES LOOK COMPLETELY DIFFERENT FROM WHEN SHE'S ANGRY...
Her facial muscles moved a bit differently too.
staaare
Has become more observant
...I ALWAYS MADE SURE...
...EVER SINCE I WAS LITTLE...
...THAT I COULD READ HER FROWNS IN A FLASH.

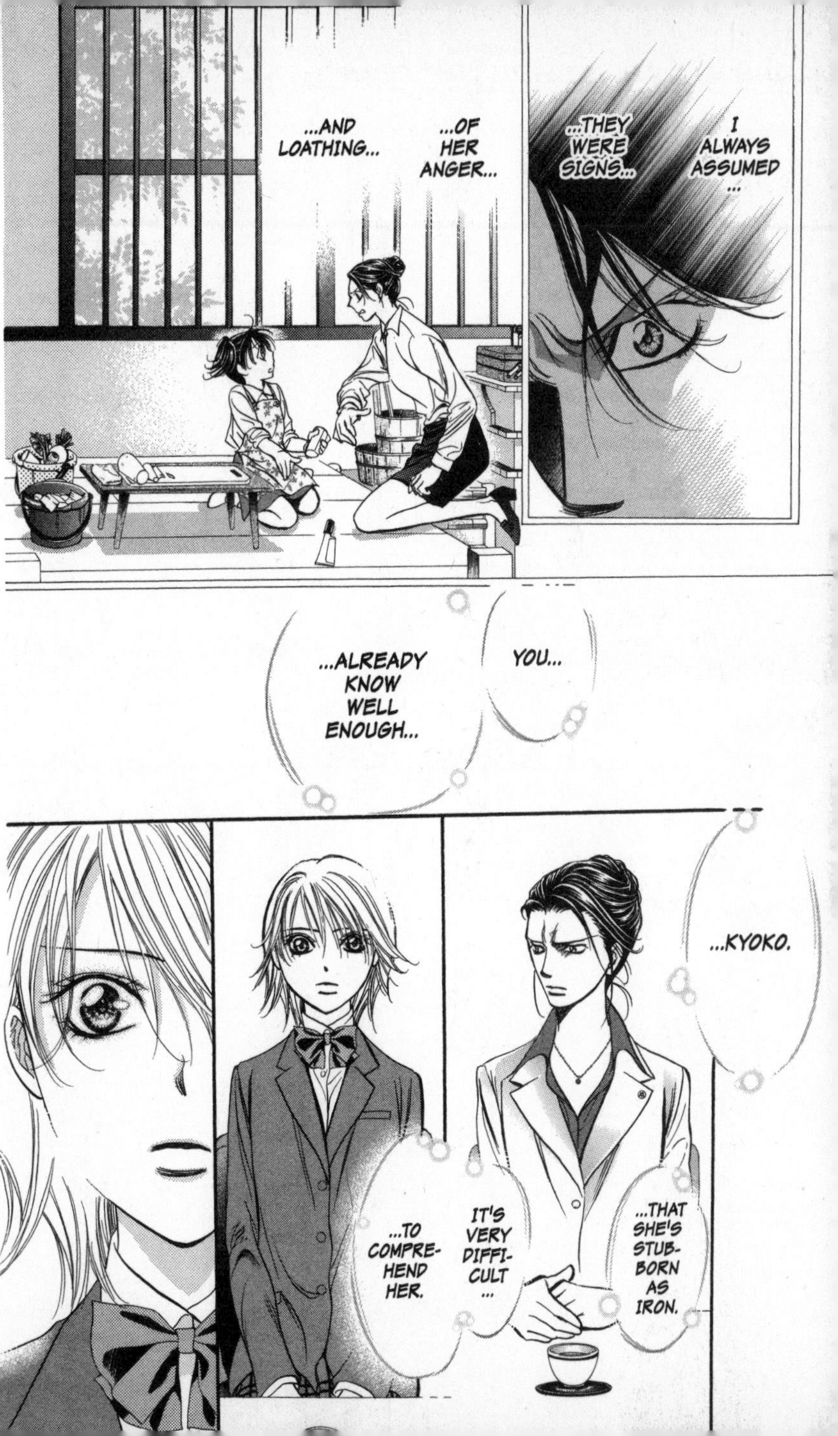
I ALWAYS ASSUMED...
...THEY WERE SIGNS...
...OF HER ANGER...
...AND LOATHING...
YOU...
...ALREADY KNOW WELL ENOUGH...
...KYOKO.
...THAT SHE'S STUB-BORN AS IRON.
IT'S VERY DIFFI-CULT...
...TO COMPRE-HEND HER.

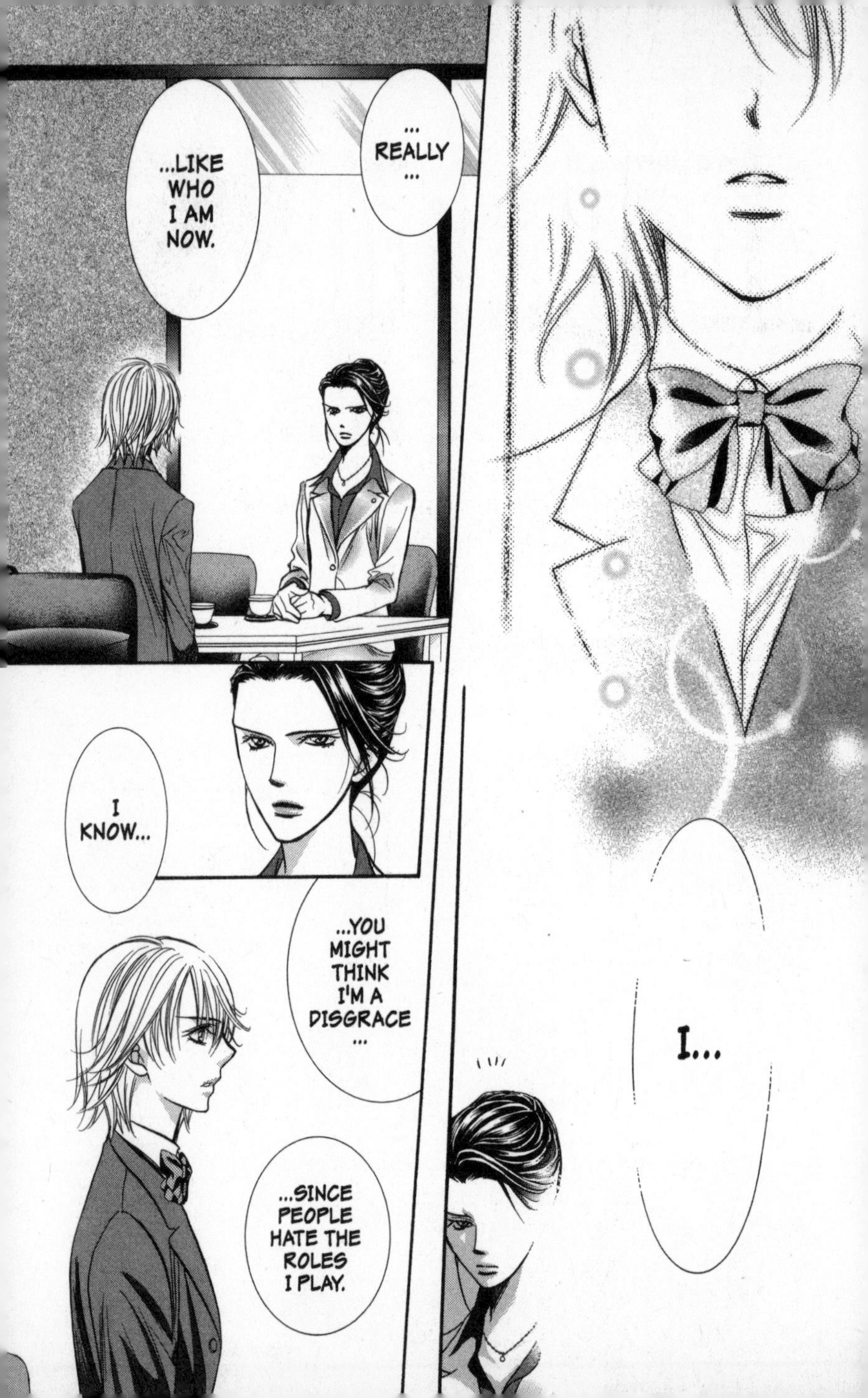
I...
...REALLY...
...LIKE WHO I AM NOW.
I KNOW...
...YOU MIGHT THINK I'M A DISGRACE...
...SINCE PEOPLE HATE THE ROLES I PLAY.

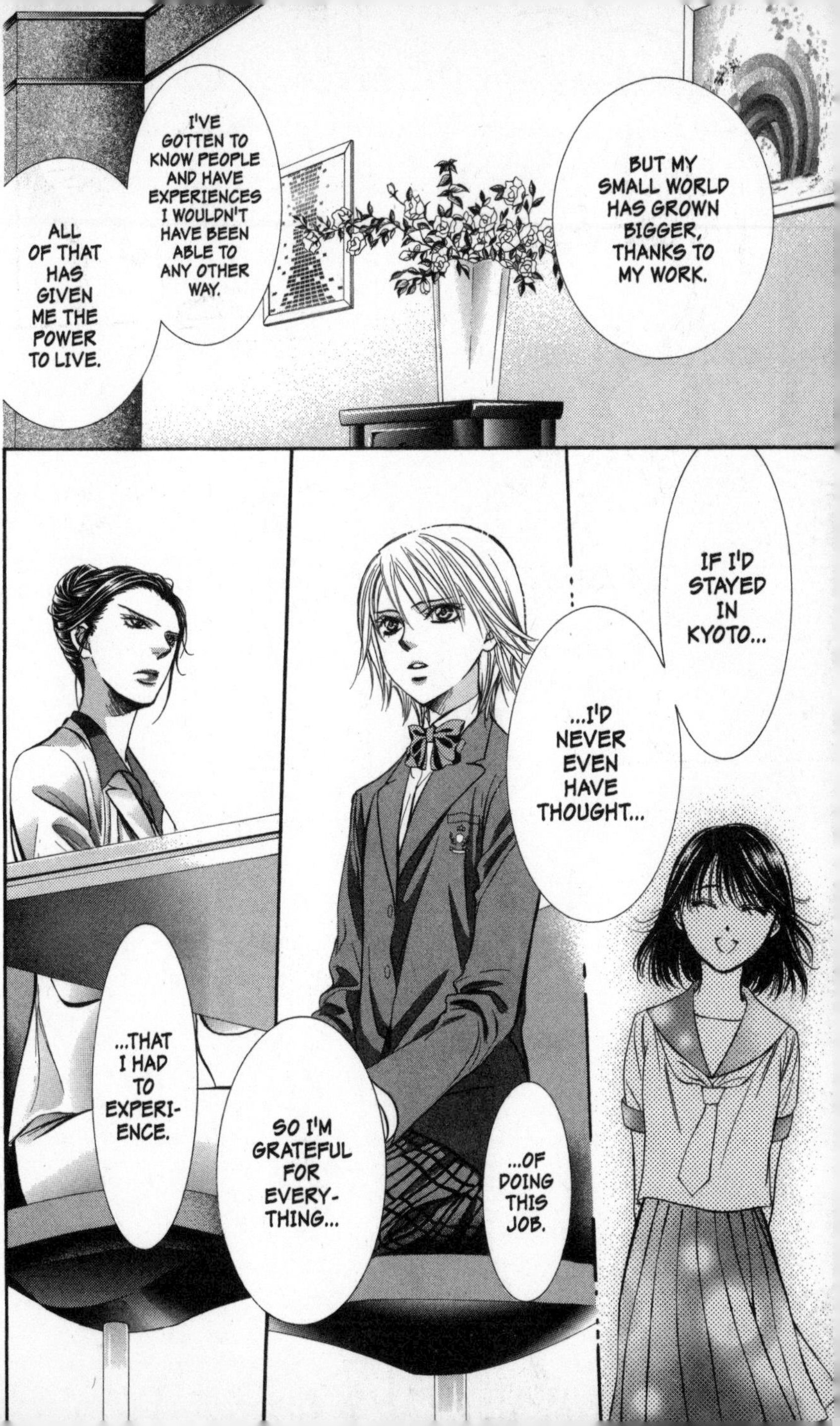
BUT MY SMALL WORLD HAS GROWN BIGGER, THANKS TO MY WORK.
I'VE GOTTEN TO KNOW PEOPLE AND HAVE EXPERIENCES I WOULDN'T HAVE BEEN ABLE TO ANY OTHER WAY.
ALL OF THAT HAS GIVEN ME THE POWER TO LIVE.
IF I'D STAYED IN KYOTO...
...I'D NEVER EVEN HAVE THOUGHT...
...OF DOING THIS JOB.
SO I'M GRATEFUL FOR EVERY-THING...
...THAT I HAD TO EXPERI-ENCE.

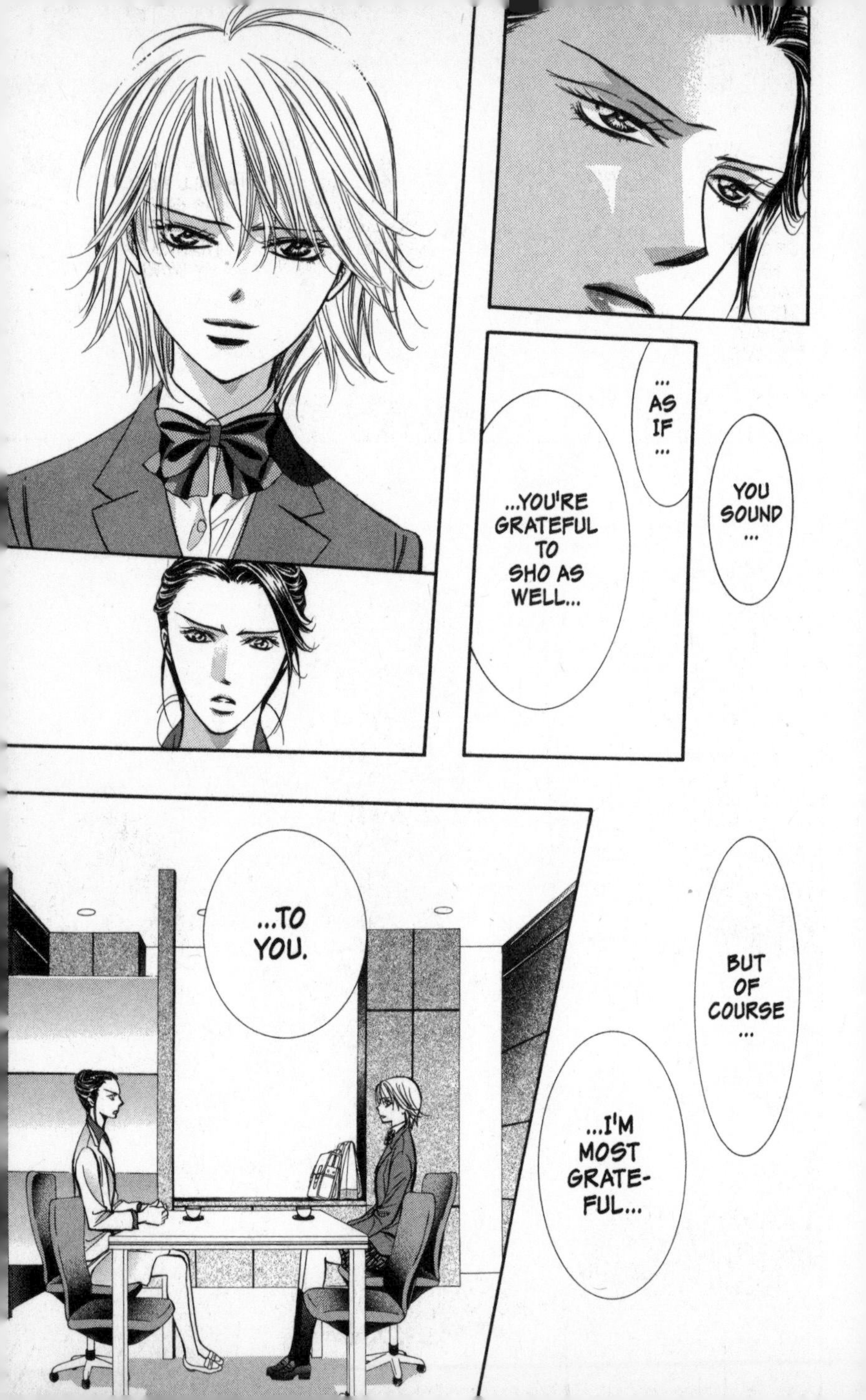
YOU SOUND...
...AS IF...
...YOU'RE GRATEFUL TO SHO AS WELL...
BUT OF COURSE...
...I'M MOST GRATE-FUL...
...TO YOU.

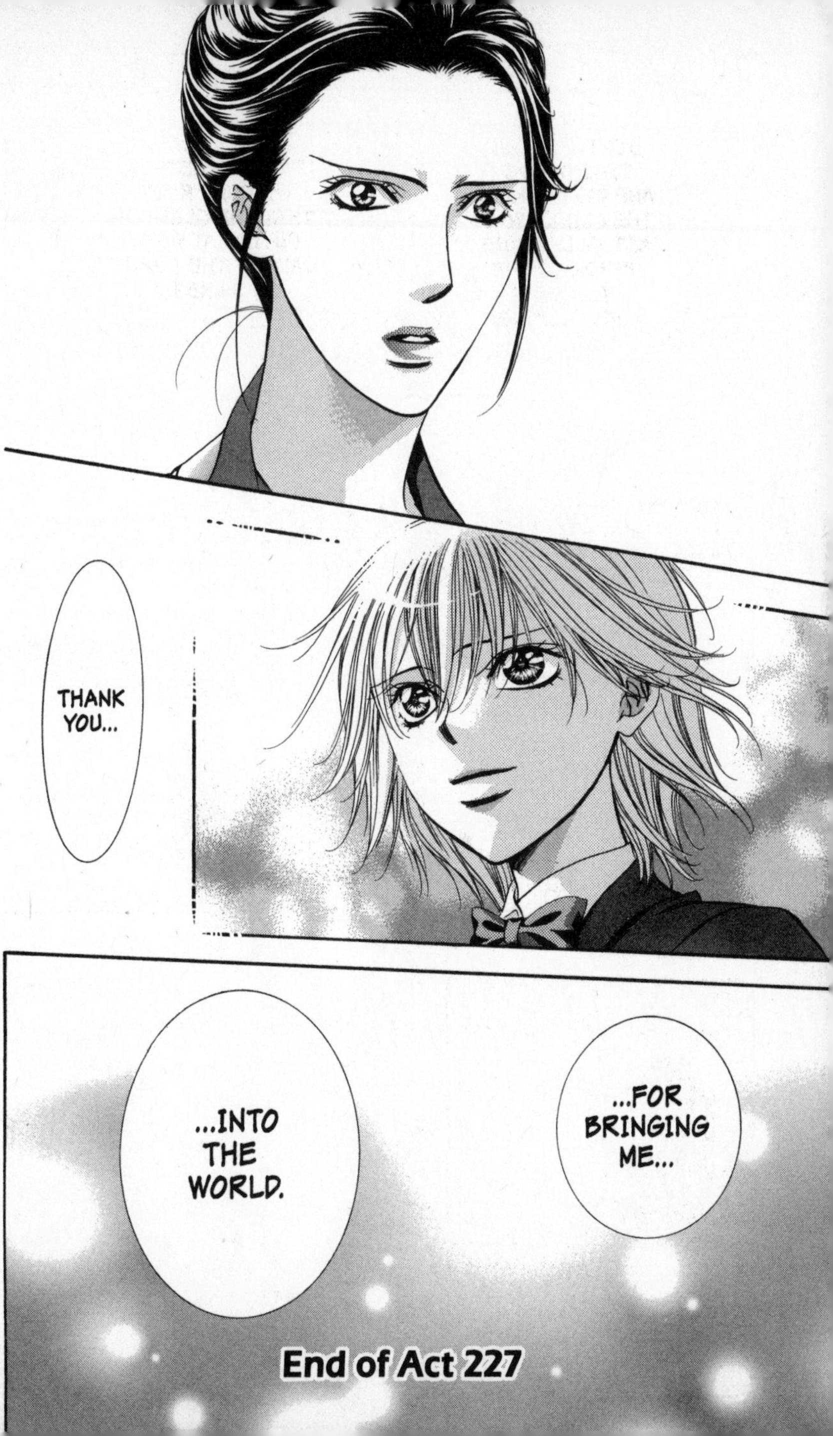
THANK YOU...
...FOR BRINGING ME...
...INTO THE WORLD.
End of Act 227

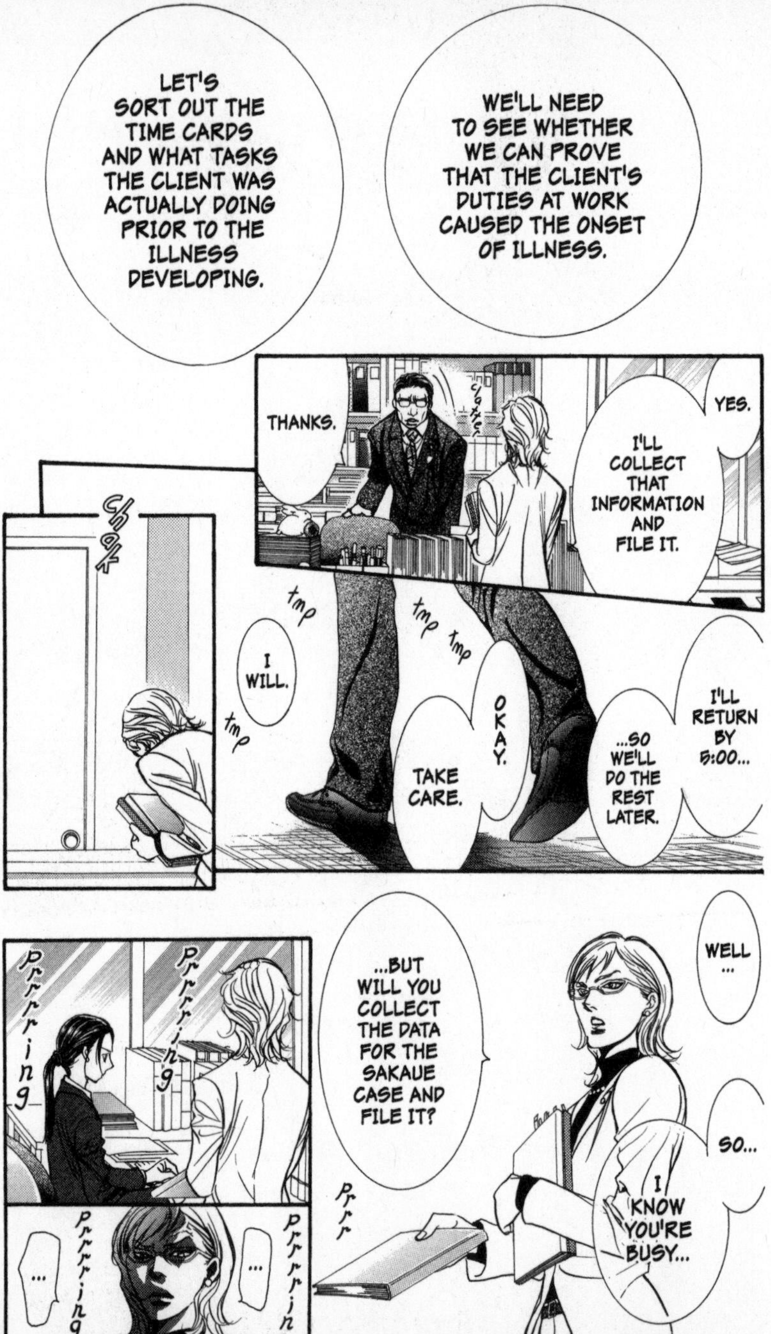
WE'LL NEED TO SEE WHETHER WE CAN PROVE THAT THE CLIENT'S DUTIES AT WORK CAUSED THE ONSET OF ILLNESS.
LET'S SORT OUT THE TIME CARDS AND WHAT TASKS THE CLIENT WAS ACTUALLY DOING PRIOR TO THE ILLNESS DEVELOPING.
YES.
I'LL COLLECT THAT INFORMATION AND FILE IT.
clatter
THANKS.
I'LL RETURN BY 5:00...
...SO WE'LL DO THE REST LATER.
OKAY.
TAKE CARE.
tmp tmp
tmp
I WILL.
tmp
chak
WELL...
SO...
I KNOW YOU'RE BUSY...
...BUT WILL YOU COLLECT THE DATA FOR THE SAKAUE CASE AND FILE IT?
Prrr
Prrrring
Prrrring
...
...
Prrrring
Prrrring

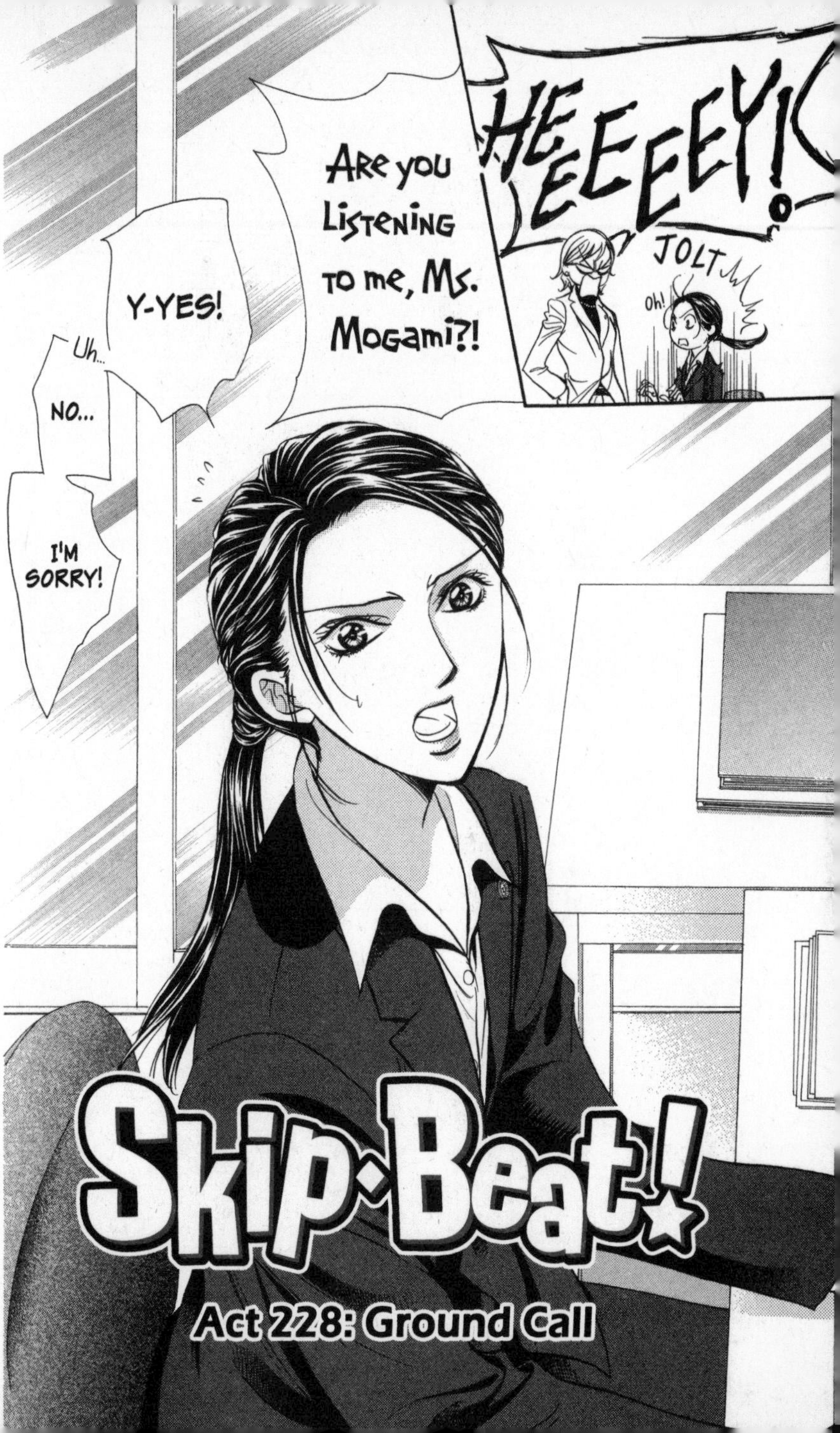
HEEEEEY!
JOLT
Oh!
Are you listening to me, Ms. Mogami?!
Y-YES!
Uh... NO... I'M SORRY!
Skip·Beat!
Act 228: Ground Call

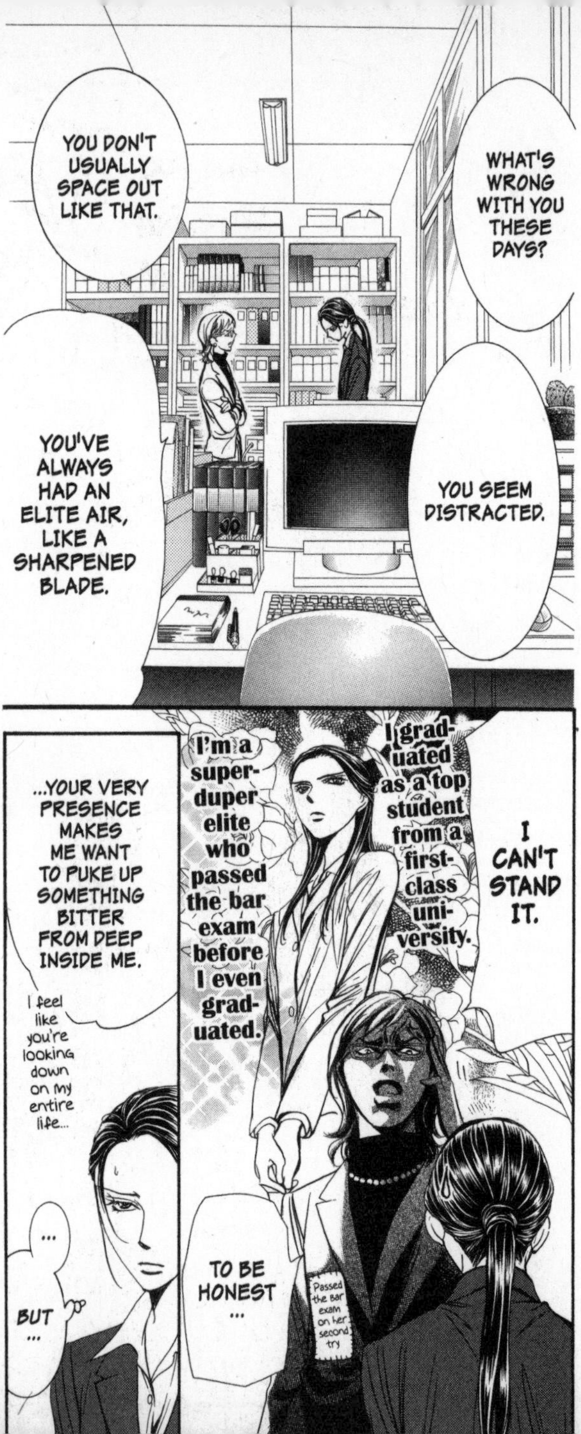
WHAT'S WRONG WITH YOU THESE DAYS?
YOU SEEM DISTRACTED.
YOU DON'T USUALLY SPACE OUT LIKE THAT.
YOU'VE ALWAYS HAD AN ELITE AIR, LIKE A SHARPENED BLADE.
I CAN'T STAND IT.
I graduated as a top student from a first-class university.
I'm a super-duper elite who passed the bar exam before I even graduated.
...YOUR VERY PRESENCE MAKES ME WANT TO PUKE UP SOMETHING BITTER FROM DEEP INSIDE ME.
I feel like you're looking down on my entire life...
Passed the bar exam on her second try
TO BE HONEST ...
...
BUT ...
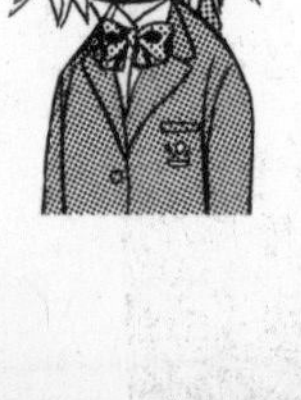

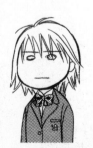

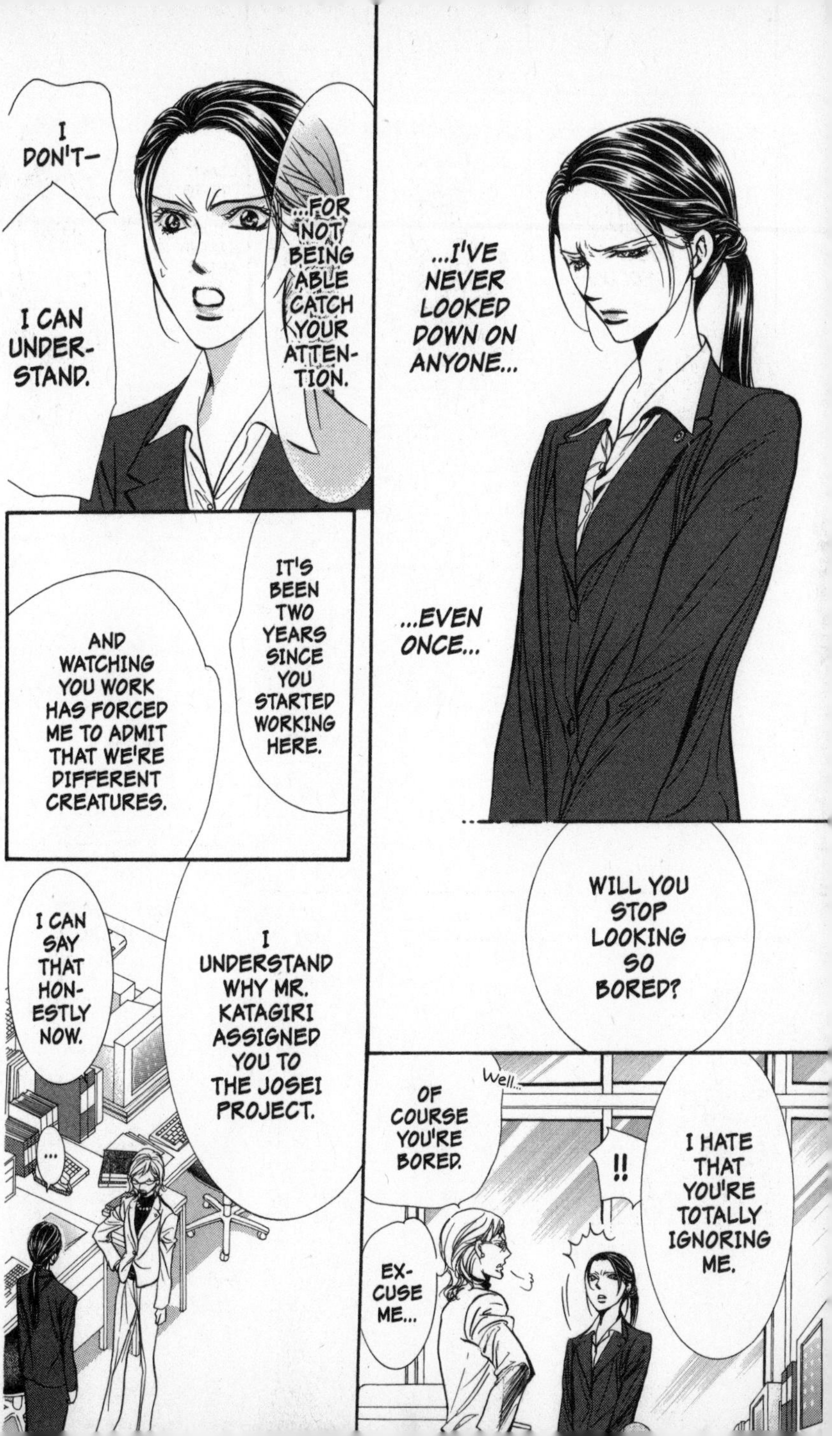
...I'VE NEVER LOOKED DOWN ON ANYONE...
...EVEN ONCE...
WILL YOU STOP LOOKING SO BORED?
I HATE THAT YOU'RE TOTALLY IGNORING ME.
!!
Well...
OF COURSE YOU'RE BORED.
EX-CUSE ME...
...FOR NOT BEING ABLE CATCH YOUR ATTEN-TION.
I DON'T—
I CAN UNDER-STAND.
IT'S BEEN TWO YEARS SINCE YOU STARTED WORKING HERE.
AND WATCHING YOU WORK HAS FORCED ME TO ADMIT THAT WE'RE DIFFERENT CREATURES.
I UNDERSTAND WHY MR. KATAGIRI ASSIGNED YOU TO THE JOSEI PROJECT.
I CAN SAY THAT HON-ESTLY NOW.
...

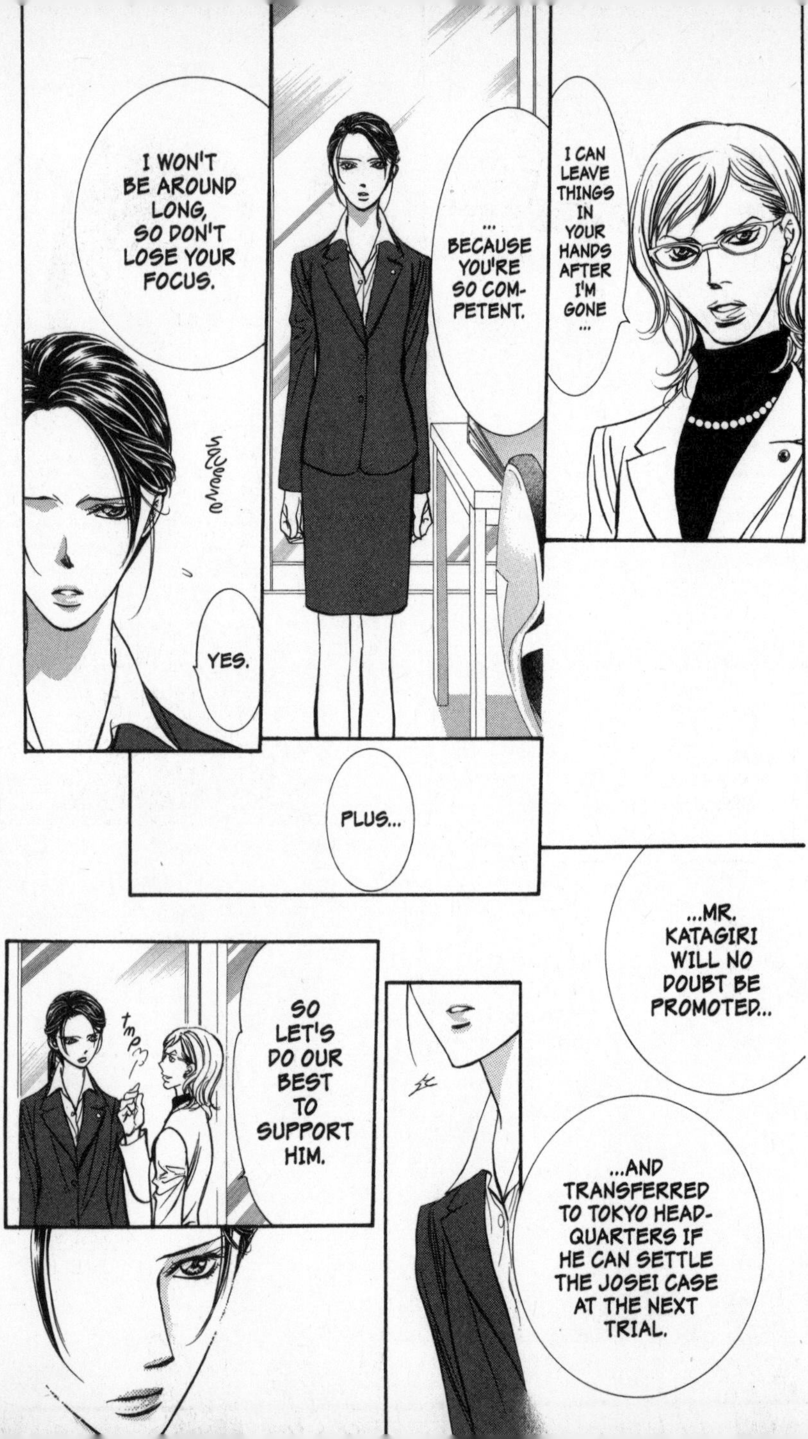
I CAN LEAVE THINGS IN YOUR HANDS AFTER I'M GONE...
...BECAUSE YOU'RE SO COM-PETENT.
I WON'T BE AROUND LONG, SO DON'T LOSE YOUR FOCUS.
squeeze
YES.
PLUS...
...MR. KATAGIRI WILL NO DOUBT BE PROMOTED...
...AND TRANSFERRED TO TOKYO HEAD-QUARTERS IF HE CAN SETTLE THE JOSEI CASE AT THE NEXT TRIAL.
SO LET'S DO OUR BEST TO SUPPORT HIM.

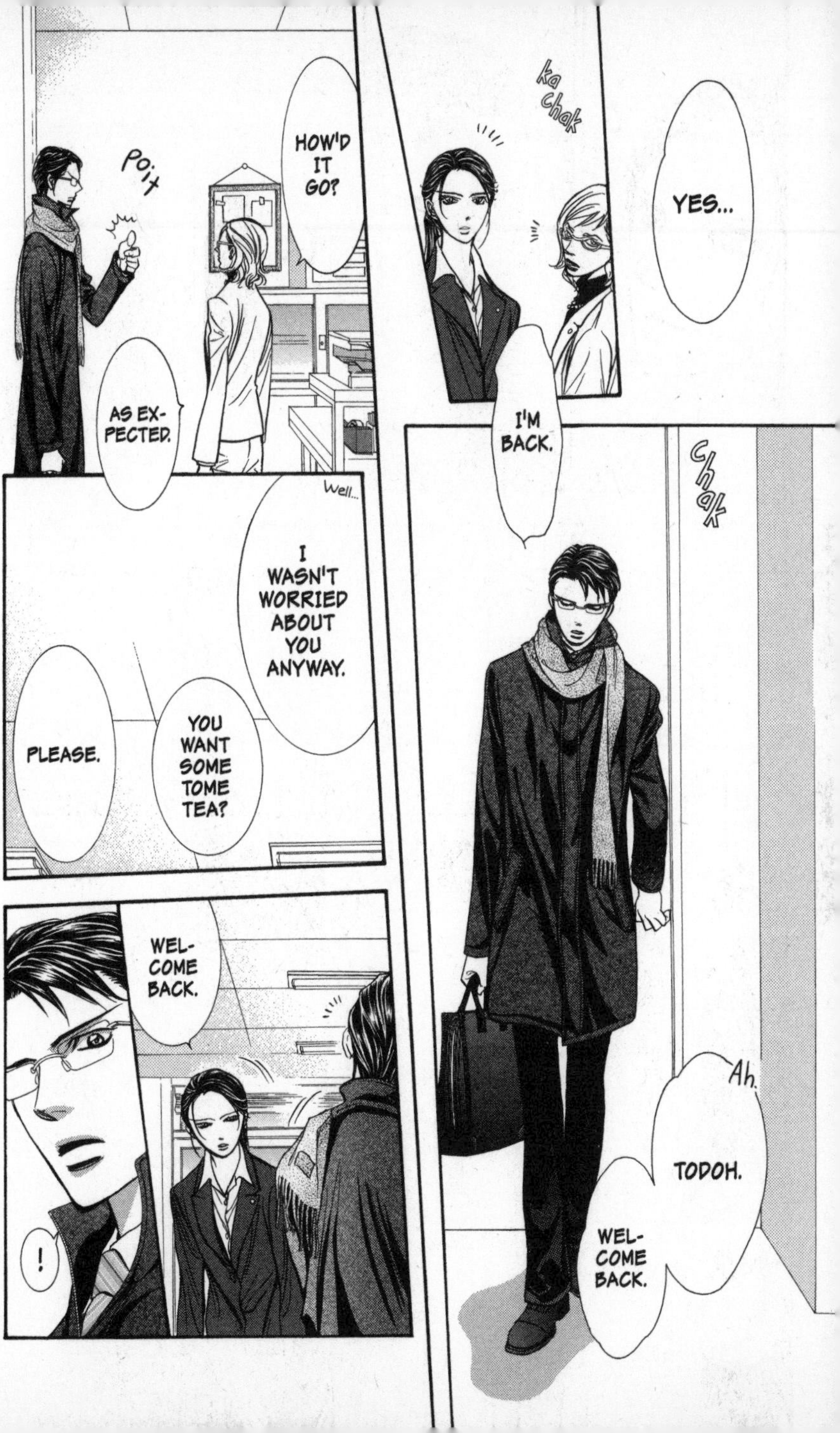

ka chak
YES...
I'M BACK.
HOW'D IT GO?
Poit
AS EX-PECTED.
Chak
Ah.
TODOH.
WEL-COME BACK.
Well...
I WASN'T WORRIED ABOUT YOU ANYWAY.
YOU WANT SOME TOME TEA?
PLEASE.
WEL-COME BACK.
!

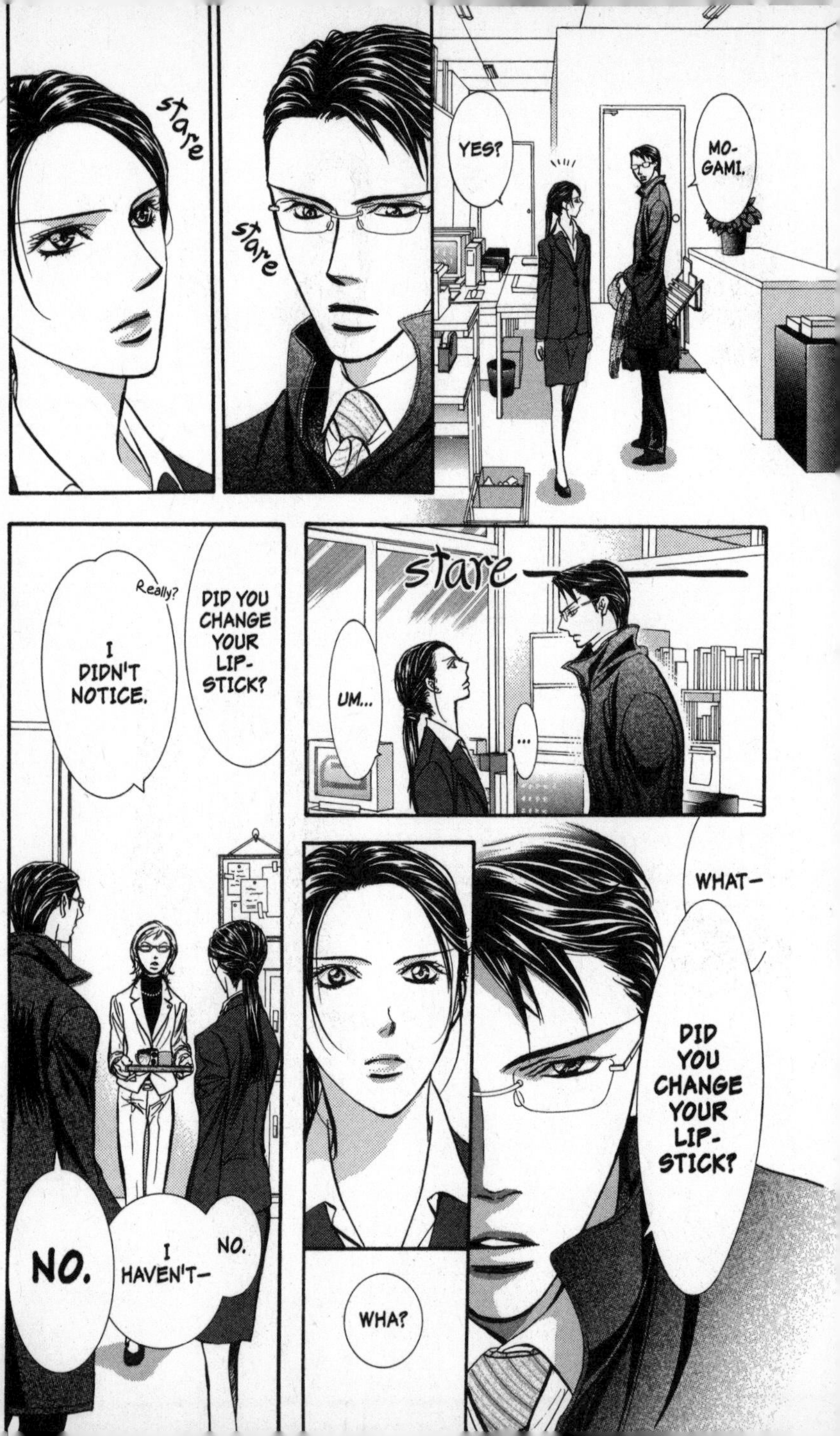
MO-GAMI.
YES?
stare
stare
stare
...
UM...
DID YOU CHANGE YOUR LIP-STICK?
Really?
I DIDN'T NOTICE.
WHAT-
DID YOU CHANGE YOUR LIP-STICK?
WHA?
NO.
I HAVEN'T-
NO.

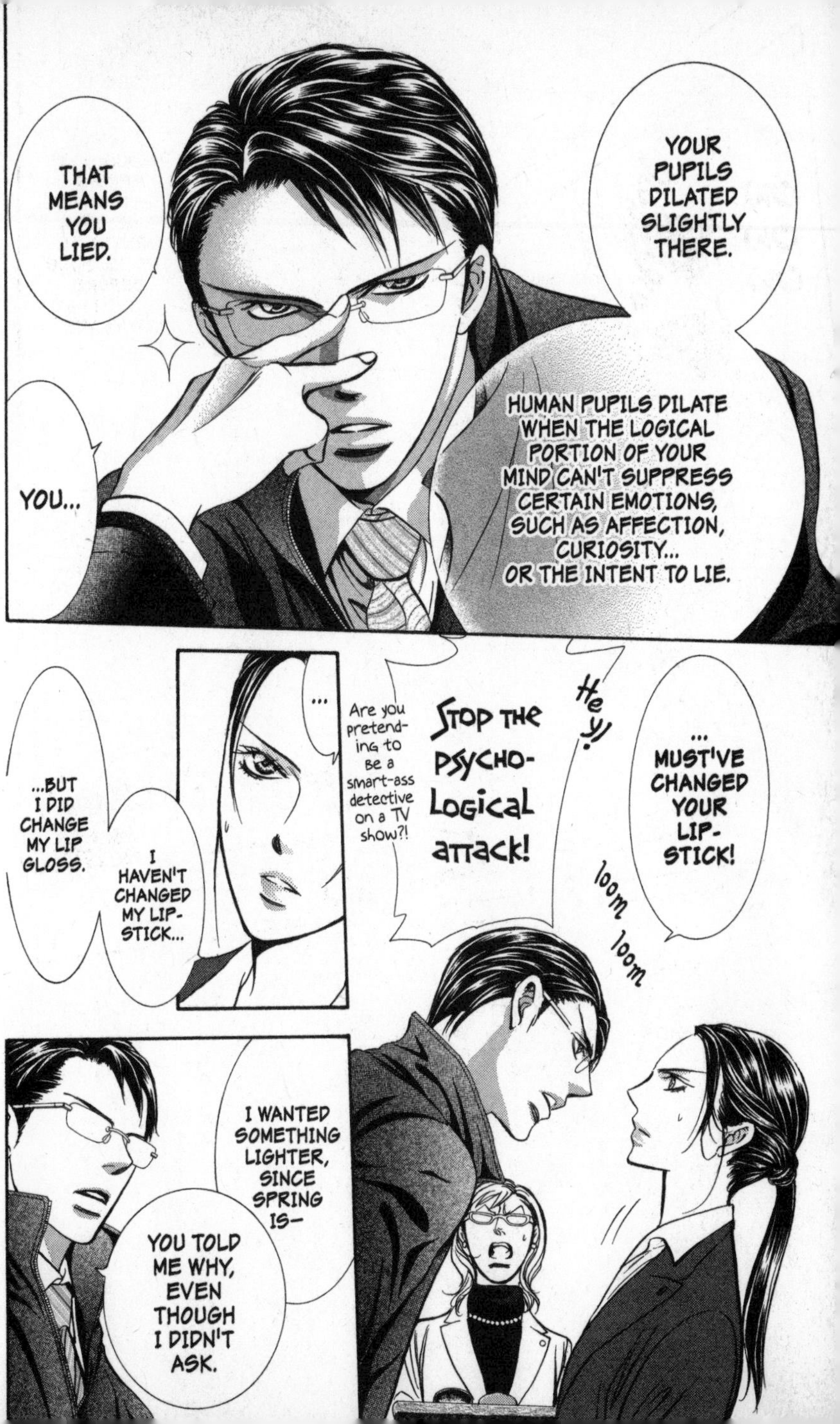
YOUR PUPILS DILATED SLIGHTLY THERE.
THAT MEANS YOU LIED.
HUMAN PUPILS DILATE WHEN THE LOGICAL PORTION OF YOUR MIND CAN'T SUPPRESS CERTAIN EMOTIONS, SUCH AS AFFECTION, CURIOSITY... OR THE INTENT TO LIE.
YOU...
... MUST'VE CHANGED YOUR LIP-STICK!
Hey!
loom loom
STOP THE PSYCHO-LOGICAL attack!
Are you pretend-ing to be a smart-ass detective on a TV show?!
...
I HAVEN'T CHANGED MY LIP-STICK...
...BUT I DID CHANGE MY LIP GLOSS.
I WANTED SOMETHING LIGHTER, SINCE SPRING IS—
YOU TOLD ME WHY, EVEN THOUGH I DIDN'T ASK.

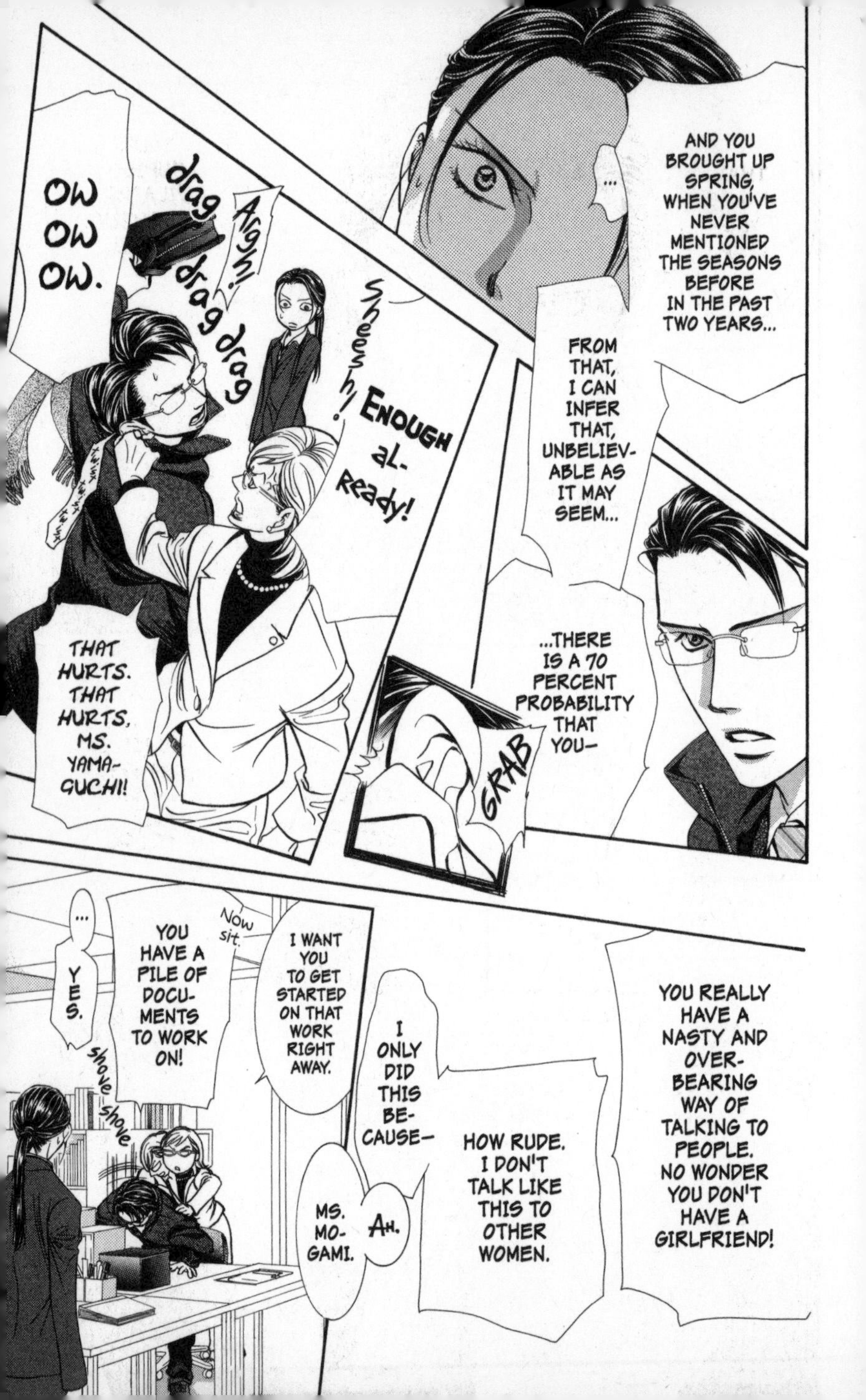
...
AND YOU BROUGHT UP SPRING, WHEN YOU'VE NEVER MENTIONED THE SEASONS BEFORE IN THE PAST TWO YEARS...
FROM THAT, I CAN INFER THAT, UNBELIEVABLE AS IT MAY SEEM...
...THERE IS A 70 PERCENT PROBABILITY THAT YOU—
GRAB
Sheesh!
ENOUGH al-ready!
Argh!
drag drag drag drag
OW OW OW.
THAT HURTS. THAT HURTS, MS. YAMAGUCHI!
YOU REALLY HAVE A NASTY AND OVER-BEARING WAY OF TALKING TO PEOPLE. NO WONDER YOU DON'T HAVE A GIRLFRIEND!
HOW RUDE. I DON'T TALK LIKE THIS TO OTHER WOMEN.
I ONLY DID THIS BE-CAUSE—
Ah.
MS. MO-GAMI.
I WANT YOU TO GET STARTED ON THAT WORK RIGHT AWAY.
Now sit.
YOU HAVE A PILE OF DOCU-MENTS TO WORK ON!
... YES.
shove shove

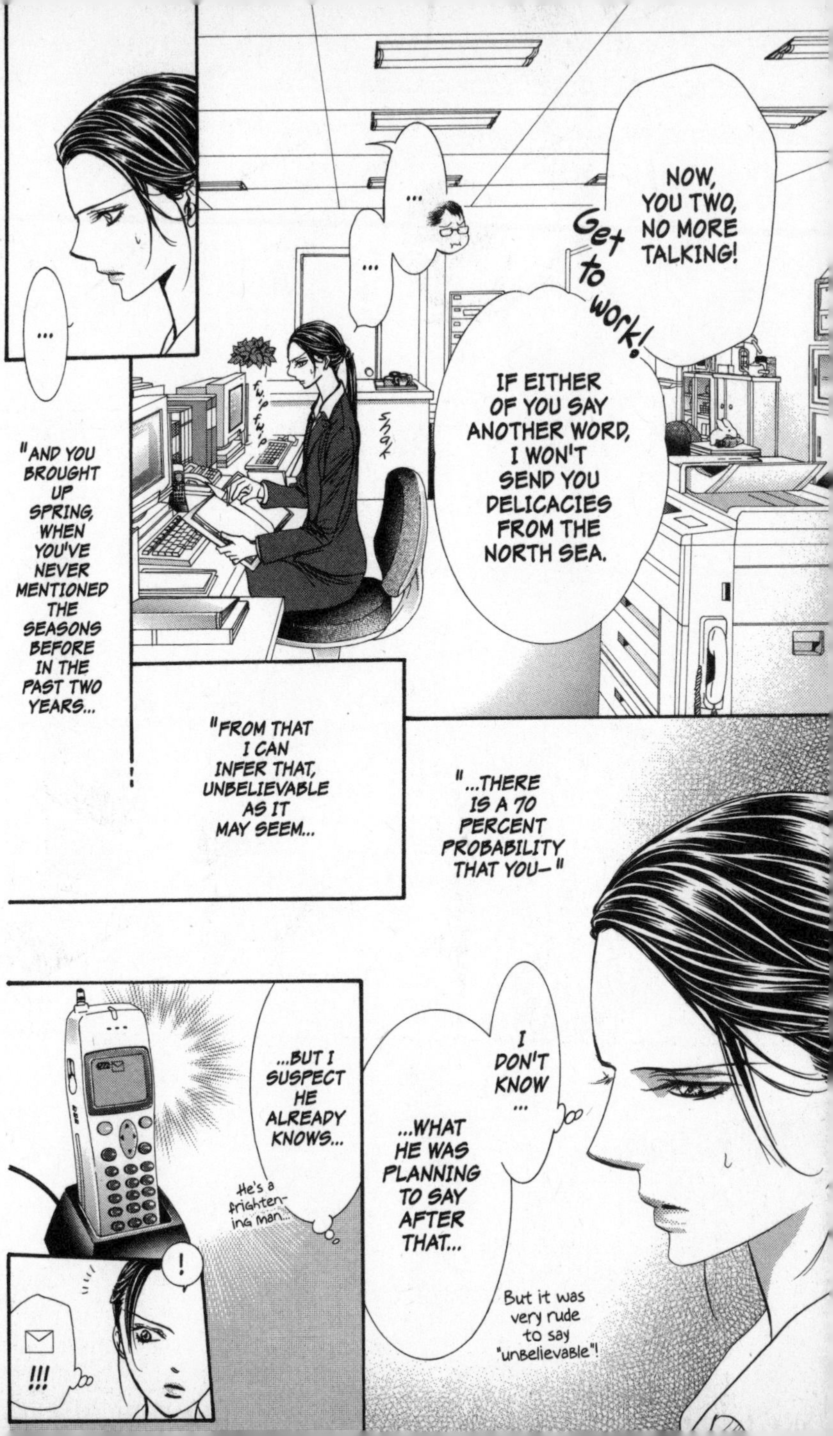
NOW, YOU TWO, NO MORE TALKING!
Get to work!
IF EITHER OF YOU SAY ANOTHER WORD, I WON'T SEND YOU DELICACIES FROM THE NORTH SEA.
...
...
fwip fwip
shak
...
"AND YOU BROUGHT UP SPRING, WHEN YOU'VE NEVER MENTIONED THE SEASONS BEFORE IN THE PAST TWO YEARS...
"FROM THAT I CAN INFER THAT, UNBELIEVABLE AS IT MAY SEEM...
"...THERE IS A 70 PERCENT PROBABILITY THAT YOU–"
I DON'T KNOW...
...WHAT HE WAS PLANNING TO SAY AFTER THAT...
But it was very rude to say "unbelievable"!
...BUT I SUSPECT HE ALREADY KNOWS...
He's a frightening man...
!
!!!

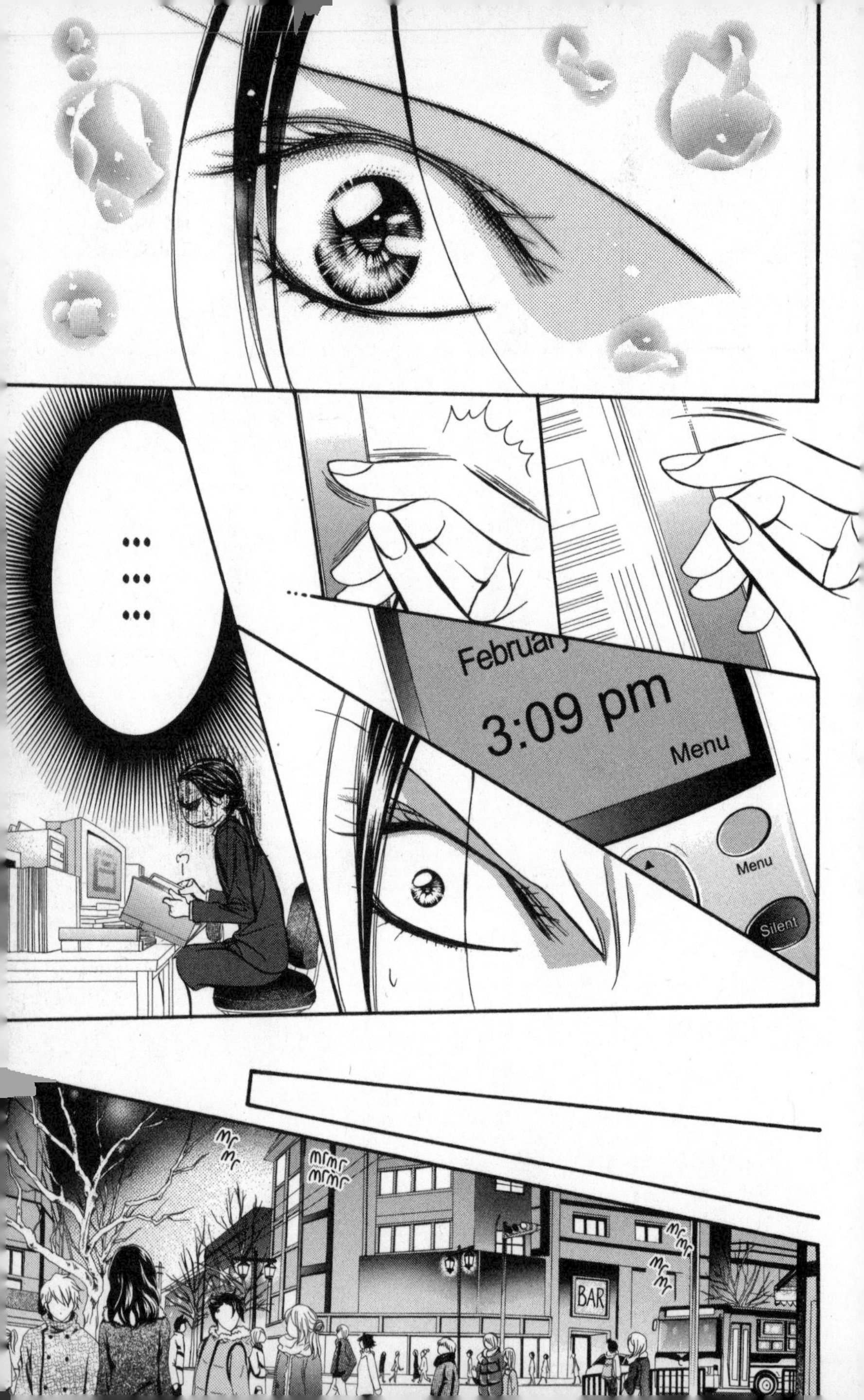
February
3:09 pm
Menu
Menu
Silent
...
... ...
mr mr
mr mr
BAR
mrmr mrmr
mr mr

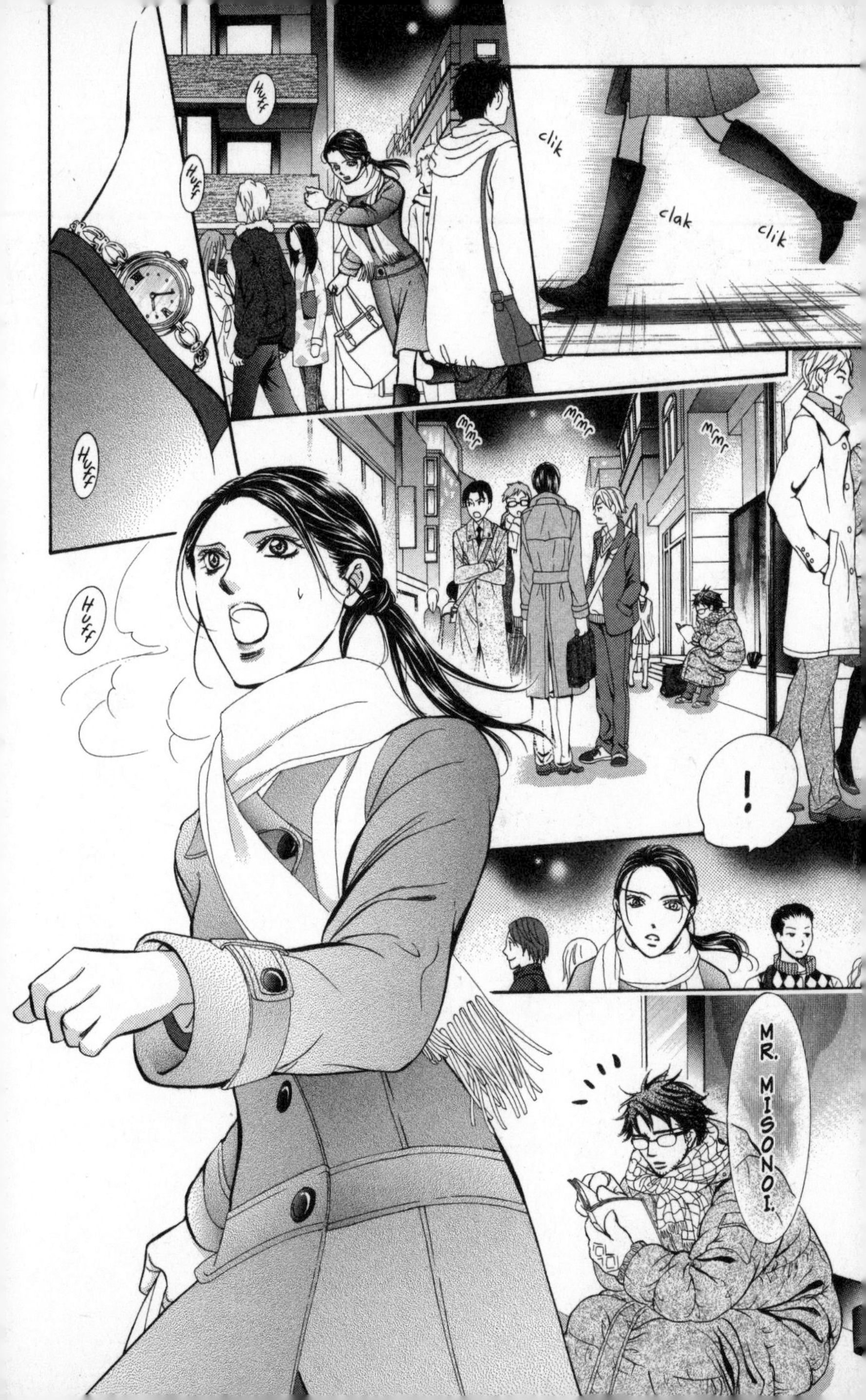
clik
clak
clik
Huff
Huff
mrmr
mrmr
mrmr
!
MR. MISONOI.
Huff
Huff

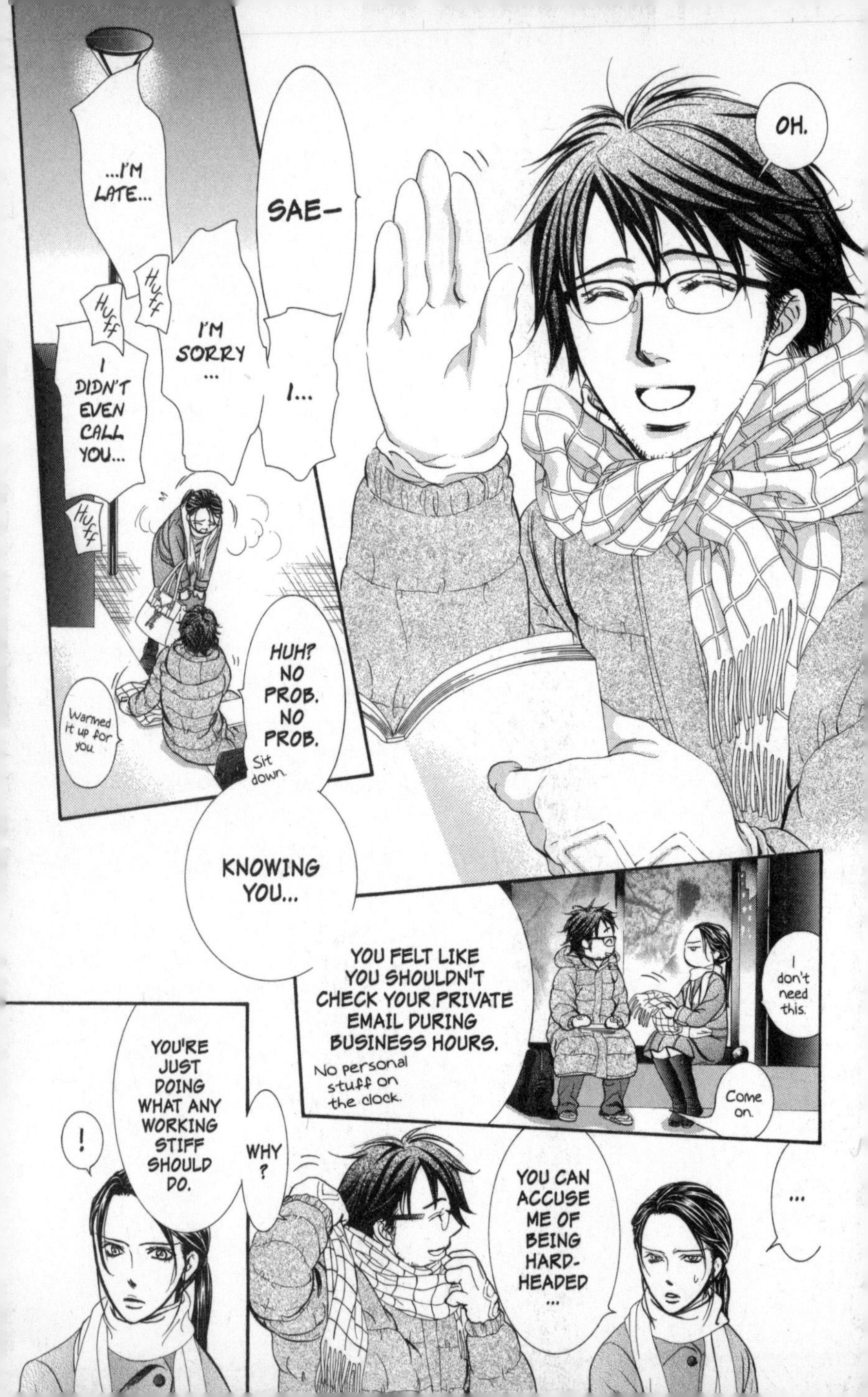
OH.
SAE—
I...
I'M SORRY ...
...I'M LATE...
Huff
Huff
I DIDN'T EVEN CALL YOU...
Huff
HUH? NO PROB. NO PROB.
Sit down.
Warmed it up for you.
KNOWING YOU...
I don't need this.
Come on.
YOU FELT LIKE YOU SHOULDN'T CHECK YOUR PRIVATE EMAIL DURING BUSINESS HOURS.
No personal stuff on the clock.
...
YOU CAN ACCUSE ME OF BEING HARD-HEADED ...
WHY?
YOU'RE JUST DOING WHAT ANY WORKING STIFF SHOULD DO.
!

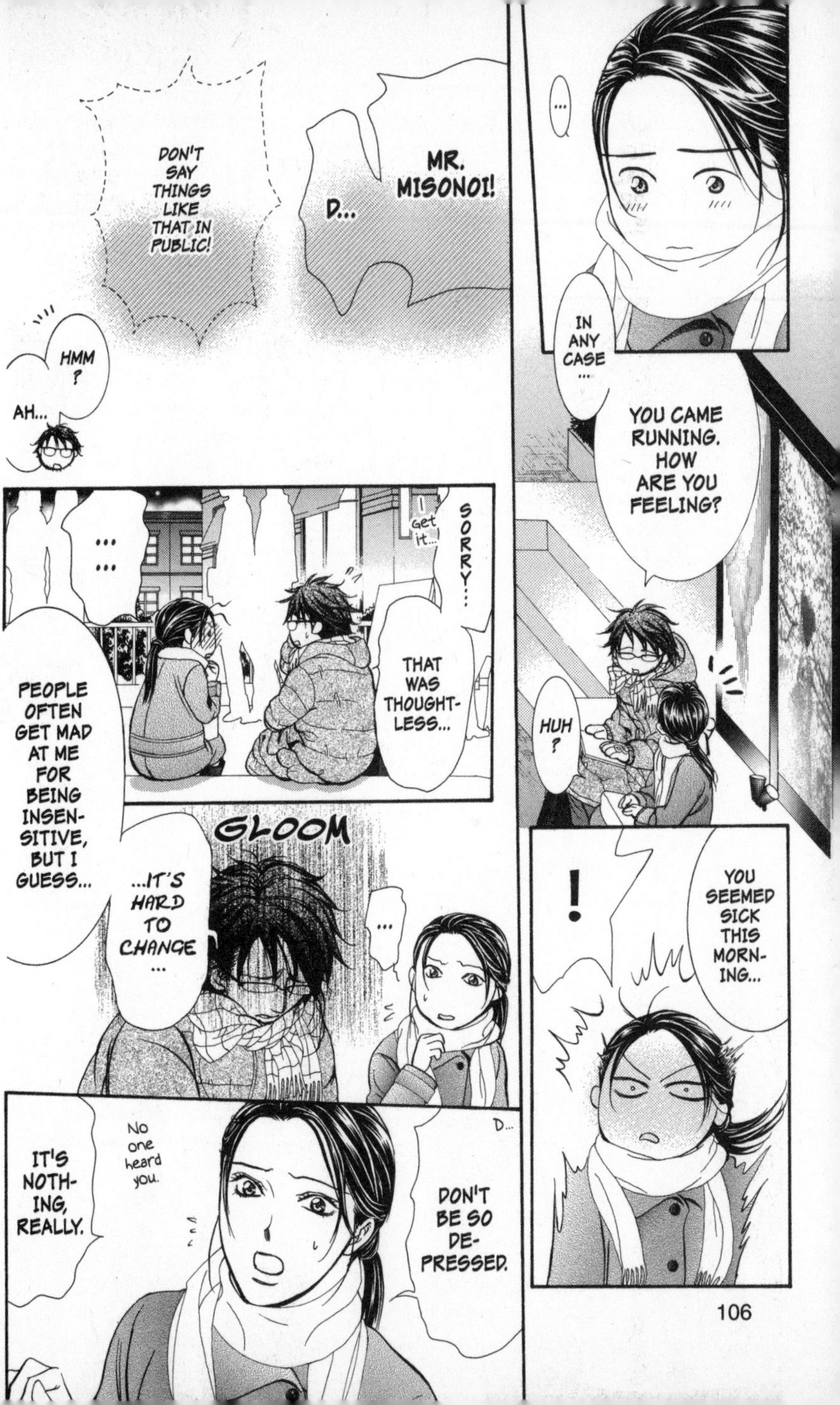
...
IN ANY CASE...
YOU CAME RUNNING. HOW ARE YOU FEELING?
HUH?
YOU SEEMED SICK THIS MORNING...
!
D...
MR. MISONO!!
DON'T SAY THINGS LIKE THAT IN PUBLIC!
HMM?
AH...
SORRY...
I get it...
THAT WAS THOUGHTLESS...
... ...
PEOPLE OFTEN GET MAD AT ME FOR BEING INSENSITIVE, BUT I GUESS...
GLOOM
...IT'S HARD TO CHANGE...
...
D...
DON'T BE SO DEPRESSED.
No one heard you.
IT'S NOTHING, REALLY.

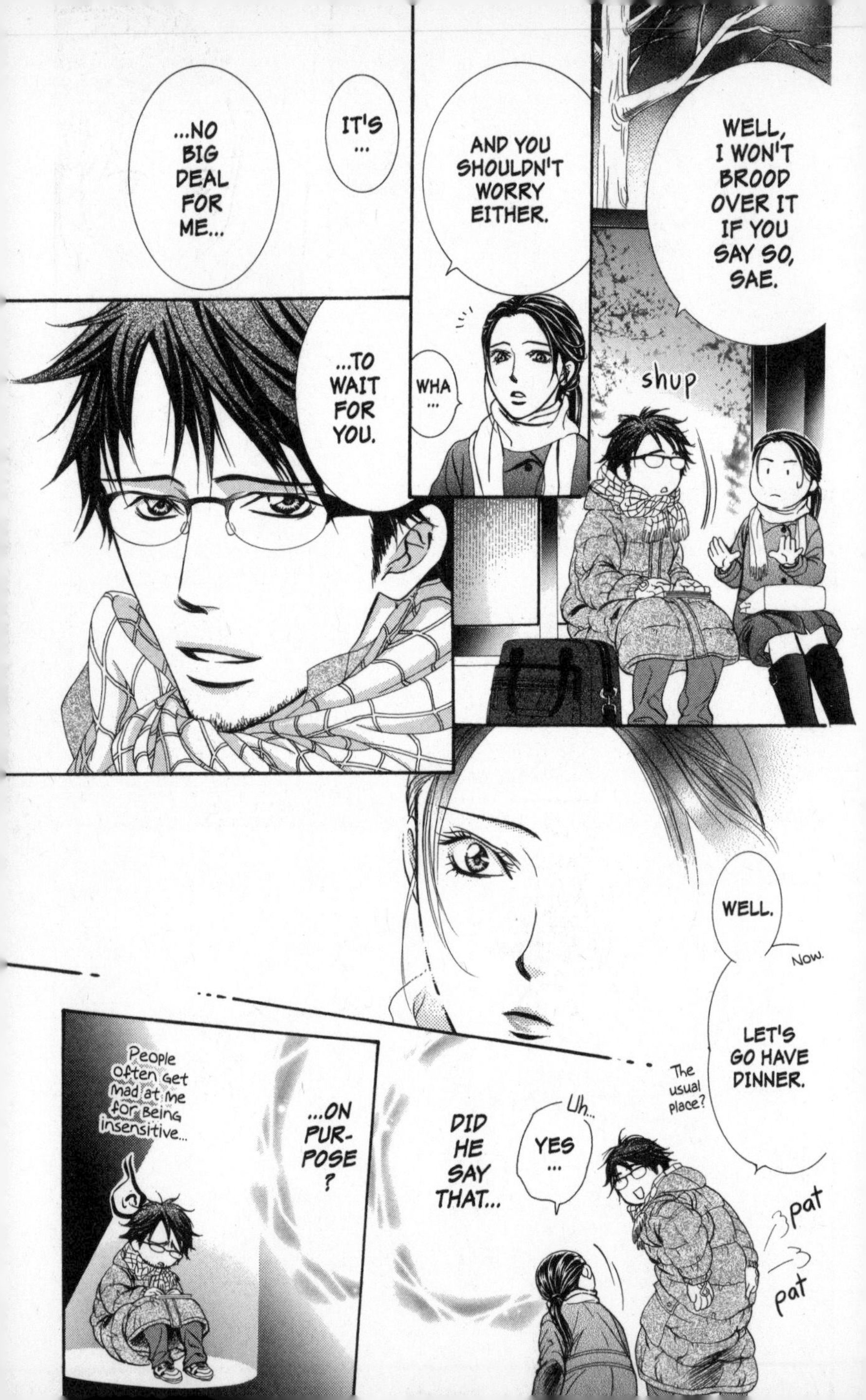
WELL, I WON'T BROOD OVER IT IF YOU SAY SO, SAE.
shup
AND YOU SHOULDN'T WORRY EITHER.
IT'S...
...NO BIG DEAL FOR ME...
...TO WAIT FOR YOU.
WHA...
WELL.
Now.
LET'S GO HAVE DINNER.
The usual place?
Uh...
YES...
pat
pat
DID HE SAY THAT...
...ON PURPOSE?
People often get mad at me for being insensitive...

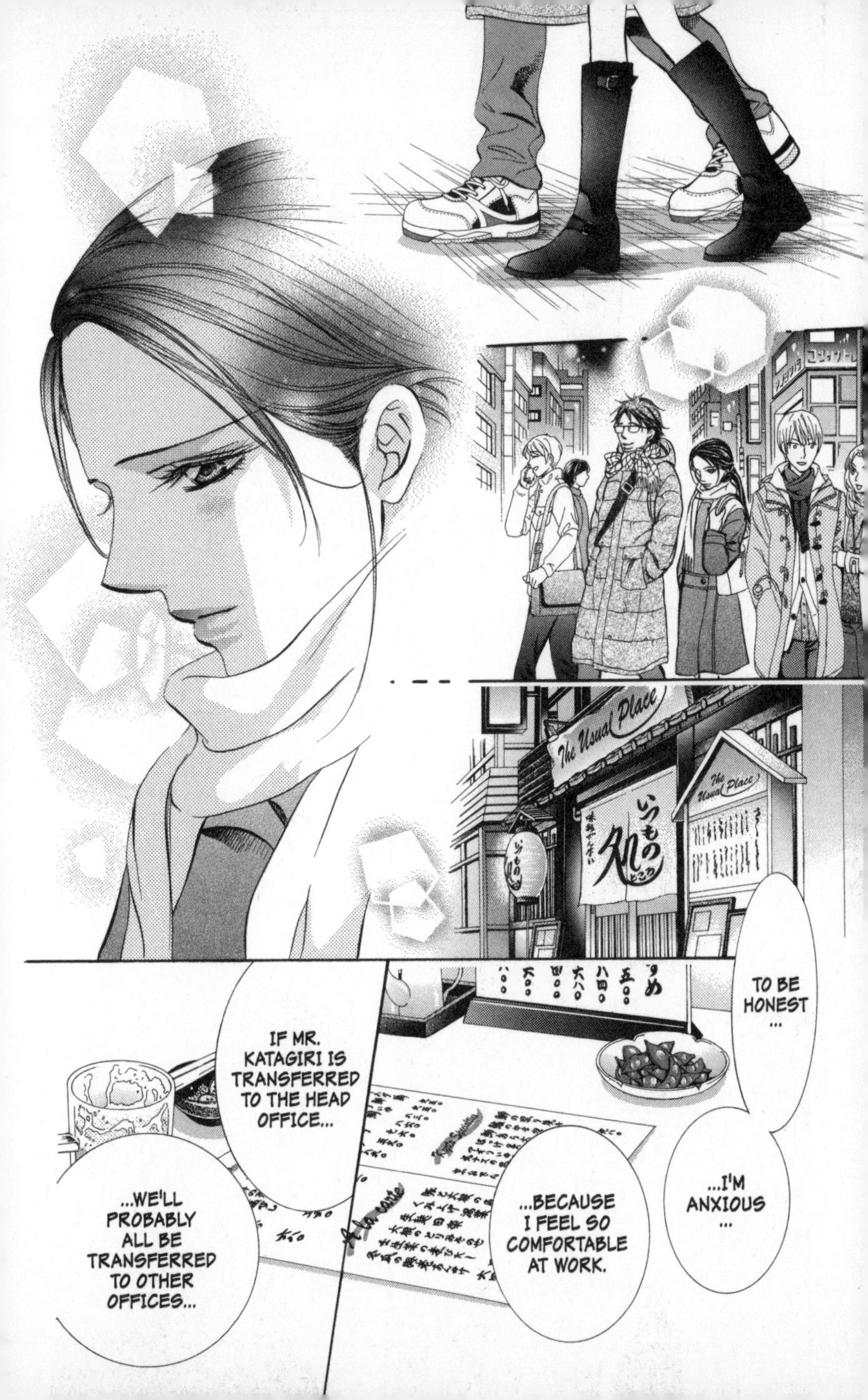
The Usual Place
The Usual Place
TO BE HONEST ...
...I'M ANXIOUS ...
...BECAUSE I FEEL SO COMFORTABLE AT WORK.
IF MR. KATAGIRI IS TRANSFERRED TO THE HEAD OFFICE...
...WE'LL PROBABLY ALL BE TRANSFERRED TO OTHER OFFICES...

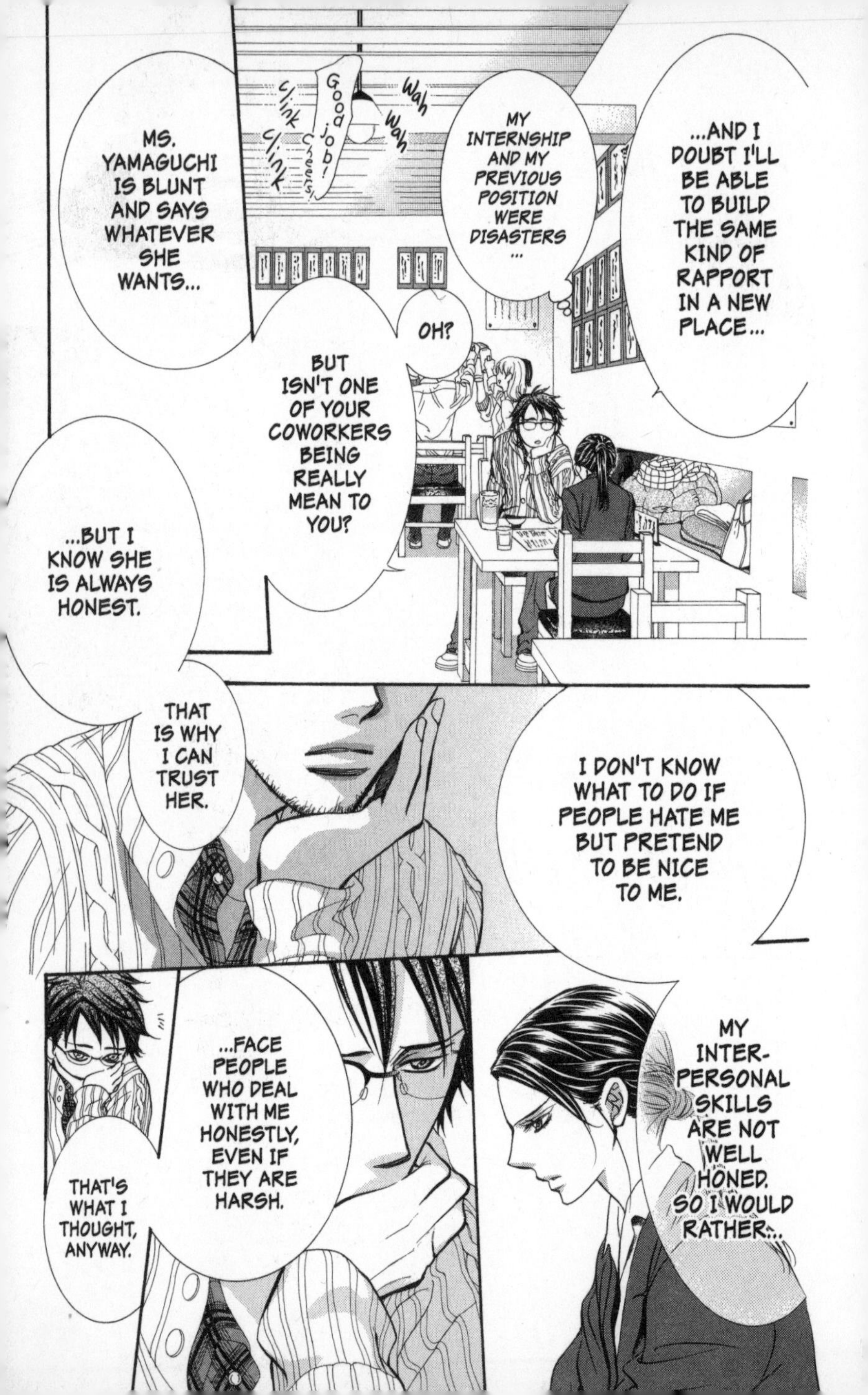

Wah Wah
Good job! Cheers!
clink clink
MY INTERNSHIP AND MY PREVIOUS POSITION WERE DISASTERS...
...AND I DOUBT I'LL BE ABLE TO BUILD THE SAME KIND OF RAPPORT IN A NEW PLACE...
OH?
BUT ISN'T ONE OF YOUR COWORKERS BEING REALLY MEAN TO YOU?
MS. YAMAGUCHI IS BLUNT AND SAYS WHATEVER SHE WANTS...
...BUT I KNOW SHE IS ALWAYS HONEST.
THAT IS WHY I CAN TRUST HER.
I DON'T KNOW WHAT TO DO IF PEOPLE HATE ME BUT PRETEND TO BE NICE TO ME.
MY INTER-PERSONAL SKILLS ARE NOT WELL HONED. SO I WOULD RATHER...
...FACE PEOPLE WHO DEAL WITH ME HONESTLY, EVEN IF THEY ARE HARSH.
THAT'S WHAT I THOUGHT, ANYWAY.

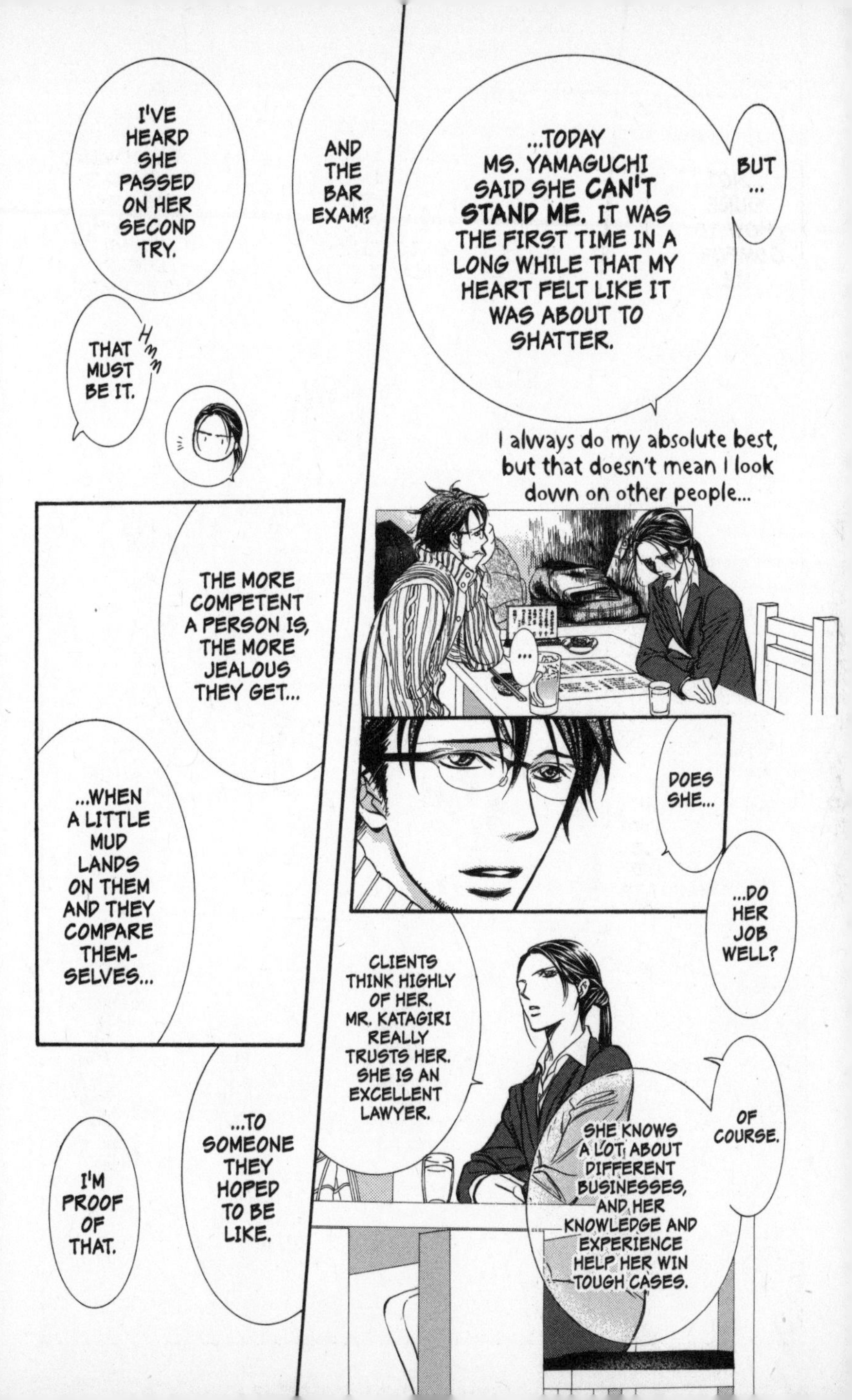
BUT...
...TODAY MS. YAMAGUCHI SAID SHE CAN'T STAND ME. IT WAS THE FIRST TIME IN A LONG WHILE THAT MY HEART FELT LIKE IT WAS ABOUT TO SHATTER.
I always do my absolute best, but that doesn't mean I look down on other people...
...
DOES SHE...
...DO HER JOB WELL?
OF COURSE.
CLIENTS THINK HIGHLY OF HER. MR. KATAGIRI REALLY TRUSTS HER. SHE IS AN EXCELLENT LAWYER.
SHE KNOWS A LOT ABOUT DIFFERENT BUSINESSES, AND HER KNOWLEDGE AND EXPERIENCE HELP HER WIN TOUGH CASES.
AND THE BAR EXAM?
I'VE HEARD SHE PASSED ON HER SECOND TRY.
Hmm
THAT MUST BE IT.
THE MORE COMPETENT A PERSON IS, THE MORE JEALOUS THEY GET...
...WHEN A LITTLE MUD LANDS ON THEM AND THEY COMPARE THEM-SELVES...
...TO SOMEONE THEY HOPED TO BE LIKE.
I'M PROOF OF THAT.

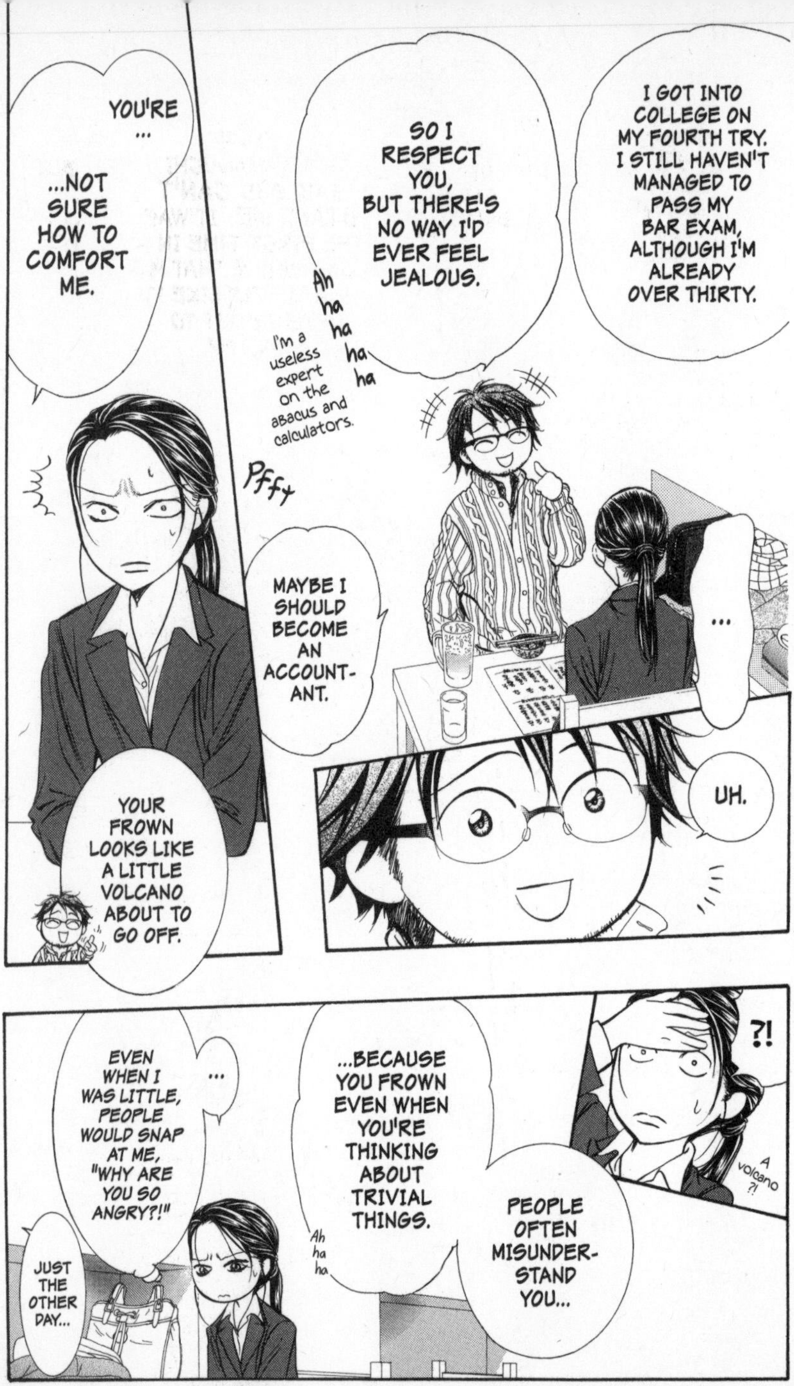
I GOT INTO COLLEGE ON MY FOURTH TRY. I STILL HAVEN'T MANAGED TO PASS MY BAR EXAM, ALTHOUGH I'M ALREADY OVER THIRTY.
SO I RESPECT YOU, BUT THERE'S NO WAY I'D EVER FEEL JEALOUS.
Ah ha ha ha ha
I'm a useless expert on the abacus and calculators.
Pffft
MAYBE I SHOULD BECOME AN ACCOUNT-ANT.
...
UH.
YOU'RE ...
...NOT SURE HOW TO COMFORT ME.
YOUR FROWN LOOKS LIKE A LITTLE VOLCANO ABOUT TO GO OFF.
?!
A volcano ?!
PEOPLE OFTEN MISUNDER-STAND YOU...
...BECAUSE YOU FROWN EVEN WHEN YOU'RE THINKING ABOUT TRIVIAL THINGS.
Ah ha ha
...
EVEN WHEN I WAS LITTLE, PEOPLE WOULD SNAP AT ME, "WHY ARE YOU SO ANGRY?!"
JUST THE OTHER DAY...

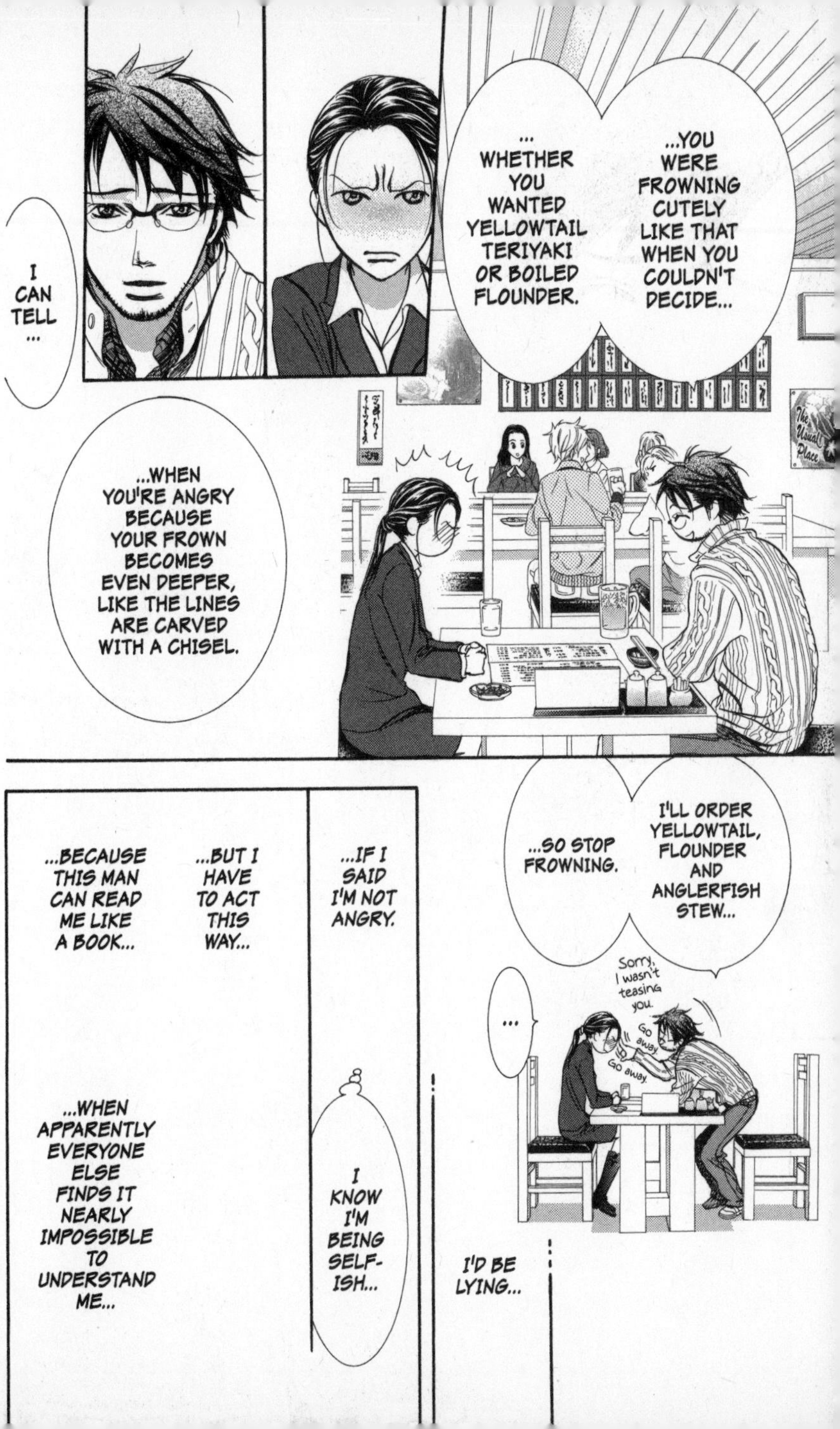
...YOU WERE FROWNING CUTELY LIKE THAT WHEN YOU COULDN'T DECIDE...
... WHETHER YOU WANTED YELLOWTAIL TERIYAKI OR BOILED FLOUNDER.
The Usual Place
I CAN TELL...
...WHEN YOU'RE ANGRY BECAUSE YOUR FROWN BECOMES EVEN DEEPER, LIKE THE LINES ARE CARVED WITH A CHISEL.
I'LL ORDER YELLOWTAIL, FLOUNDER AND ANGLERFISH STEW...
...SO STOP FROWNING.
Sorry, I wasn't teasing you.
Go away.
Go away.
...
I'D BE LYING...
...IF I SAID I'M NOT ANGRY.
I KNOW I'M BEING SELF-ISH...
...BUT I HAVE TO ACT THIS WAY...
...BECAUSE THIS MAN CAN READ ME LIKE A BOOK...
...WHEN APPARENTLY EVERYONE ELSE FINDS IT NEARLY IMPOSSIBLE TO UNDERSTAND ME...

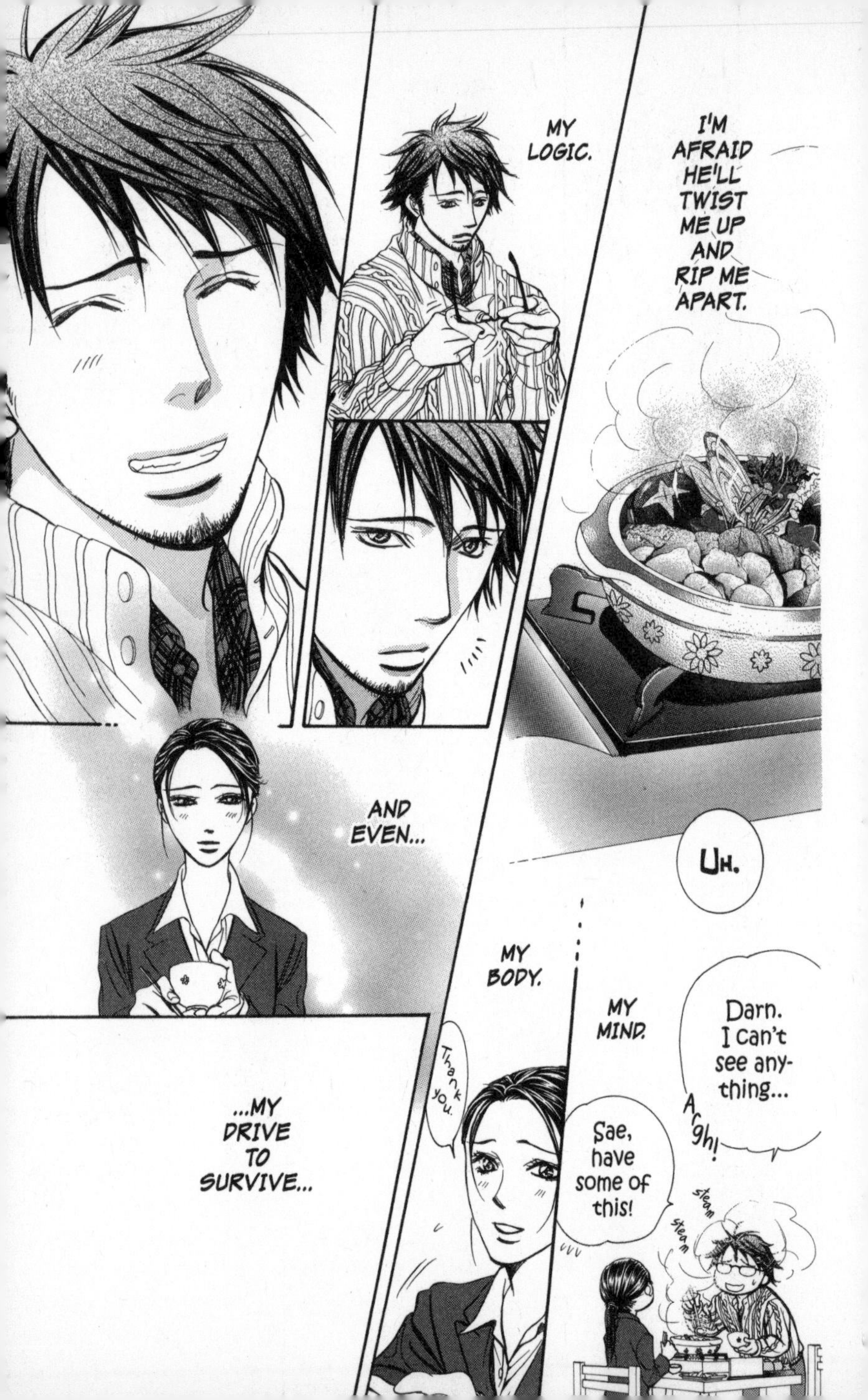
I'M AFRAID HE'LL TWIST ME UP AND RIP ME APART.
MY LOGIC.
UH.
AND EVEN...
MY BODY.
MY MIND.
Darn. I can't see anything...
Argh!
Sae, have some of this!
steam
steam
Thank you.
...MY DRIVE TO SURVIVE...

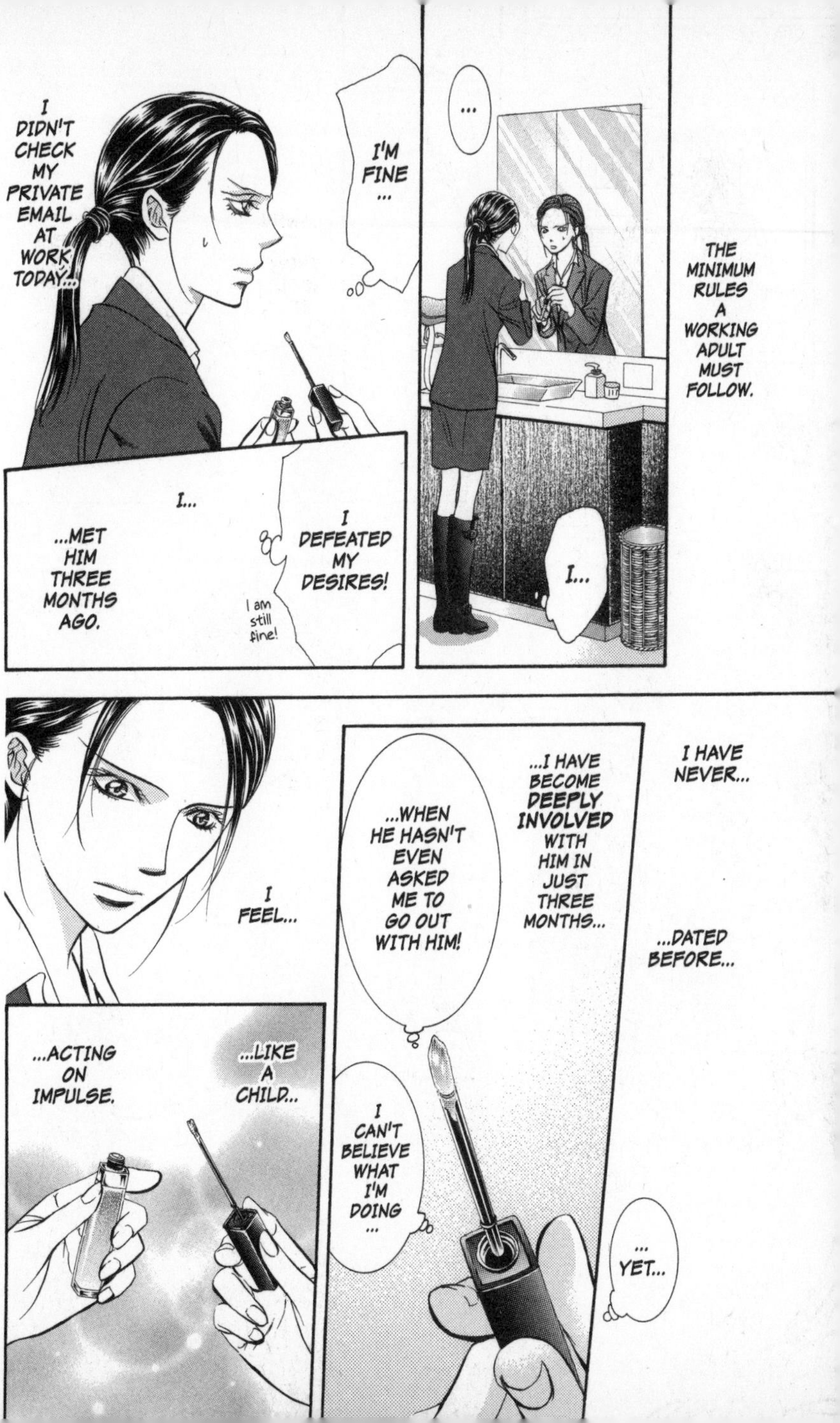
...
THE MINIMUM RULES A WORKING ADULT MUST FOLLOW.
I...
I'M FINE ...
I DIDN'T CHECK MY PRIVATE EMAIL AT WORK TODAY...
I DEFEATED MY DESIRES!
I am still fine!
I...
...MET HIM THREE MONTHS AGO.
I HAVE NEVER...
...DATED BEFORE...
...I HAVE BECOME DEEPLY INVOLVED WITH HIM IN JUST THREE MONTHS...
...WHEN HE HASN'T EVEN ASKED ME TO GO OUT WITH HIM!
I FEEL...
... YET...
I CAN'T BELIEVE WHAT I'M DOING ...
...LIKE A CHILD...
...ACTING ON IMPULSE.

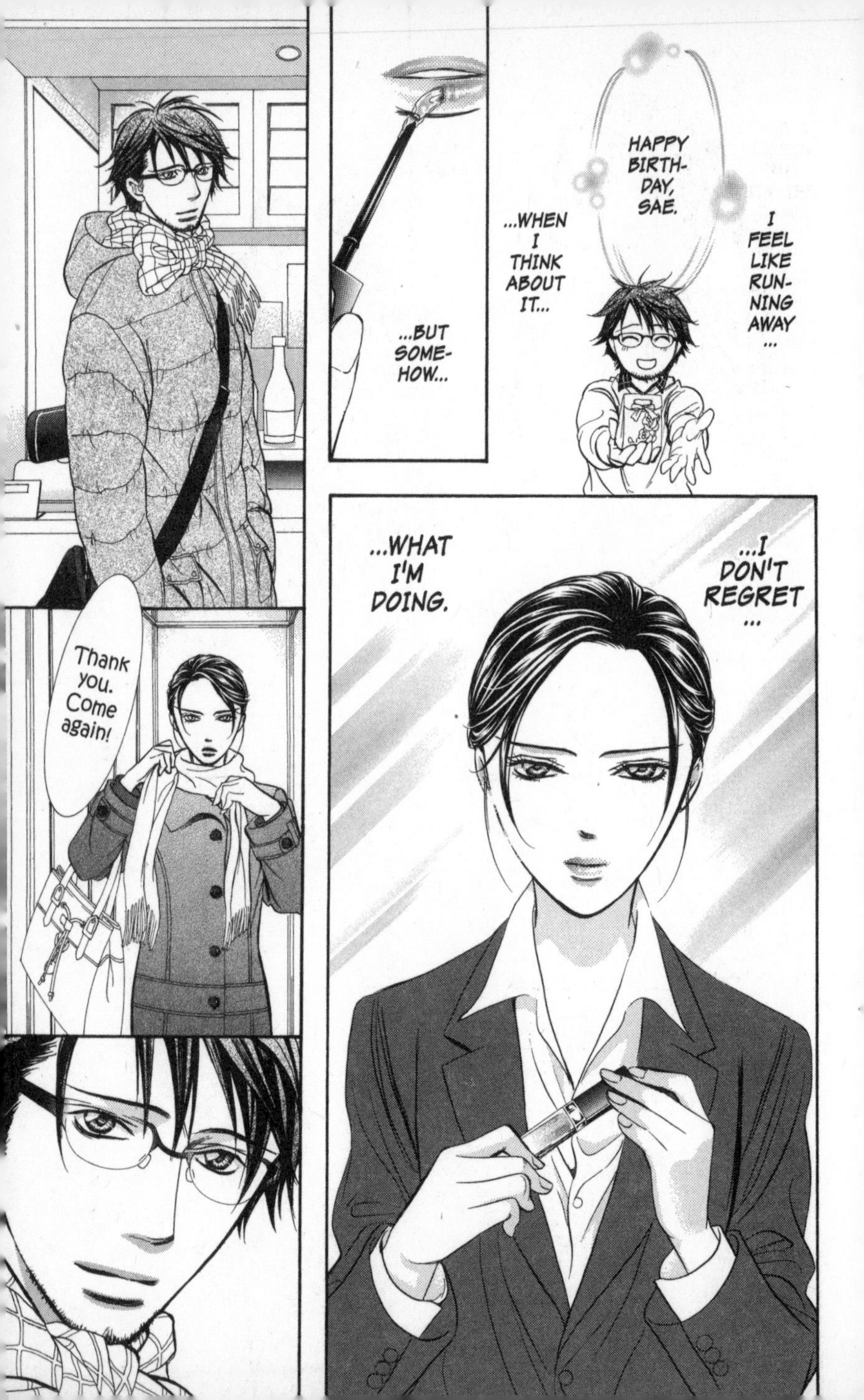
I FEEL LIKE RUN-NING AWAY...
HAPPY BIRTH-DAY, SAE.
...WHEN I THINK ABOUT IT...
...BUT SOME-HOW...
...I DON'T REGRET...
...WHAT I'M DOING.
Thank you. Come again!

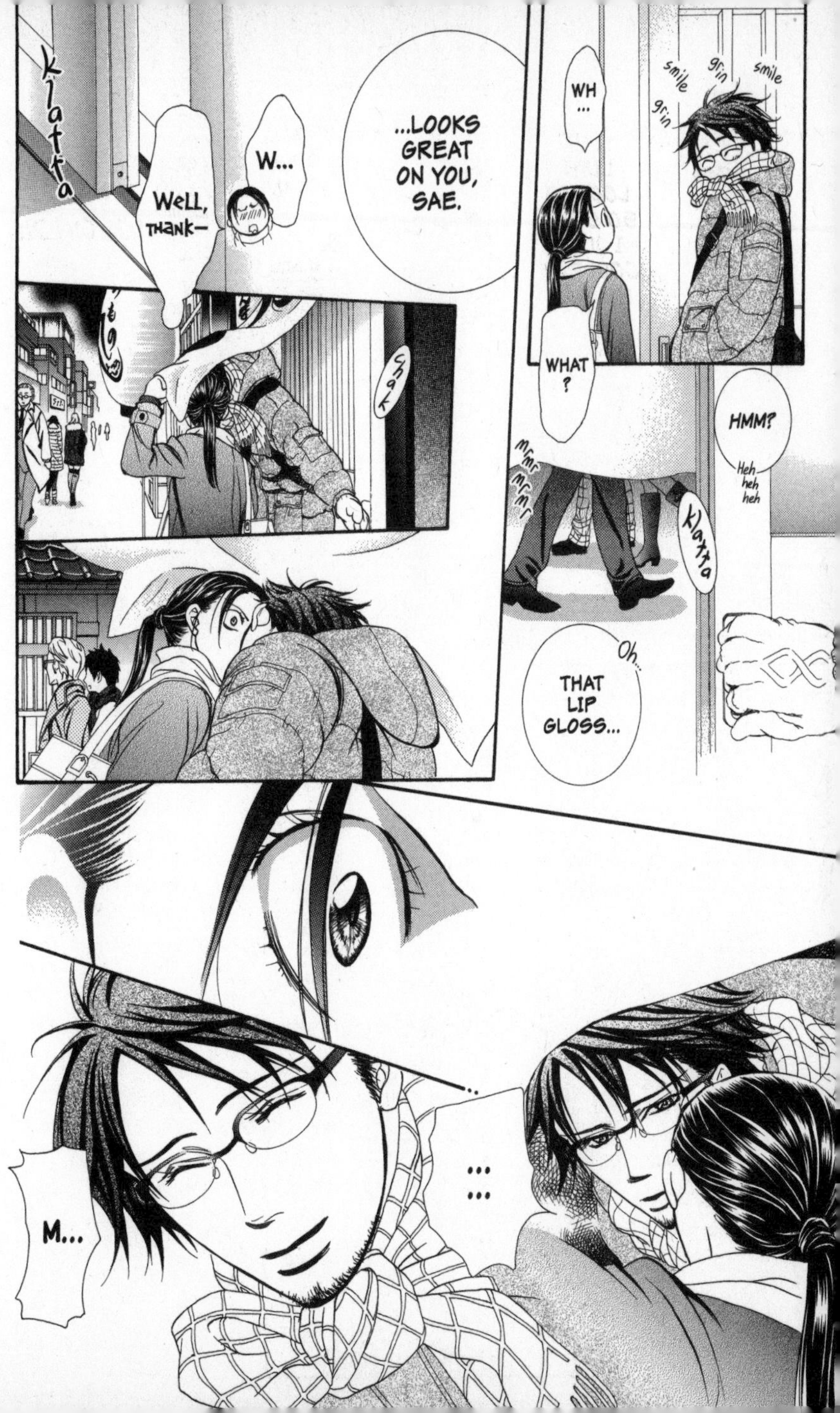

WH...
smile
grin
grin
smile
WHAT?
HMM?
Heh heh heh
mrmrmrmr
klatta
Oh...
THAT LIP GLOSS...
...LOOKS GREAT ON YOU, SAE.
W...
Well, thank—
klatta
chak
...
...
...
M...

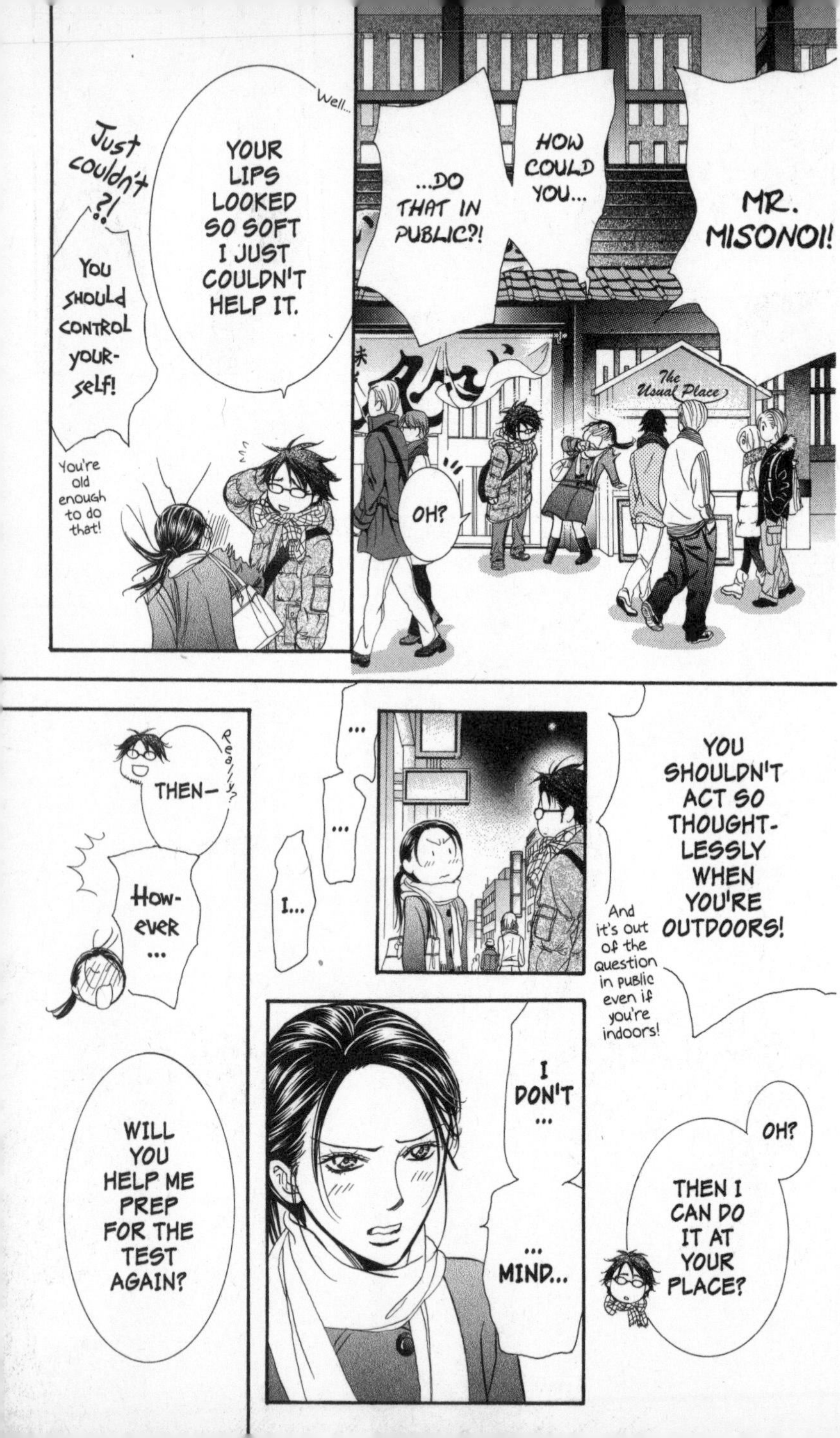

MR. MISONO!!
HOW COULD YOU...
...DO THAT IN PUBLIC?!
The Usual Place
OH?
Well...
YOUR LIPS LOOKED SO SOFT I JUST COULDN'T HELP IT.
Just couldn't ?!
You should control your-self!
You're old enough to do that!
YOU SHOULDN'T ACT SO THOUGHT-LESSLY WHEN YOU'RE OUTDOORS!
And it's out of the question in public even if you're indoors!
...
...
I...
OH?
THEN I CAN DO IT AT YOUR PLACE?
I DON'T ...
... MIND...
Really?
THEN—
How-ever ...
WILL YOU HELP ME PREP FOR THE TEST AGAIN?

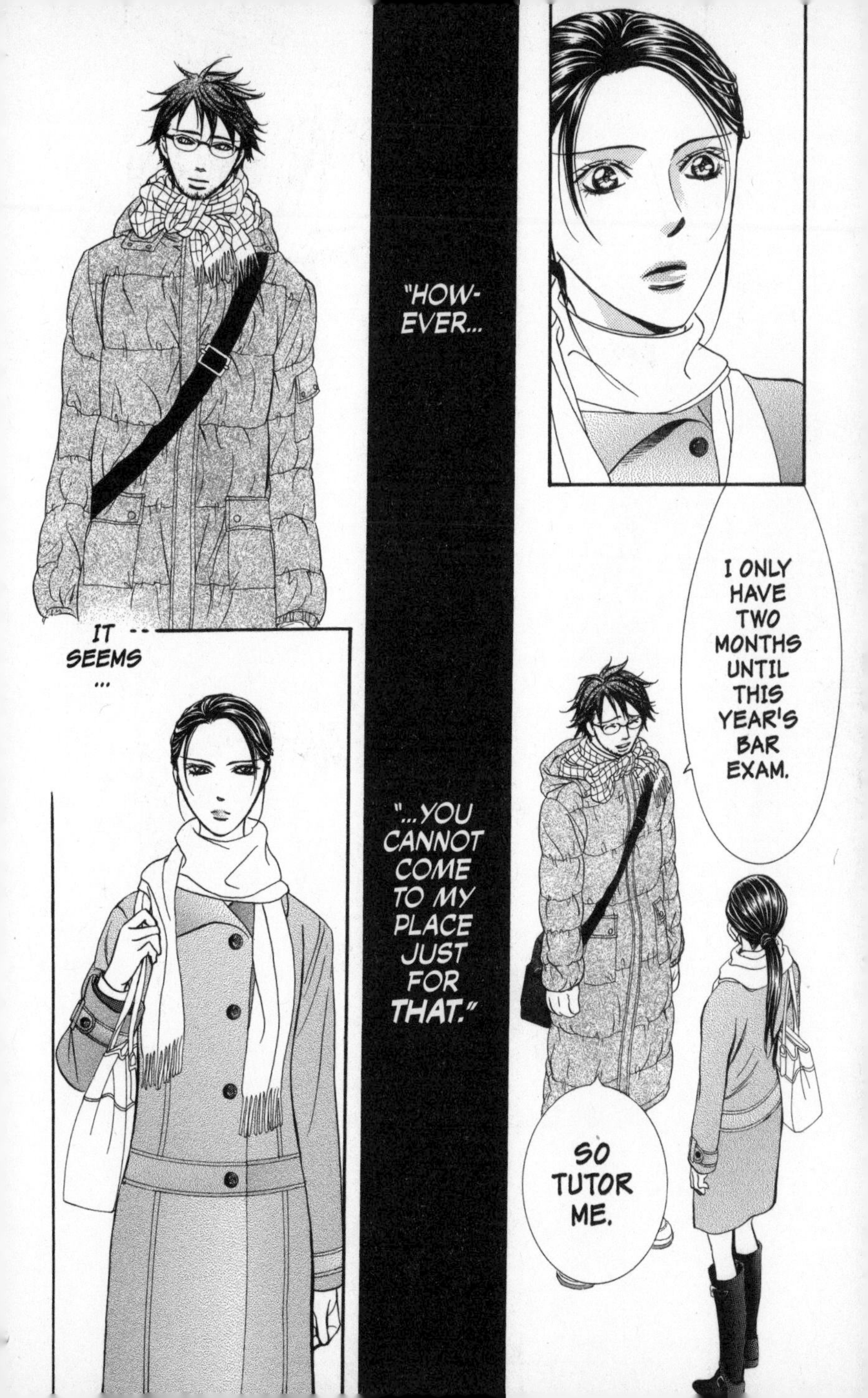
I ONLY HAVE TWO MONTHS UNTIL THIS YEAR'S BAR EXAM.
SO TUTOR ME.
"HOW-EVER...
"...YOU CANNOT COME TO MY PLACE JUST FOR THAT."
IT SEEMS ...

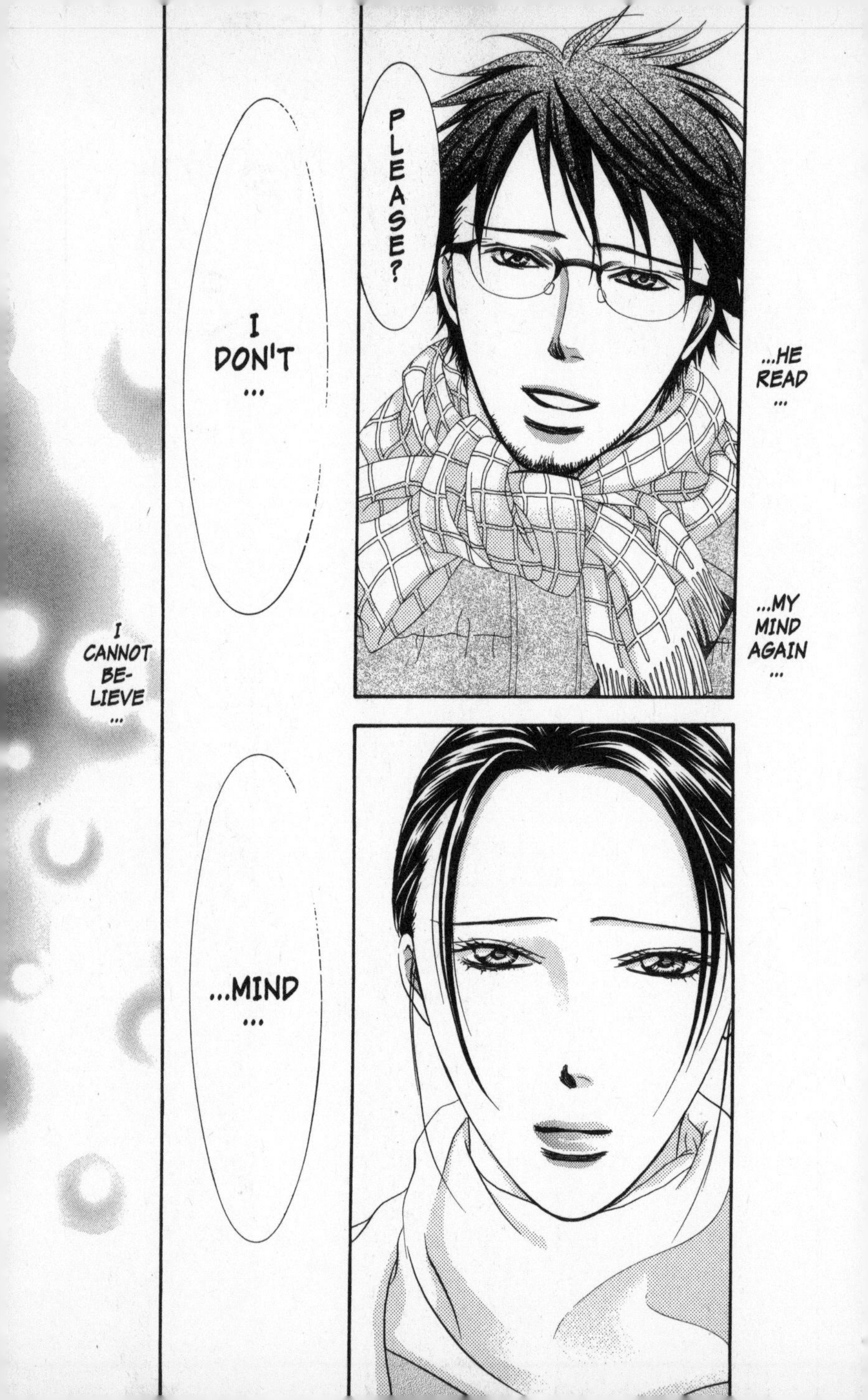
...HE READ ...
...MY MIND AGAIN ...
PLEASE?
I DON'T ...
...MIND ...
I CANNOT BE-LIEVE ...

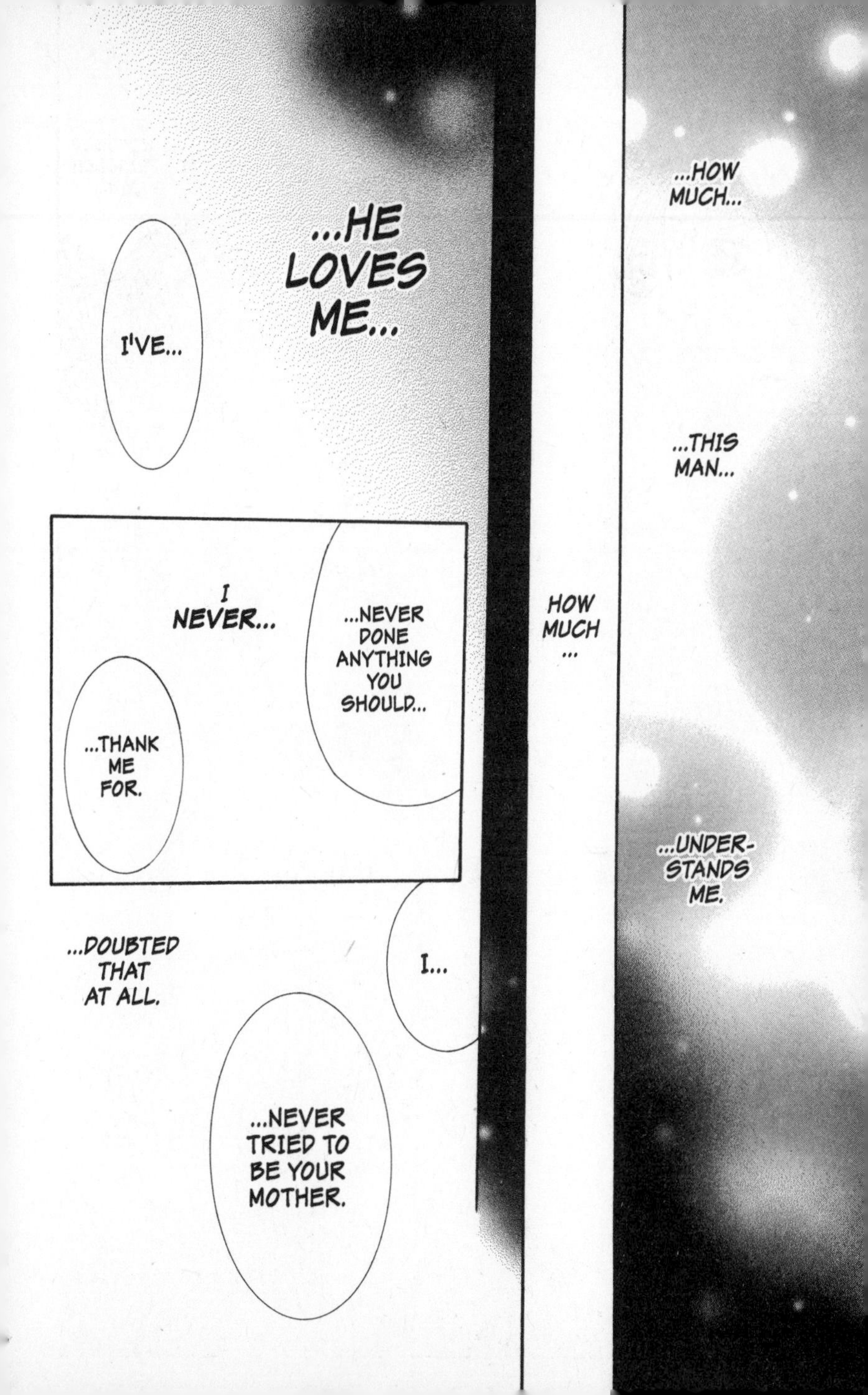
...HOW MUCH...
...THIS MAN...
...UNDER-STANDS ME.
HOW MUCH ...
...HE LOVES ME...
I'VE...
...NEVER DONE ANYTHING YOU SHOULD...
I NEVER...
...THANK ME FOR.
I...
...DOUBTED THAT AT ALL.
...NEVER TRIED TO BE YOUR MOTHER.

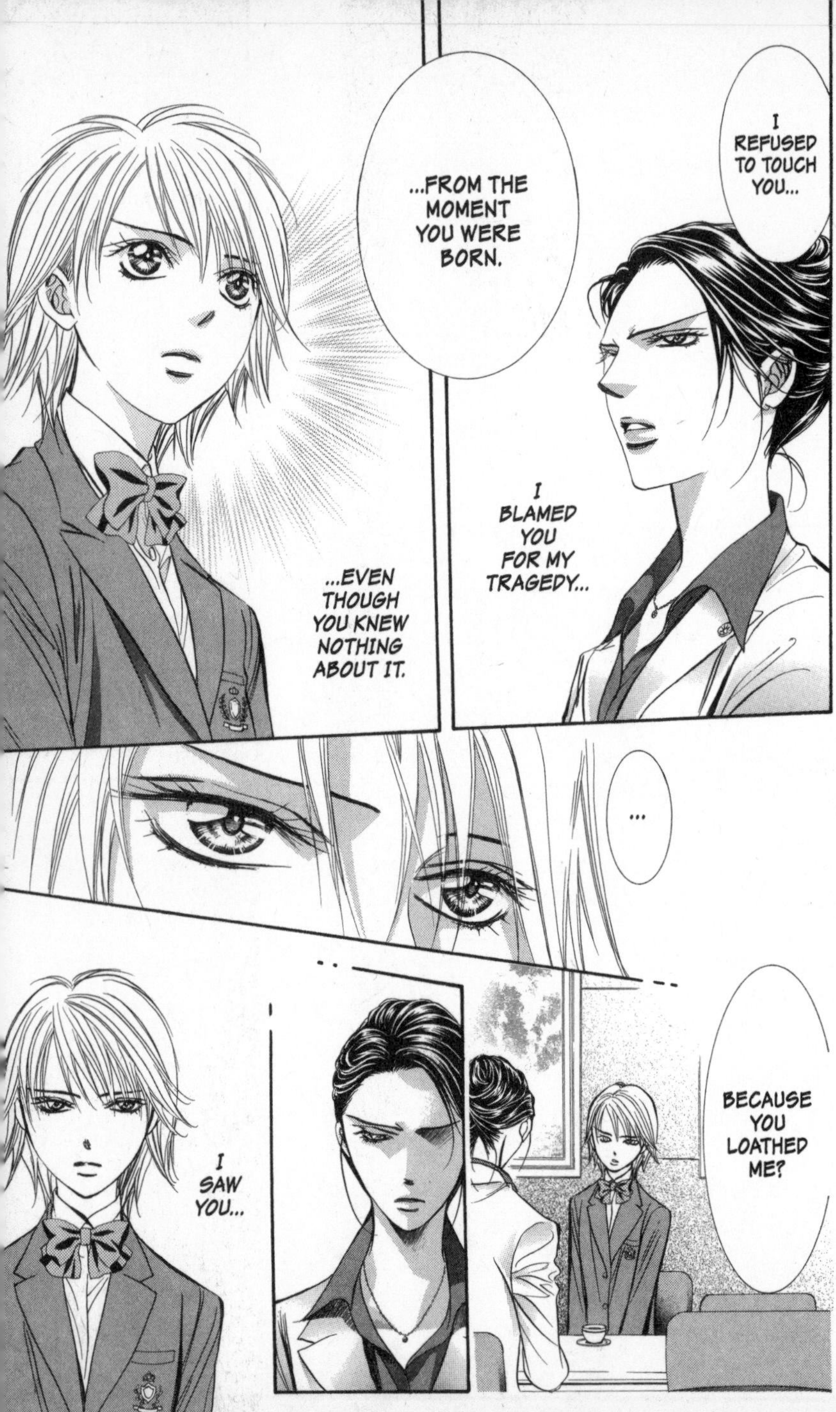
I REFUSED TO TOUCH YOU...
...FROM THE MOMENT YOU WERE BORN.
I BLAMED YOU FOR MY TRAGEDY...
...EVEN THOUGH YOU KNEW NOTHING ABOUT IT.
...
BECAUSE YOU LOATHED ME?
I SAW YOU...

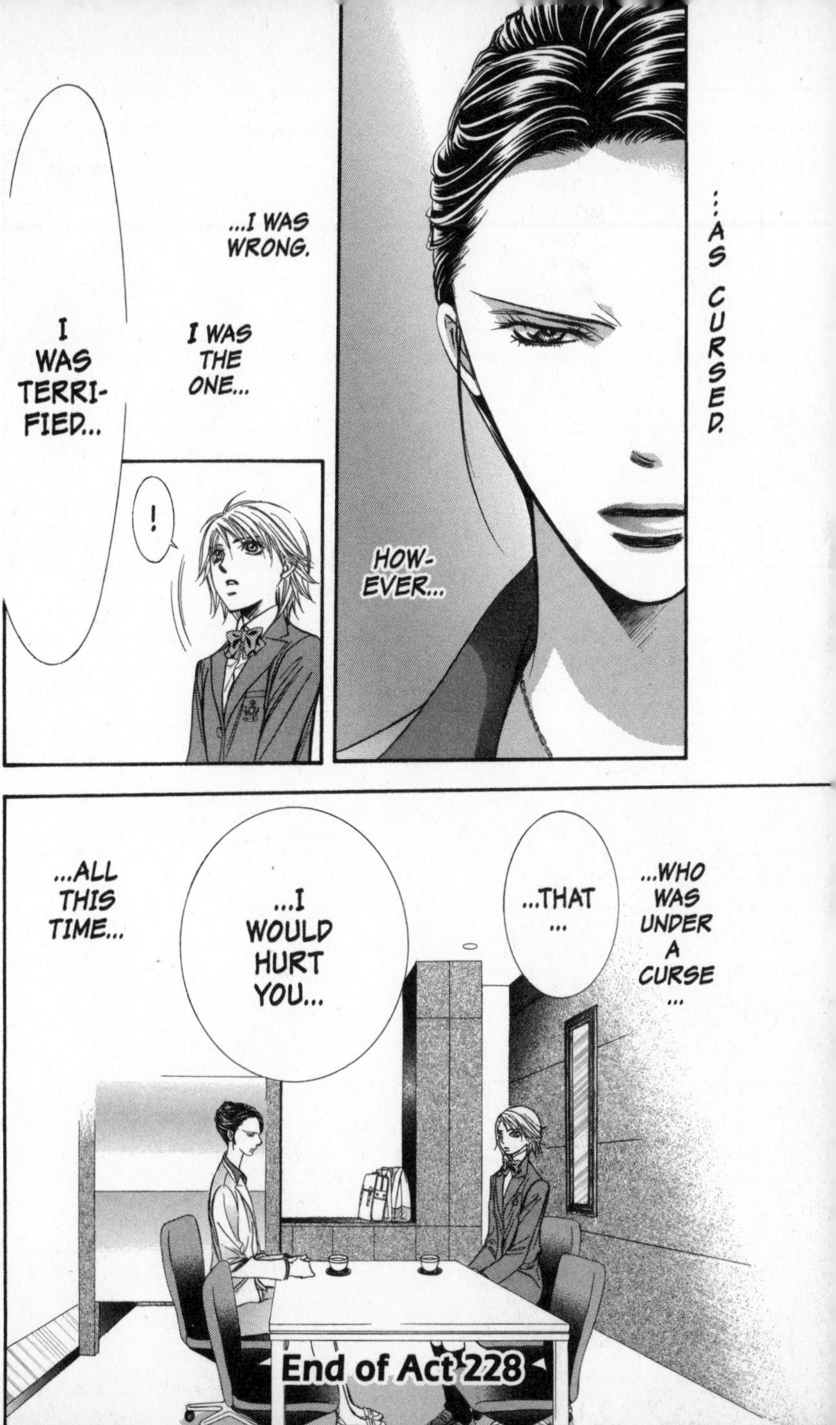
...AS CURSED.
HOW-EVER...
...I WAS WRONG.
I WAS THE ONE...
I WAS TERRI-FIED...
!
...WHO WAS UNDER A CURSE...
...THAT...
...I WOULD HURT YOU...
...ALL THIS TIME...
End of Act 228

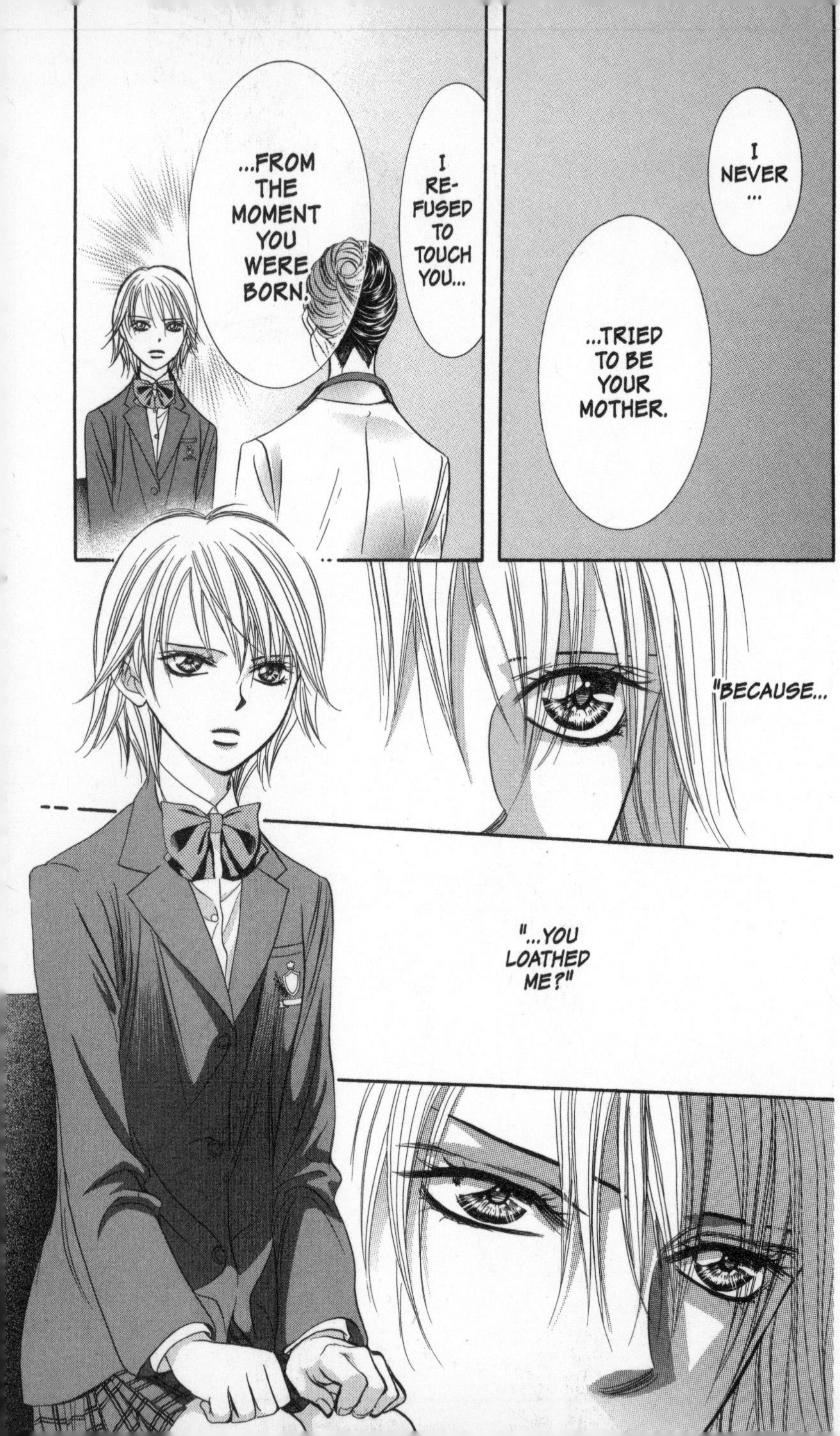
I NEVER...
...TRIED TO BE YOUR MOTHER.
I RE-FUSED TO TOUCH YOU...
...FROM THE MOMENT YOU WERE BORN.
"BECAUSE...
"...YOU LOATHED ME?"

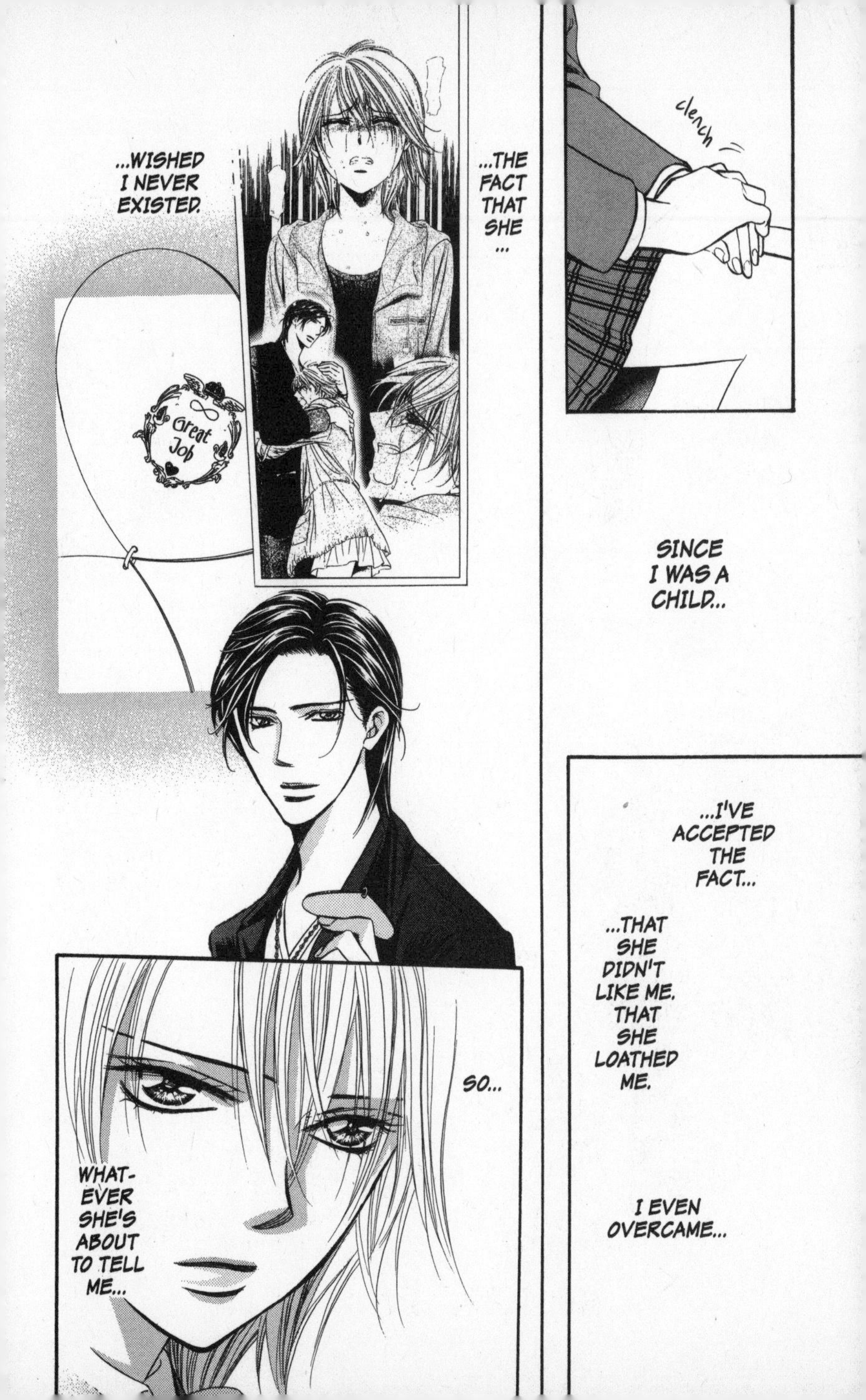
clench
SINCE I WAS A CHILD...
...I'VE ACCEPTED THE FACT...
...THAT SHE DIDN'T LIKE ME. THAT SHE LOATHED ME.
I EVEN OVERCAME...
...THE FACT THAT SHE ...
...WISHED I NEVER EXISTED.
Great Job
SO...
WHAT-EVER SHE'S ABOUT TO TELL ME...

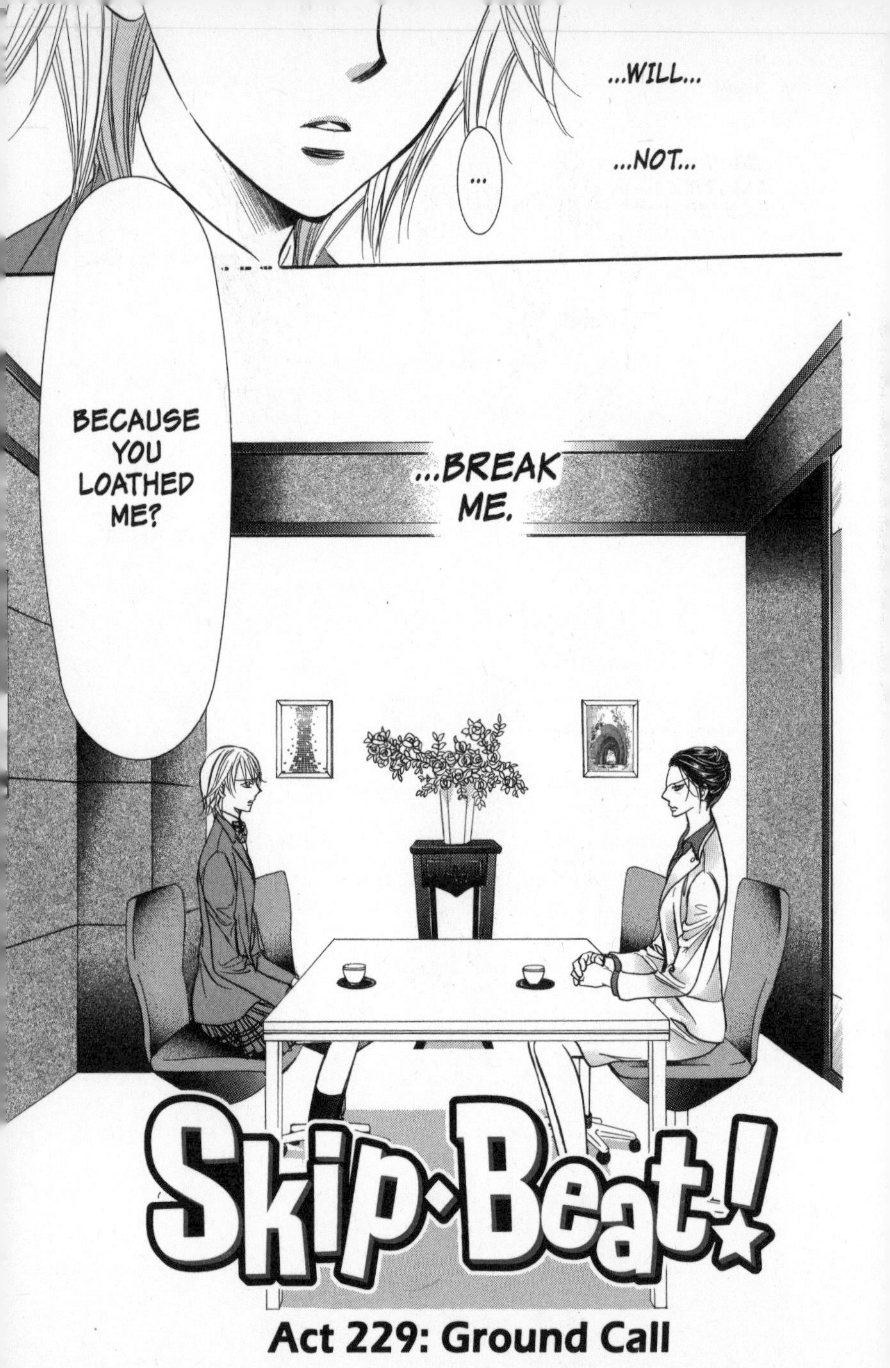
...WILL...
...NOT...
...
...BREAK ME.
BECAUSE YOU LOATHED ME?
Skip·Beat!

Act 229: Ground Call

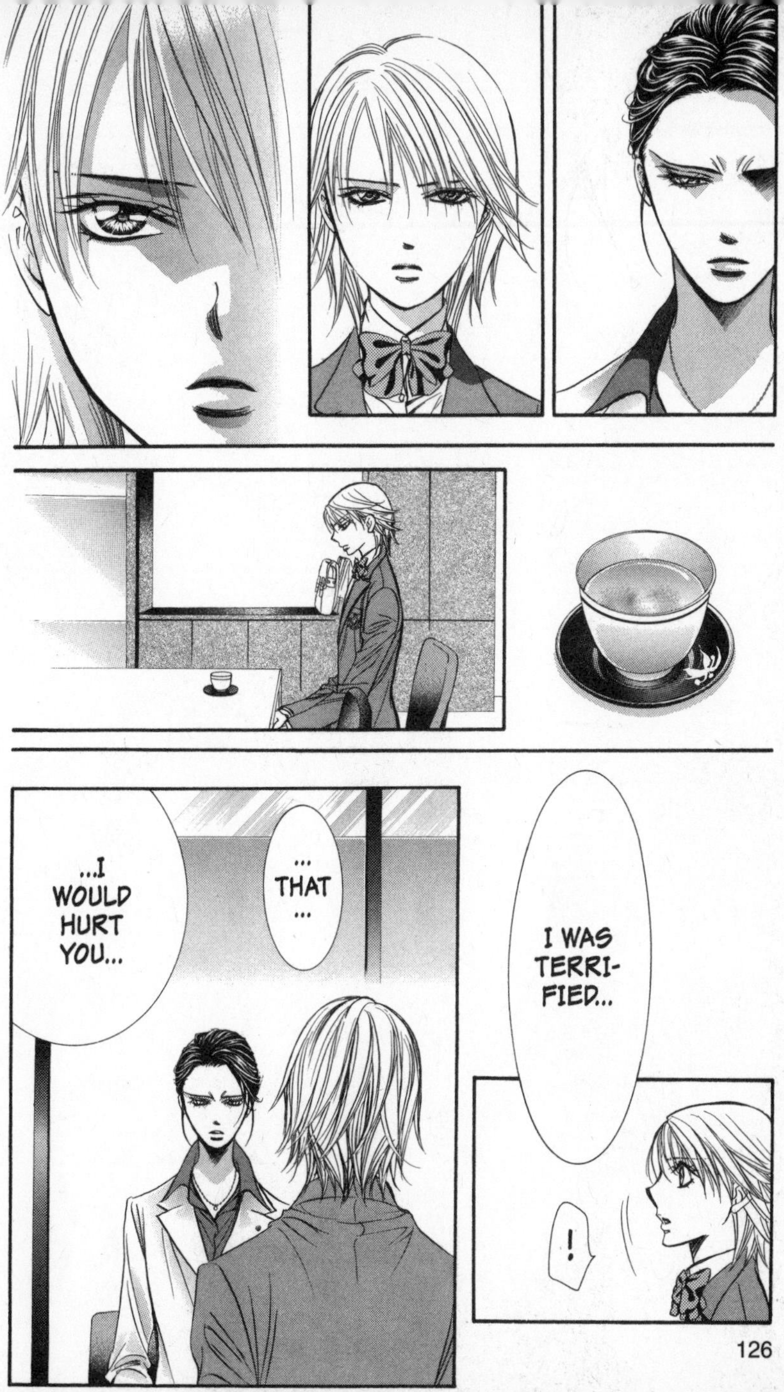
I WAS TERRI-FIED...
!
...THAT...
...I WOULD HURT YOU...

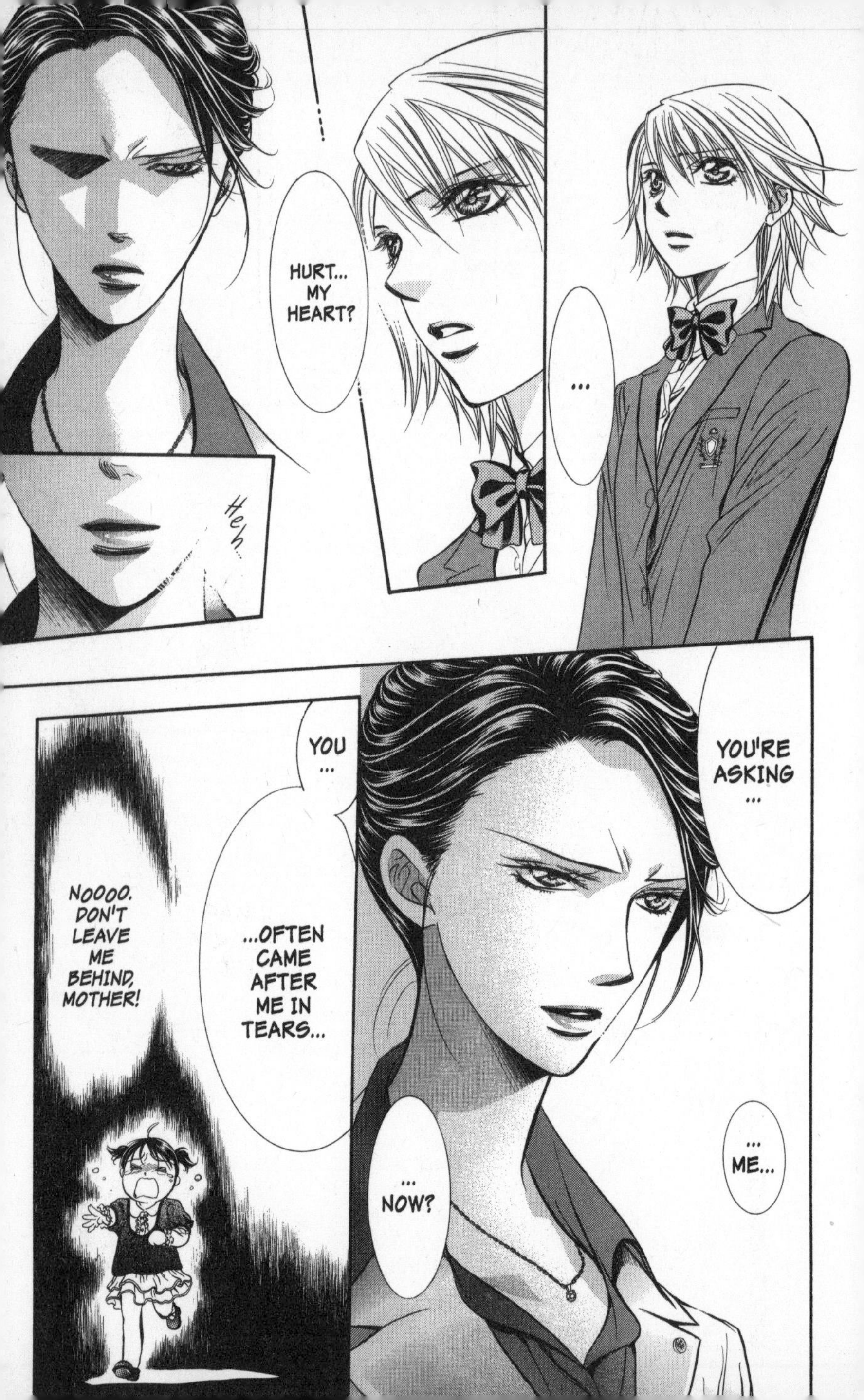
...
HURT... MY HEART?
Heh...
YOU'RE ASKING ...
... ME...
... NOW?
YOU ...
...OFTEN CAME AFTER ME IN TEARS...
NOOOO. DON'T LEAVE ME BEHIND, MOTHER!

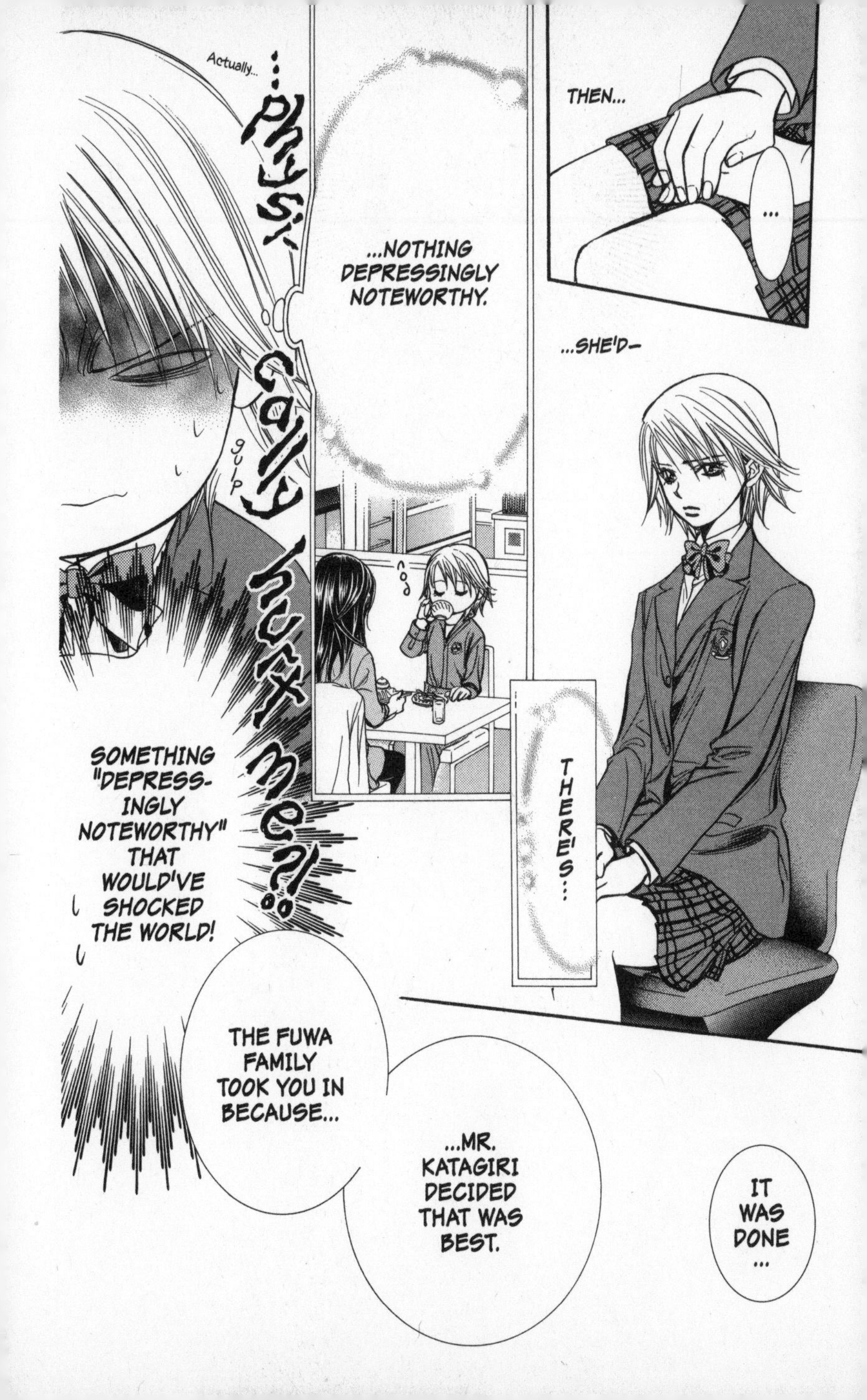
THEN...
...
...SHE'D–
THERE'S...
...NOTHING DEPRESSINGLY NOTEWORTHY.
nod
Actually...
...PHYSICALLY HURT ME?!
gulp
SOMETHING "DEPRESS-INGLY NOTEWORTHY" THAT WOULD'VE SHOCKED THE WORLD!
IT WAS DONE...
...MR. KATAGIRI DECIDED THAT WAS BEST.
THE FUWA FAMILY TOOK YOU IN BECAUSE...

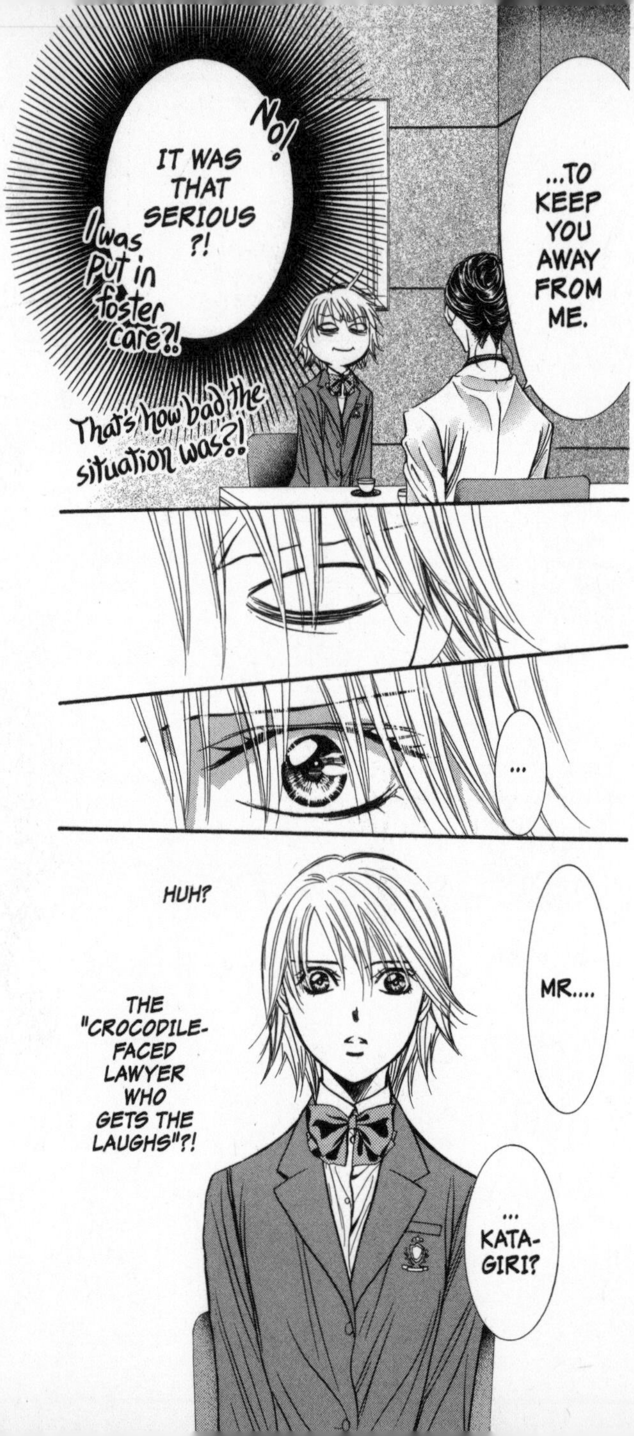
...TO KEEP YOU AWAY FROM ME.
No!
IT WAS THAT SERIOUS?!
I was put in foster care?!
That's how bad the situation was?!
...
MR....
...KATA-GIRI?
HUH?
THE "CROCODILE-FACED LAWYER WHO GETS THE LAUGHS"?!

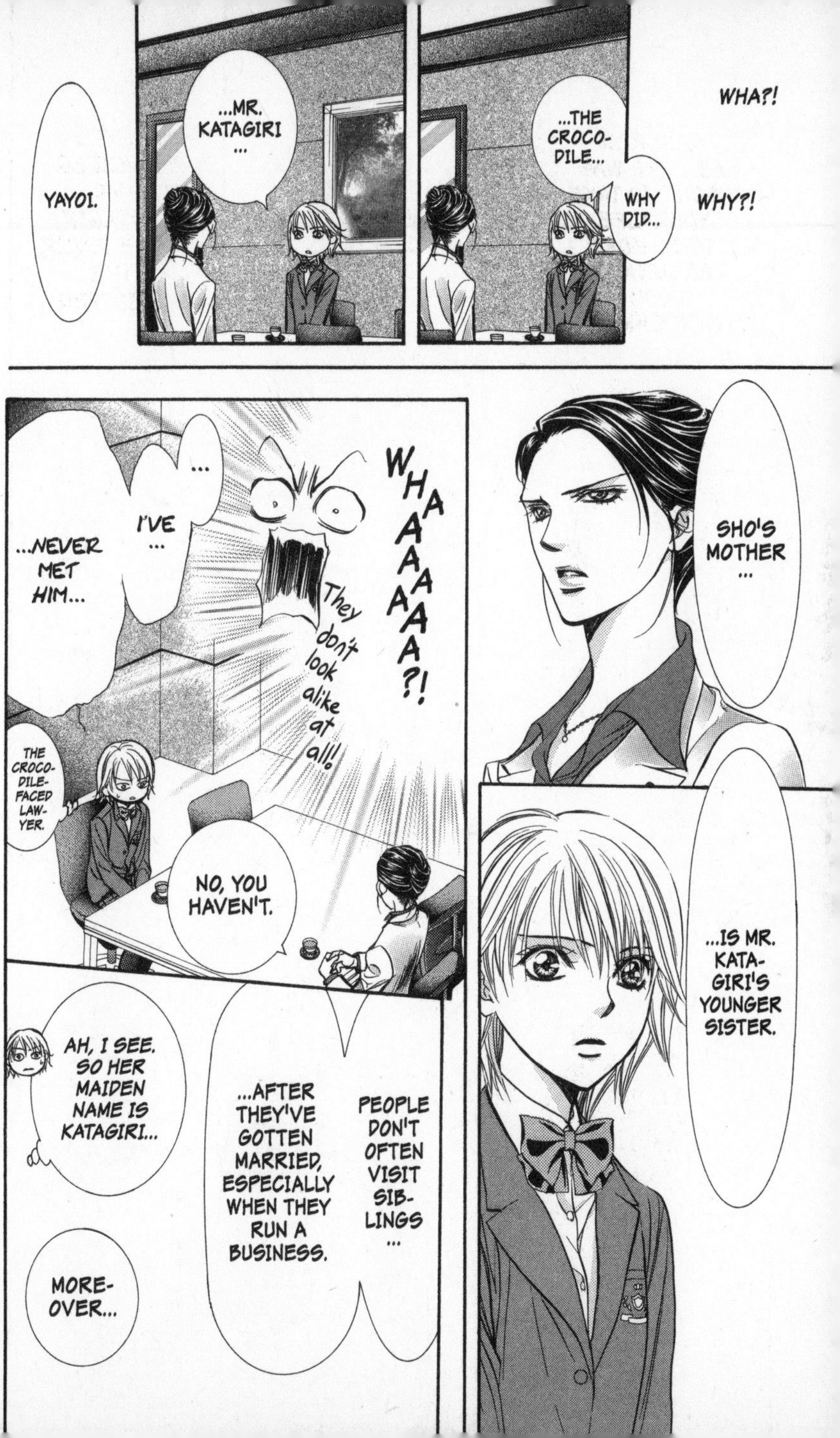

WHA?!
WHY?!
...THE CROCO-DILE...
WHY DID...
...MR. KATAGIRI...
YAYOI.
SHO'S MOTHER...
...IS MR. KATA-GIRI'S YOUNGER SISTER.
WHAAAAAAA?!
They don't look alike at all!
...
I'VE...
...NEVER MET HIM...
THE CROCO-DILE-FACED LAW-YER.
NO, YOU HAVEN'T.
PEOPLE DON'T OFTEN VISIT SIB-LINGS...
...AFTER THEY'VE GOTTEN MARRIED, ESPECIALLY WHEN THEY RUN A BUSINESS.
AH, I SEE. SO HER MAIDEN NAME IS KATAGIRI...
MORE-OVER...

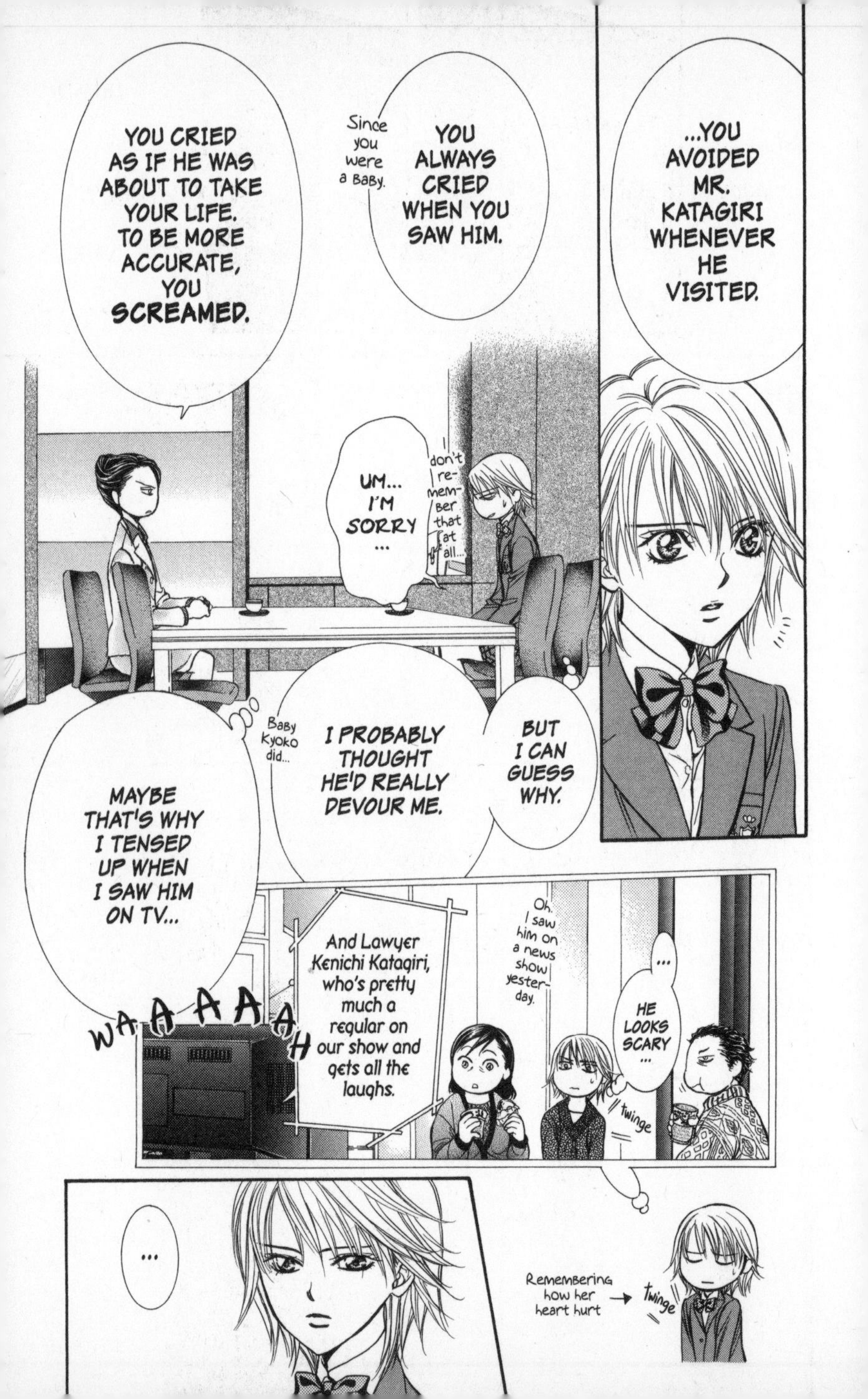
...YOU AVOIDED MR. KATAGIRI WHENEVER HE VISITED.
Since you were a Baby.
YOU ALWAYS CRIED WHEN YOU SAW HIM.
YOU CRIED AS IF HE WAS ABOUT TO TAKE YOUR LIFE. TO BE MORE ACCURATE, YOU SCREAMED.
I don't remember that at all...
UM... I'M SORRY...
BUT I CAN GUESS WHY.
Baby Kyoko did...
I PROBABLY THOUGHT HE'D REALLY DEVOUR ME.
MAYBE THAT'S WHY I TENSED UP WHEN I SAW HIM ON TV...
Oh. I saw him on a news show yester-day.
...
HE LOOKS SCARY...
twinge
And Lawyer Kenichi Katagiri, who's pretty much a regular on our show and gets all the laughs.
WAAAAAH
Remembering how her heart hurt → twinge
...

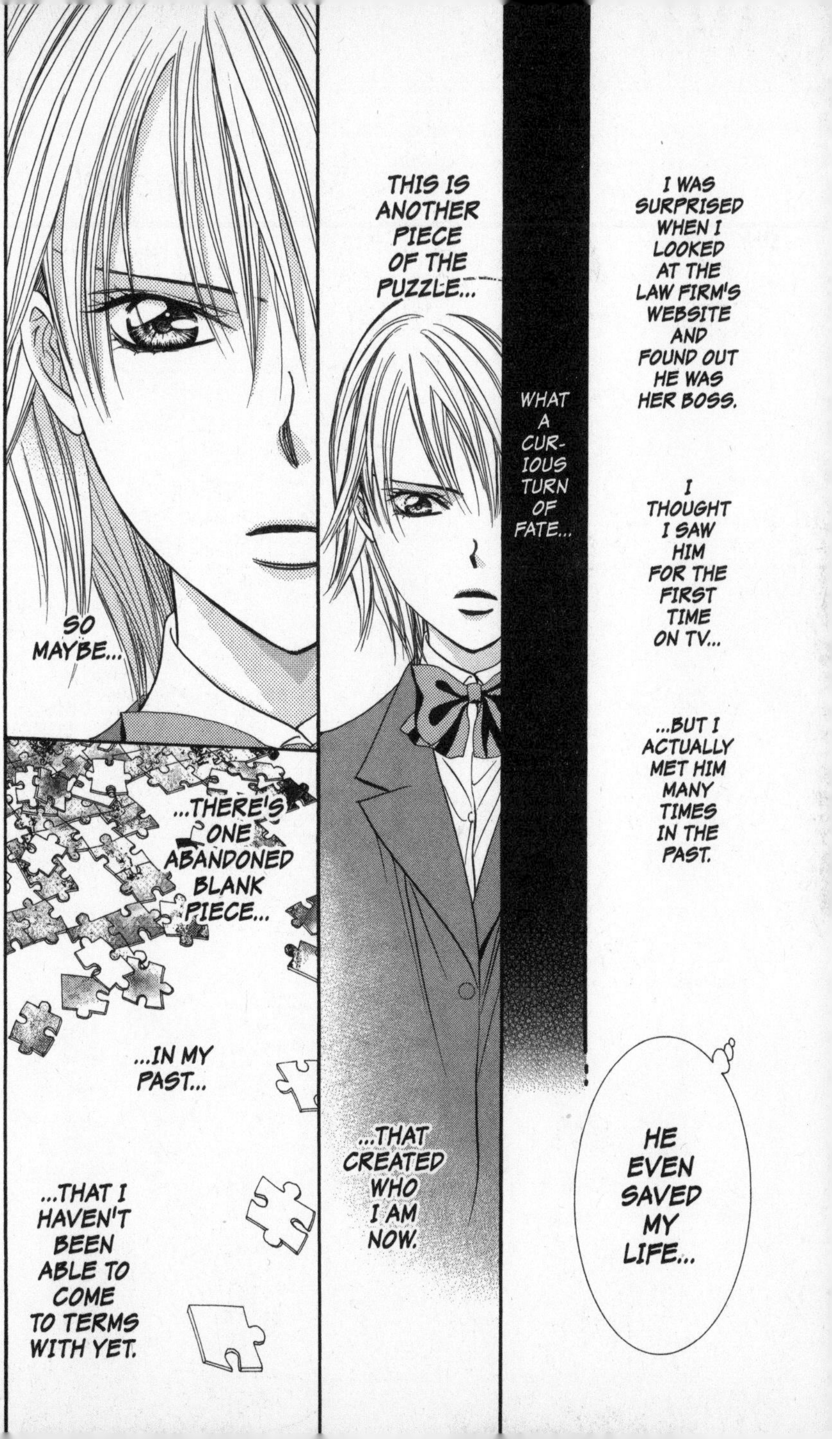
I WAS SURPRISED WHEN I LOOKED AT THE LAW FIRM'S WEBSITE AND FOUND OUT HE WAS HER BOSS.
I THOUGHT I SAW HIM FOR THE FIRST TIME ON TV...
...BUT I ACTUALLY MET HIM MANY TIMES IN THE PAST.
HE EVEN SAVED MY LIFE...
WHAT A CURIOUS TURN OF FATE...
THIS IS ANOTHER PIECE OF THE PUZZLE...
...THAT CREATED WHO I AM NOW.
SO MAYBE...
...THERE'S ONE ABANDONED BLANK PIECE...
...IN MY PAST...
...THAT I HAVEN'T BEEN ABLE TO COME TO TERMS WITH YET.

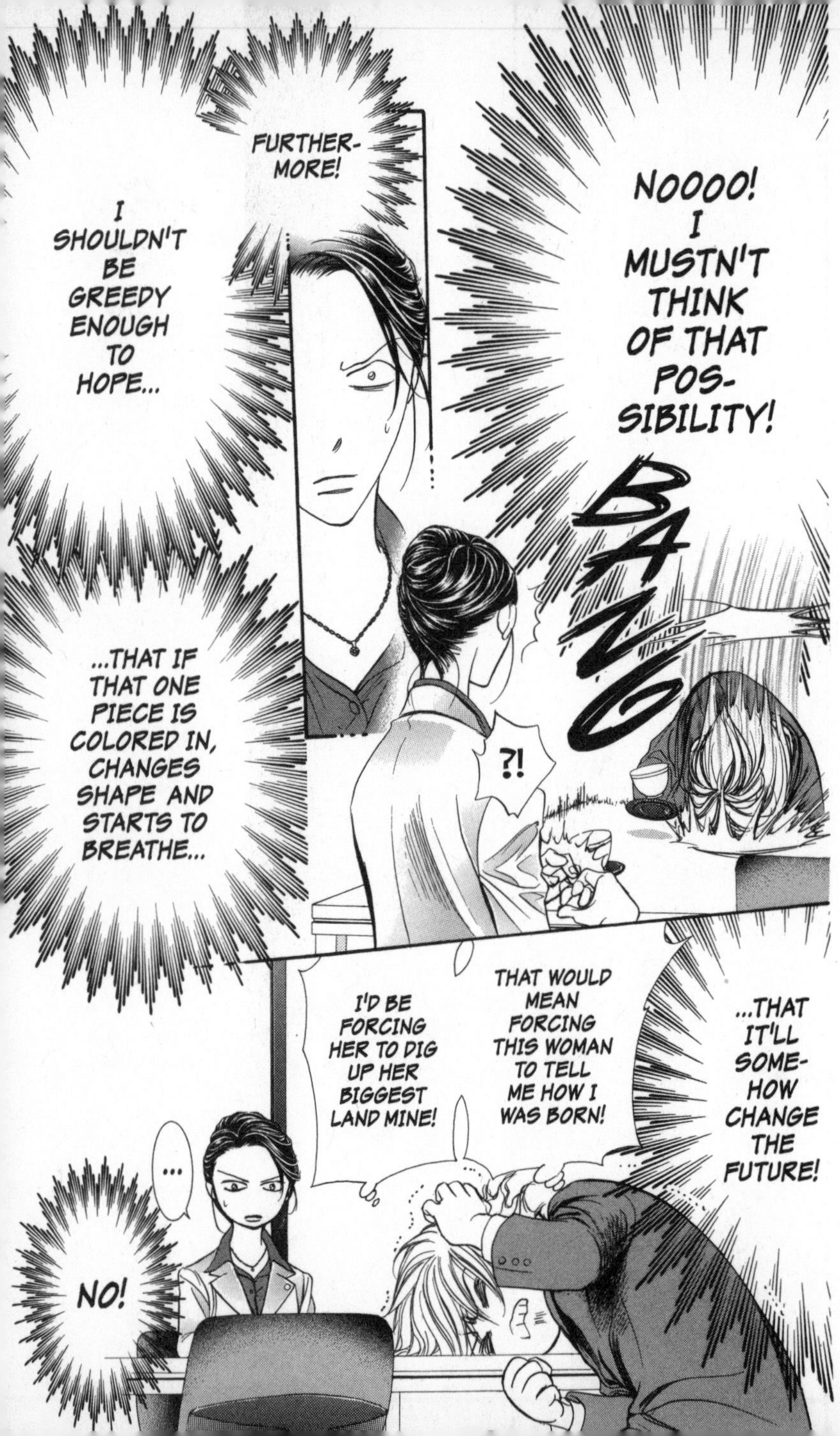
FURTHER-MORE!
I SHOULDN'T BE GREEDY ENOUGH TO HOPE...
...THAT IF THAT ONE PIECE IS COLORED IN, CHANGES SHAPE AND STARTS TO BREATHE...
...THAT IT'LL SOMEHOW CHANGE THE FUTURE!
NOOOO! I MUSTN'T THINK OF THAT POS-SIBILITY!
BANG
?!
THAT WOULD MEAN FORCING THIS WOMAN TO TELL ME HOW I WAS BORN!
I'D BE FORCING HER TO DIG UP HER BIGGEST LAND MINE!
...
NO!

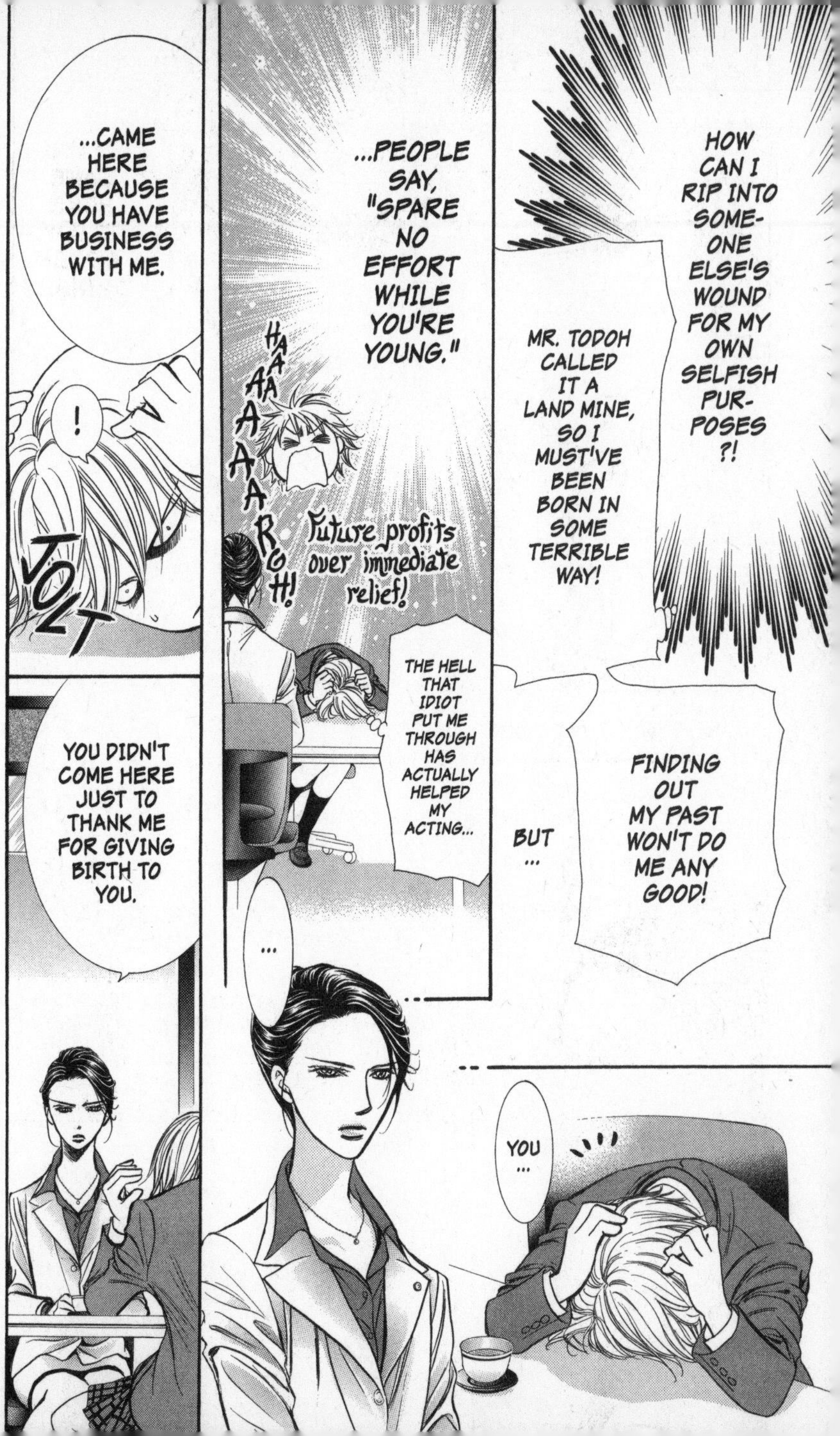
HOW CAN I RIP INTO SOME-ONE ELSE'S WOUND FOR MY OWN SELFISH PUR-POSES ?!
MR. TODOH CALLED IT A LAND MINE, SO I MUST'VE BEEN BORN IN SOME TERRIBLE WAY!
FINDING OUT MY PAST WON'T DO ME ANY GOOD!
BUT ...
THE HELL THAT IDIOT PUT ME THROUGH HAS ACTUALLY HELPED MY ACTING...
...PEOPLE SAY, "SPARE NO EFFORT WHILE YOU'RE YOUNG."
HAAAAAAARGH!
Future profits over immediate relief!
...CAME HERE BECAUSE YOU HAVE BUSINESS WITH ME.
!
JOLT
YOU ...
...
YOU DIDN'T COME HERE JUST TO THANK ME FOR GIVING BIRTH TO YOU.

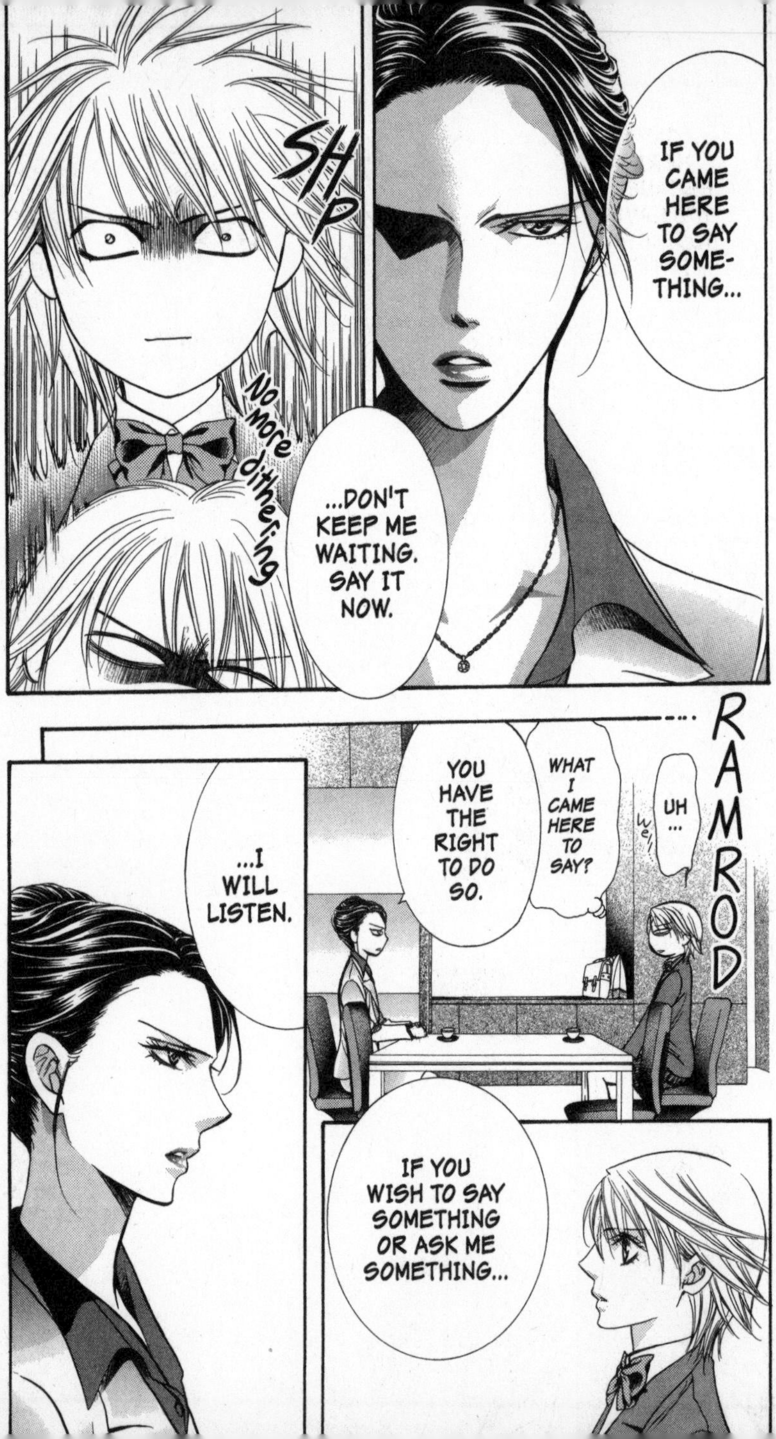
IF YOU CAME HERE TO SAY SOME-THING...
...DON'T KEEP ME WAITING. SAY IT NOW.
SHP
No more dithering
RAMROD
UH ...
Well
WHAT I CAME HERE TO SAY?
YOU HAVE THE RIGHT TO DO SO.
IF YOU WISH TO SAY SOMETHING OR ASK ME SOMETHING...
...I WILL LISTEN.

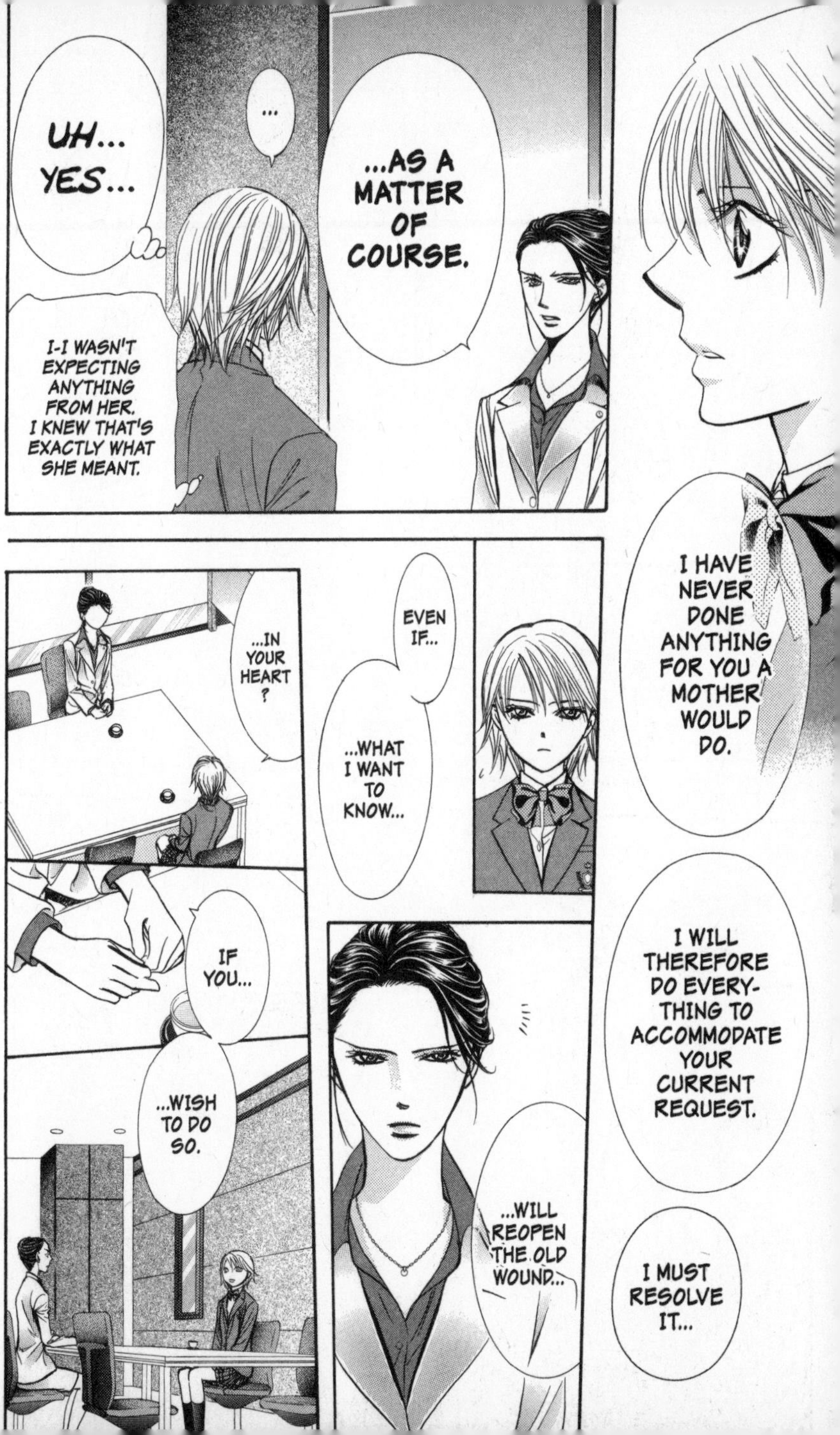
I HAVE NEVER DONE ANYTHING FOR YOU A MOTHER WOULD DO.
I WILL THEREFORE DO EVERY-THING TO ACCOMMODATE YOUR CURRENT REQUEST.
I MUST RESOLVE IT...
...AS A MATTER OF COURSE.
...
UH... YES...
I-I WASN'T EXPECTING ANYTHING FROM HER. I KNEW THAT'S EXACTLY WHAT SHE MEANT.
EVEN IF...
...WHAT I WANT TO KNOW...
...IN YOUR HEART?
...WILL REOPEN THE OLD WOUND...
IF YOU...
...WISH TO DO SO.

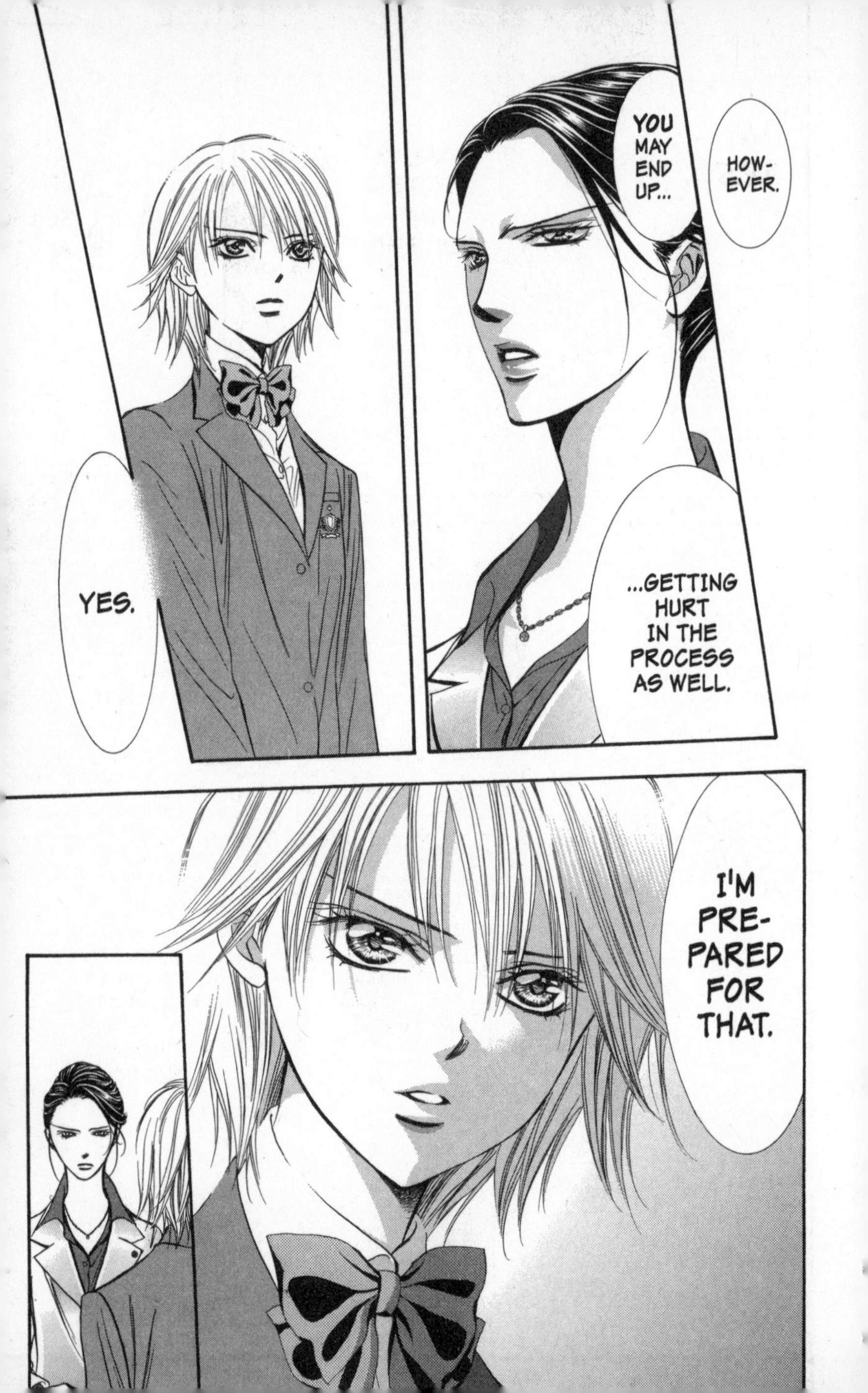
HOW-EVER.
YOU MAY END UP...
...GETTING HURT IN THE PROCESS AS WELL.
YES.
I'M PRE-PARED FOR THAT.

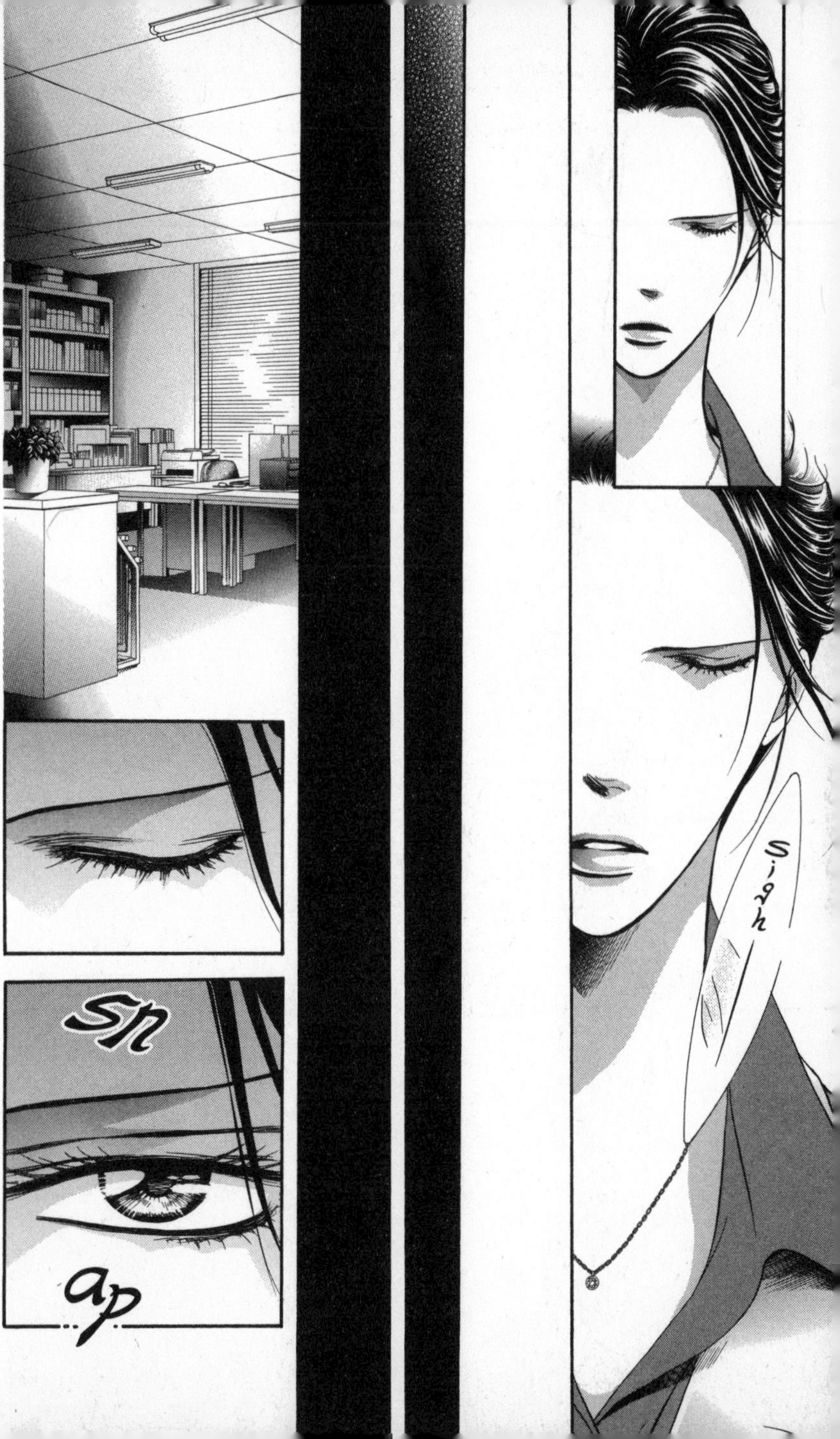
Sigh
Sn
ap

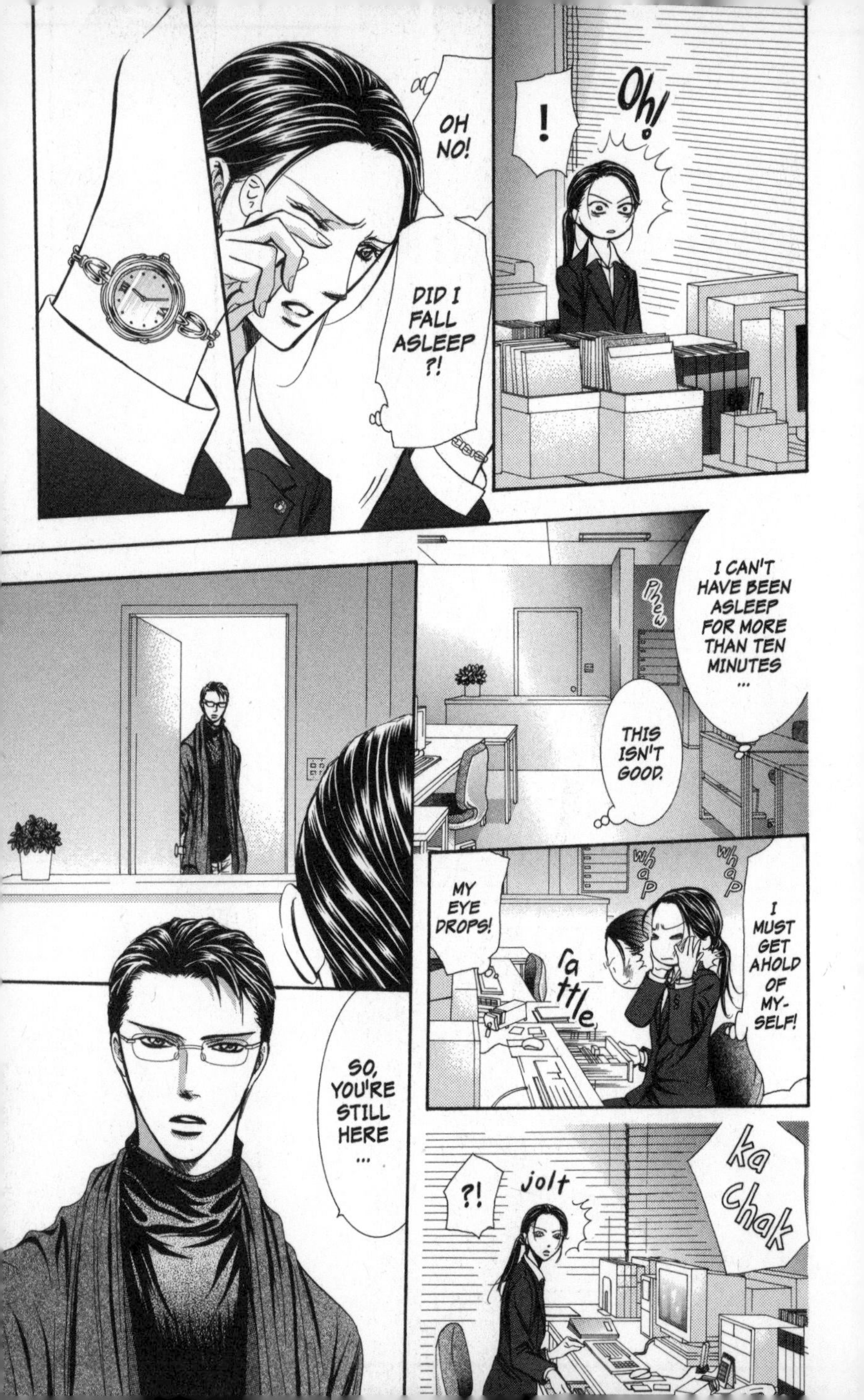

!
Oh!
OH NO!
DID I FALL ASLEEP ?!
I CAN'T HAVE BEEN ASLEEP FOR MORE THAN TEN MINUTES ...
Phew
THIS ISN'T GOOD.
whap
whap
I MUST GET AHOLD OF MY-SELF!
MY EYE DROPS!
rattle
ka chak
jolt
?!
SO, YOU'RE STILL HERE ...

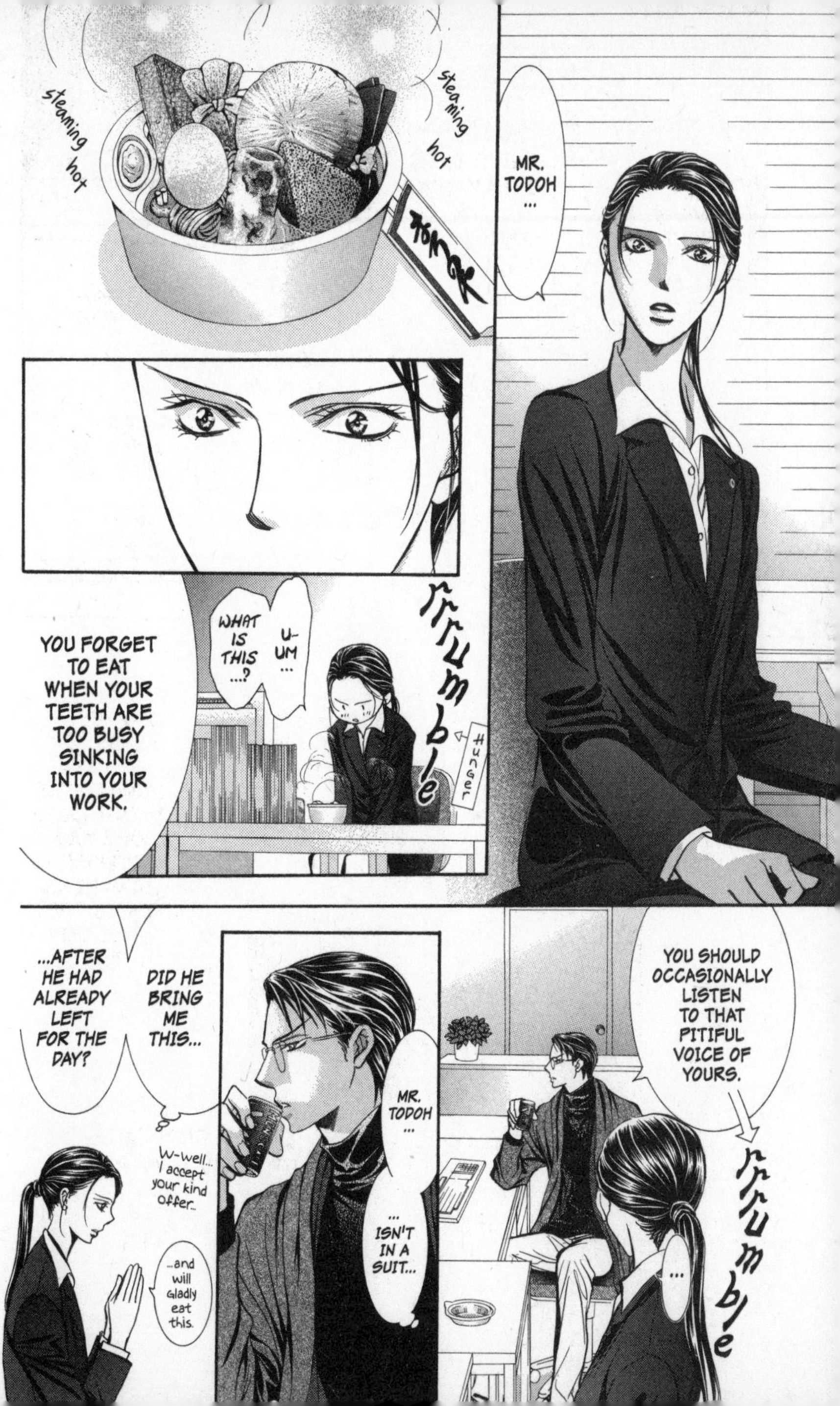
MR. TODOH ...
steaming hot
steaming hot
rrrumble
Hunger
U-UM ...
WHAT IS THIS ...?
YOU FORGET TO EAT WHEN YOUR TEETH ARE TOO BUSY SINKING INTO YOUR WORK.
YOU SHOULD OCCASIONALLY LISTEN TO THAT PITIFUL VOICE OF YOURS.
rrrumble
...
MR. TODOH ...
... ISN'T IN A SUIT...
DID HE BRING ME THIS...
...AFTER HE HAD ALREADY LEFT FOR THE DAY?
W-well... I accept your kind offer..
...and will gladly eat this.

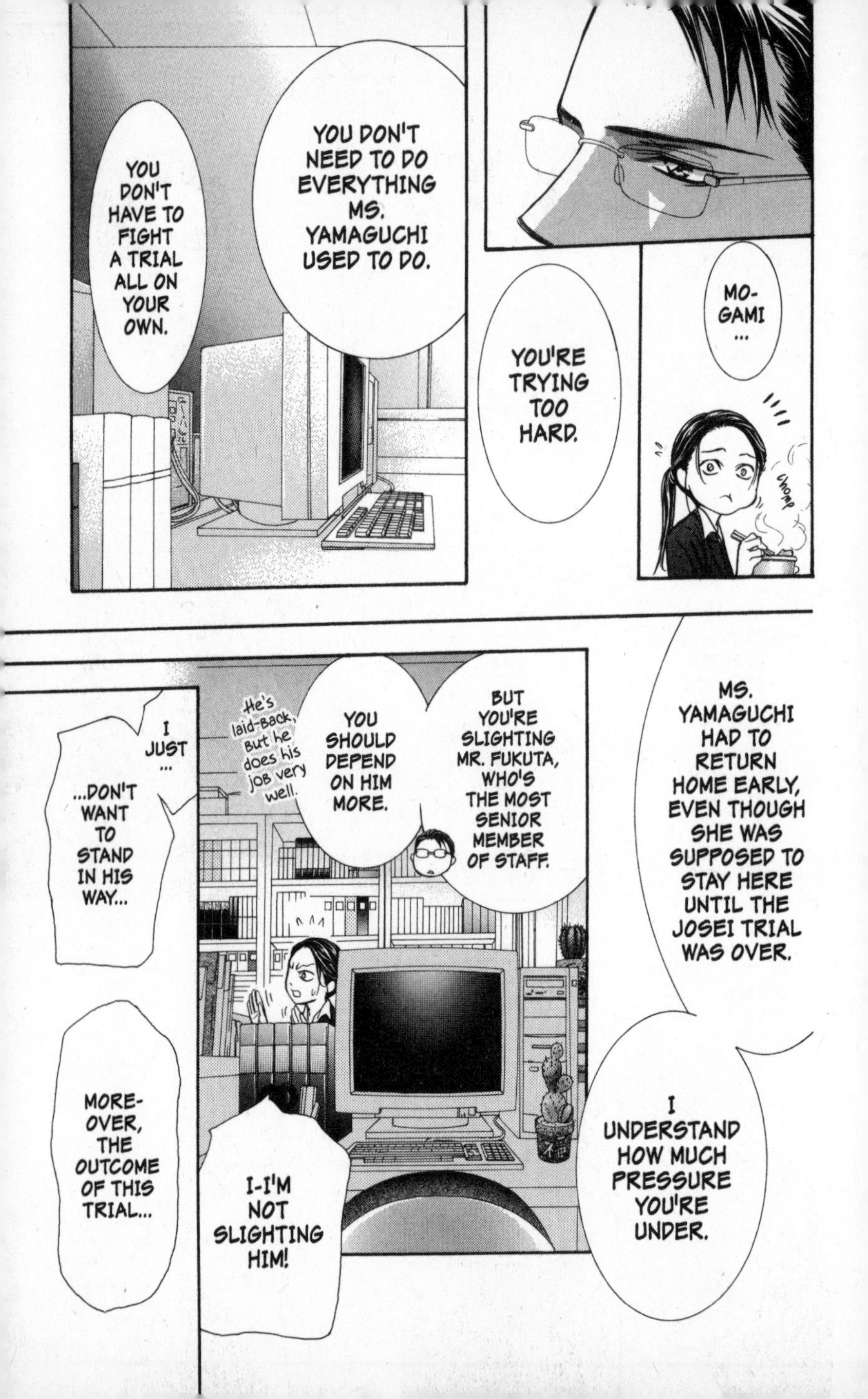
MO-GAMI...
CHOMP
YOU'RE TRYING TOO HARD.
YOU DON'T NEED TO DO EVERYTHING MS. YAMAGUCHI USED TO DO.
YOU DON'T HAVE TO FIGHT A TRIAL ALL ON YOUR OWN.
MS. YAMAGUCHI HAD TO RETURN HOME EARLY, EVEN THOUGH SHE WAS SUPPOSED TO STAY HERE UNTIL THE JOSEI TRIAL WAS OVER.
I UNDERSTAND HOW MUCH PRESSURE YOU'RE UNDER.
BUT YOU'RE SLIGHTING MR. FUKUTA, WHO'S THE MOST SENIOR MEMBER OF STAFF.
YOU SHOULD DEPEND ON HIM MORE.
He's laid-back, but he does his job very well.
I-I'M NOT SLIGHTING HIM!
I JUST...
...DON'T WANT TO STAND IN HIS WAY...
MORE-OVER, THE OUTCOME OF THIS TRIAL...

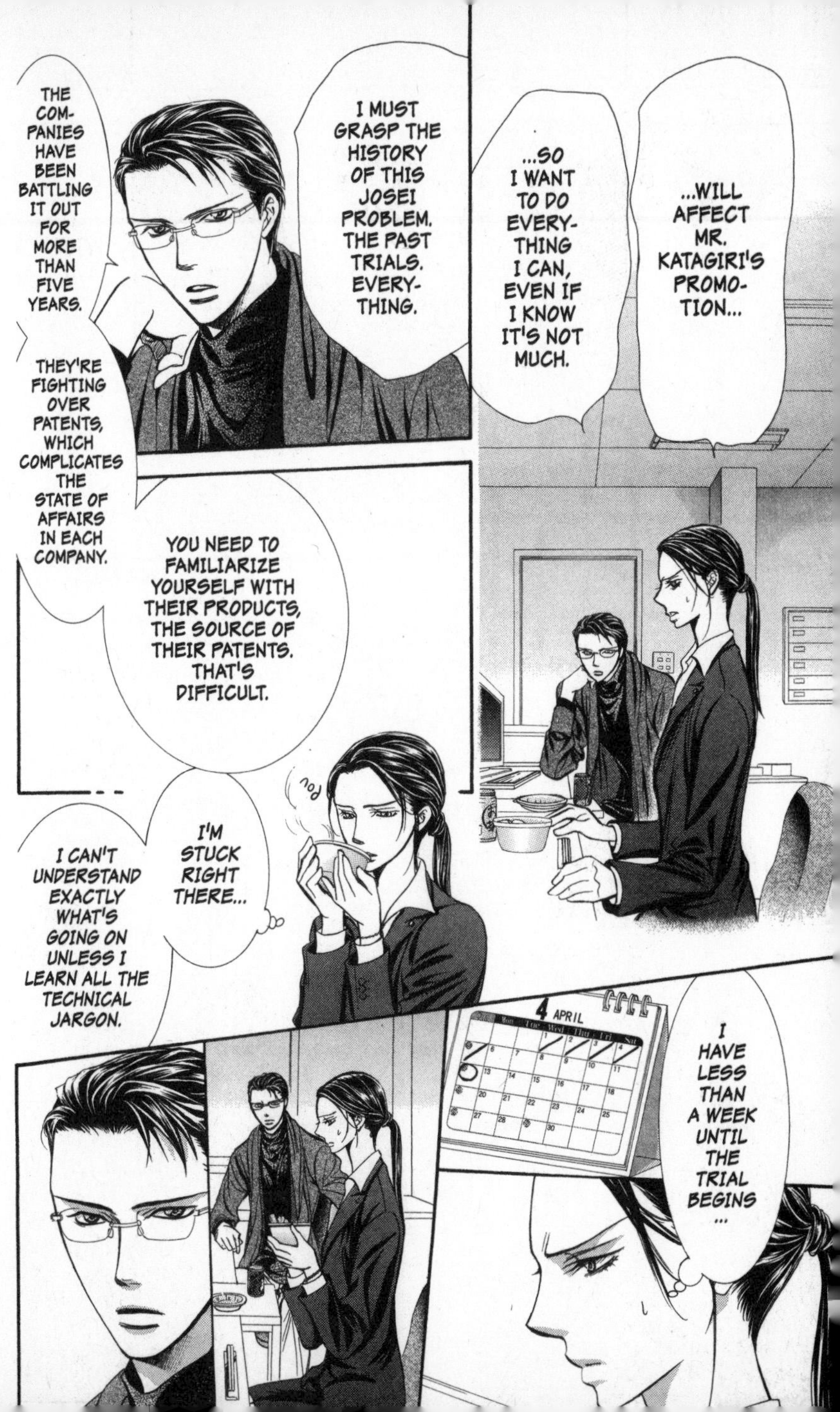
...WILL AFFECT MR. KATAGIRI'S PROMOTION...
...SO I WANT TO DO EVERYTHING I CAN, EVEN IF I KNOW IT'S NOT MUCH.
I MUST GRASP THE HISTORY OF THIS JOSEI PROBLEM. THE PAST TRIALS. EVERYTHING.
THE COMPANIES HAVE BEEN BATTLING IT OUT FOR MORE THAN FIVE YEARS.
THEY'RE FIGHTING OVER PATENTS, WHICH COMPLICATES THE STATE OF AFFAIRS IN EACH COMPANY.
YOU NEED TO FAMILIARIZE YOURSELF WITH THEIR PRODUCTS, THE SOURCE OF THEIR PATENTS. THAT'S DIFFICULT.
Pou
I'M STUCK RIGHT THERE...
I CAN'T UNDERSTAND EXACTLY WHAT'S GOING ON UNLESS I LEARN ALL THE TECHNICAL JARGON.
4 APRIL
I HAVE LESS THAN A WEEK UNTIL THE TRIAL BEGINS...

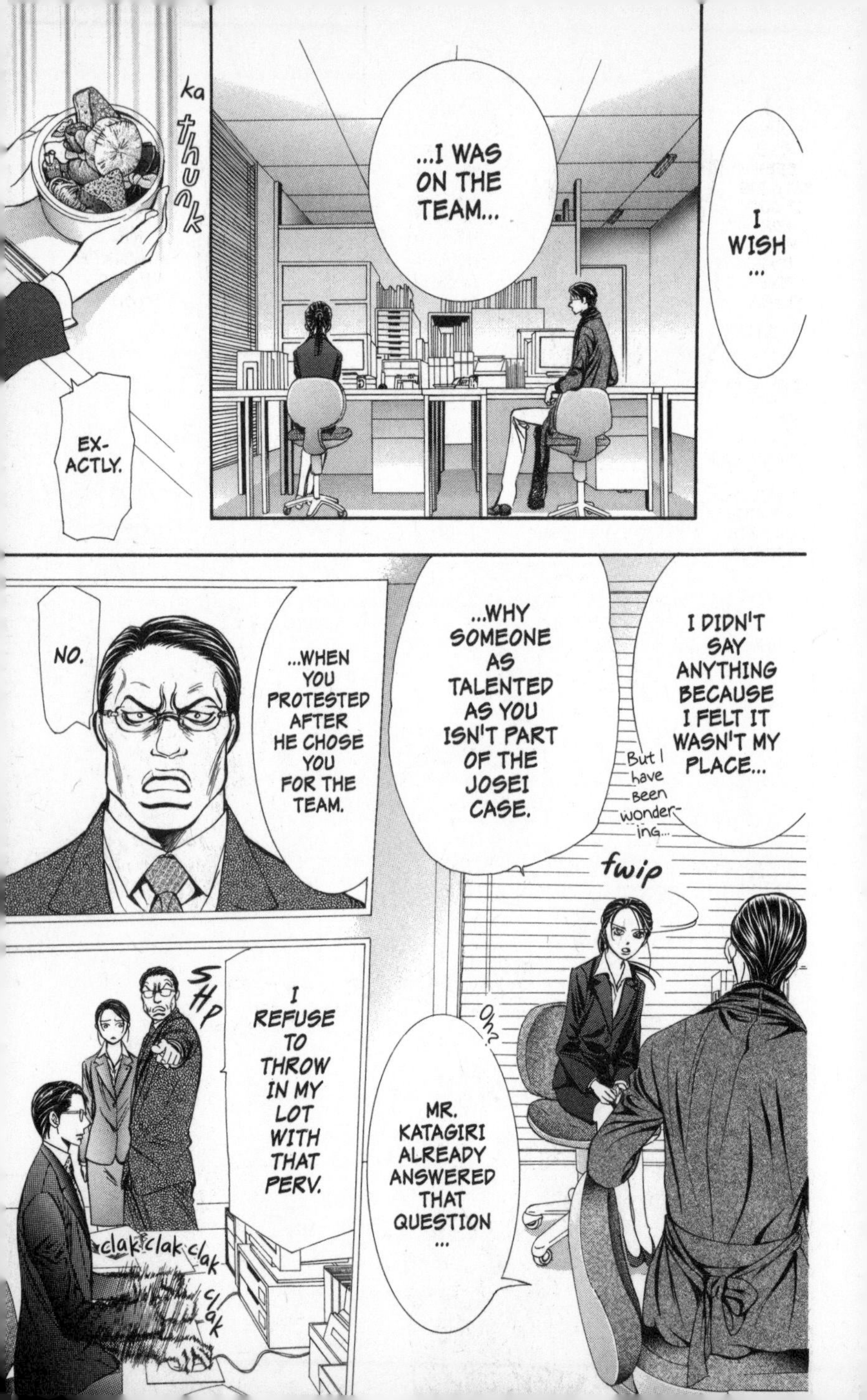
I WISH ...
...I WAS ON THE TEAM...
ka thunk
EX-ACTLY.
I DIDN'T SAY ANYTHING BECAUSE I FELT IT WASN'T MY PLACE...
But I have been wondering...
...WHY SOMEONE AS TALENTED AS YOU ISN'T PART OF THE JOSEI CASE.
fwip
Oh?
MR. KATAGIRI ALREADY ANSWERED THAT QUESTION ...
...WHEN YOU PROTESTED AFTER HE CHOSE YOU FOR THE TEAM.
NO.
I REFUSE TO THROW IN MY LOT WITH THAT PERV.
SHP
clak clak clak clak

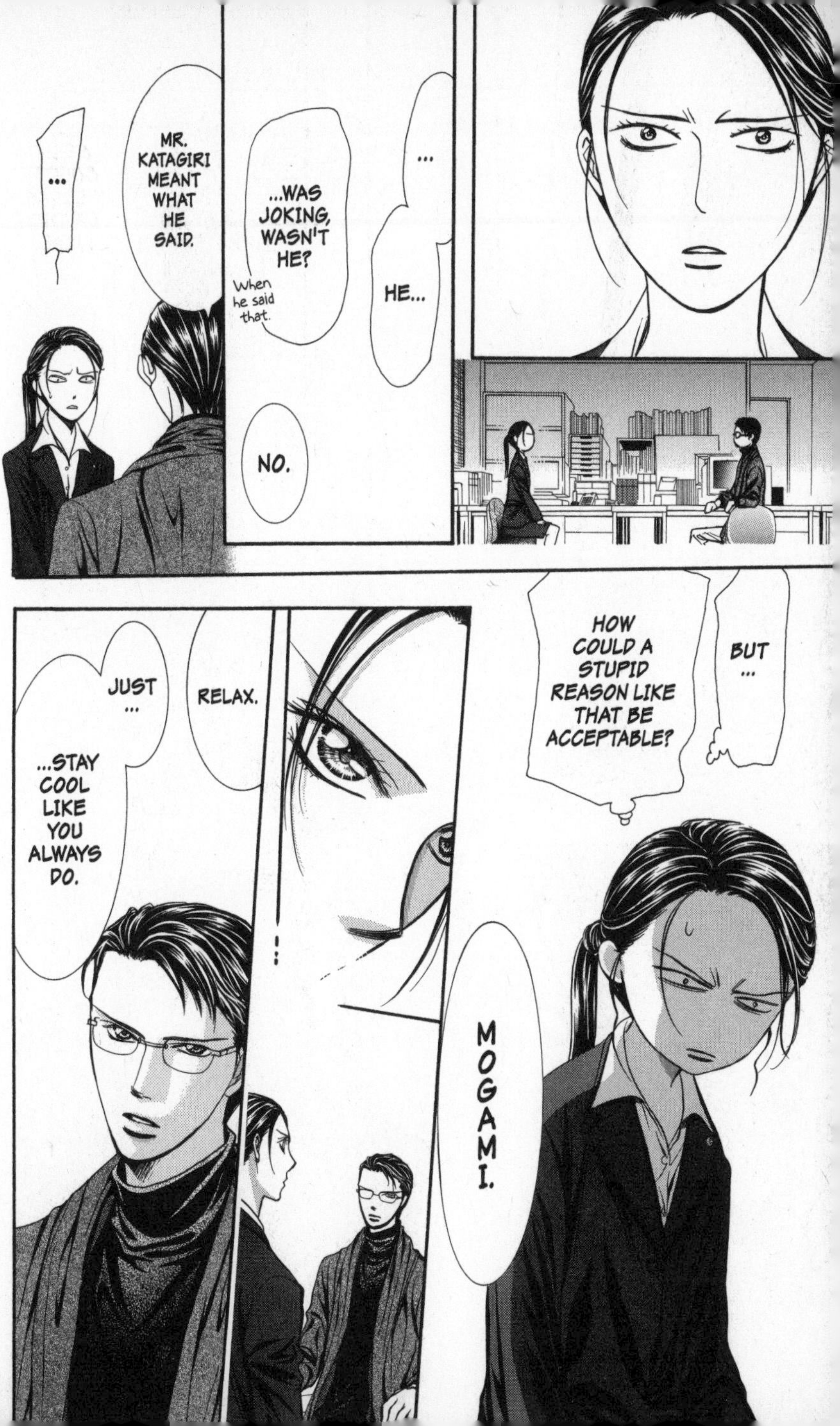
...
HE...
...WAS JOKING, WASN'T HE?
When he said that.
NO.
MR. KATAGIRI MEANT WHAT HE SAID.
...
BUT ...
HOW COULD A STUPID REASON LIKE THAT BE ACCEPTABLE?
MOGAMI.
RELAX.
JUST ...
...STAY COOL LIKE YOU ALWAYS DO.

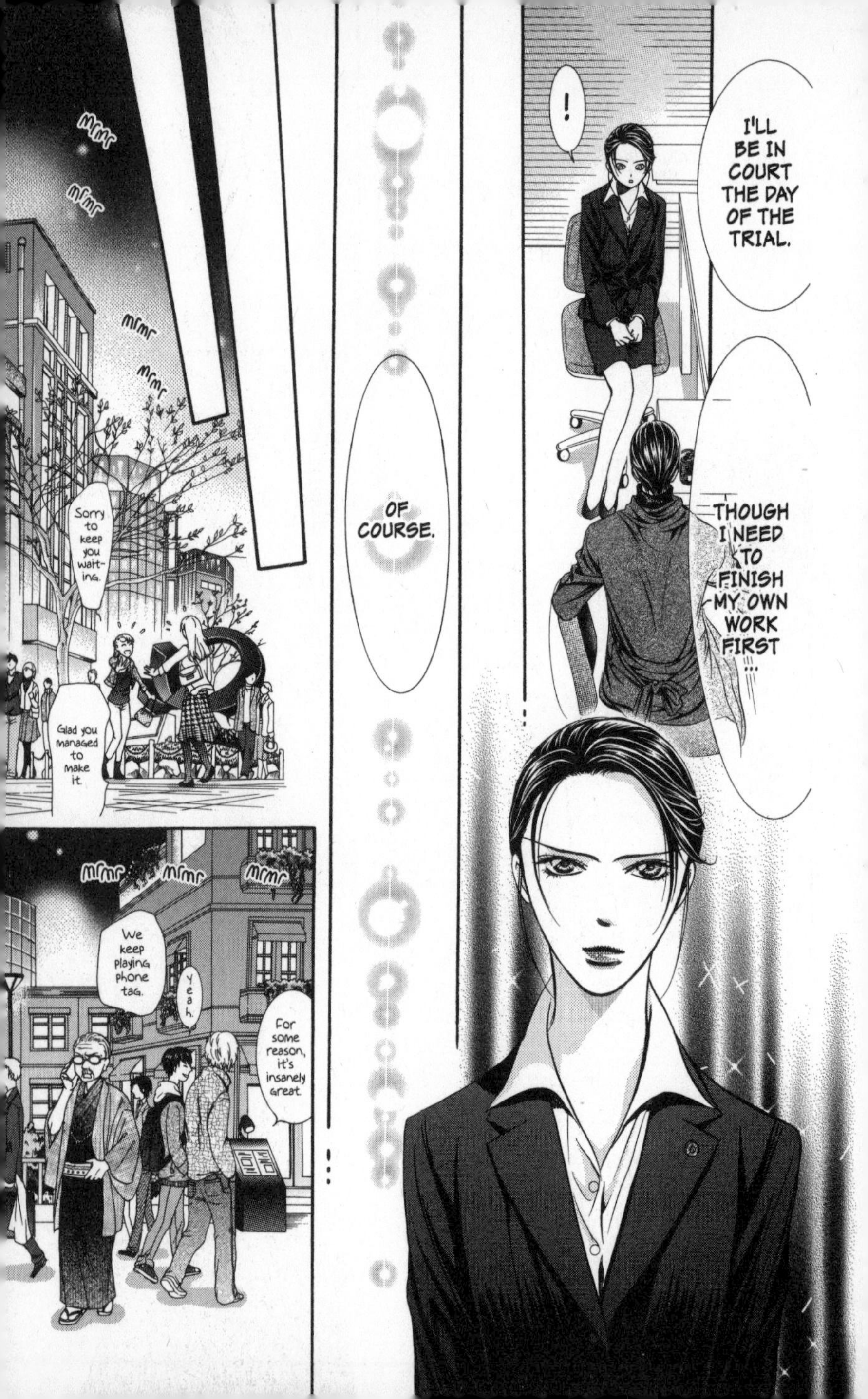
I'LL BE IN COURT THE DAY OF THE TRIAL.
!
THOUGH I NEED TO FINISH MY OWN WORK FIRST...
OF COURSE.
mrmr
mrmr
mrmr
mrmr
Sorry to keep you waiting.
Glad you managed to make it.
mrmr
mrmr
mrmr
We keep playing phone tag.
Yeah.
For some reason, it's insanely great.

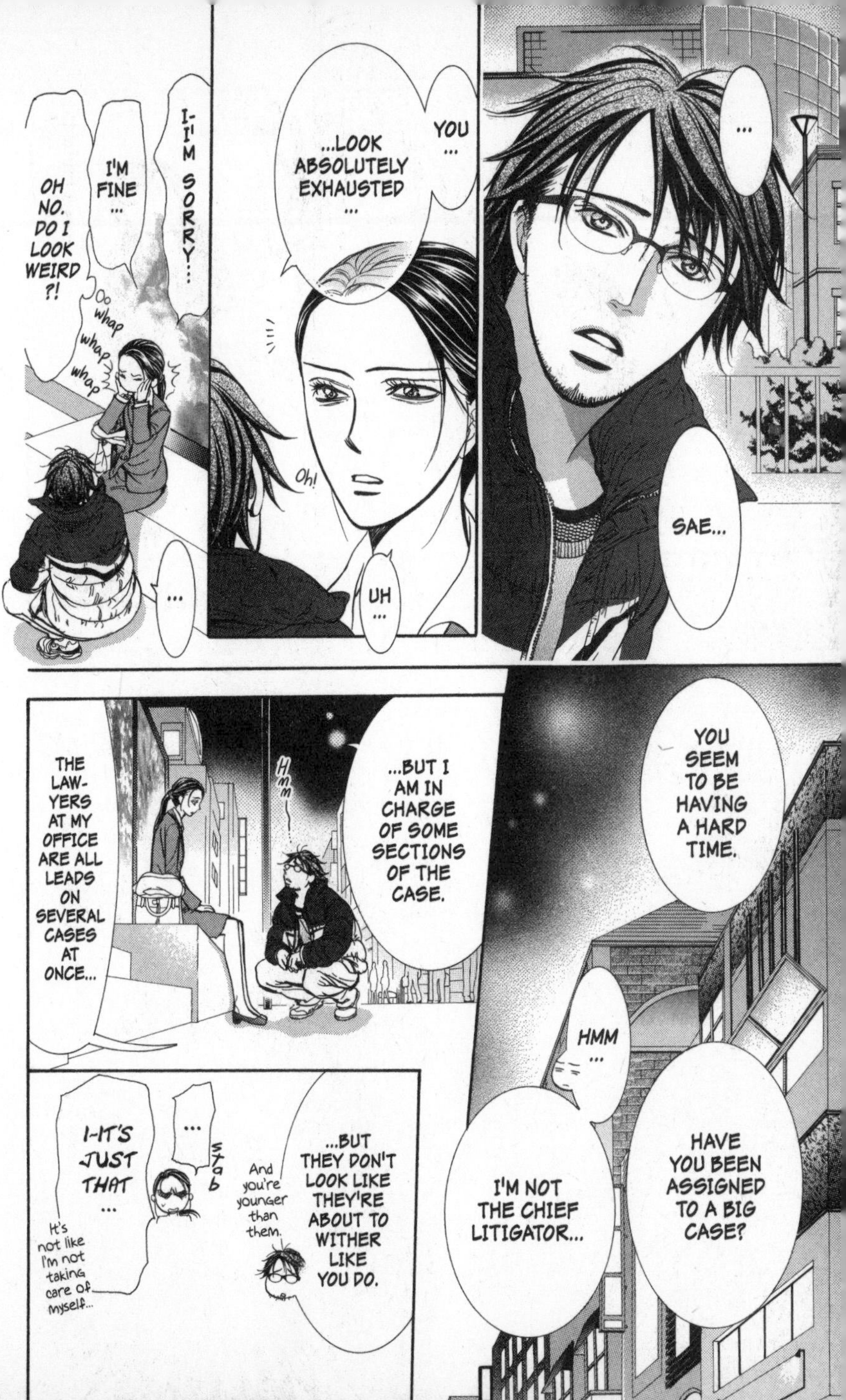
...
SAE...
YOU ...
...LOOK ABSOLUTELY EXHAUSTED ...
Oh!
UH ...
I-I'M SORRY...
I'M FINE ...
OH NO. DO I LOOK WEIRD ?!
Oo whap whap whap
...
YOU SEEM TO BE HAVING A HARD TIME.
HAVE YOU BEEN ASSIGNED TO A BIG CASE?
HMM ...
I'M NOT THE CHIEF LITIGATOR...
...BUT I AM IN CHARGE OF SOME SECTIONS OF THE CASE.
Hmm~
THE LAWYERS AT MY OFFICE ARE ALL LEADS ON SEVERAL CASES AT ONCE...
...BUT THEY DON'T LOOK LIKE THEY'RE ABOUT TO WITHER LIKE YOU DO.
And you're younger than them.
...
stab
I-IT'S JUST THAT ...
It's not like I'm not taking care of myself...

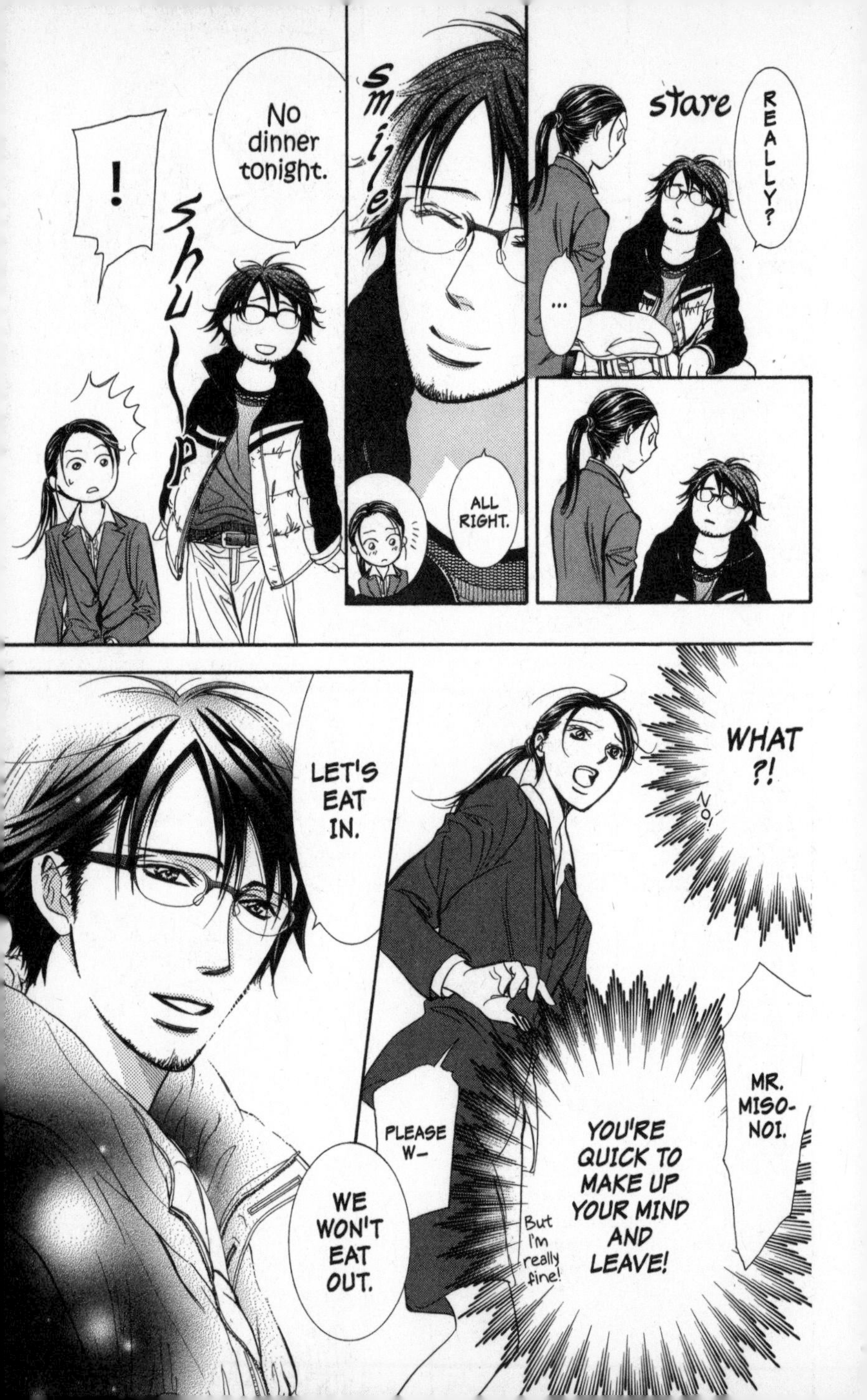

REALLY?
stare
...
smile
ALL RIGHT.
No dinner tonight.
SHU-P
!
WHAT?!
NO!
MR. MISO-NOI.
YOU'RE QUICK TO MAKE UP YOUR MIND AND LEAVE!
But I'm really fine!
PLEASE W—
LET'S EAT IN.
WE WON'T EAT OUT.

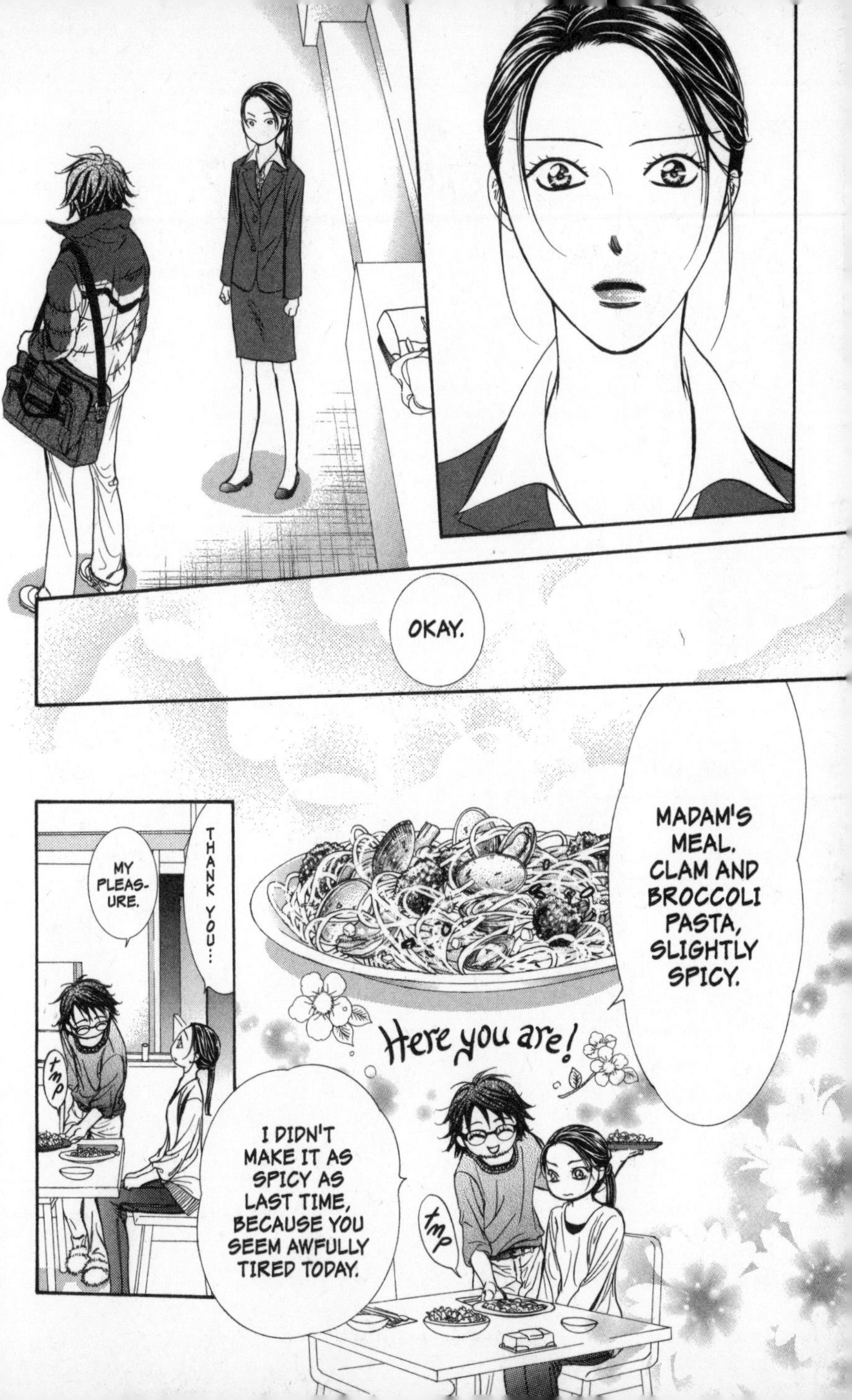
OKAY.
MADAM'S MEAL. CLAM AND BROCCOLI PASTA, SLIGHTLY SPICY.
Here you are!
tmp
I DIDN'T MAKE IT AS SPICY AS LAST TIME, BECAUSE YOU SEEM AWFULLY TIRED TODAY.
THANK YOU...
MY PLEASURE.
tmp

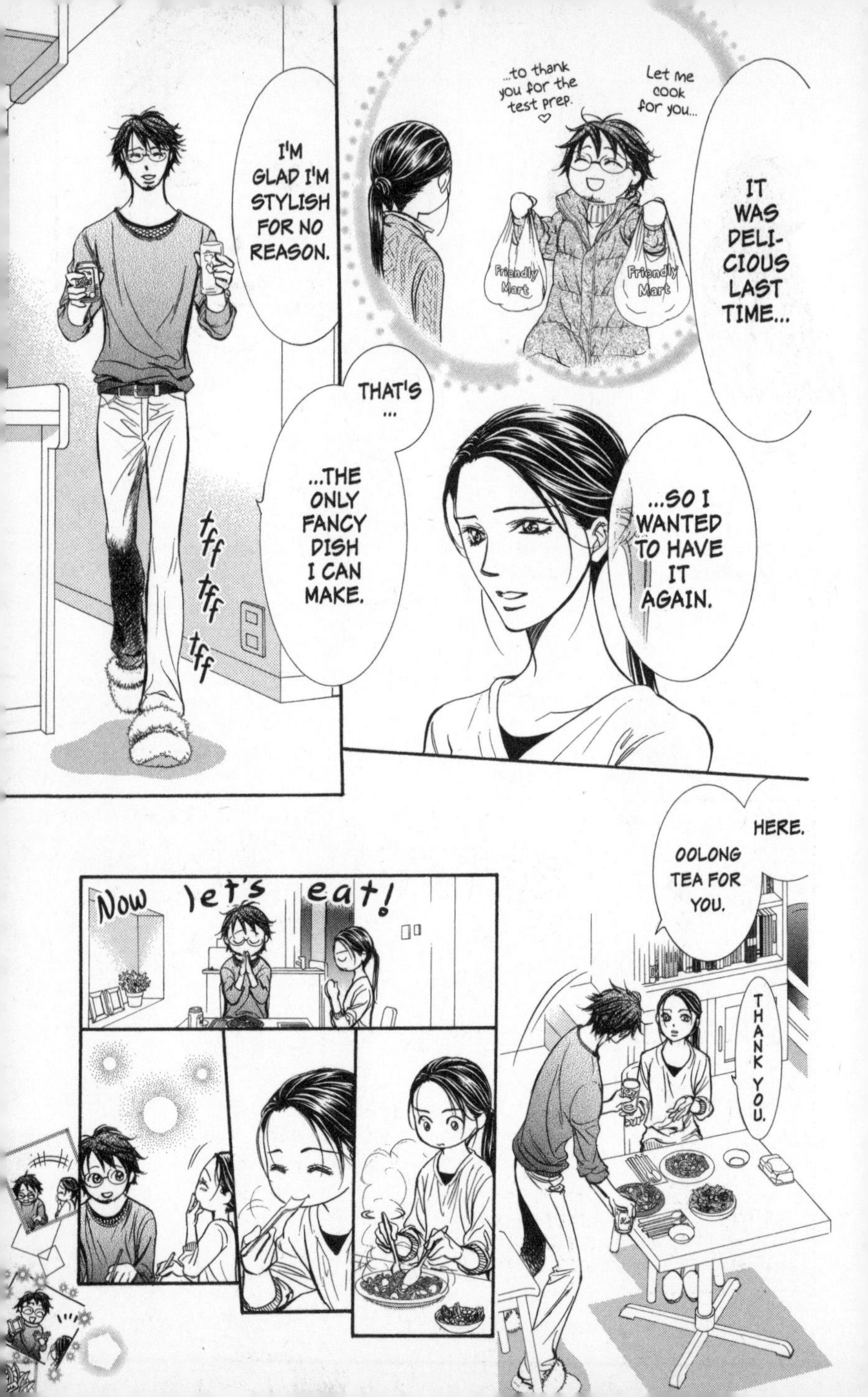
Let me cook for you...
...to thank you for the test prep.
Friendly Mart
Friendly Mart
IT WAS DELICIOUS LAST TIME...
...SO I WANTED TO HAVE IT AGAIN.
THAT'S...
...THE ONLY FANCY DISH I CAN MAKE.
I'M GLAD I'M STYLISH FOR NO REASON.
tff tff tff
HERE. OOLONG TEA FOR YOU.
THANK YOU.
Now let's eat!

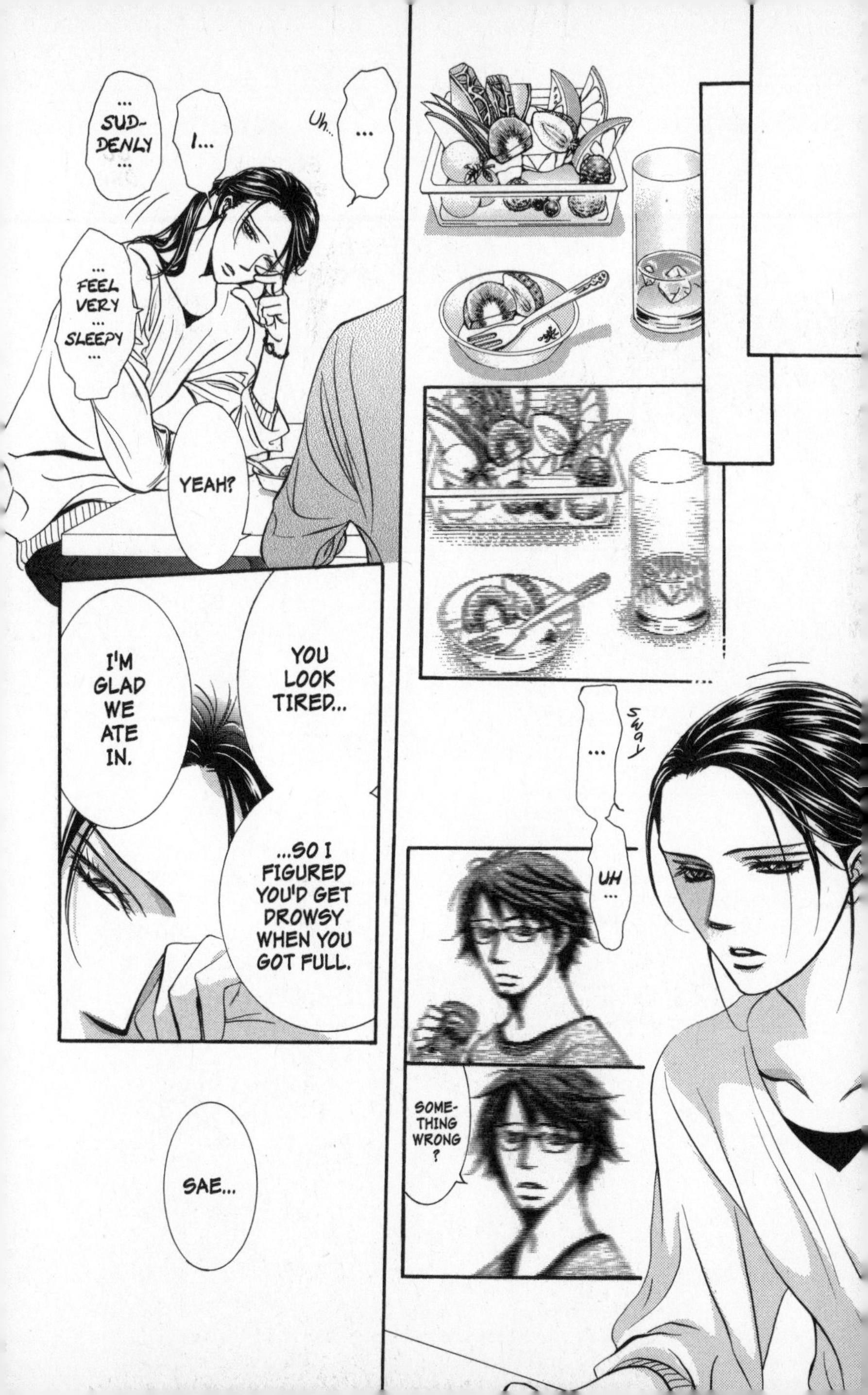
...
SWAY
UH...
SOMETHING WRONG?
Uh... ...
I...
...SUD-DENLY...
...FEEL VERY...SLEEPY...
YEAH?
YOU LOOK TIRED...
...SO I FIGURED YOU'D GET DROWSY WHEN YOU GOT FULL.
I'M GLAD WE ATE IN.
SAE...

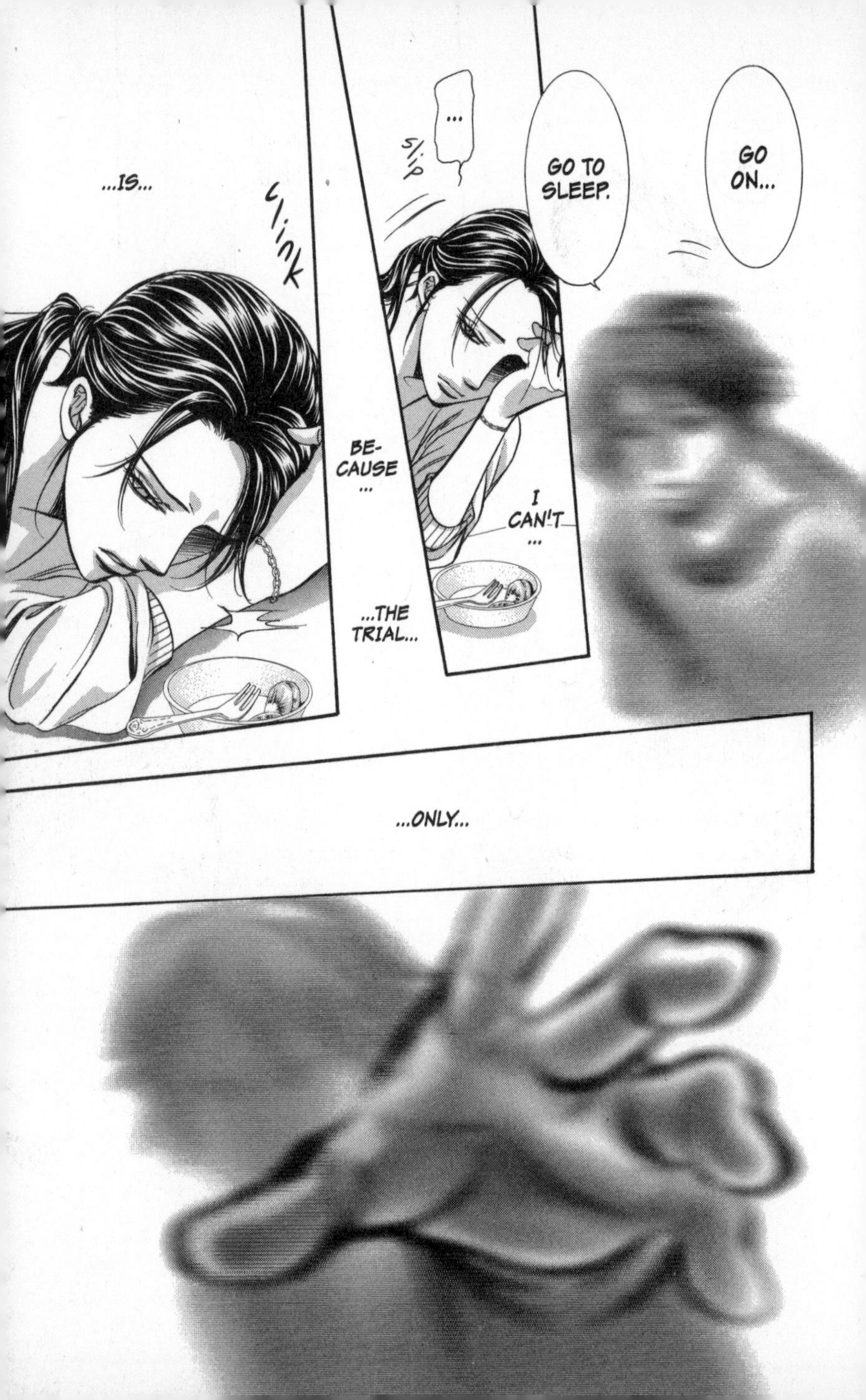
GO ON...
GO TO SLEEP.
...
slip
I CAN'T...
BE-CAUSE...
...THE TRIAL...
...IS...
...ONLY...

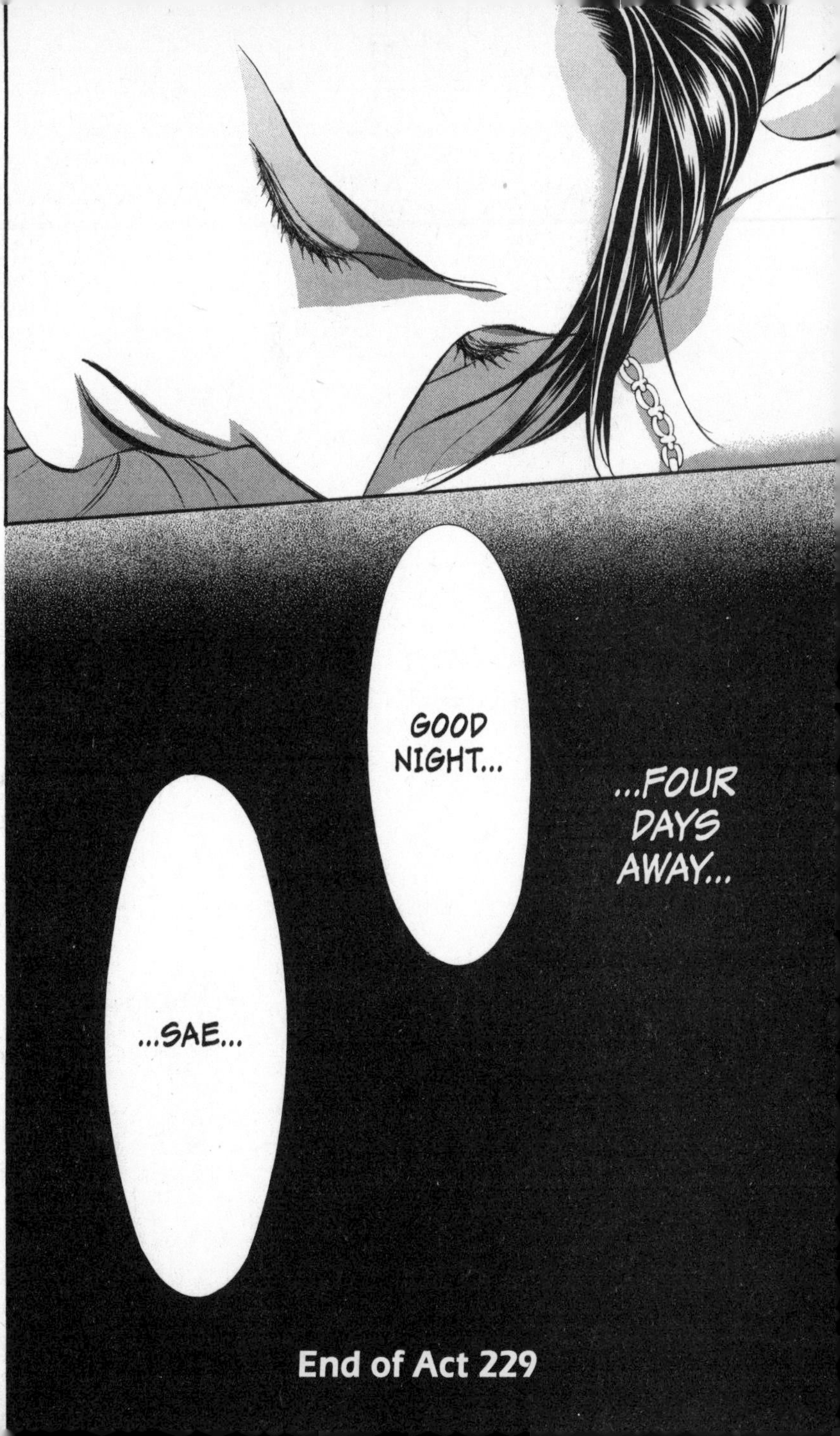
...FOUR DAYS AWAY...
GOOD NIGHT...
...SAE...
End of Act 229

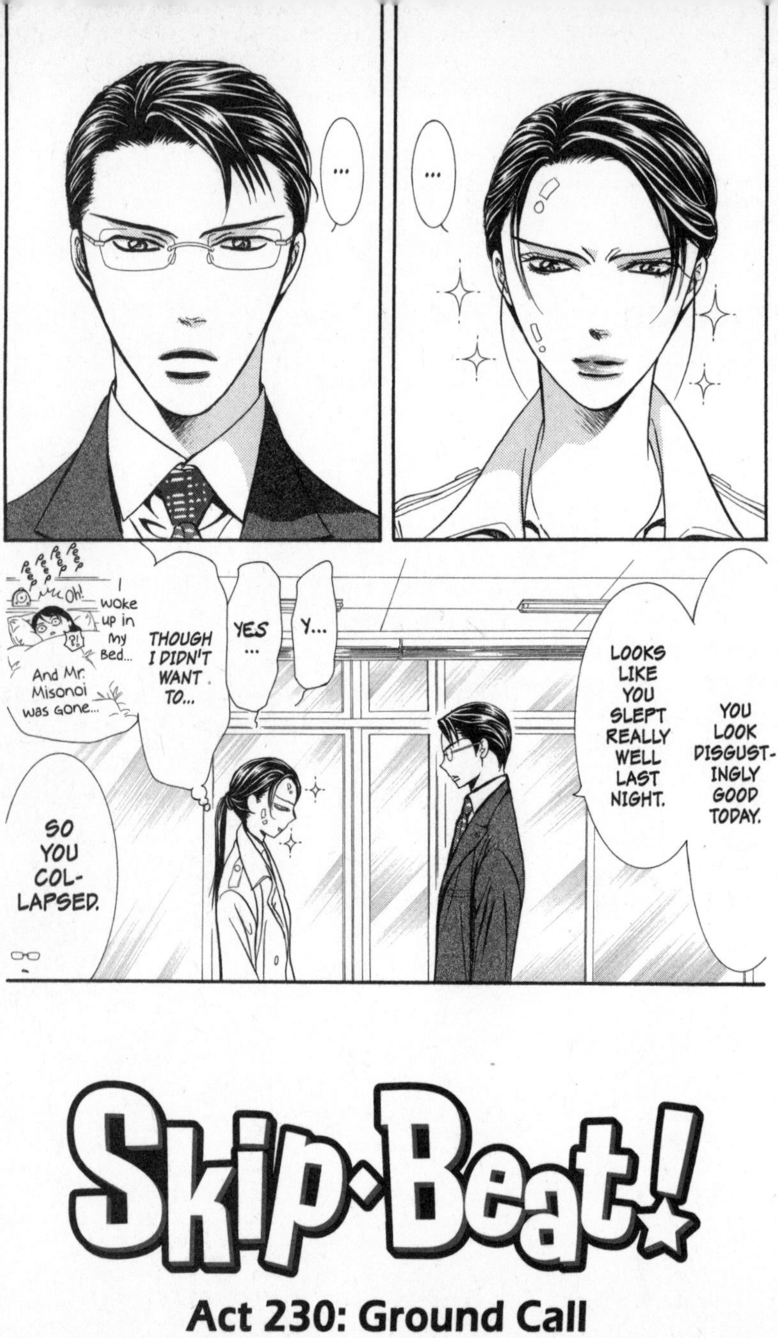
...
...
YOU LOOK DISGUST-INGLY GOOD TODAY.
LOOKS LIKE YOU SLEPT REALLY WELL LAST NIGHT.
Y...
YES...
THOUGH I DIDN'T WANT TO...
Peep Peep Peep Peep Peep
Oh!
?!
I woke up in my bed...
And Mr. Misonoi was gone...
SO YOU COL-LAPSED.

Skip·Beat!

Act 230: Ground Call

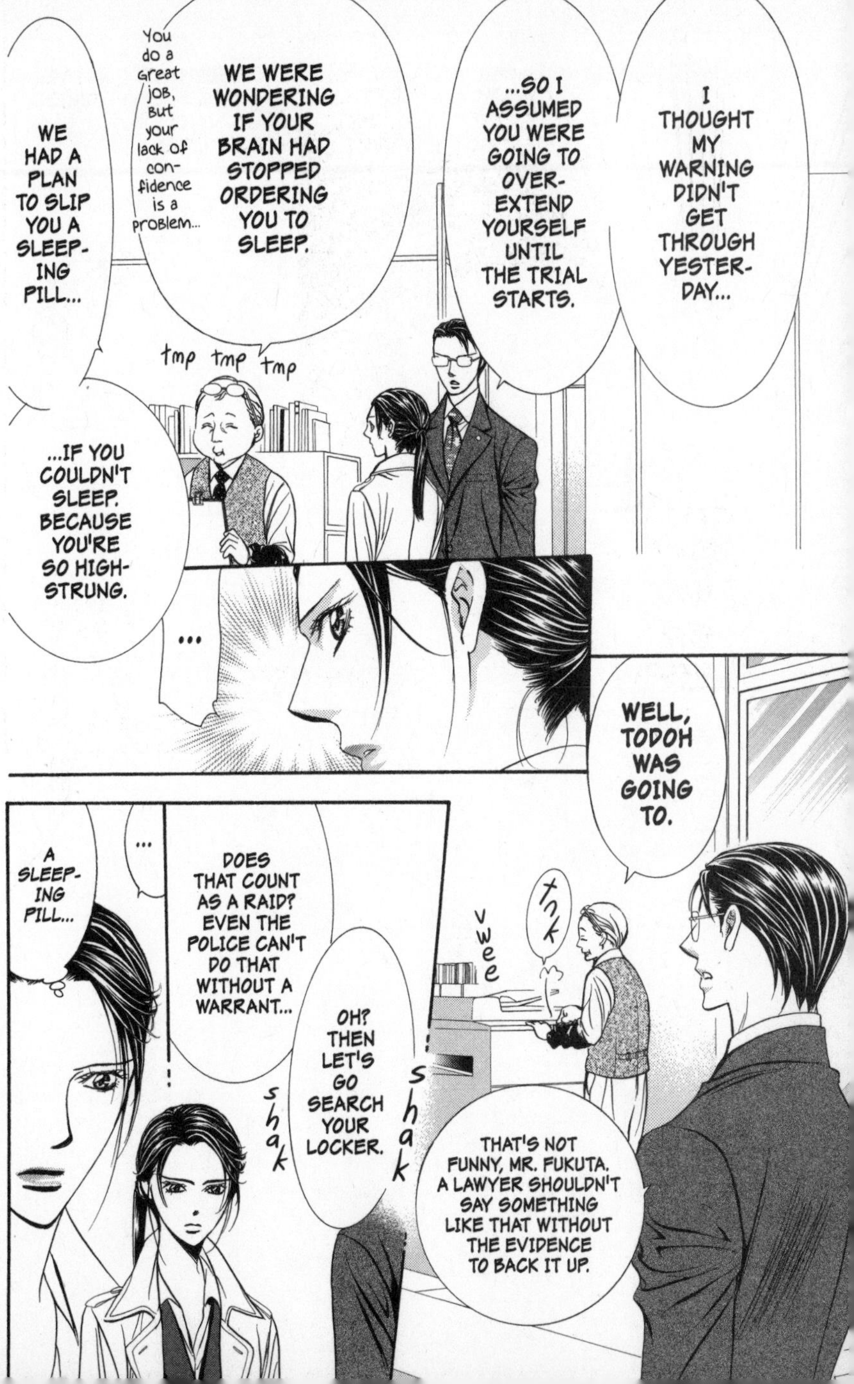

I THOUGHT MY WARNING DIDN'T GET THROUGH YESTERDAY...
...SO I ASSUMED YOU WERE GOING TO OVER-EXTEND YOURSELF UNTIL THE TRIAL STARTS.
WE WERE WONDERING IF YOUR BRAIN HAD STOPPED ORDERING YOU TO SLEEP.
You do a Great job, but your lack of confidence is a problem...
tmp tmp tmp
WE HAD A PLAN TO SLIP YOU A SLEEPING PILL...
...IF YOU COULDN'T SLEEP. BECAUSE YOU'RE SO HIGH-STRUNG.
...
WELL, TODOH WAS GOING TO.
tnk
vwee
THAT'S NOT FUNNY, MR. FUKUTA. A LAWYER SHOULDN'T SAY SOMETHING LIKE THAT WITHOUT THE EVIDENCE TO BACK IT UP.
shak shak
OH? THEN LET'S GO SEARCH YOUR LOCKER.
DOES THAT COUNT AS A RAID? EVEN THE POLICE CAN'T DO THAT WITHOUT A WARRANT...
...
A SLEEPING PILL...

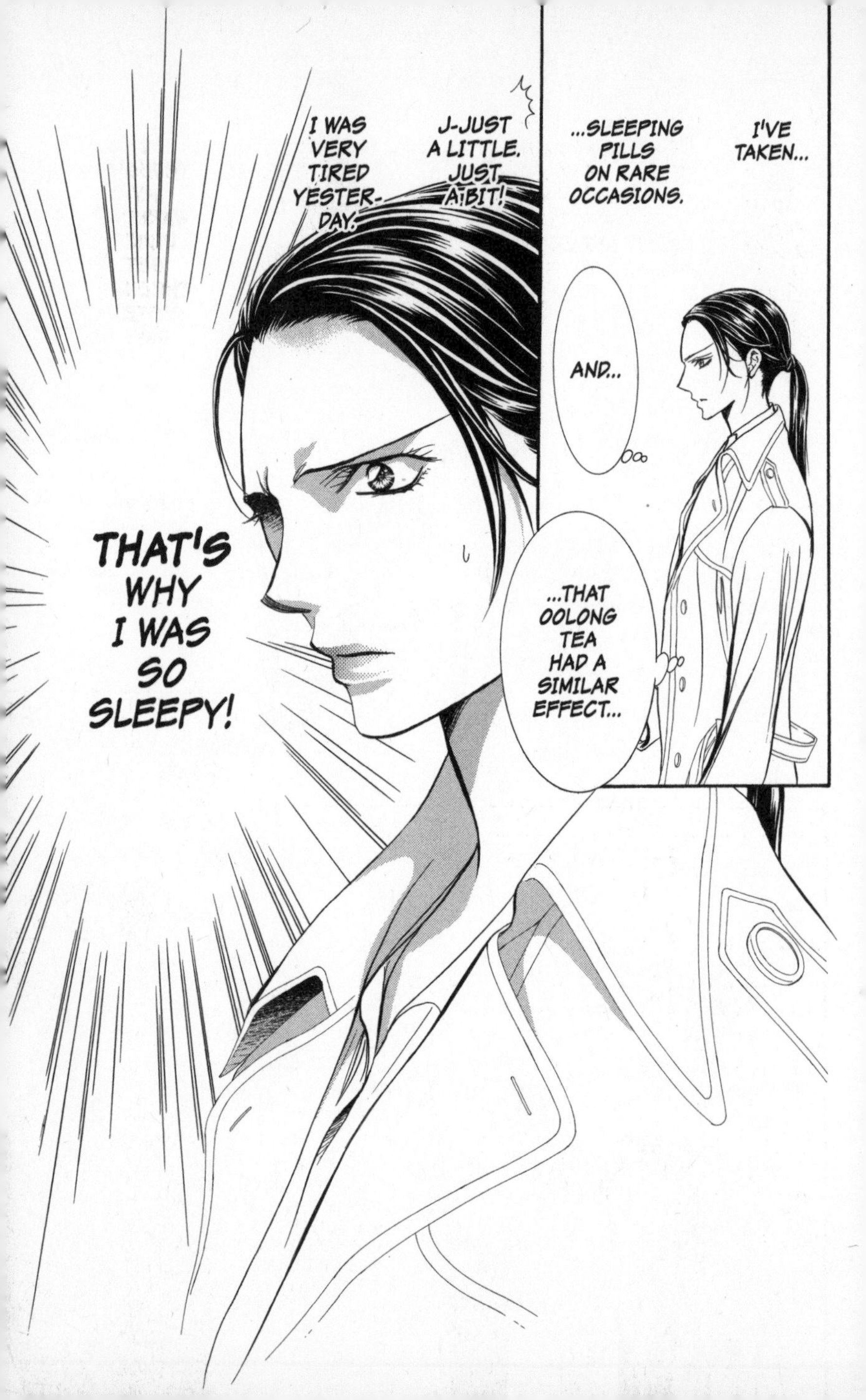
I'VE TAKEN...
...SLEEPING PILLS ON RARE OCCASIONS.
AND...
...THAT OOLONG TEA HAD A SIMILAR EFFECT...
J-JUST A LITTLE. JUST A BIT!
I WAS VERY TIRED YESTER-DAY.
THAT'S WHY I WAS SO SLEEPY!

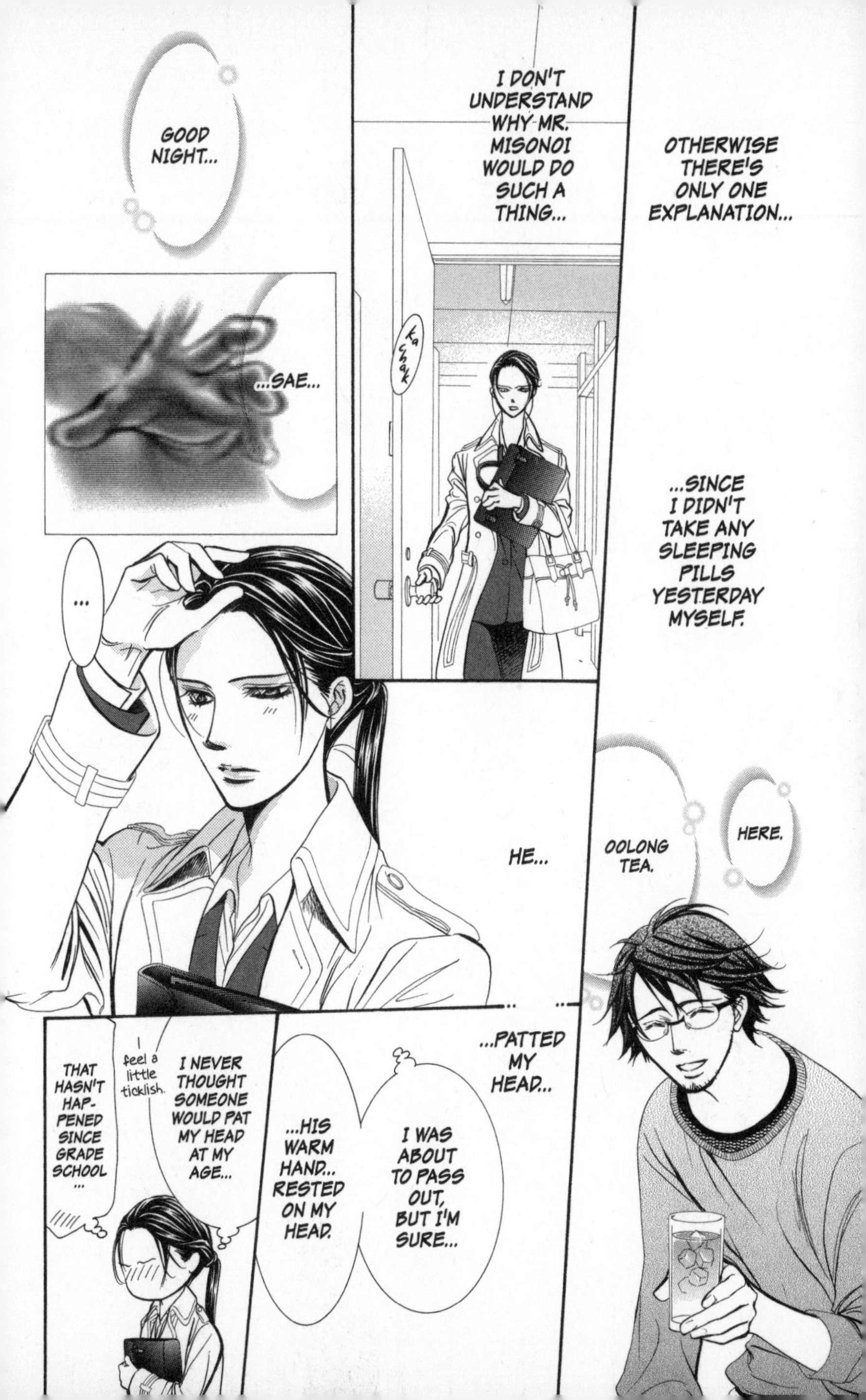
OTHERWISE THERE'S ONLY ONE EXPLANATION...
...SINCE I DIDN'T TAKE ANY SLEEPING PILLS YESTERDAY MYSELF.
I DON'T UNDERSTAND WHY MR. MISONOI WOULD DO SUCH A THING...
ka chak
GOOD NIGHT...
...SAE...
...
HERE.
OOLONG TEA.
HE...
......
...PATTED MY HEAD...
I WAS ABOUT TO PASS OUT, BUT I'M SURE...
...HIS WARM HAND... RESTED ON MY HEAD.
I NEVER THOUGHT SOMEONE WOULD PAT MY HEAD AT MY AGE...
I feel a little ticklish.
THAT HASN'T HAP-PENED SINCE GRADE SCHOOL...

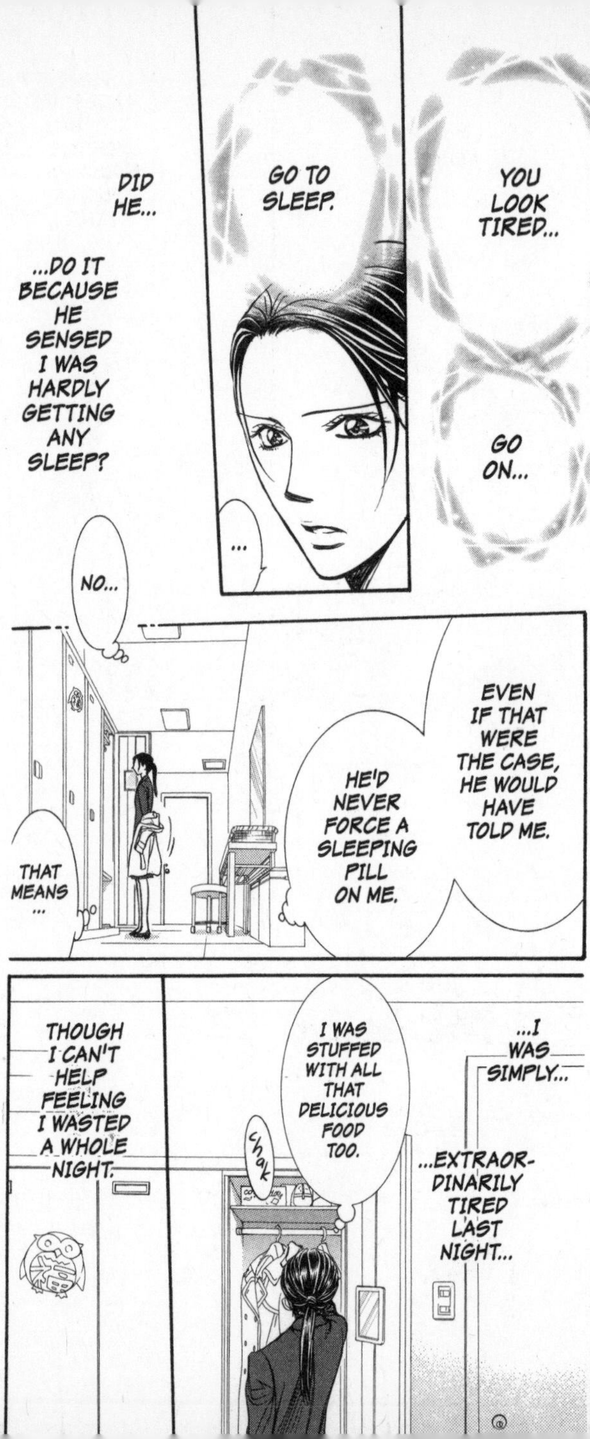
YOU LOOK TIRED...
GO ON...
GO TO SLEEP.
...
DID HE...
...DO IT BECAUSE HE SENSED I WAS HARDLY GETTING ANY SLEEP?
NO...
EVEN IF THAT WERE THE CASE, HE WOULD HAVE TOLD ME.
HE'D NEVER FORCE A SLEEPING PILL ON ME.
THAT MEANS...
...I WAS SIMPLY...
...EXTRAOR-DINARILY TIRED LAST NIGHT...
I WAS STUFFED WITH ALL THAT DELICIOUS FOOD TOO.
chak
THOUGH I CAN'T HELP FEELING I WASTED A WHOLE NIGHT.

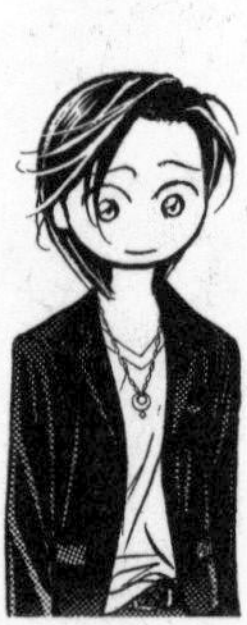

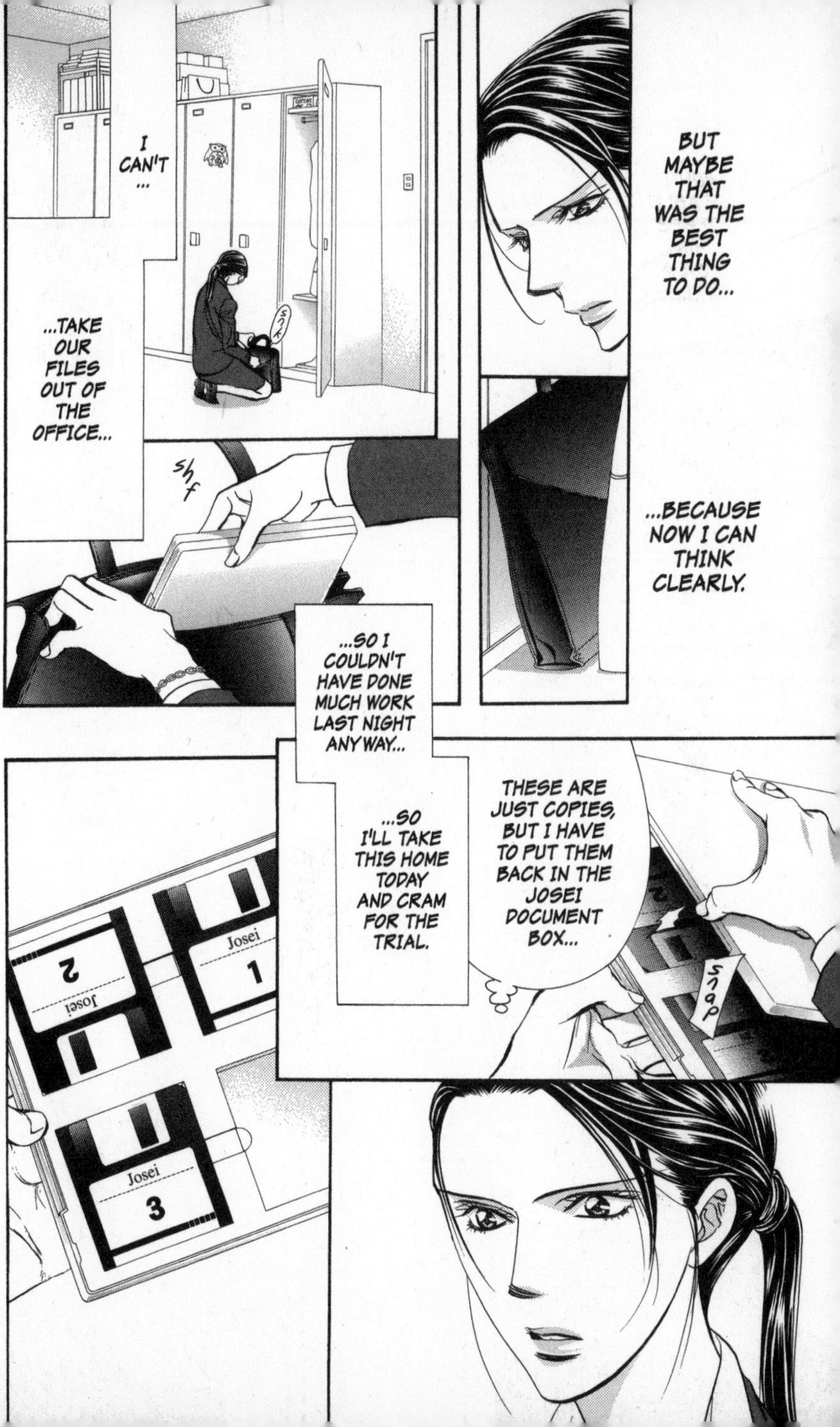

I CAN'T ...
...TAKE OUR FILES OUT OF THE OFFICE...
snk
shf
...SO I COULDN'T HAVE DONE MUCH WORK LAST NIGHT ANYWAY...
BUT MAYBE THAT WAS THE BEST THING TO DO...
...BECAUSE NOW I CAN THINK CLEARLY.
Josei 2
Josei 1
Josei 3
THESE ARE JUST COPIES, BUT I HAVE TO PUT THEM BACK IN THE JOSEI DOCUMENT BOX...
snap
...SO I'LL TAKE THIS HOME TODAY AND CRAM FOR THE TRIAL.

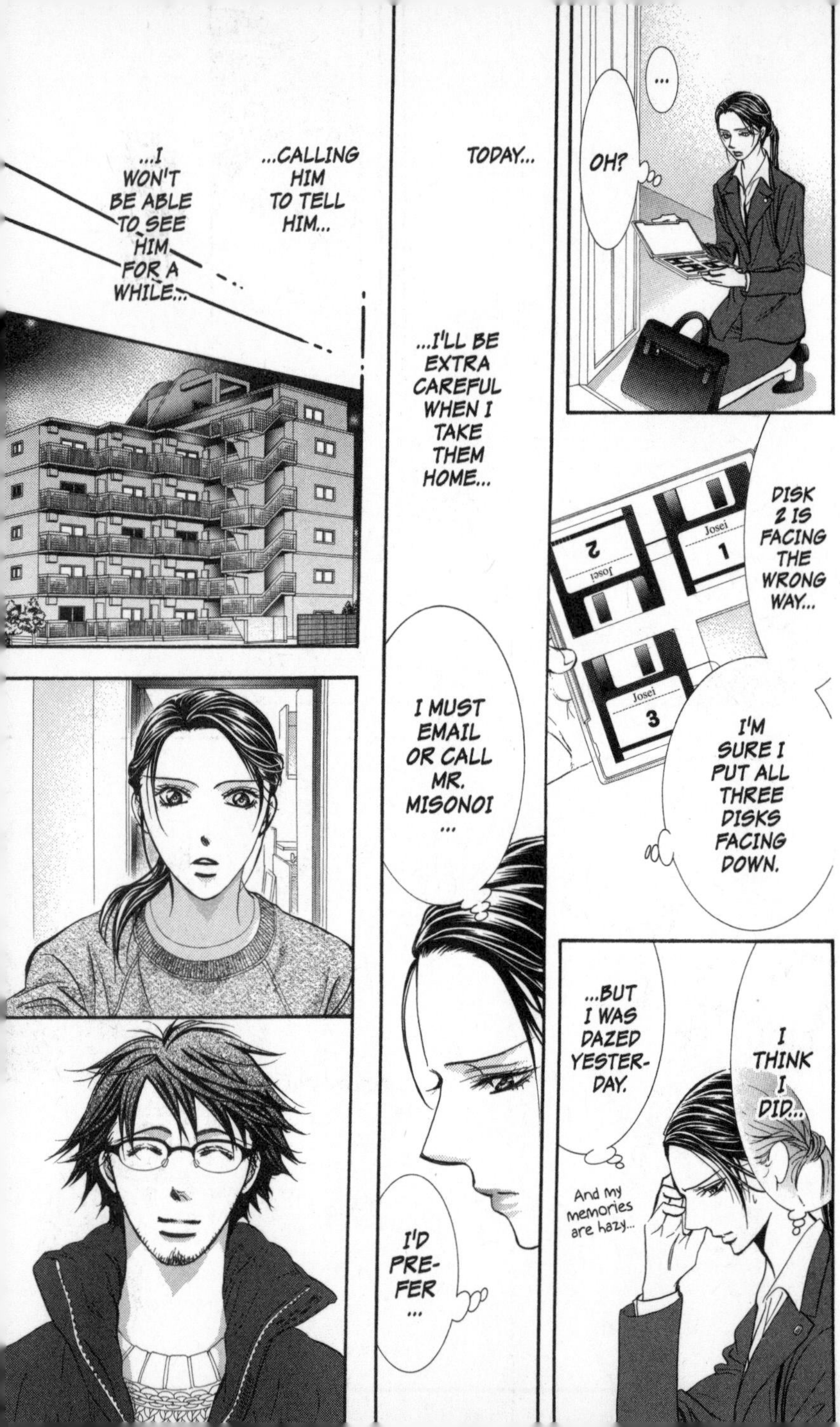
...
OH?
Josei 1
Josei 2
Josei 3
DISK 2 IS FACING THE WRONG WAY...
I'M SURE I PUT ALL THREE DISKS FACING DOWN.
I THINK I DID...
...BUT I WAS DAZED YESTER-DAY.
And my memories are hazy...
TODAY...
...I'LL BE EXTRA CAREFUL WHEN I TAKE THEM HOME...
I MUST EMAIL OR CALL MR. MISONOI ...
I'D PRE-FER ...
...CALLING HIM TO TELL HIM...
...I WON'T BE ABLE TO SEE HIM FOR A WHILE...

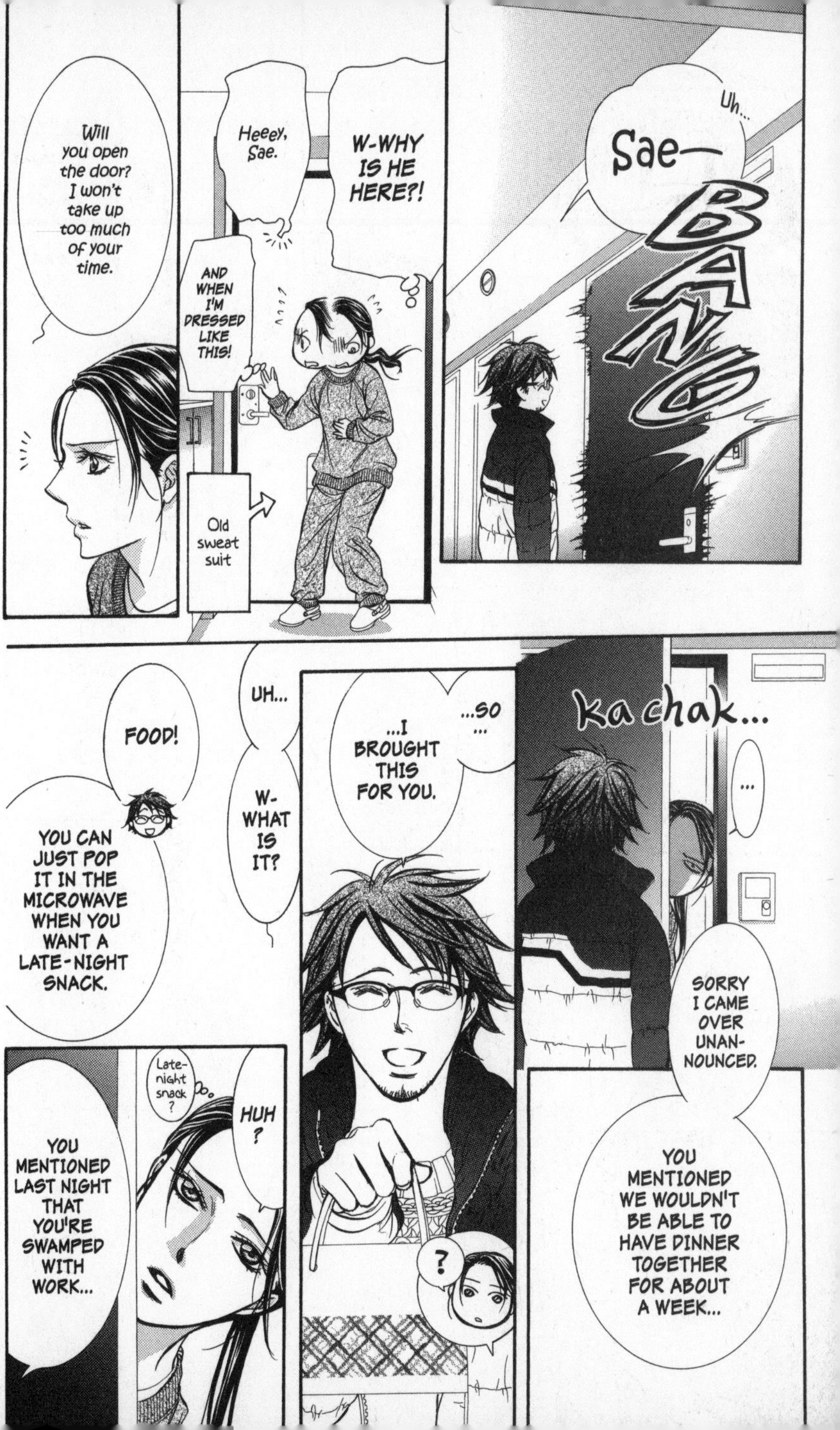
Uh...
Sae—
BANG
Heeey, Sae.
W-WHY IS HE HERE?!
AND WHEN I'M DRESSED LIKE THIS!
Old sweat suit
Will you open the door? I won't take up too much of your time.
ka chak...
...
SORRY I CAME OVER UNAN-NOUNCED.
YOU MENTIONED WE WOULDN'T BE ABLE TO HAVE DINNER TOGETHER FOR ABOUT A WEEK...
...SO ...
...I BROUGHT THIS FOR YOU.
?
UH...
W-WHAT IS IT?
FOOD!
YOU CAN JUST POP IT IN THE MICROWAVE WHEN YOU WANT A LATE-NIGHT SNACK.
HUH?
Late-night snack?
YOU MENTIONED LAST NIGHT THAT YOU'RE SWAMPED WITH WORK...

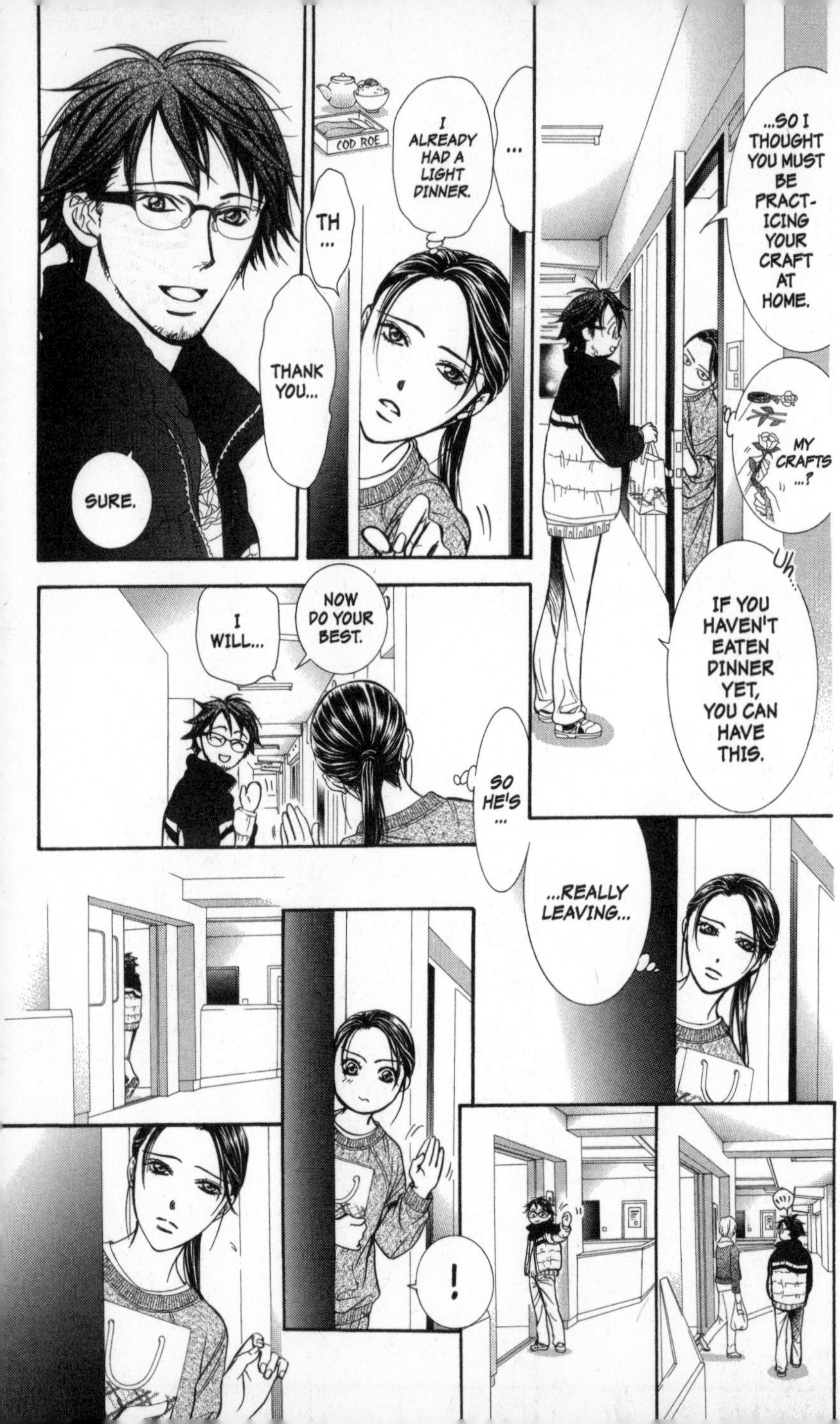
...SO I THOUGHT YOU MUST BE PRACTICING YOUR CRAFT AT HOME.
MY CRAFTS ...?
Uh...
IF YOU HAVEN'T EATEN DINNER YET, YOU CAN HAVE THIS.
...
I ALREADY HAD A LIGHT DINNER.
COD ROE
TH ...
THANK YOU...
SURE.
NOW DO YOUR BEST.
I WILL...
SO HE'S ...
...REALLY LEAVING...
!

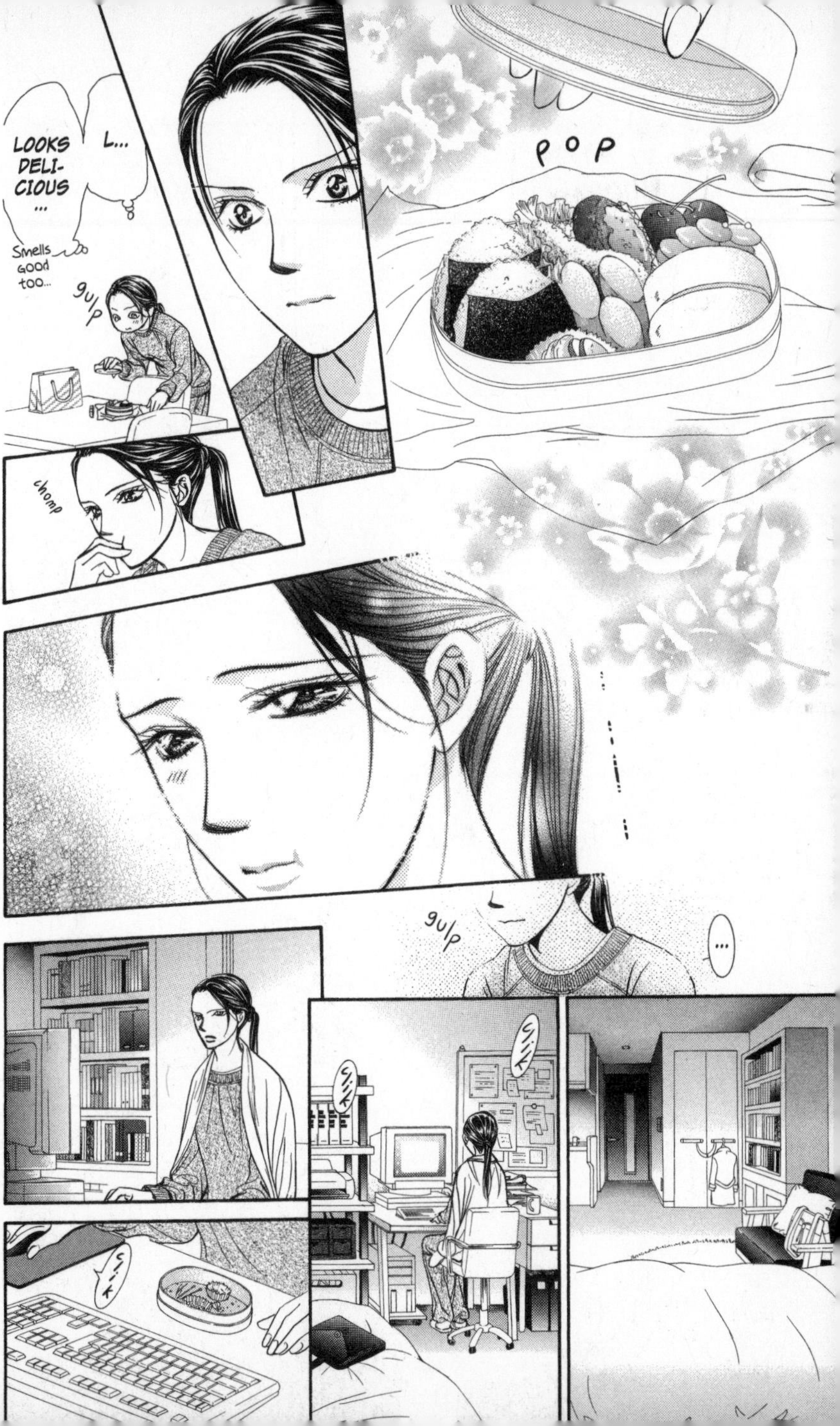
POP
L...
LOOKS DELI-CIOUS ...
Smells good too...
gulp
chomp
...!!
gulp
...
clik
clik
clik

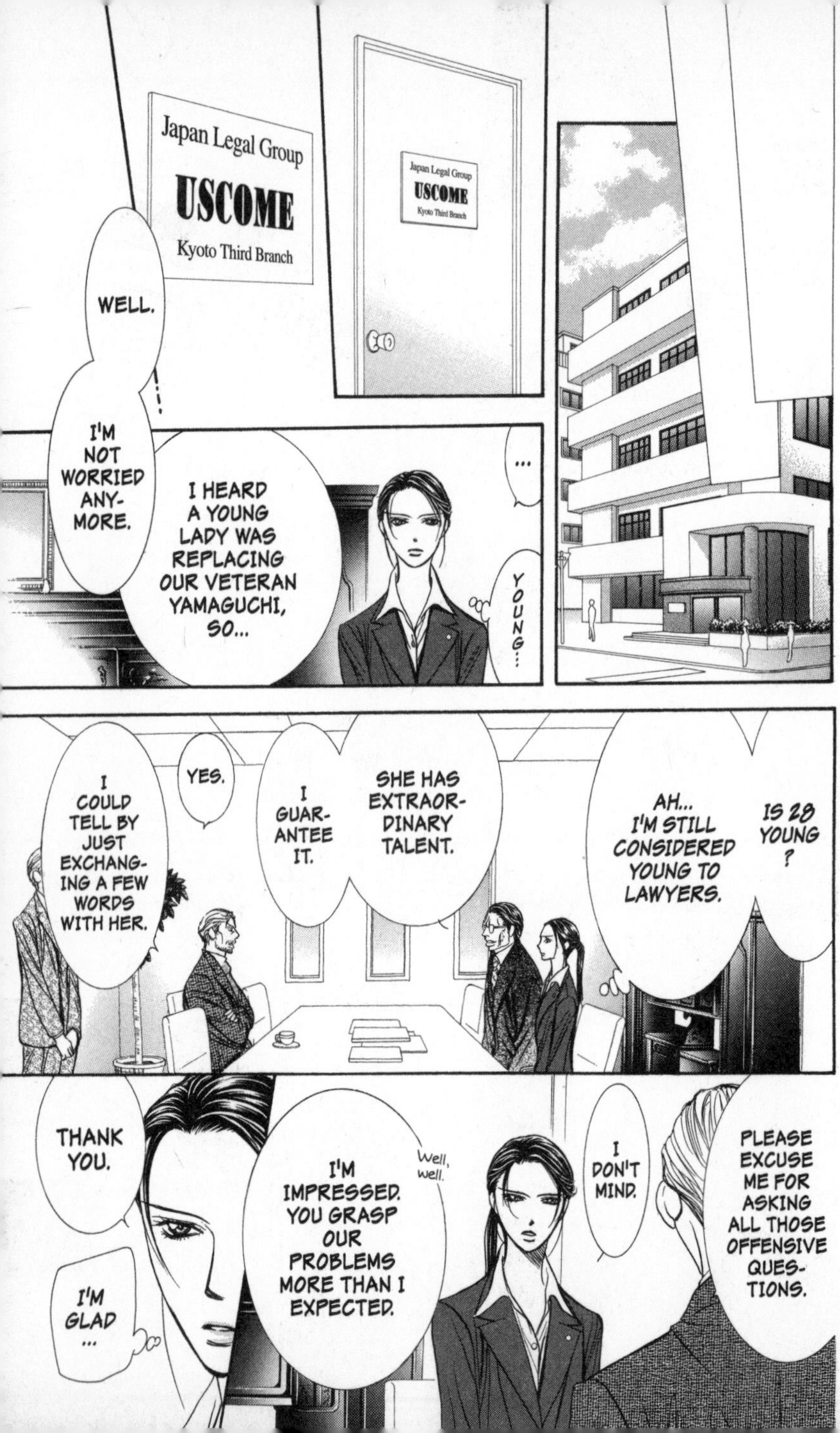
Japan Legal Group USCOME Kyoto Third Branch
Japan Legal Group USCOME Kyoto Third Branch
...
YOUNG...
I HEARD A YOUNG LADY WAS REPLACING OUR VETERAN YAMAGUCHI, SO...
WELL.
I'M NOT WORRIED ANY-MORE.
IS 28 YOUNG?
AH... I'M STILL CONSIDERED YOUNG TO LAWYERS.
SHE HAS EXTRAOR-DINARY TALENT.
I GUAR-ANTEE IT.
YES.
I COULD TELL BY JUST EXCHANG-ING A FEW WORDS WITH HER.
PLEASE EXCUSE ME FOR ASKING ALL THOSE OFFENSIVE QUES-TIONS.
I DON'T MIND.
Well, well.
I'M IMPRESSED. YOU GRASP OUR PROBLEMS MORE THAN I EXPECTED.
THANK YOU.
I'M GLAD...

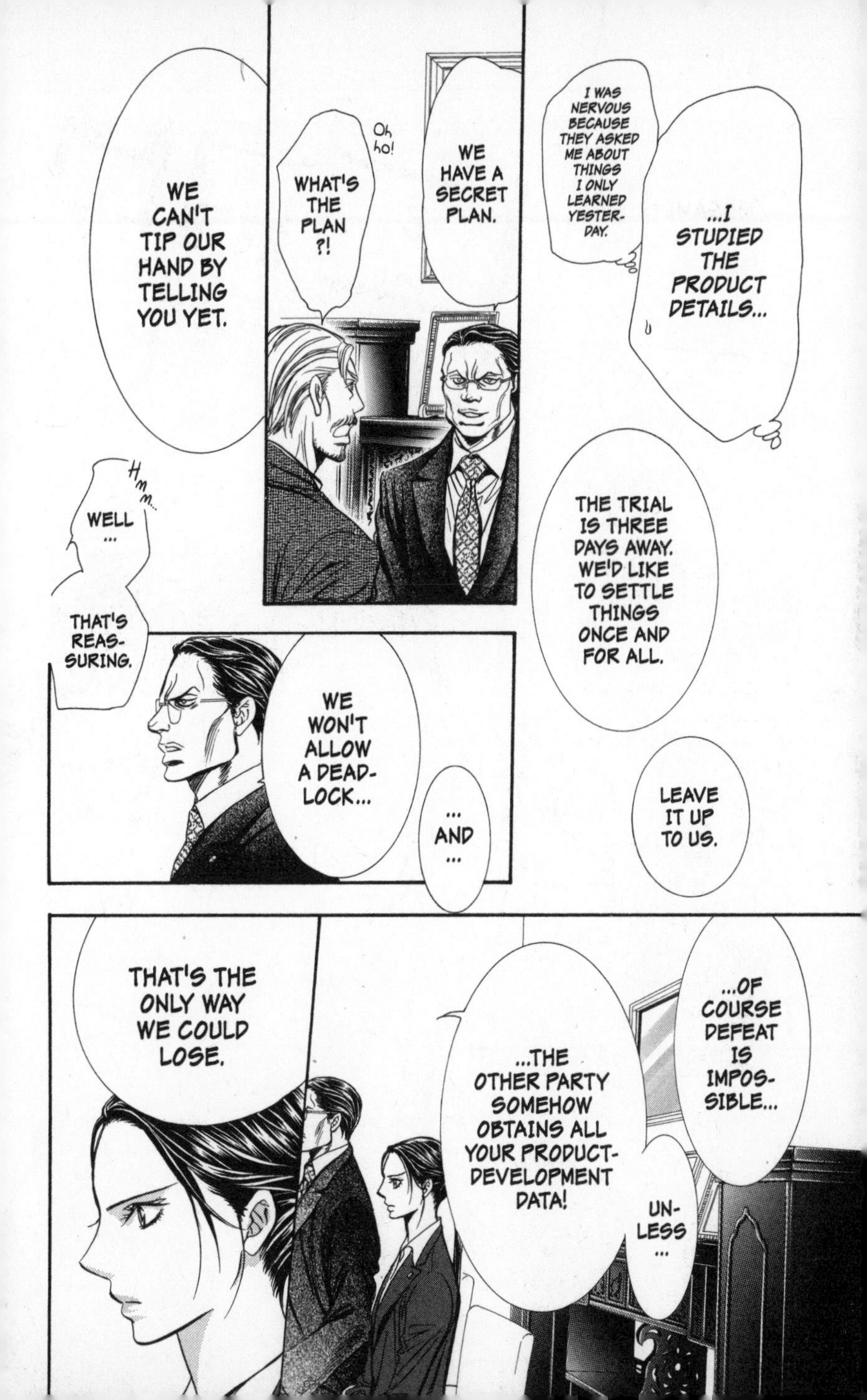
...I STUDIED THE PRODUCT DETAILS...
I WAS NERVOUS BECAUSE THEY ASKED ME ABOUT THINGS I ONLY LEARNED YESTER-DAY.
WE HAVE A SECRET PLAN.
Oh ho!
WHAT'S THE PLAN?!
WE CAN'T TIP OUR HAND BY TELLING YOU YET.
Hmm...
WELL...
THAT'S REAS-SURING.
THE TRIAL IS THREE DAYS AWAY. WE'D LIKE TO SETTLE THINGS ONCE AND FOR ALL.
LEAVE IT UP TO US.
WE WON'T ALLOW A DEAD-LOCK...
...AND...
...OF COURSE DEFEAT IS IMPOS-SIBLE...
UN-LESS...
...THE OTHER PARTY SOMEHOW OBTAINS ALL YOUR PRODUCT-DEVELOPMENT DATA!
THAT'S THE ONLY WAY WE COULD LOSE.

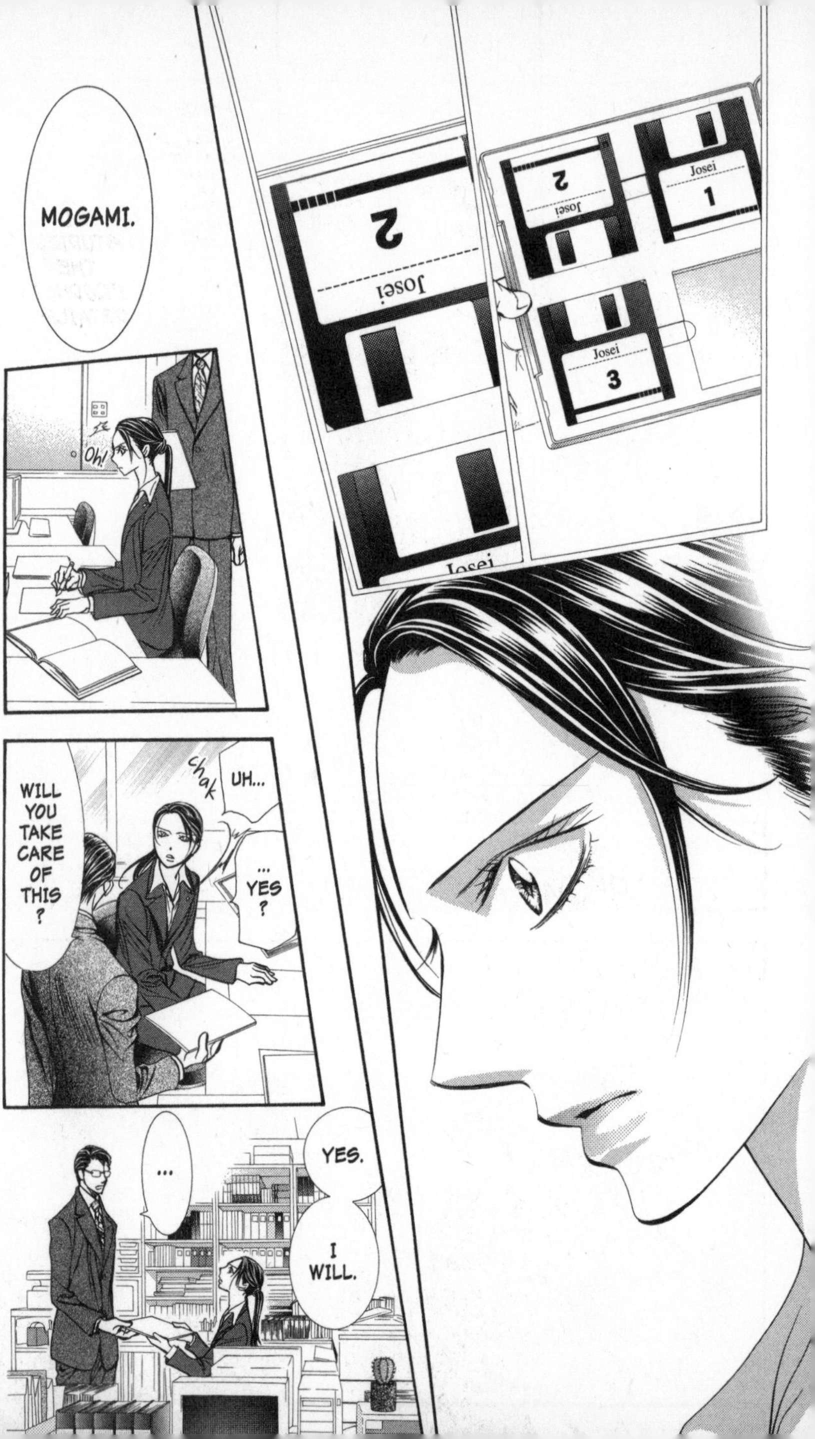
Josei
2
Josei
1
Josei
2
Josei
3
Josei
MOGAMI.
Oh!
chak
UH...
... YES?
WILL YOU TAKE CARE OF THIS?
YES.
I WILL.
...

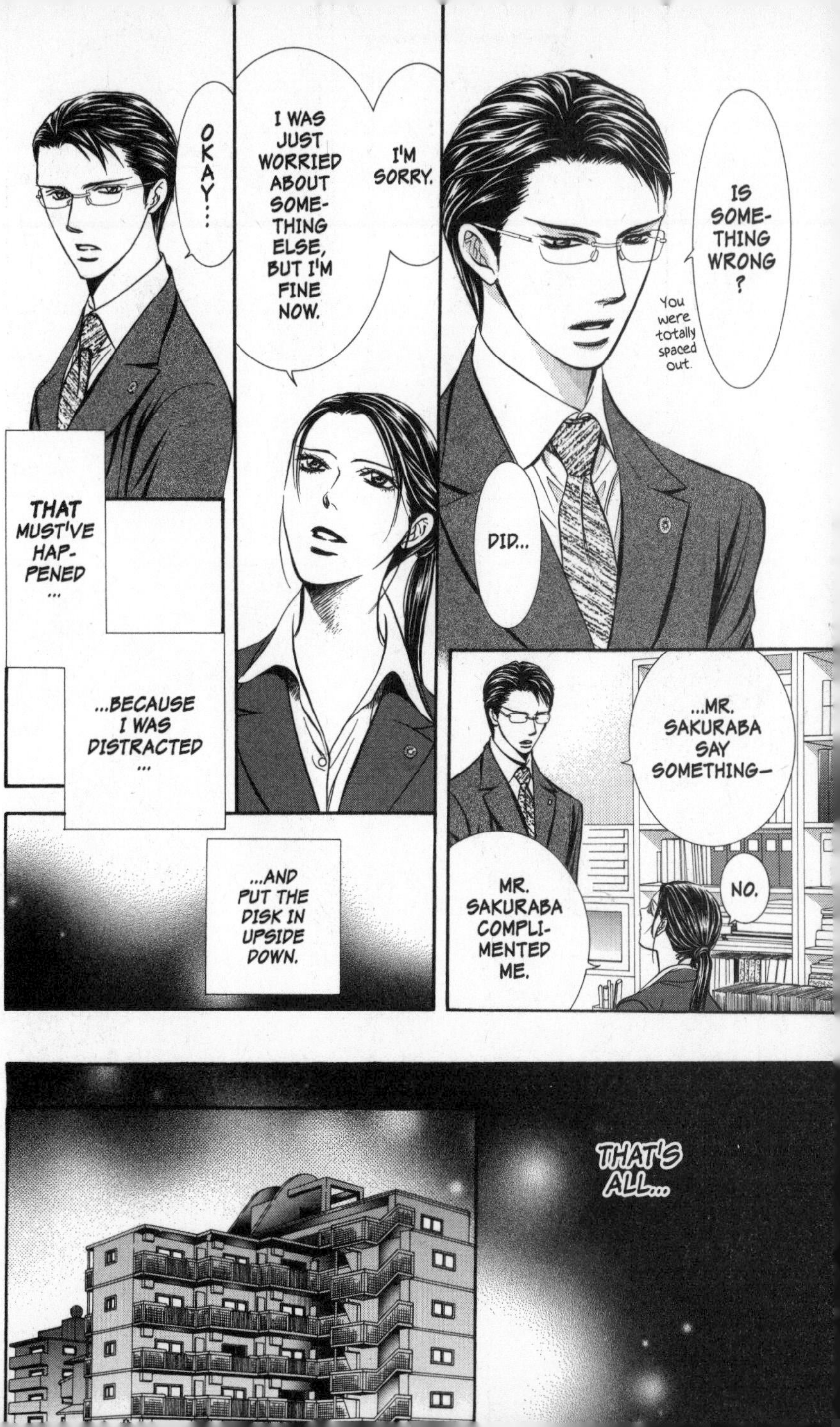
IS SOMETHING WRONG?
You were totally spaced out.
DID...
I'M SORRY.
I WAS JUST WORRIED ABOUT SOMETHING ELSE, BUT I'M FINE NOW.
OKAY...
...MR. SAKURABA SAY SOMETHING—
NO.
MR. SAKURABA COMPLIMENTED ME.
THAT MUST'VE HAPPENED...
...BECAUSE I WAS DISTRACTED...
...AND PUT THE DISK IN UPSIDE DOWN.
THAT'S ALL...

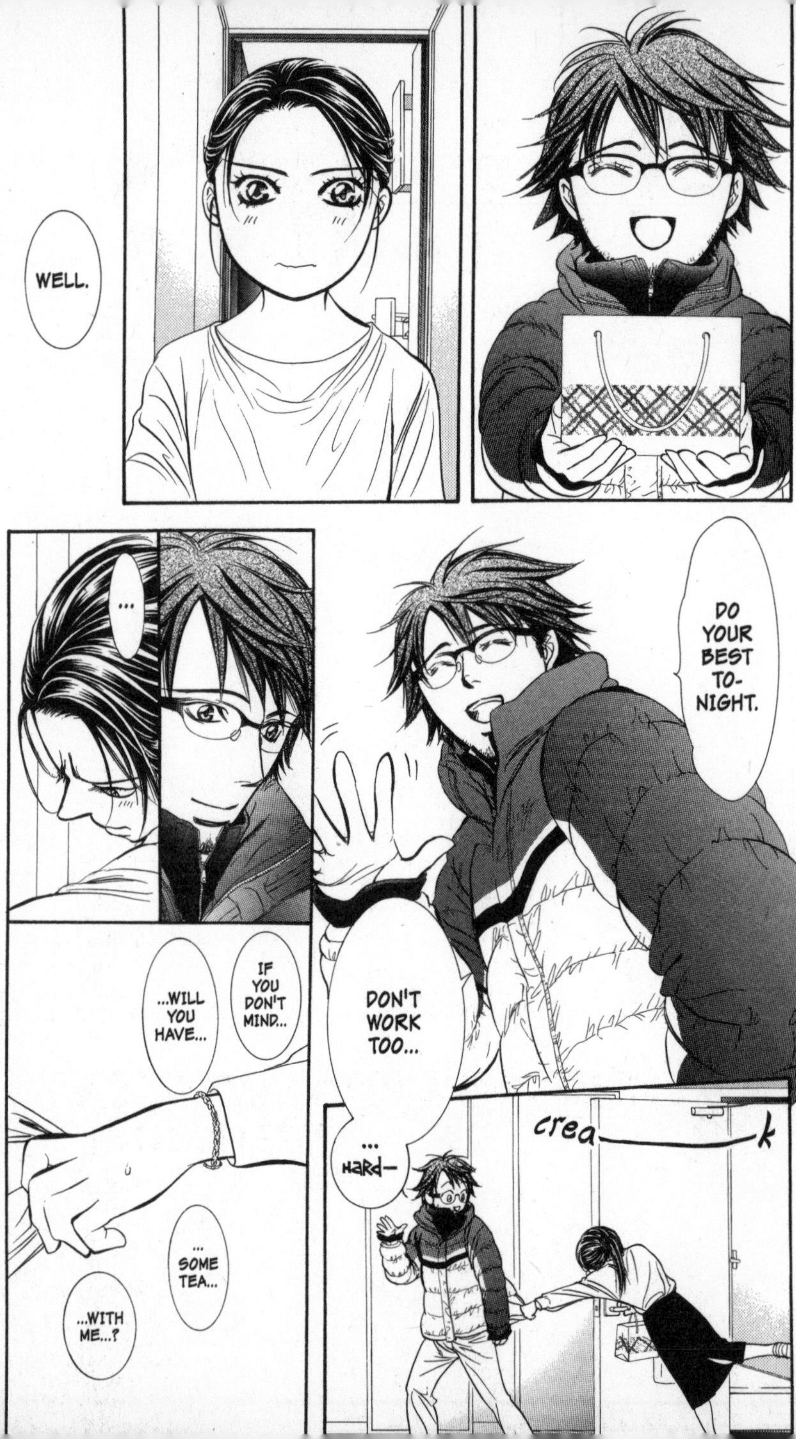
WELL.
DO YOUR BEST TO-NIGHT.
DON'T WORK TOO...
...HARD—
...
crea———k
IF YOU DON'T MIND...
...WILL YOU HAVE...
...SOME TEA...
...WITH ME...?

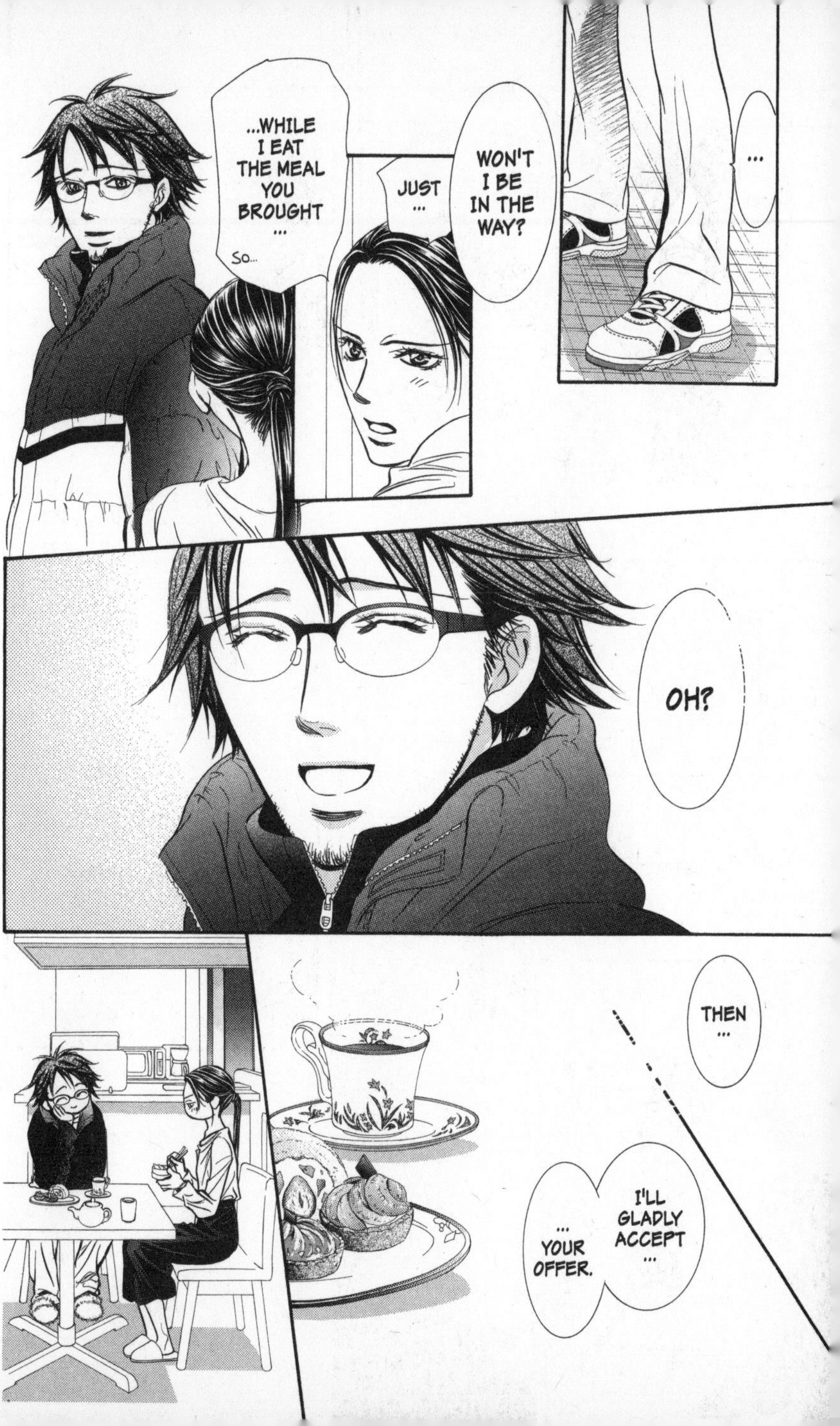
...
WON'T I BE IN THE WAY?
JUST ...
...WHILE I EAT THE MEAL YOU BROUGHT ...
So...
OH?
THEN ...
I'LL GLADLY ACCEPT ...
... YOUR OFFER.

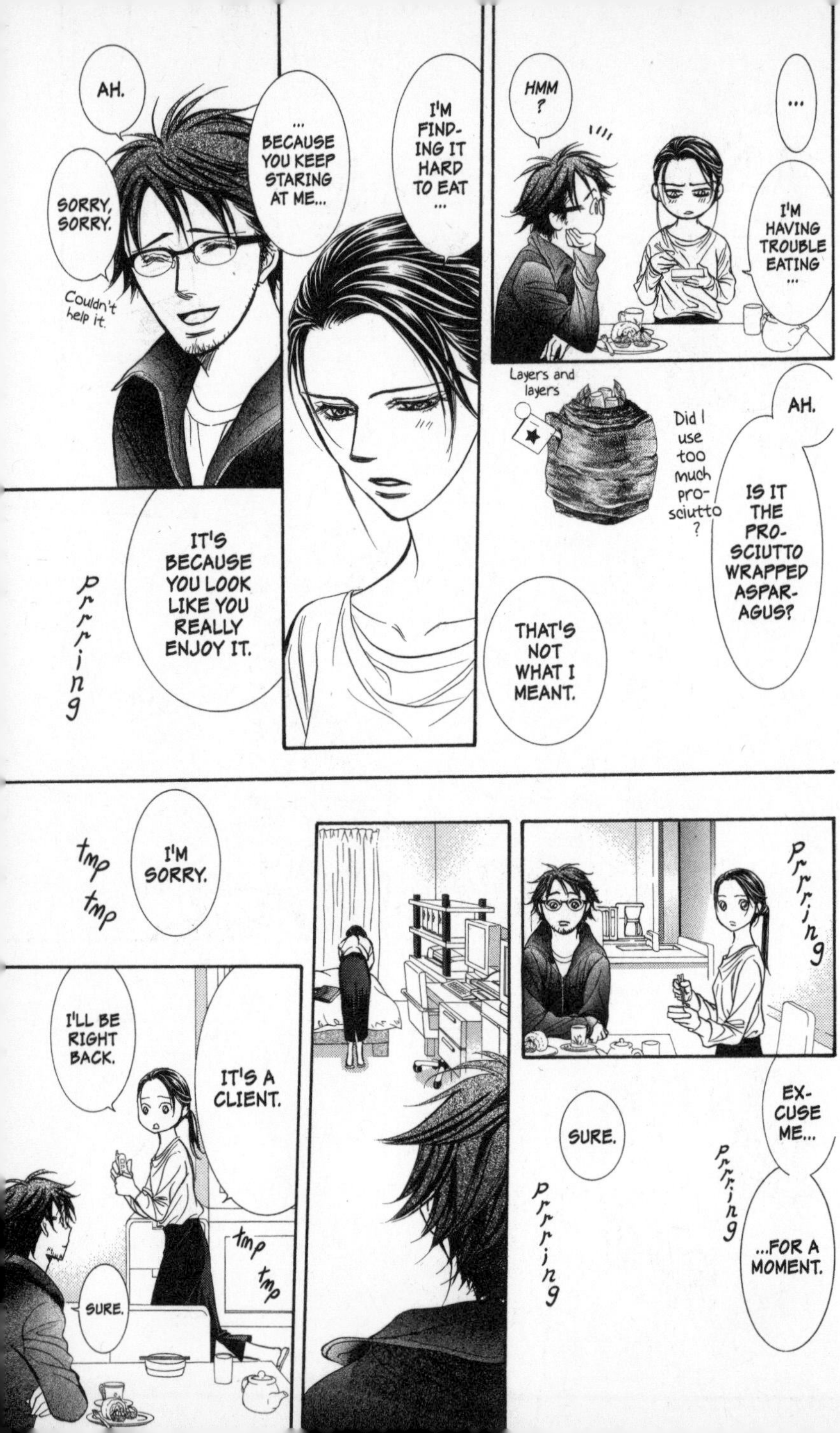
...
I'M HAVING TROUBLE EATING ...
HMM ?
AH.
IS IT THE PRO-SCIUTTO WRAPPED ASPAR-AGUS?
Layers and layers
Did I use too much pro-sciutto?
THAT'S NOT WHAT I MEANT.
I'M FINDING IT HARD TO EAT ...
... BECAUSE YOU KEEP STARING AT ME...
AH.
SORRY, SORRY.
Couldn't help it.
IT'S BECAUSE YOU LOOK LIKE YOU REALLY ENJOY IT.
Prrring
Prrring
EX-CUSE ME...
...FOR A MOMENT.
Prrring
SURE.
Prrring
I'M SORRY.
tmp tmp
IT'S A CLIENT.
I'LL BE RIGHT BACK.
tmp tmp
SURE.

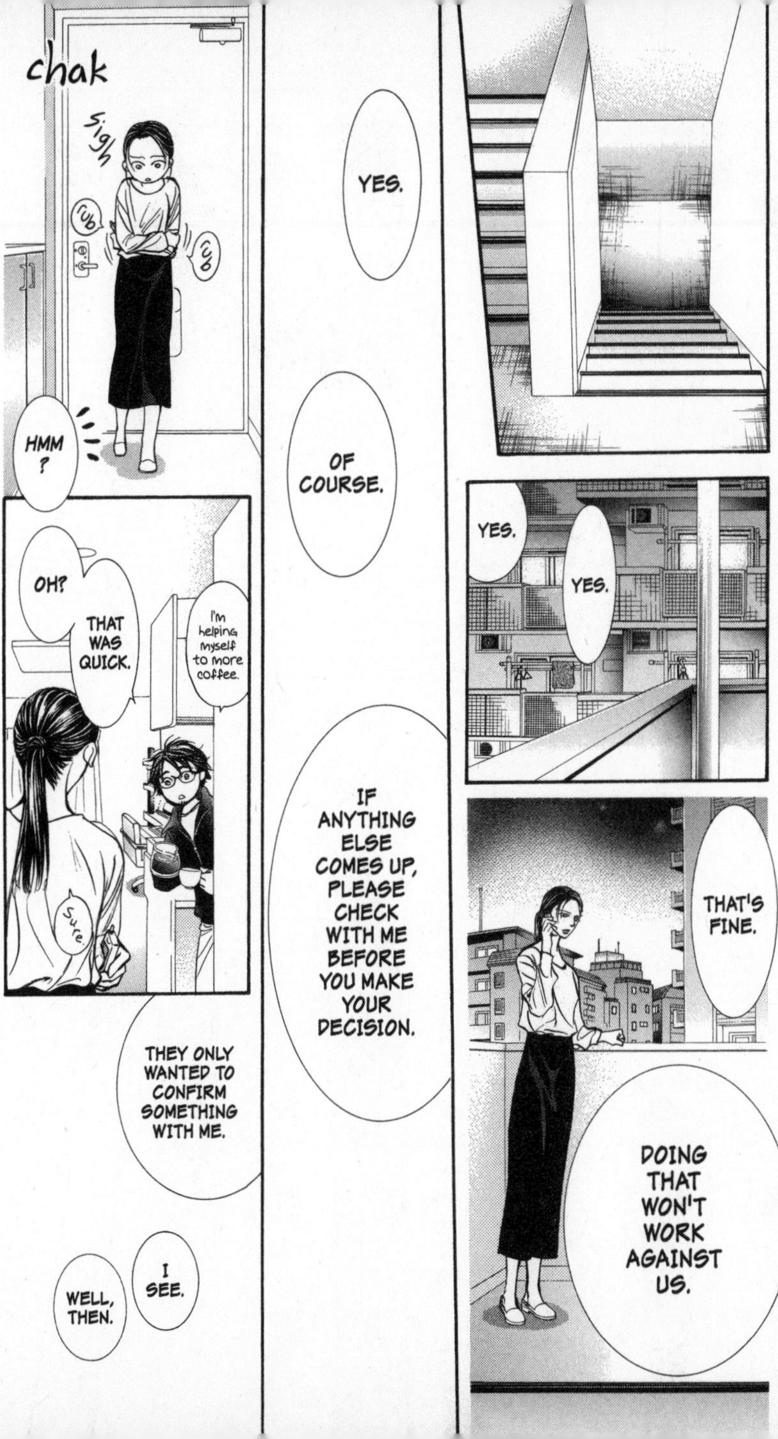
YES.
YES.
THAT'S FINE.
DOING THAT WON'T WORK AGAINST US.
YES.
OF COURSE.
IF ANYTHING ELSE COMES UP, PLEASE CHECK WITH ME BEFORE YOU MAKE YOUR DECISION.
chak
sigh
rub
rub
HMM?
I'm helping myself to more coffee.
OH?
THAT WAS QUICK.
Sure.
THEY ONLY WANTED TO CONFIRM SOMETHING WITH ME.
I SEE.
WELL, THEN.

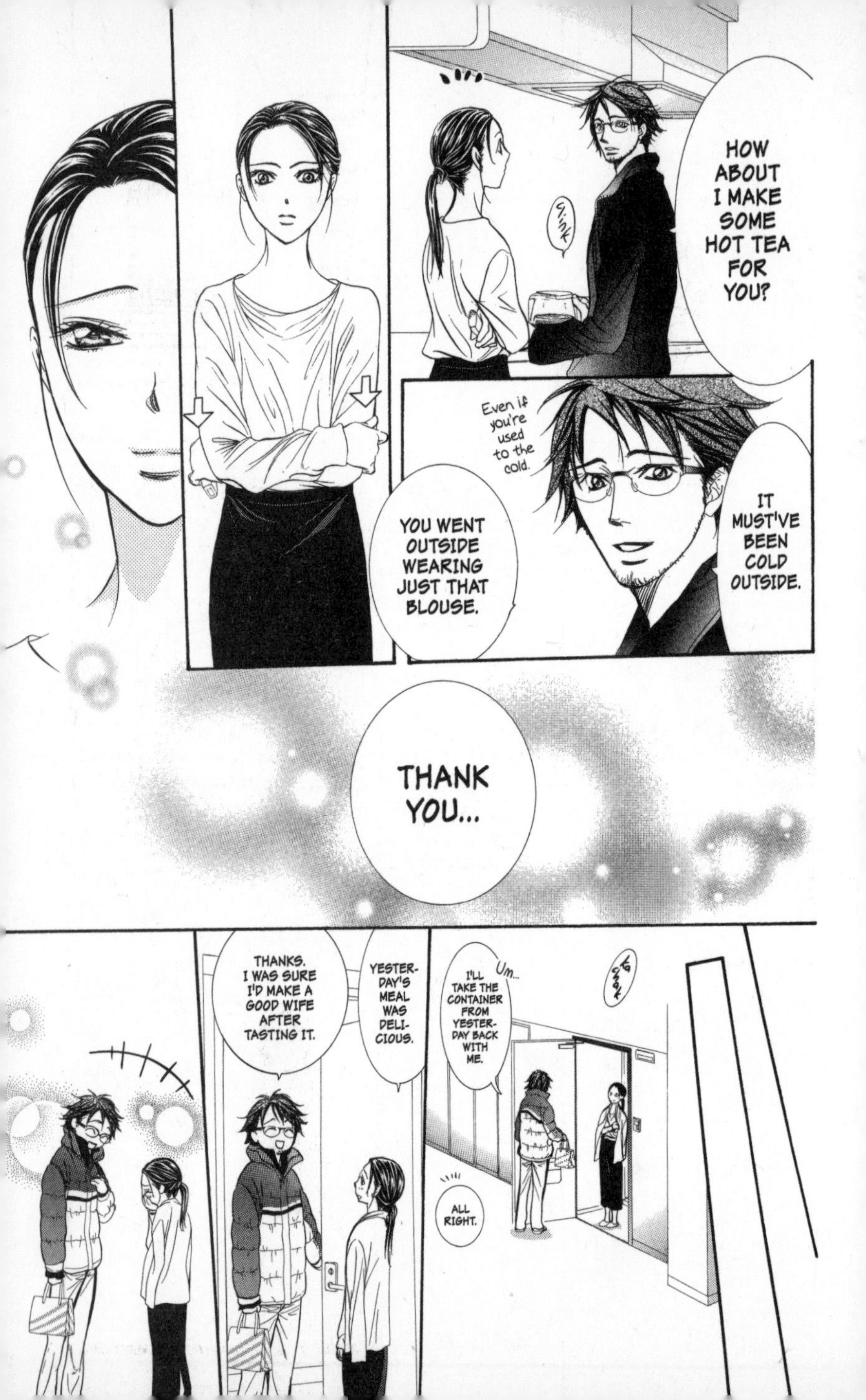
HOW ABOUT I MAKE SOME HOT TEA FOR YOU?
IT MUST'VE BEEN COLD OUTSIDE.
Even if you're used to the cold.
YOU WENT OUTSIDE WEARING JUST THAT BLOUSE.
THANK YOU...
Um...
I'LL TAKE THE CONTAINER FROM YESTER-DAY BACK WITH ME.
ALL RIGHT.
YESTER-DAY'S MEAL WAS DELI-CIOUS.
THANKS. I WAS SURE I'D MAKE A GOOD WIFE AFTER TASTING IT.

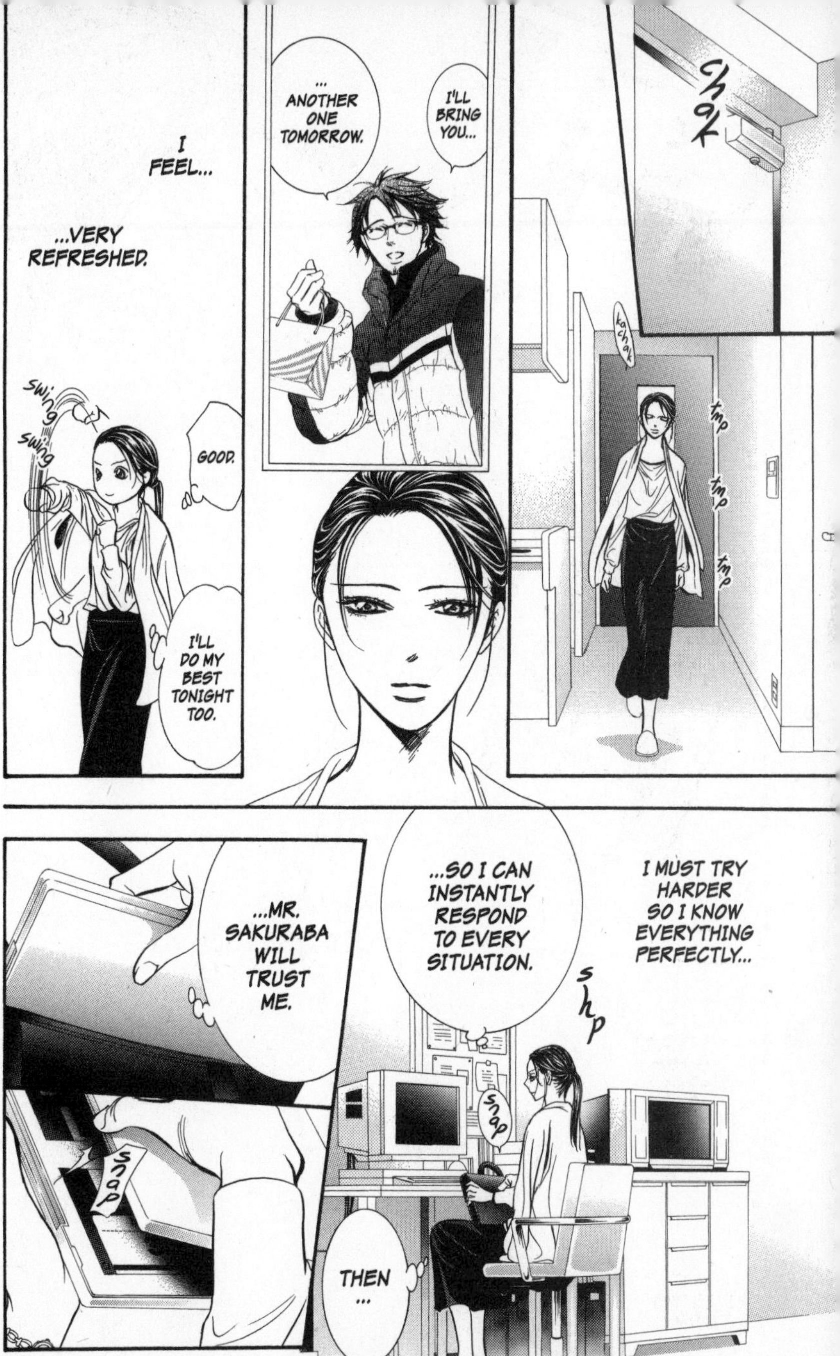
chak
kachak
tmp
tmp
tmp
I'LL BRING YOU...
... ANOTHER ONE TOMORROW.
I FEEL...
...VERY REFRESHED.
swing swing
GOOD.
I'LL DO MY BEST TONIGHT TOO.
I MUST TRY HARDER SO I KNOW EVERYTHING PERFECTLY...
...SO I CAN INSTANTLY RESPOND TO EVERY SITUATION.
shp
snap
THEN ...
...MR. SAKURABA WILL TRUST ME.
snap

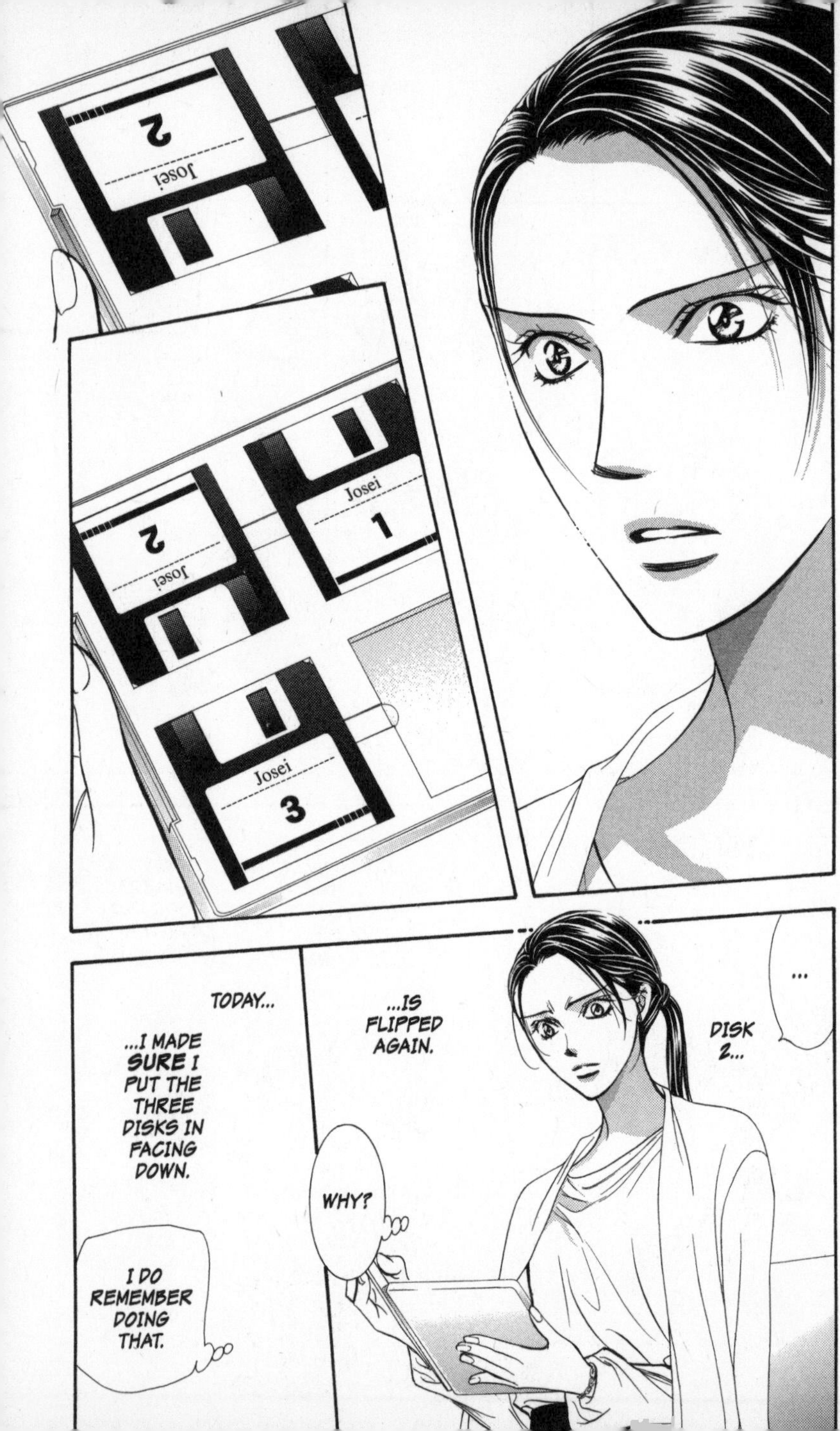
Josei
2
Josei
1
Josei
2
Josei
3
...
DISK 2...
...IS FLIPPED AGAIN.
WHY?
TODAY...
...I MADE SURE I PUT THE THREE DISKS IN FACING DOWN.
I DO REMEMBER DOING THAT.

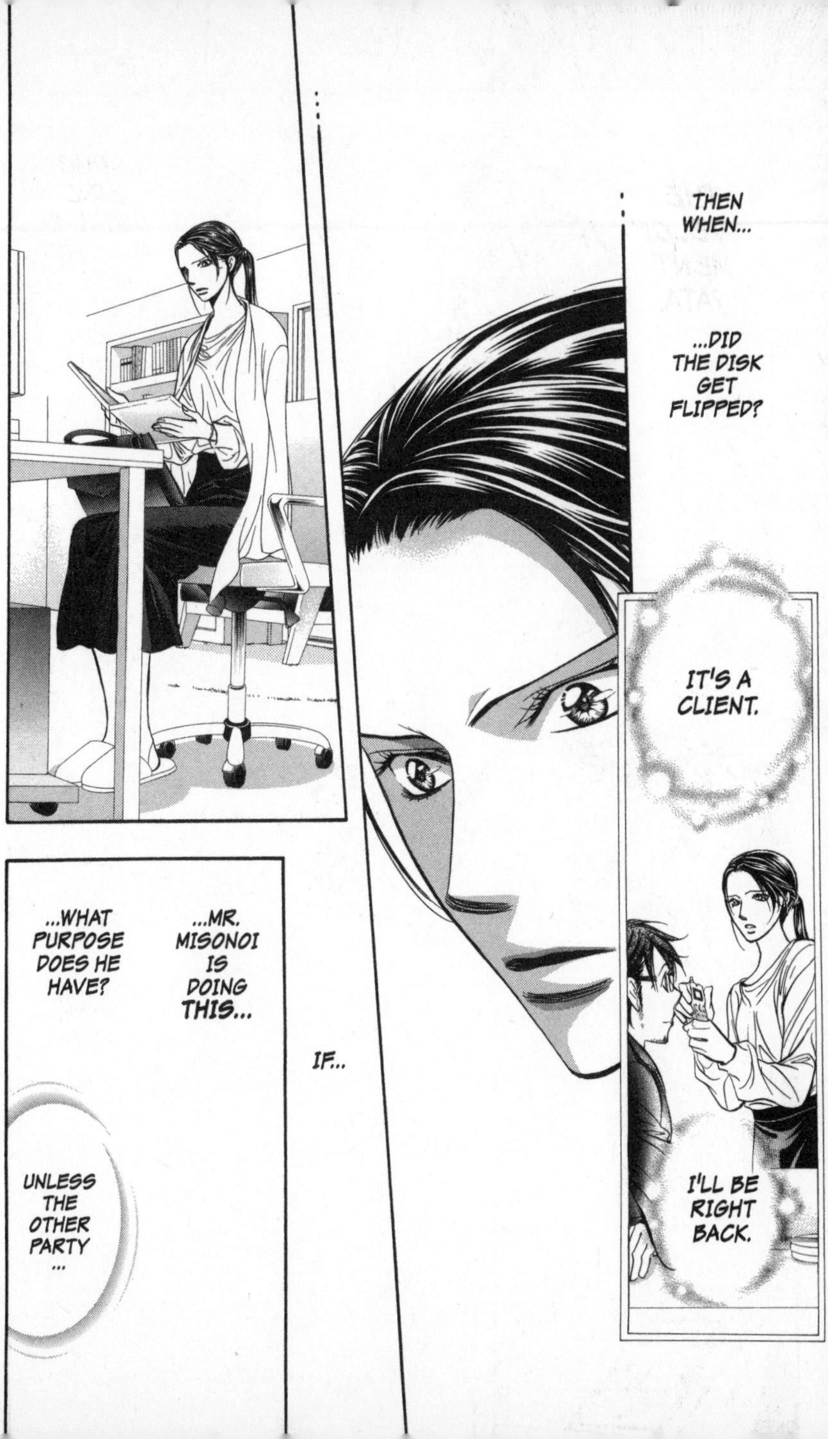
THEN WHEN...
...DID THE DISK GET FLIPPED?
IT'S A CLIENT.
I'LL BE RIGHT BACK.
IF...
...MR. MISONOI IS DOING THIS...
...WHAT PURPOSE DOES HE HAVE?
UNLESS THE OTHER PARTY ...

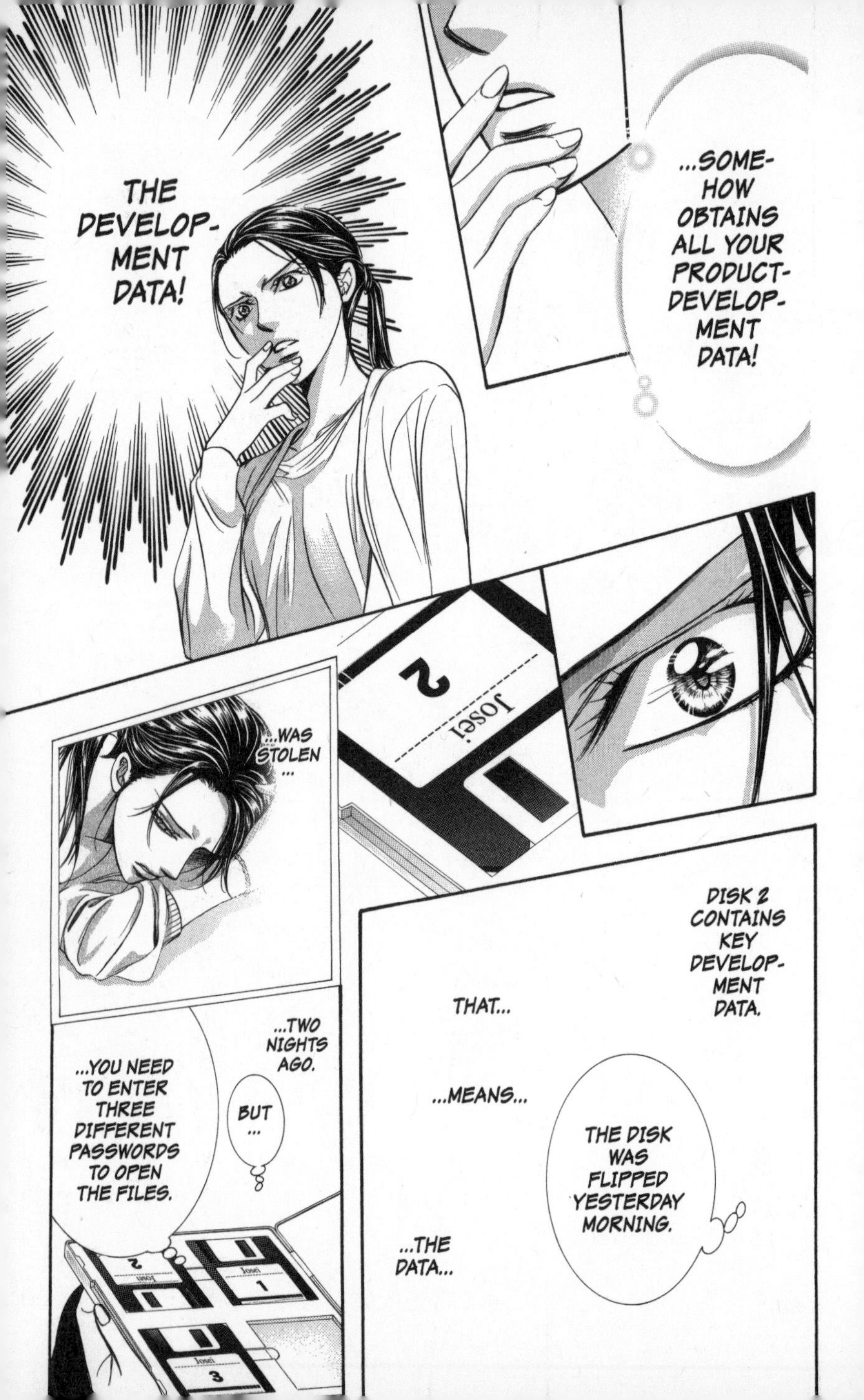
...SOME-HOW OBTAINS ALL YOUR PRODUCT-DEVELOPMENT DATA!
THE DEVELOPMENT DATA!
2
Josei
DISK 2 CONTAINS KEY DEVELOPMENT DATA.
THAT...
...MEANS...
THE DISK WAS FLIPPED YESTERDAY MORNING.
...THE DATA...
...WAS STOLEN ...
...TWO NIGHTS AGO.
BUT ...
...YOU NEED TO ENTER THREE DIFFERENT PASSWORDS TO OPEN THE FILES.

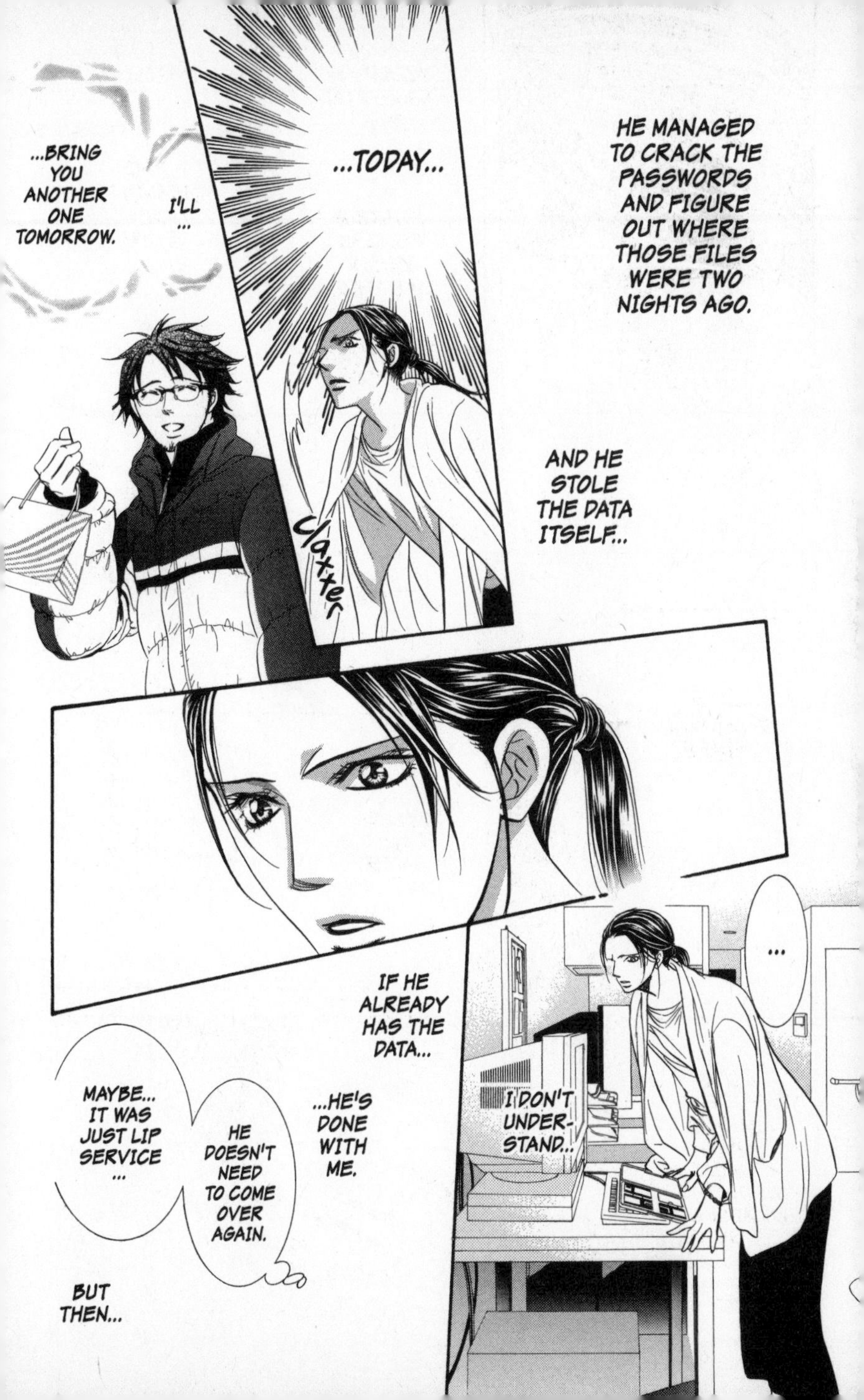
HE MANAGED TO CRACK THE PASSWORDS AND FIGURE OUT WHERE THOSE FILES WERE TWO NIGHTS AGO.
AND HE STOLE THE DATA ITSELF...
...TODAY...
claxter
I'LL ...
...BRING YOU ANOTHER ONE TOMORROW.
...
I DON'T UNDER-STAND...
IF HE ALREADY HAS THE DATA...
...HE'S DONE WITH ME.
HE DOESN'T NEED TO COME OVER AGAIN.
MAYBE... IT WAS JUST LIP SERVICE ...
BUT THEN...

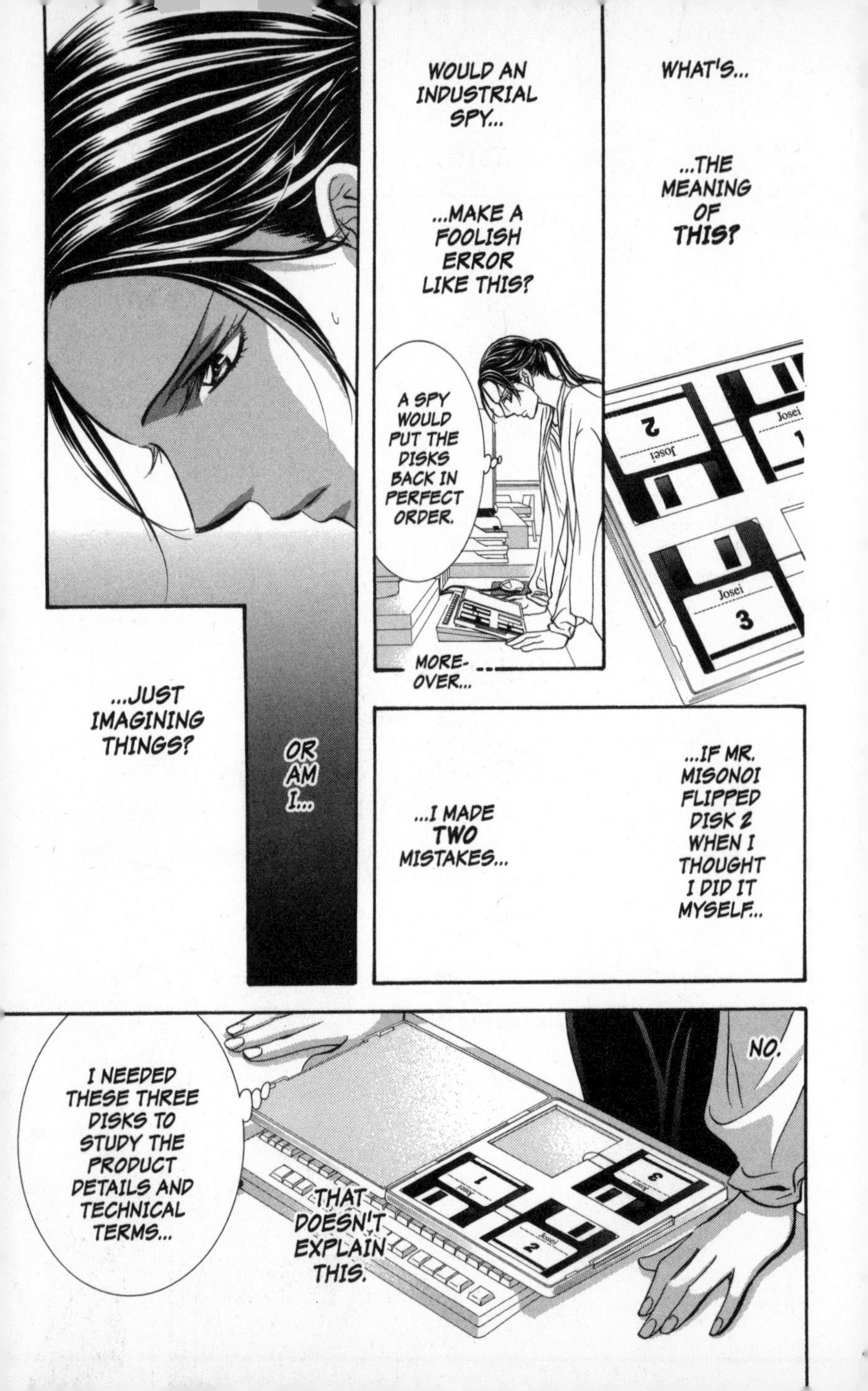
WHAT'S...
...THE MEANING OF THIS?
WOULD AN INDUSTRIAL SPY...
...MAKE A FOOLISH ERROR LIKE THIS?
A SPY WOULD PUT THE DISKS BACK IN PERFECT ORDER.
MORE-OVER...
...IF MR. MISONOI FLIPPED DISK 2 WHEN I THOUGHT I DID IT MYSELF...
...I MADE TWO MISTAKES...
OR AM I...
...JUST IMAGINING THINGS?
NO.
I NEEDED THESE THREE DISKS TO STUDY THE PRODUCT DETAILS AND TECHNICAL TERMS...
THAT DOESN'T EXPLAIN THIS.

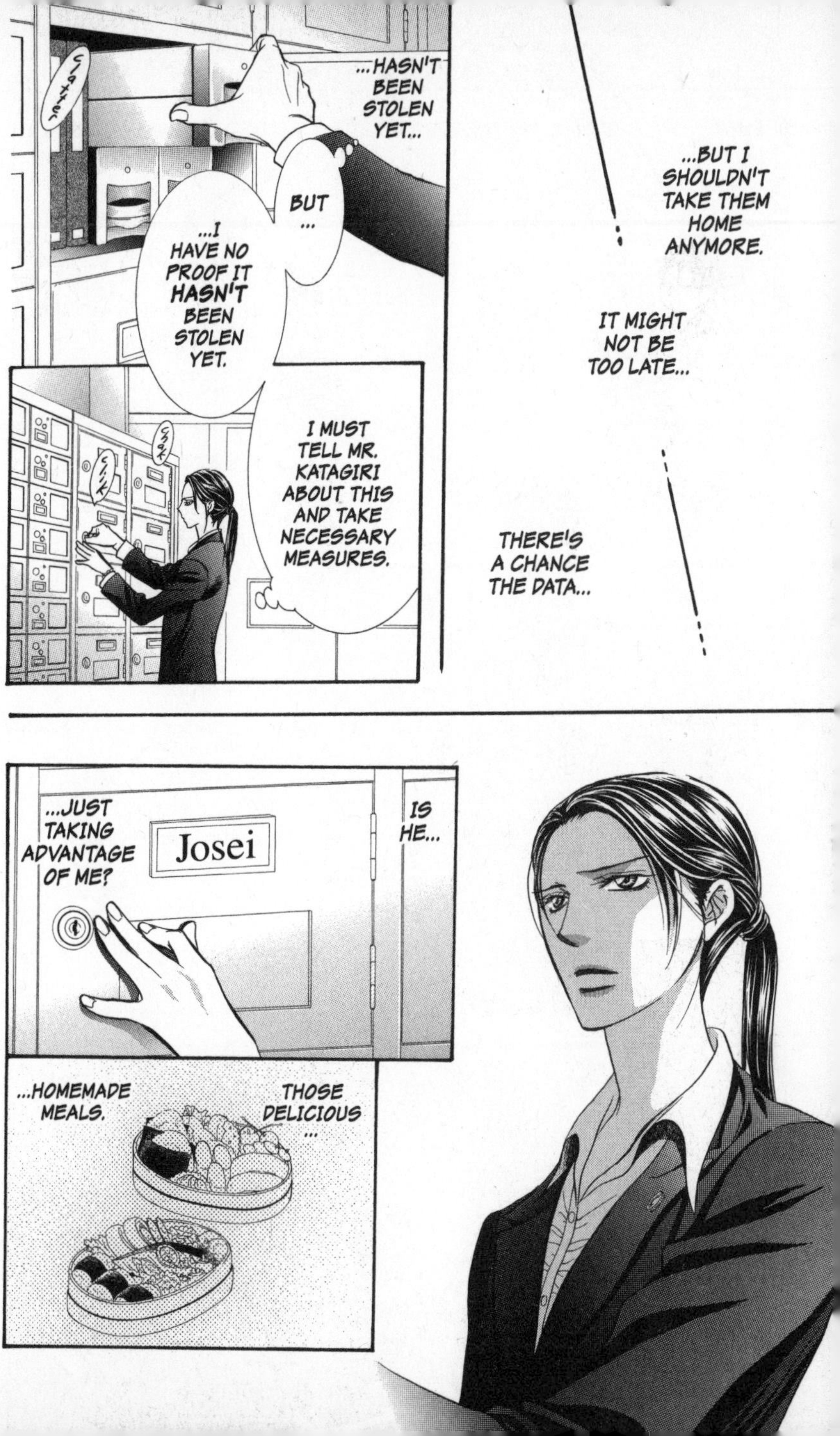
...BUT I SHOULDN'T TAKE THEM HOME ANYMORE.
IT MIGHT NOT BE TOO LATE...
THERE'S A CHANCE THE DATA...
...HASN'T BEEN STOLEN YET...
BUT ...
...I HAVE NO PROOF IT HASN'T BEEN STOLEN YET.
I MUST TELL MR. KATAGIRI ABOUT THIS AND TAKE NECESSARY MEASURES.
IS HE...
...JUST TAKING ADVANTAGE OF ME?
Josei
THOSE DELICIOUS ...
...HOMEMADE MEALS.

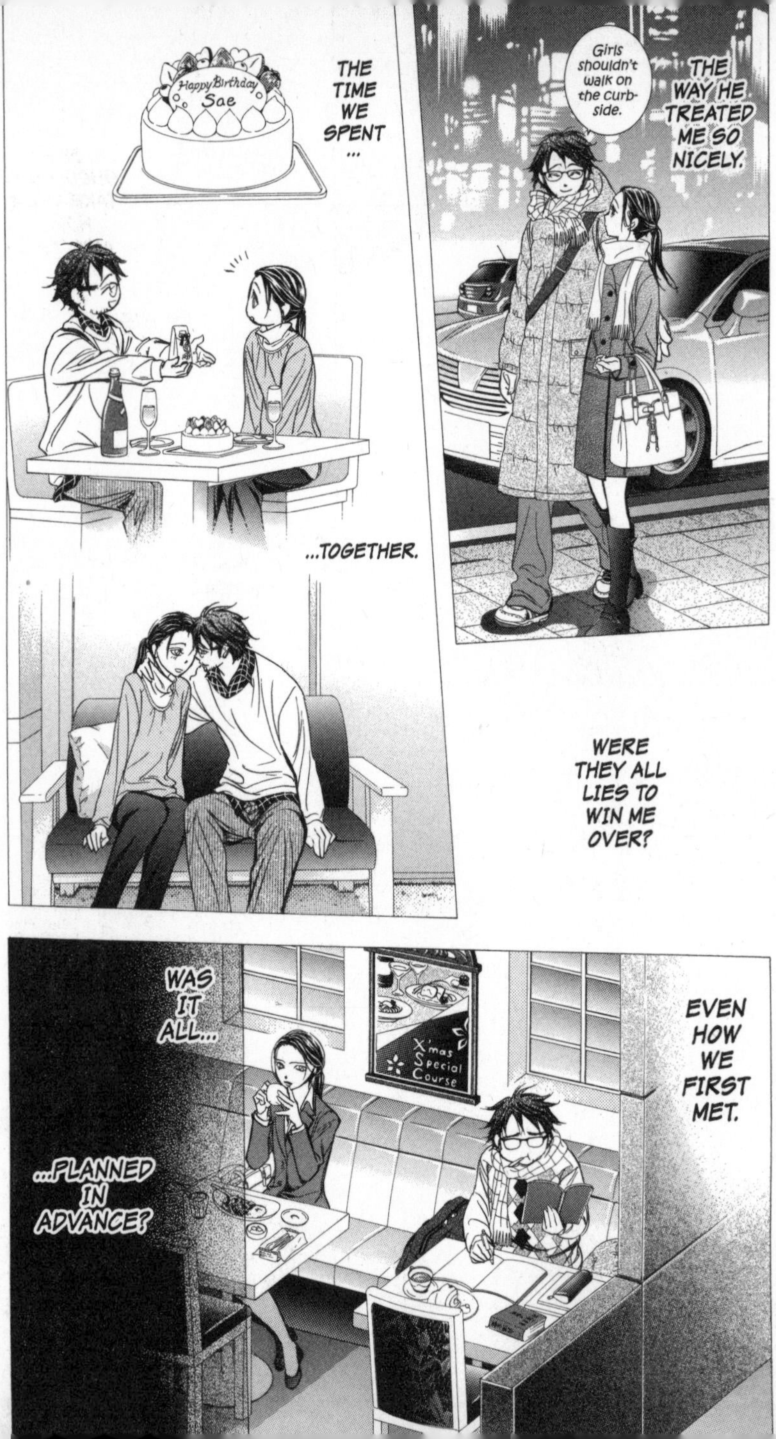
Girls shouldn't walk on the curb-side.
THE WAY HE TREATED ME SO NICELY.
THE TIME WE SPENT ...
Happy Birthday Sae
...TOGETHER.
WERE THEY ALL LIES TO WIN ME OVER?
EVEN HOW WE FIRST MET.
X'mas Special Course
WAS IT ALL...
...PLANNED IN ADVANCE?

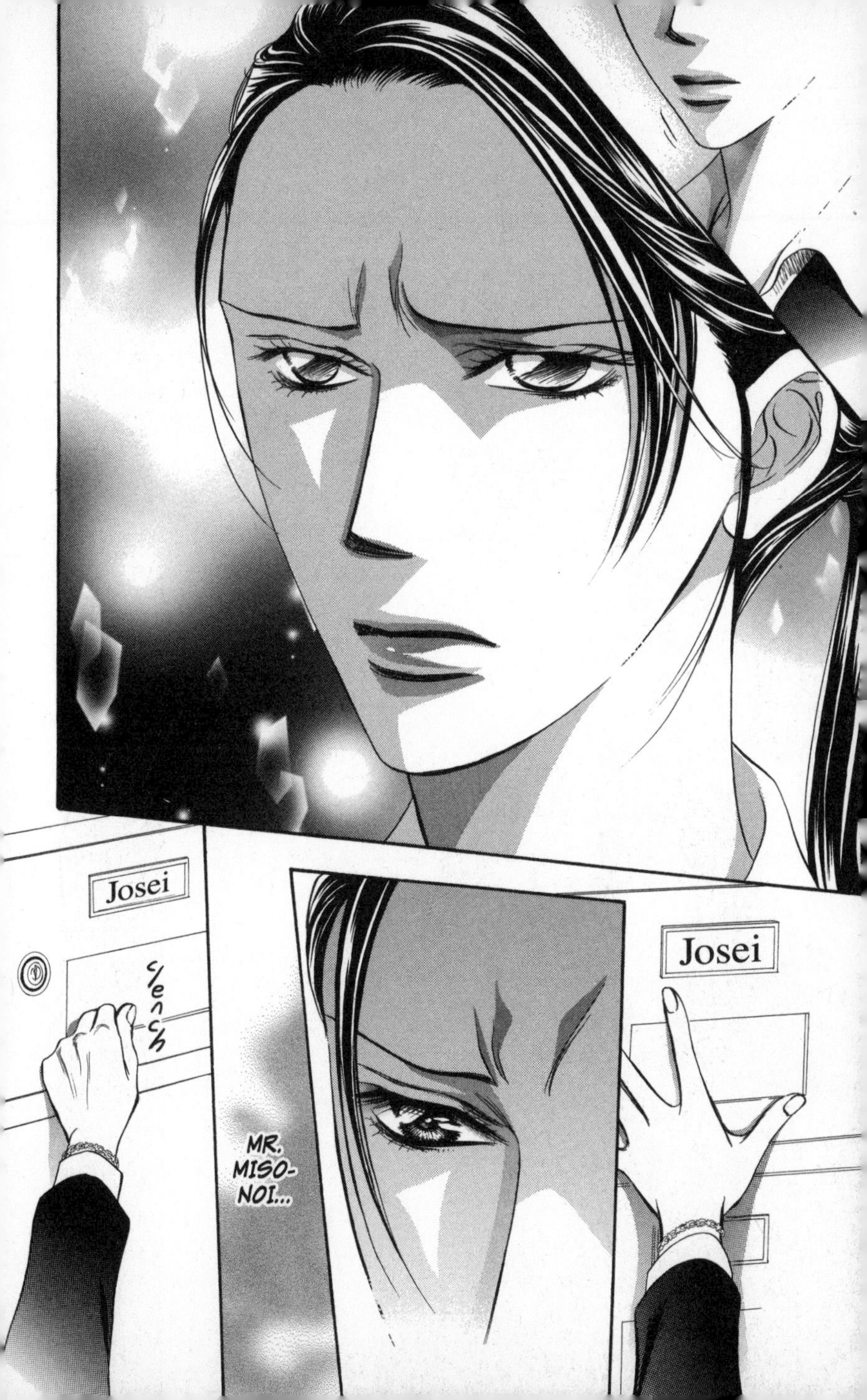
Josei
MR. MISONOI...
Josei
clench

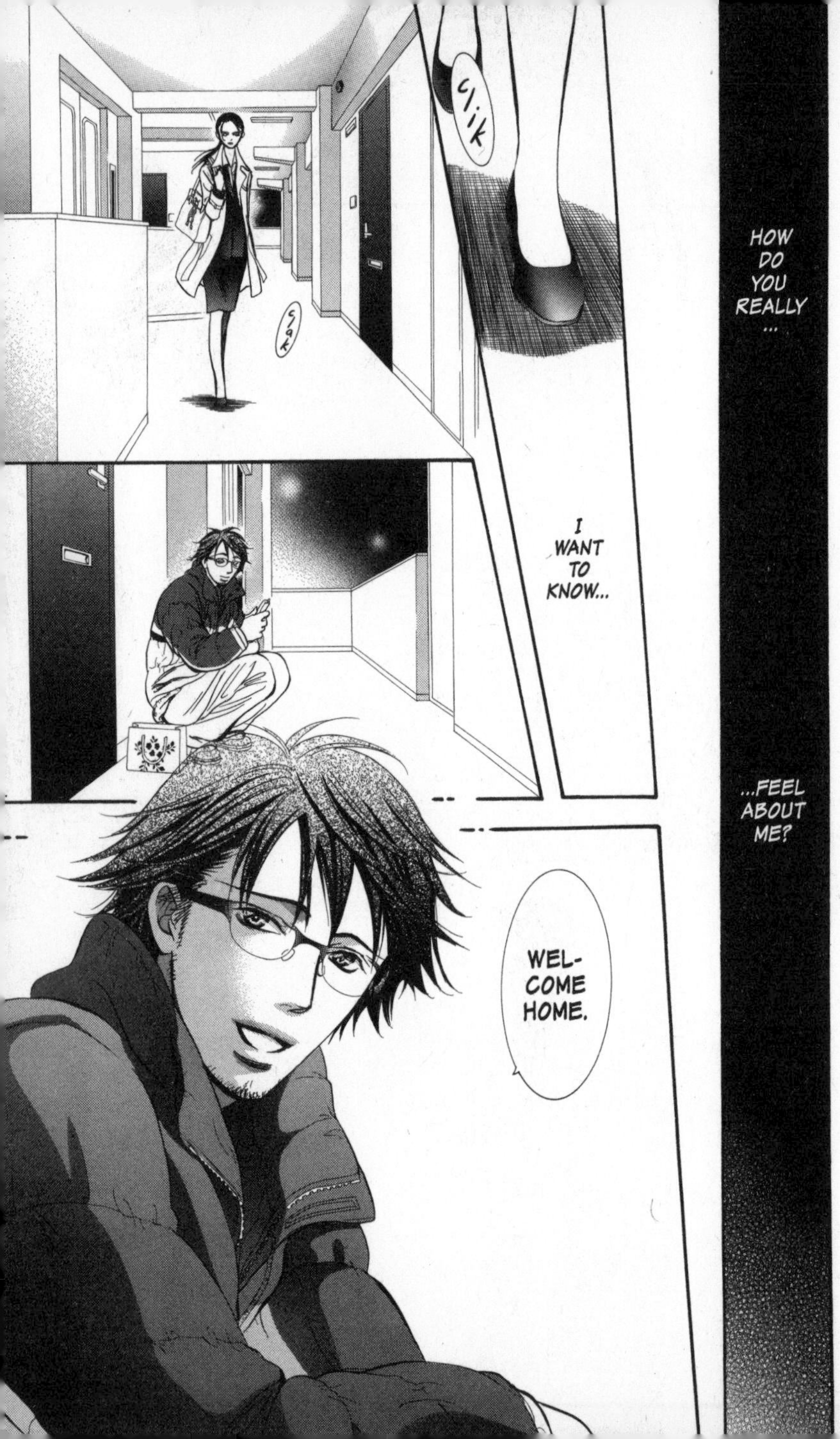
HOW DO YOU REALLY ...
...FEEL ABOUT ME?
clik
clak
I WANT TO KNOW...
WEL-COME HOME.

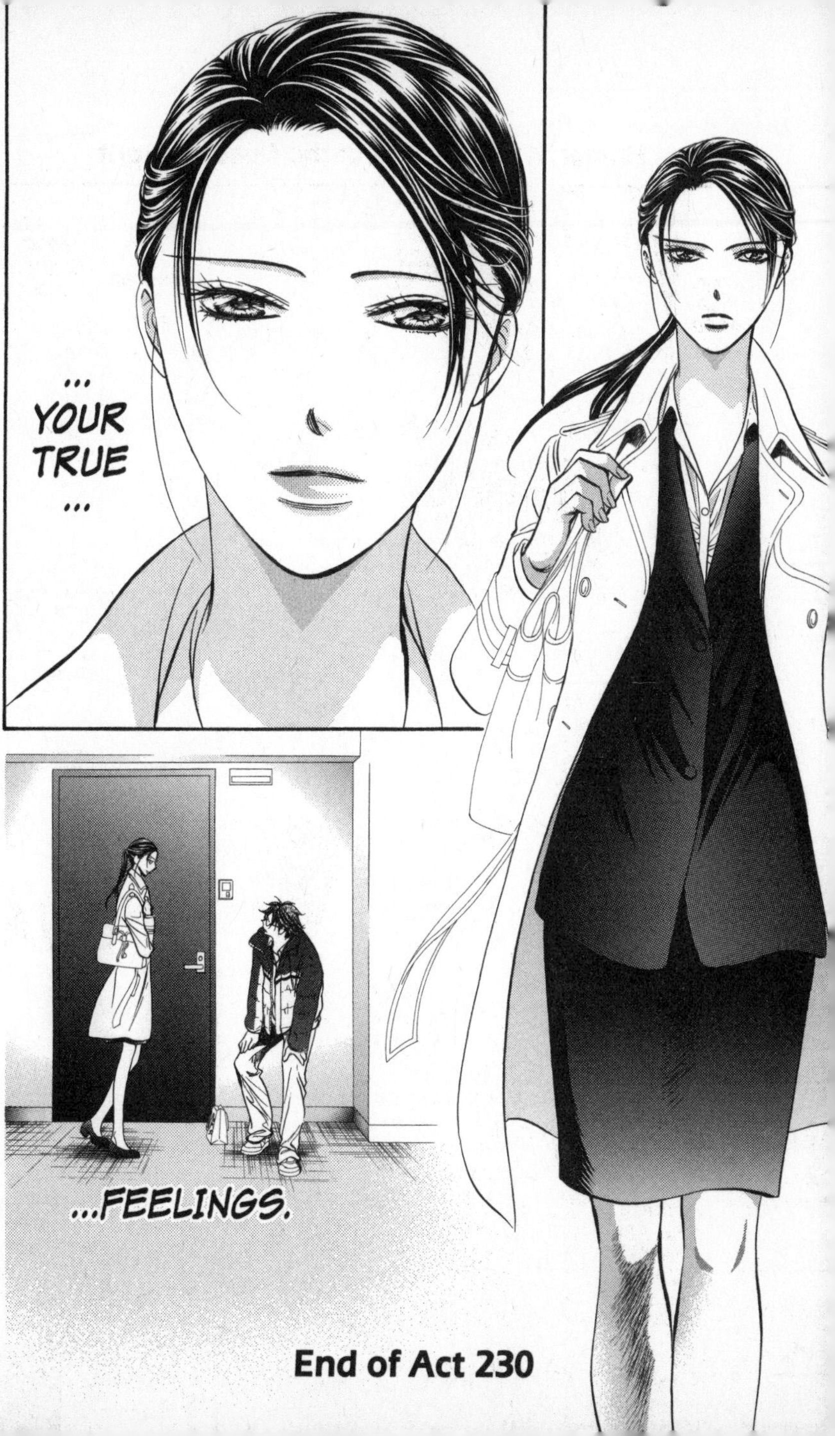
... YOUR TRUE ...
...FEELINGS.
End of Act 230

How They Acted Then: Human Kaleidoscope in the Dead of Night

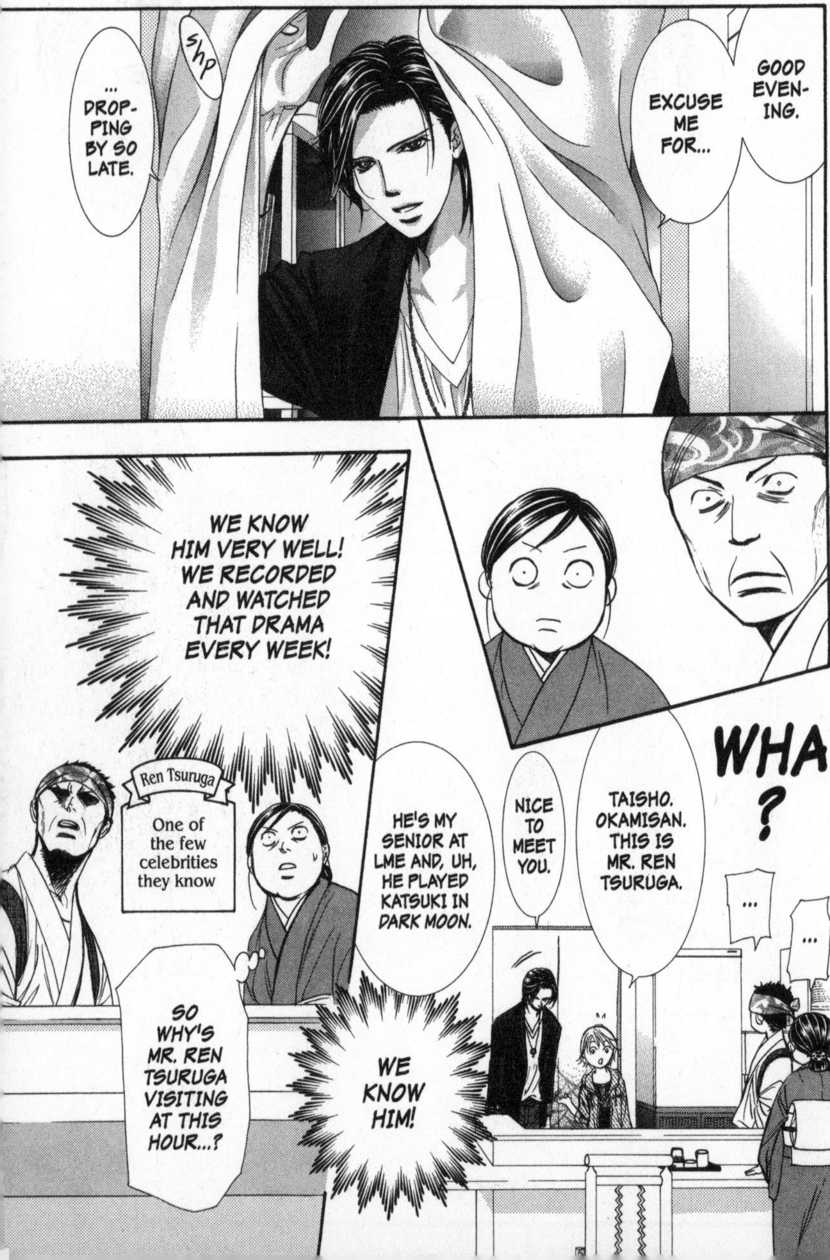
GOOD EVENING.
EXCUSE ME FOR...
shp
...DROP-PING BY SO LATE.
WHA ?
TAISHO. OKAMISAN. THIS IS MR. REN TSURUGA.
NICE TO MEET YOU.
HE'S MY SENIOR AT LME AND, UH, HE PLAYED KATSUKI IN DARK MOON.
...
...
Ren Tsuruga
One of the few celebrities they know
WE KNOW HIM VERY WELL! WE RECORDED AND WATCHED THAT DRAMA EVERY WEEK!
SO WHY'S MR. REN TSURUGA VISITING AT THIS HOUR...?
WE KNOW HIM!

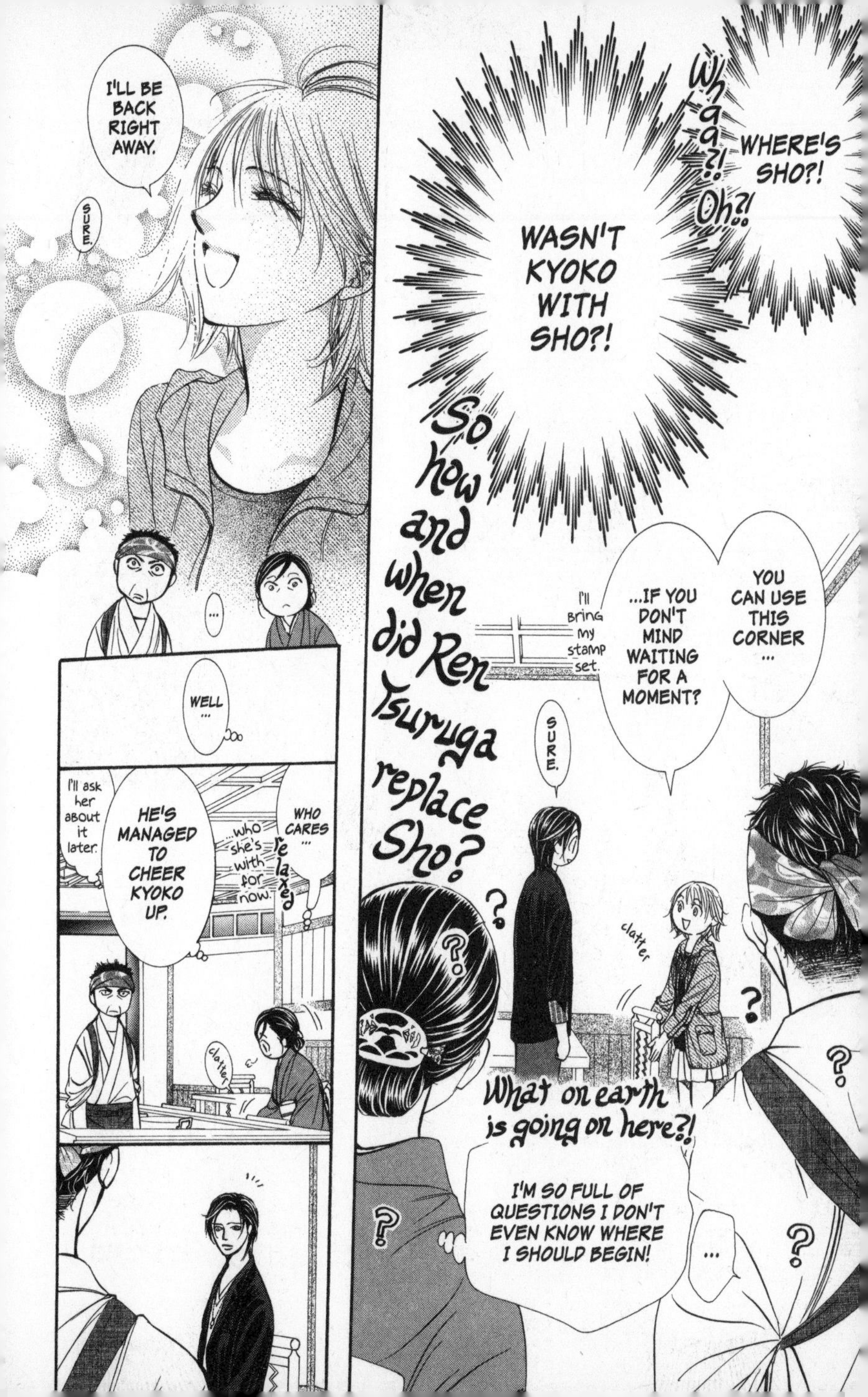
Whaa?! Oh?!
WHERE'S SHO?!
WASN'T KYOKO WITH SHO?!
So how and when did Ren Tsuruga replace Sho?
YOU CAN USE THIS CORNER ...
...IF YOU DON'T MIND WAITING FOR A MOMENT?
I'll bring my stamp set.
SURE.
clatter
What on earth is going on here?!
...
I'M SO FULL OF QUESTIONS I DON'T EVEN KNOW WHERE I SHOULD BEGIN!
I'LL BE BACK RIGHT AWAY.
SURE.
...
WELL ...
WHO CARES ...
relaxed
...who she's with for now.
HE'S MANAGED TO CHEER KYOKO UP.
I'll ask her about it later.
clatter

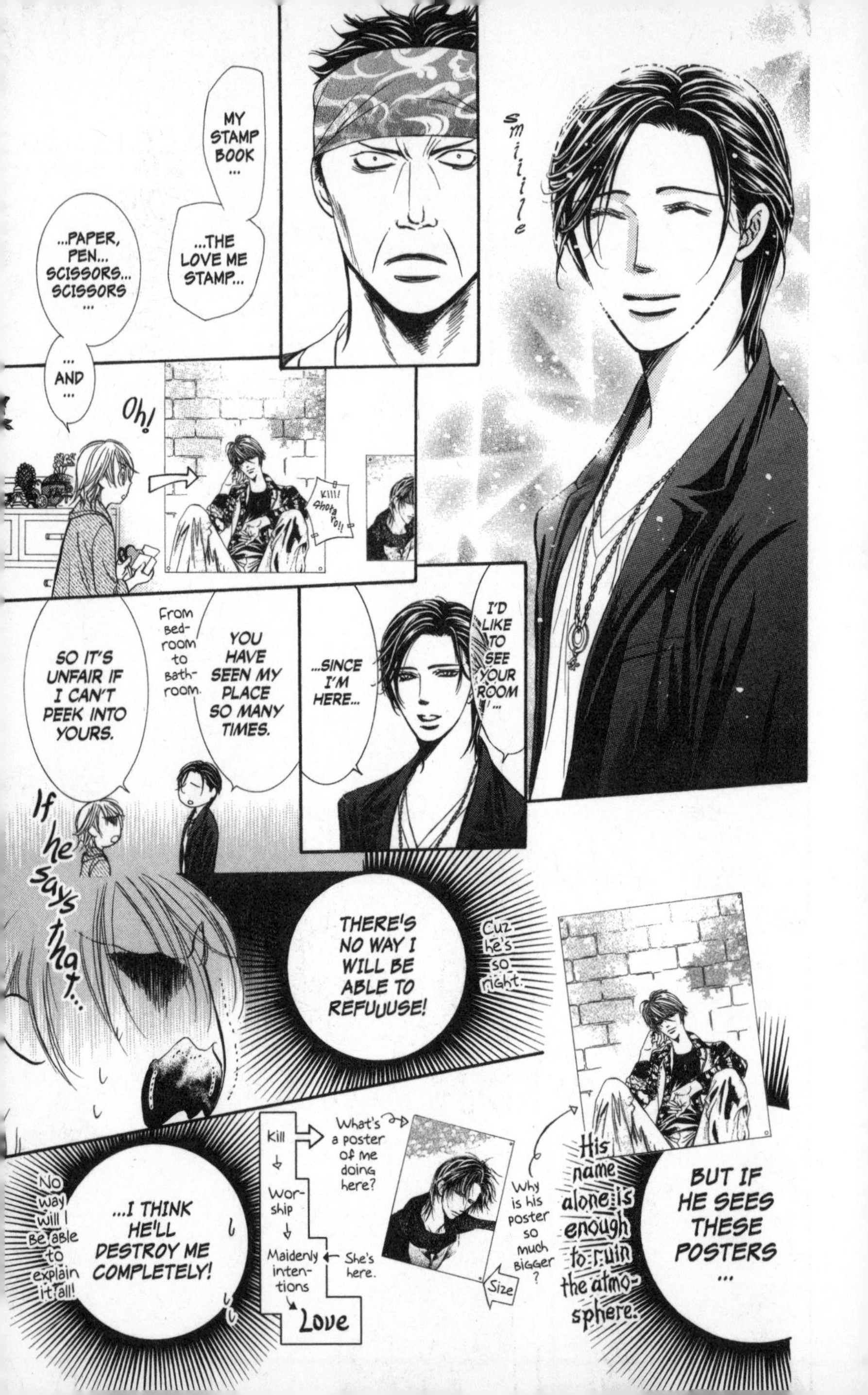
MY STAMP BOOK ...
...THE LOVE ME STAMP...
...PAPER, PEN... SCISSORS... SCISSORS ...
... AND ...
Oh!
Kill! Shotaro!!
smiiile
...SINCE I'M HERE...
I'D LIKE TO SEE YOUR ROOM ...
YOU HAVE SEEN MY PLACE SO MANY TIMES.
From bedroom to bathroom.
SO IT'S UNFAIR IF I CAN'T PEEK INTO YOURS.
If he says that...
THERE'S NO WAY I WILL BE ABLE TO REFUUUSE!
Cuz he's so right.
BUT IF HE SEES THESE POSTERS ...
His name alone is enough to ruin the atmosphere.
Why is his poster so much bigger?
Size
What's a poster of me doing here?
Kill
Worship
Maidenly intentions
Love
She's here.
...I THINK HE'LL DESTROY ME COMPLETELY!
No way will I be able to explain it all!

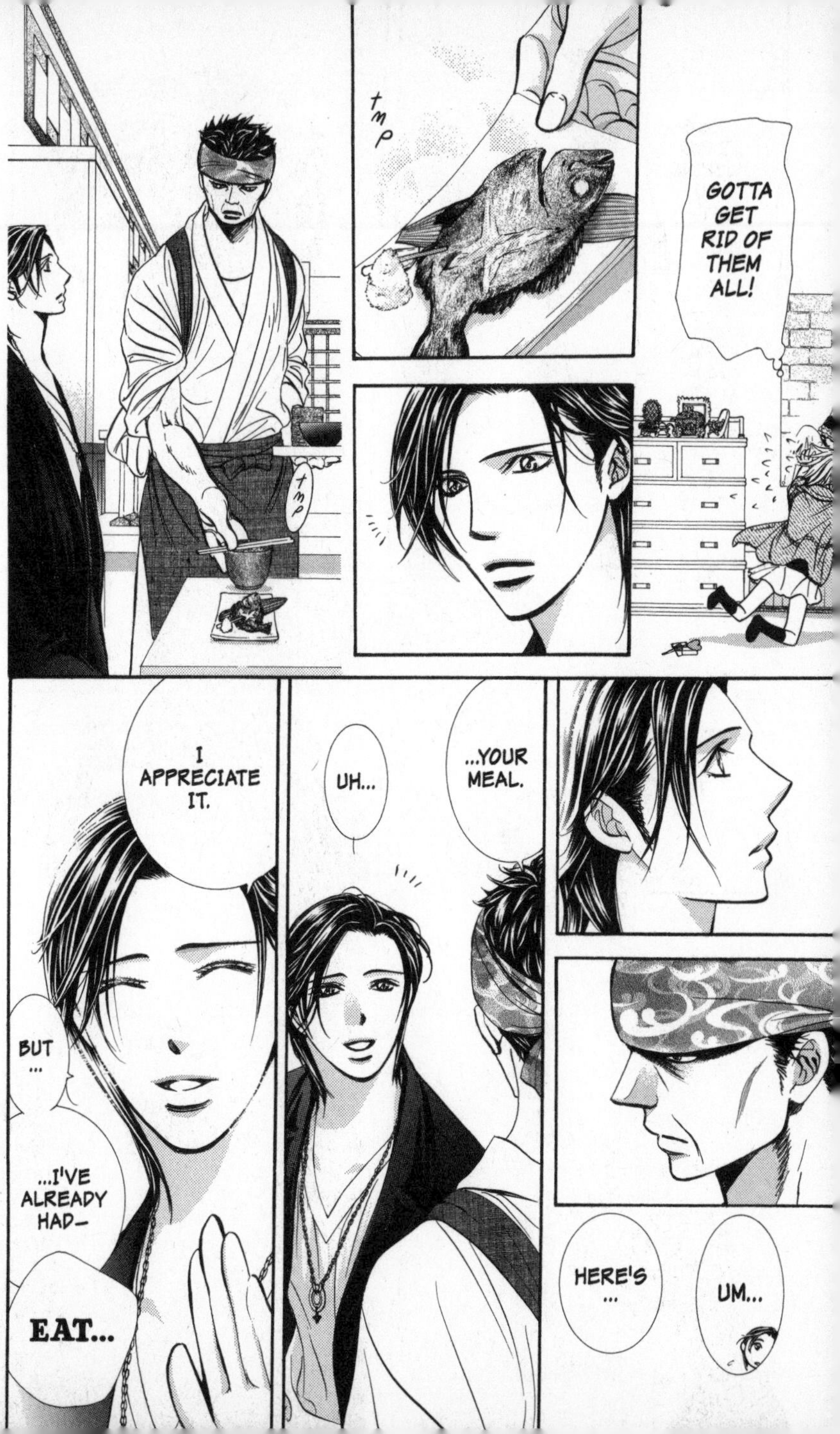
GOTTA GET RID OF THEM ALL!
tmp
tmp
UM...
HERE'S...
...YOUR MEAL.
UH...
I APPRECIATE IT.
BUT...
...I'VE ALREADY HAD—
EAT...

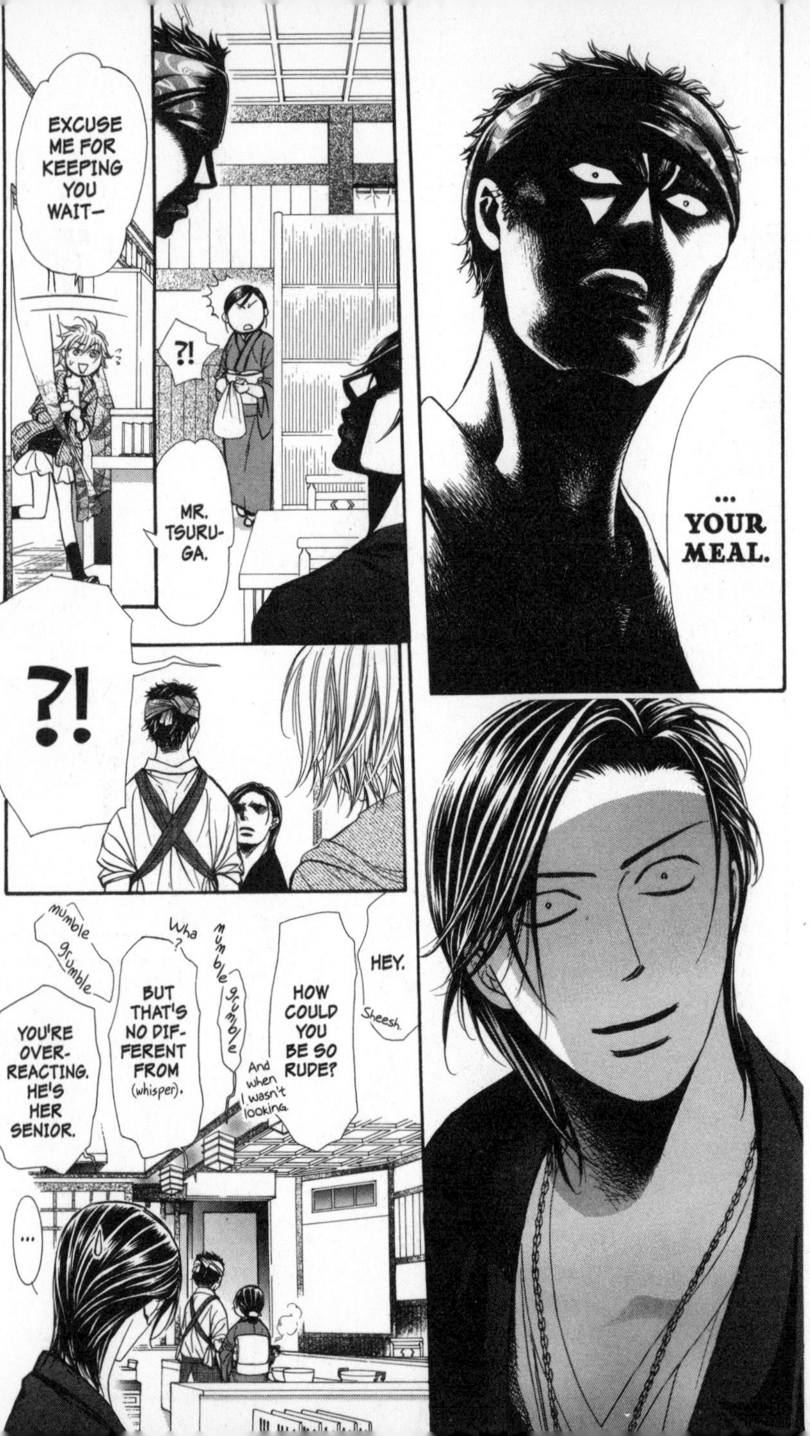
... YOUR MEAL.
EXCUSE ME FOR KEEPING YOU WAIT—
?!
MR. TSURUGA.
?!
HEY.
Sheesh.
HOW COULD YOU BE SO RUDE?
And when I wasn't looking.
mumble grumble
Wha?
BUT THAT'S NO DIF-FERENT FROM (whisper).
mumble grumble
YOU'RE OVER-REACTING. HE'S HER SENIOR.
...

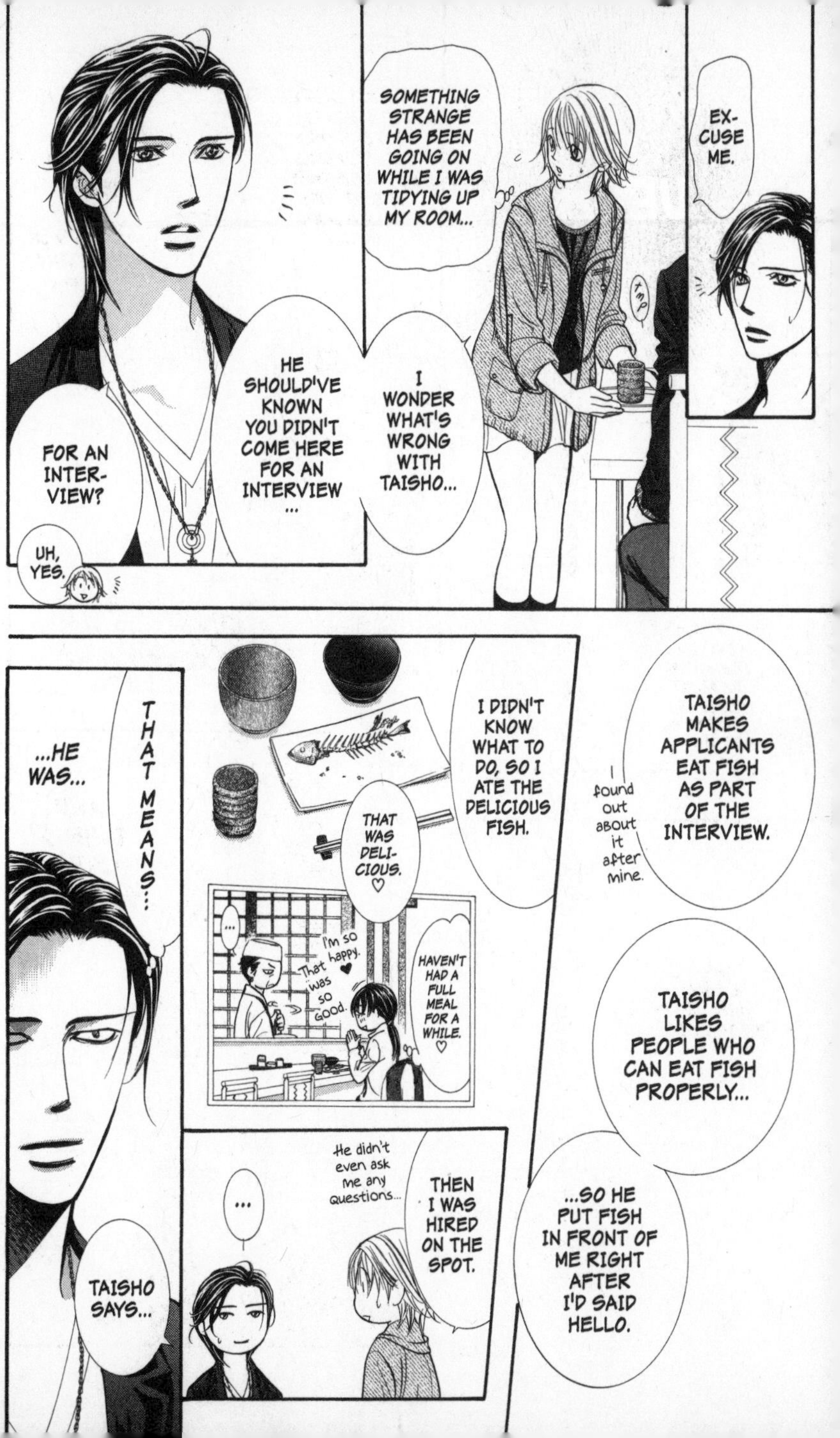

EX-CUSE ME.
SOMETHING STRANGE HAS BEEN GOING ON WHILE I WAS TIDYING UP MY ROOM...
I WONDER WHAT'S WRONG WITH TAISHO...
HE SHOULD'VE KNOWN YOU DIDN'T COME HERE FOR AN INTERVIEW ...
FOR AN INTER-VIEW?
UH, YES.
TAISHO MAKES APPLICANTS EAT FISH AS PART OF THE INTERVIEW.
I found out about it after mine.
I DIDN'T KNOW WHAT TO DO, SO I ATE THE DELICIOUS FISH.
THAT WAS DELI-CIOUS. ♡
HAVEN'T HAD A FULL MEAL FOR A WHILE. ♡
I'm so happy. ♥
That was so good.
...
TAISHO LIKES PEOPLE WHO CAN EAT FISH PROPERLY...
...SO HE PUT FISH IN FRONT OF ME RIGHT AFTER I'D SAID HELLO.
THEN I WAS HIRED ON THE SPOT.
He didn't even ask me any questions...
...
TAISHO SAYS...
THAT MEANS...
...HE WAS...

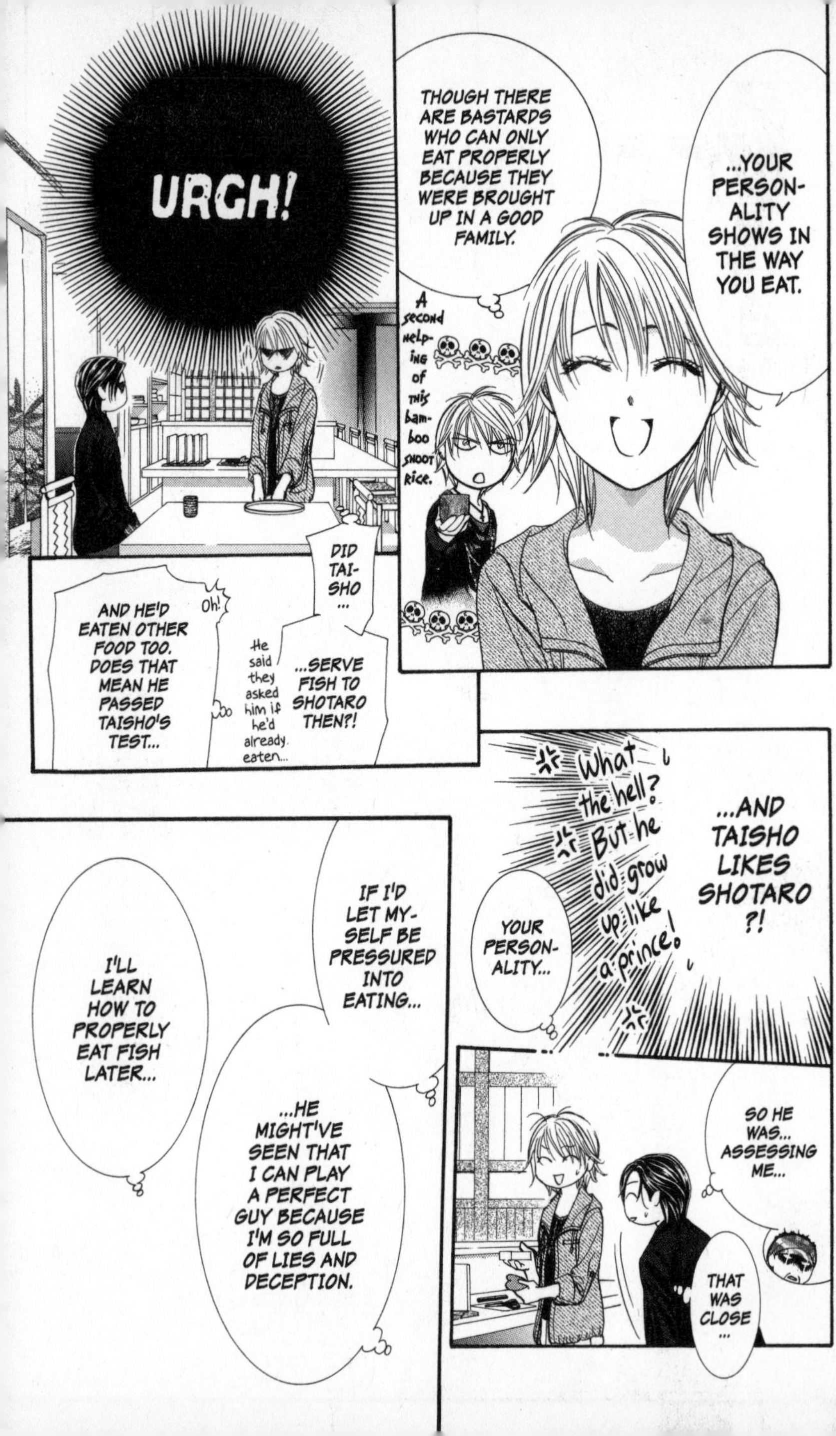
...YOUR PERSONALITY SHOWS IN THE WAY YOU EAT.
THOUGH THERE ARE BASTARDS WHO CAN ONLY EAT PROPERLY BECAUSE THEY WERE BROUGHT UP IN A GOOD FAMILY.
A second helping of this bamboo shoot rice.
URGH!
DID TAISHO...
...SERVE FISH TO SHOTARO THEN?!
He said they asked him if he'd already eaten...
Oh!
AND HE'D EATEN OTHER FOOD TOO. DOES THAT MEAN HE PASSED TAISHO'S TEST...
...AND TAISHO LIKES SHOTARO?!
What the hell? But he did grow up like a prince!
YOUR PERSONALITY...
SO HE WAS... ASSESSING ME...
THAT WAS CLOSE...
IF I'D LET MYSELF BE PRESSURED INTO EATING...
...HE MIGHT'VE SEEN THAT I CAN PLAY A PERFECT GUY BECAUSE I'M SO FULL OF LIES AND DECEPTION.
I'LL LEARN HOW TO PROPERLY EAT FISH LATER...

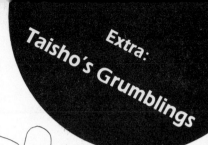

Extra: Taisho's Grumblings

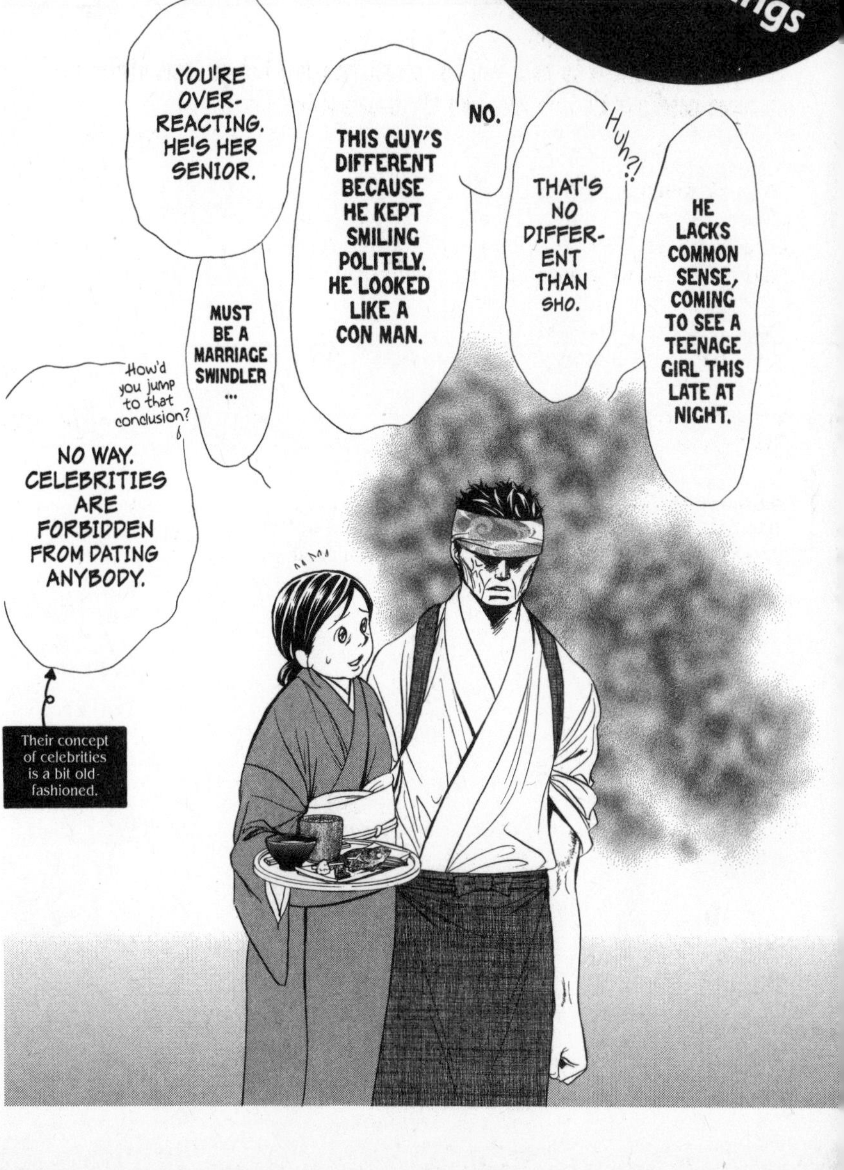
HE LACKS COMMON SENSE, COMING TO SEE A TEENAGE GIRL THIS LATE AT NIGHT.
Huh?!
THAT'S NO DIFFERENT THAN SHO.
NO.
THIS GUY'S DIFFERENT BECAUSE HE KEPT SMILING POLITELY. HE LOOKED LIKE A CON MAN.
YOU'RE OVER-REACTING. HE'S HER SENIOR.
MUST BE A MARRIAGE SWINDLER...
How'd you jump to that conclusion?
NO WAY. CELEBRITIES ARE FORBIDDEN FROM DATING ANYBODY.
Their concept of celebrities is a bit old-fashioned.

Skip-Beat! End Notes
Everyone knows how to be a fan, but sometimes cool things from other cultures need a little help crossing the language barrier.

Page 45, panel 6: Battle flags
These are based on the battle flags used by the feudal lord Singen Takeda, which had the kanji for "wind-forest-fire-mountain" and were pronounced *fuurin kazan*.

Page 59, panel 3: Taiyaki
Fish-shaped cake, usually filled with sweet red bean paste.

page 72, panel 4: Yakuza
The yakuza is the Japanese mafia.

Page 183, panel 3: Taisho, okamisan
Taisho is the term used for the proprietor of a traditional Japanese restaurant, and *okamisan* is the term used for the proprietress.

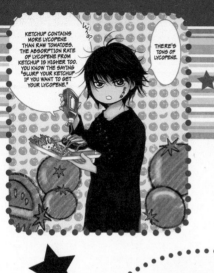

THERE'S TONS OF LYCOPENE.
KETCHUP CONTAINS MORE LYCOPENE THAN RAW TOMATOES. THE ABSORPTION RATE OF LYCOPENE FROM KETCHUP IS HIGHER TOO. YOU KNOW THE SAYING "SLURP YOUR KETCHUP IF YOU WANT TO GET YOUR LYCOPENE."

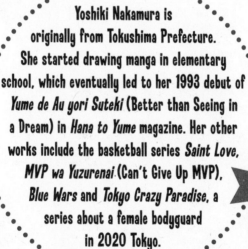

Yoshiki Nakamura is originally from Tokushima Prefecture. She started drawing manga in elementary school, which eventually led to her 1993 debut of *Yume de Au yori Suteki* (Better than Seeing in a Dream) in *Hana to Yume* magazine. Her other works include the basketball series *Saint Love*, *MVP wa Yuzurenai* (Can't Give Up MVP), *Blue Wars* and *Tokyo Crazy Paradise*, a series about a female bodyguard in 2020 Tokyo.

SKIP·BEAT!
Vol. 38
Shojo Beat Edition

STORY AND ART BY YOSHIKI NAKAMURA

English Translation & Adaptation/Tomo Kimura
Touch-up Art & Lettering/Sabrina Heep
Design/Veronica Casson
Editor/Pancha Diaz

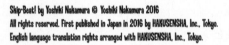

Printed in Canada

Published by VIZ Media, LLC
P.O. Box 77010
San Francisco, CA 94107

www.viz.com
www.shojobeat.com

10 9 8 7 6 5 4 3 2 1
First printing, March 2017

PARENTAL ADVISORY
SKIP·BEAT! is rated T for Teen and is recommended for ages 13 and up. This volume contains a grudge.
ratings.viz.com

IDOL *dreams*

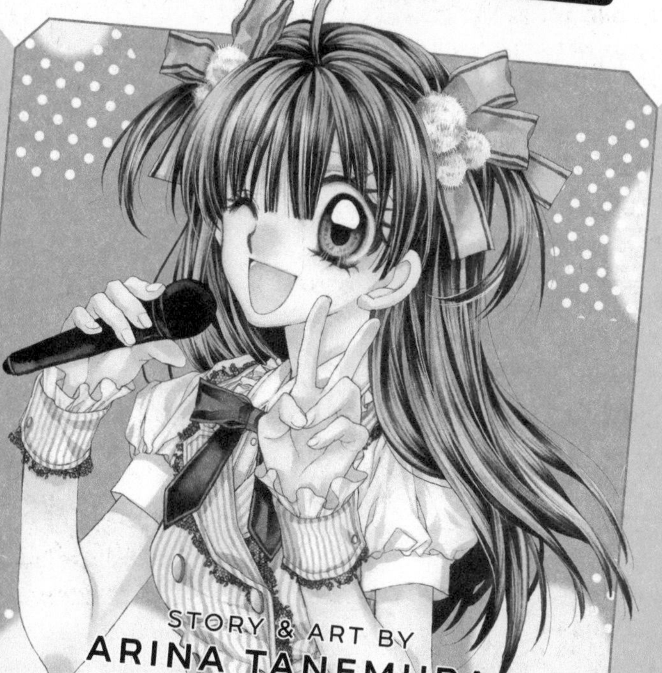
STORY & ART BY
ARINA TANEMURA

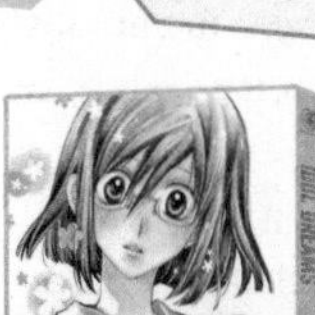
IDOL DREAMS
IDOL dreams
1
ARINA TANEMURA

At age 31, office worker Chikage Deguchi feels she missed her chances at love and success. When word gets out that she's a virgin, Chikage is humiliated and wishes she could turn back time to when she was still young and popular. She takes an experimental drug that changes her appearance back to when she was 15. Now Chikage is determined to pursue everything she missed out on all those years ago—including becoming a star!

Shojo Beat VIZ media www.viz.com

RATED T FOR TEEN ratings.viz.com

Behind the Scenes!!

From the creator of Ouran High School Host Club

STORY AND ART BY **BISCO HATORI**

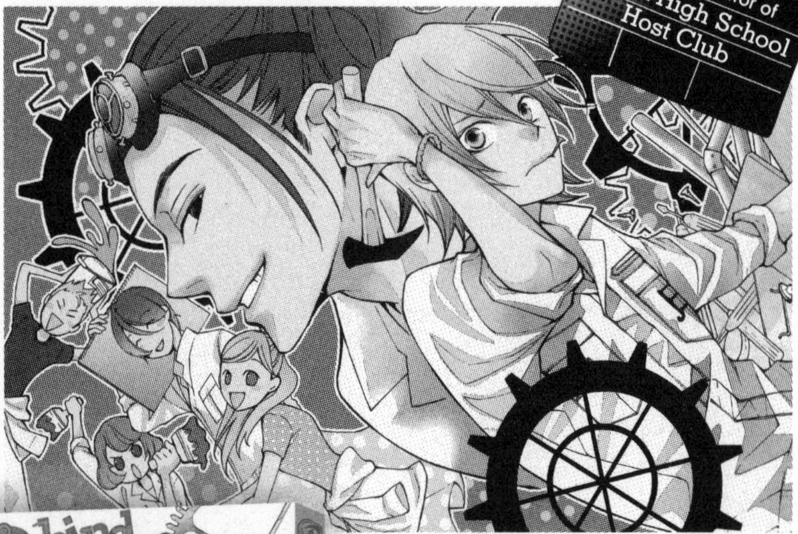

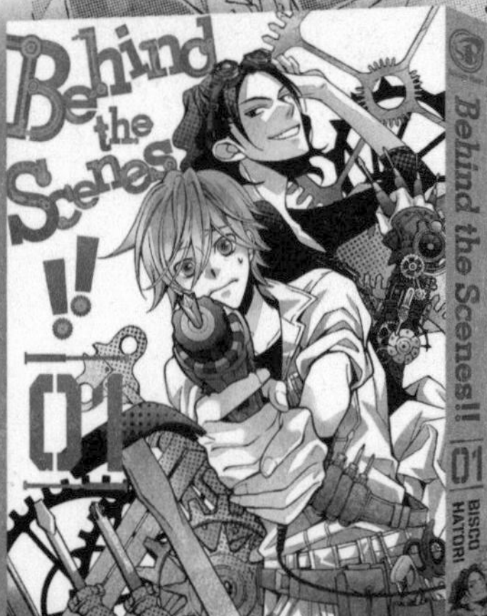
Behind the Scenes!!
01
Behind the Scenes!!
01
BISCO HATORI
STORY AND ART BY
BISCO HATORI

Ranmaru Kurisu comes from a family of hardy, rough-and-tumble fisherfolk and he sticks out at home like a delicate, artistic sore thumb. It's given him a raging inferiority complex and a permanently pessimistic outlook. Now that he's in college, he's hoping to find a sense of belonging. But after a whole life of being left out, does he even know how to fit in?!

RATED T FOR TEEN
ratings.viz.com

VIZ MEDIA
www.viz.com

Shojo Beat

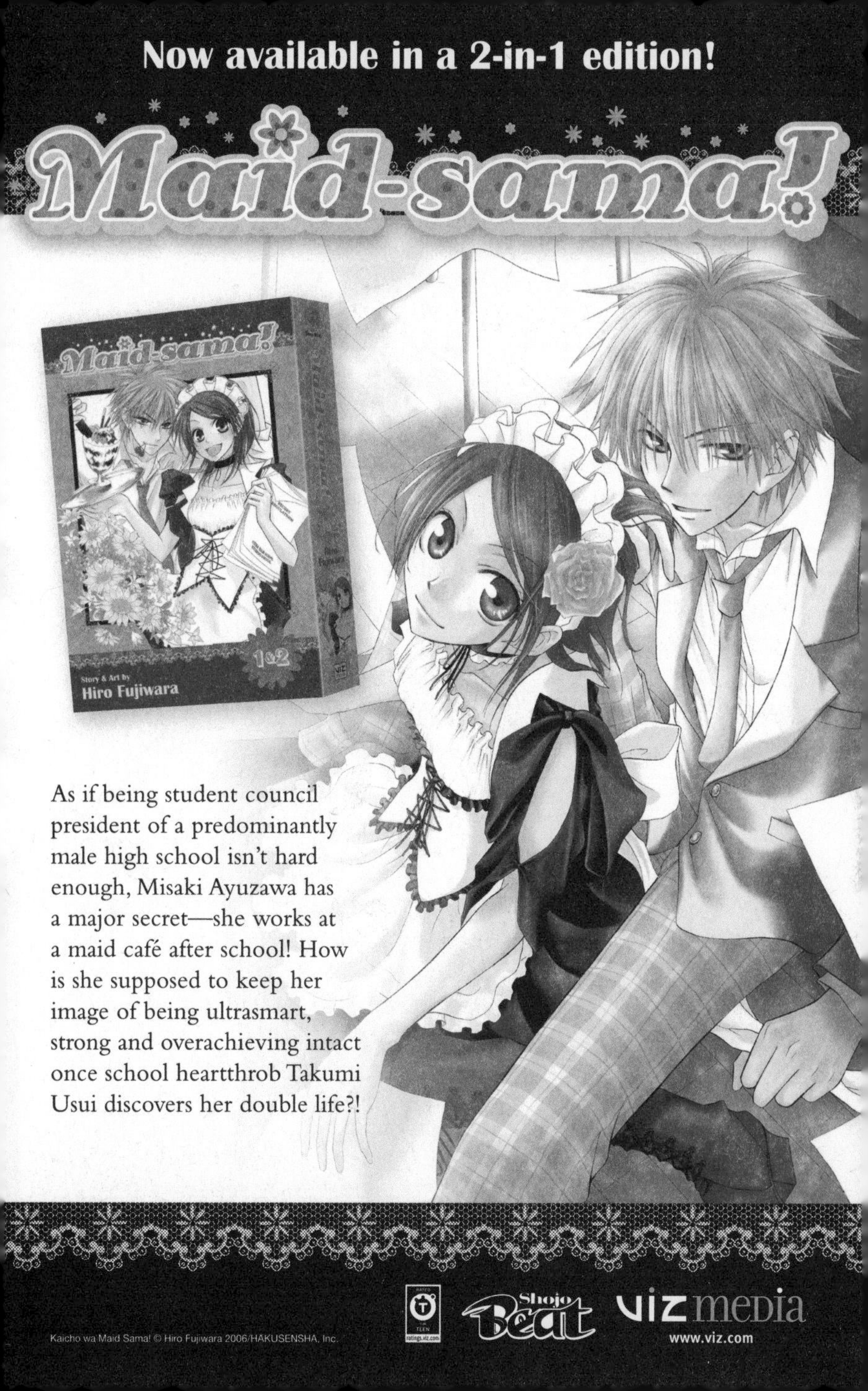
Now available in a 2-in-1 edition!
Maid-sama!
Maid-sama!
1&2
Story & Art by
Hiro Fujiwara
As if being student council president of a predominantly male high school isn't hard enough, Misaki Ayuzawa has a major secret—she works at a maid café after school! How is she supposed to keep her image of being ultrasmart, strong and overachieving intact once school heartthrob Takumi Usui discovers her double life?!
Kaicho wa Maid Sama! © Hiro Fujiwara 2006/HAKUSENSHA, Inc.
RATED T TEEN ratings.viz.com
Shojo Beat
viz media
www.viz.com

Skip·Beat!
Volume 38

CONTENTS

Shojo Beat

Skip·Beat!

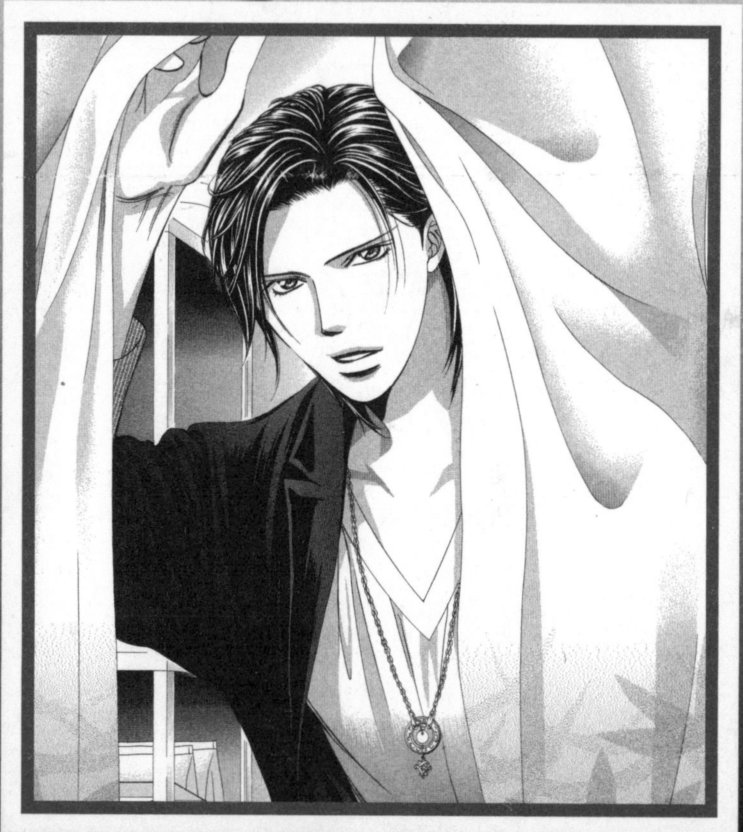

38

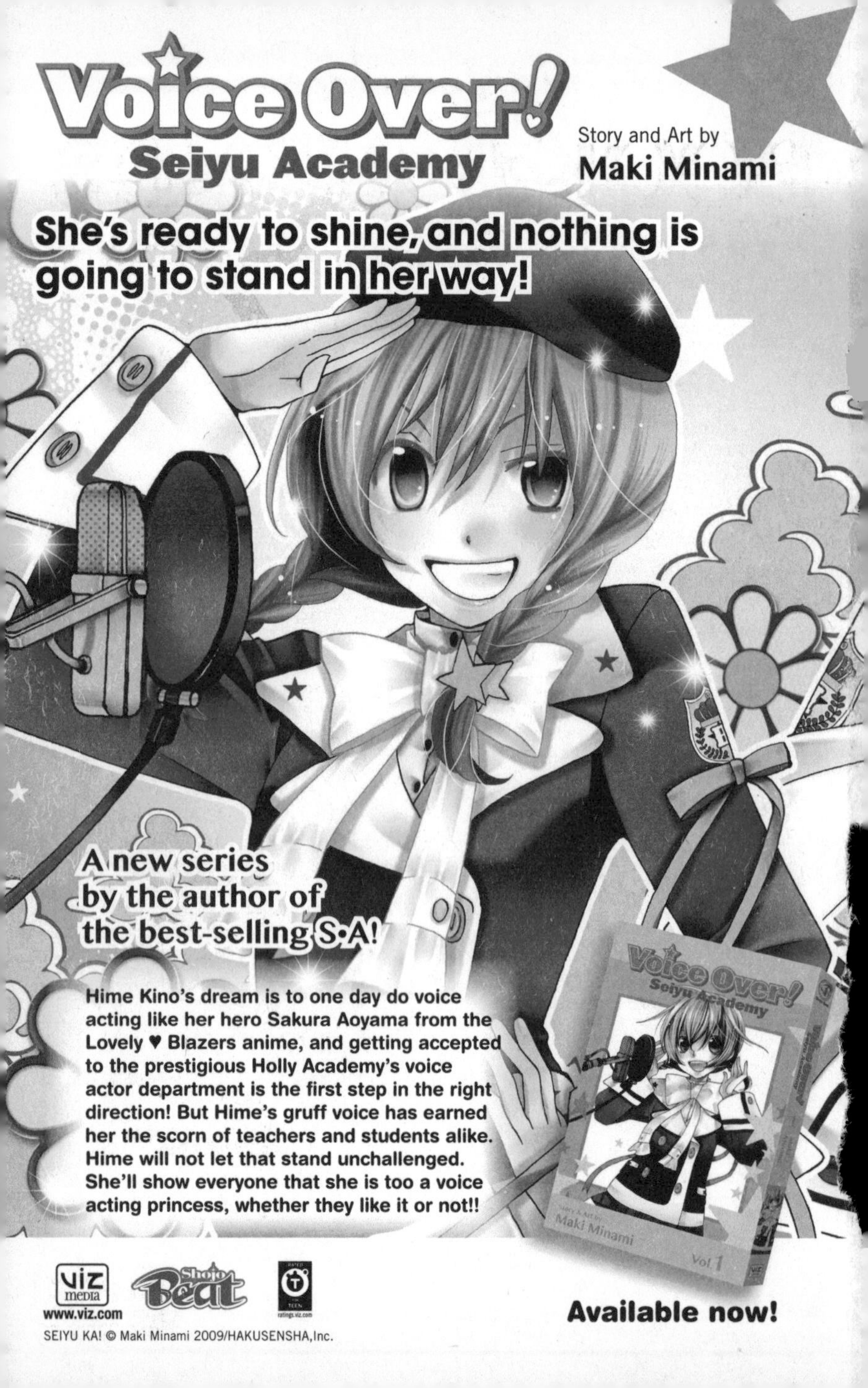
Voice Over! Seiyu Academy
Story and Art by
Maki Minami
She's ready to shine, and nothing is going to stand in her way!
A new series by the author of the best-selling S•A!
Hime Kino's dream is to one day do voice acting like her hero Sakura Aoyama from the Lovely ♥ Blazers anime, and getting accepted to the prestigious Holly Academy's voice actor department is the first step in the right direction! But Hime's gruff voice has earned her the scorn of teachers and students alike. Hime will not let that stand unchallenged. She'll show everyone that she is too a voice acting princess, whether they like it or not!!
Voice Over! Seiyu Academy
Story & Art by
Maki Minami
Vol.1
viz media
Shojo Beat
RATED T FOR TEEN
ratings.viz.com
www.viz.com
Available now!
SEIYU KA! © Maki Minami 2009/HAKUSENSHA,Inc.

D0029034

SURPRISE!

You may be reading the wrong way!

It's true: In keeping with the original Japanese comic format, this book reads from right to left—so action, sound effects, and word balloons are completely reversed. This preserves the orientation of the original artwork—plus, it's fun! Check out the diagram shown here to get the hang of things, and then turn to the other side of the book to get started!

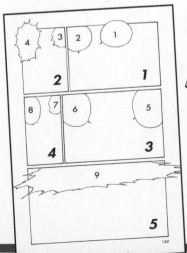